Around the World in 80 Events

Enjoy!

Matthew Lamb

Matt

#comeonthejourney

matt@aroundtheworldin80events.com

ISBN: 9781739870409

British Cataloguing Publication Data: A catalogue record of this book is available from The British Library.
Also available on Kindle.

Contents

Dear you,

Thank you for starting at the beginning of this book and not skipping the pages that everyone usually leaves out.

Thank you to the people who stuck by me throughout the journey.

Thank you to the people who texted every few weeks to check in.

Thank you to those who tried to make me stop and made sure I was eating proper food...

Thank you to those who came on the journey – both on social media and literally...

Aunt Helen... you never got to read the finished journey...

And to Mother and Father Lamb – thanks for allowing me to go and live my dream...

This one is for you.

Introduction

Around the World in 80 Events began as an idea and, over time, I started looking at flight routes online. Next, I was exploring events around the world and imagining how it would feel to be walking through the gates. I wanted to know what different events look like globally and to understand why art on walls is more than just paint. To appreciate the Penis Festival for its true worth. To volunteer at the world's largest offshore firework competition. And more – much more…

In 2018, the first flights were booked and in February 2019, I took off. By October 2019, the physical journey was over. But it never really stops. There was a book to write, events to attend, stories to tell. Get ready for moments of surprise, moments to cherish and moments to forget. Get ready for *Around the World in 80 Events*.

This is not a journey I went on alone. This book captures the experience of everyone who witnessed, commented, thought about and supported me along the way. Welcome to a book that will take you on a journey, an adventure of discovery, not only to the events I attended but also around the world. I hope it shows you what the whole trip ended up becoming – something bigger than I ever imagined.

Before we begin – a few things.

The trip was a dream. Some people don't see value in dreams, or don't understand why anyone would want to pursue a dream. Some people laughed when I told them about the adventure. But now the adventure is laid out on these pages for the world to read.

Really, I should introduce myself. I am Matthew Lamb and I love events. I hope that is clear. But more than that, I appreciate what events do for society and people and that is where my curiosity for adventuring around the world began. I started working in the events industry in 2009. For 10 years I worked in operations and management, dabbled in other positions, lectured about events. And I loved diving into different events, meeting new people and discovering new things. You could argue I had ants in my pants and always wanted to explore the next opportunity. Ten years later, in 2019, I was about to go and discover events in a different way. I wanted to come out of my comfort zone and experience the events industry in a way that had never been attempted before.

Before the trip began, long lists of tasks faced me every day; more items to be getting on with. I was going to some crazy events and some more realistic places, and the planning allowed the project to become manageable.

Discovering events in places I never knew existed was an enthralling part of the journey. I wanted to figure out what impact events had on their host city and whether it was possible for me to visit. As I planned, many things were going through my head: finances, how to choose the 80 events, transportation, what if I didn't have anywhere to stay, and what if something happened – like I was taken ill?

I had a goal. The goal was to make *Around the World in 80 Events* a reality. Nothing was going to stop me. Determination is something I have in abundance. This trip was about going on a journey and delivering the dream.

When I was developing the structure of the physical journey, I realised there was no perfect route. I was never going to be able to get to every event I wanted to. I planned different stages that would take in as many events as possible. Stage one included Australia, New Zealand, Eastern Asia, India, Dubai and Turkey. I booked the route and then checked out what events were happening. Yes, this resulted in me missing some things, but I knew that I might be able to get to other interesting events I had never come across before.

One thing I was asked prior to the adventure was: "You're spending 24 hours in some places. How can you really experience it?" That is a fair question. But for sure, in that 24 hours I can eat the local cuisine, see the main sights, talk to locals, visit tourist attractions and go to an event as well. A limited experience, but an experience nonetheless.

This book was written about the events industry the year before the COVID-19 shutdown. It is the only book that has a complete 80-event record in 26 countries and the only book that covers what the global events industry was like in 2019. And now it gives hope for the future.

Welcome to the story and enjoy the journey...

#comeonthejourney

Disclaimer

I am brutally honest about my thoughts. Everything I have written is my own opinion with regards to how I felt about the events I visited. While some names have been changed to protect people's anonymity, everyone I met knew I was writing a book and was more than happy to be part of the story. Those events that didn't ever know I was in attendance – SURPRISE! You made it into the book.

We Are Go!

<u>4th February 2019</u>

My alarm went off at 3:30am. The first part of my journey was to Auckland via Holland and Singapore, and I was booked on the 6:15am flight to Amsterdam. As I walked through Amsterdam airport at 7:30am, I watched the business travellers heading to meetings or conferences. Loud. Bustling. Busy. Noise clattered my ears with constant announcements about departing planes.

<u>Auckland</u>

I arrived in Auckland on 5th February at 23:34pm. It was warm. After being stuck on a plane for so long, the heat was quite overwhelming. There was no one waiting for me at Arrivals. No emotional greeting, no familiar face waving at me. As the bus pulled into Auckland CBD, I smiled as the scents of New Zealand doused my smell buds. I walked into the hotel and for the first time on the whole adventure I was asked "Can I please have your passport?" It really had started! Dumping my bags in the cramped room, I looked out of the window – it was pitch black. I phoned home to tell them I had arrived.

Outside my hotel was quite a hill. The hill was where I made my first friend, Dudley, who was 84 years old. He was struggling with his bags of snacks and I helped him into the hotel. He was from Australia and was in Auckland to visit some cousins and their kids. He laughed again as I told him what I was planning to do. "Can I come?" he asked. I would have loved to take Dudley on the trip. He was a sweet, lovely person. I met a thousand friendly Dudley's on my journey – but as he was my first friend, he gets a special mention.

Event 1: Waitangi Day, Auckland

6th February

This event will be the one I will always remember. The beginning. It started at 9am. The driver of the 762 bus, which left from the middle of the city centre and cost $3, laughed as I stood at the door. "Wow – there must be something going on today," he said.

"Must be," I replied. "It is called my first event. I have come from Scotland for this..." I don't think he caught what I said.

Orakei Domain Park was the location for today's Waitangi Day celebrations. As I jumped off the bus, the heat was absolutely blistering. I stood on the harbour wall at the park and thought, "Here we go!" An array of white marquees was being erected. I entered the park and tried to figure out – *how do I approach this? Who do I speak to? What do I ask?* I was not scared one bit. It worked. As I approached the information tent, four very confused individuals stared at me as I asked if I could speak to someone regarding media. I wasn't a journalist, but I found this was a way into most events.

Before we rush into the event itself, let's take a minute to understand the roots and origins of Waitangi Day. It is the day that marks the signing of the Treaty of Waitangi in 1840. Representatives of the British Crown and over 500 Māori chiefs signed what is considered to be one of New Zealand's founding documents. The national holiday was first declared in 1974 and has grown ever since.

This year, Queenstown was organising its first ever Waitangi Day events. The Māori community, the Ngati Whatua Orakei Community in Auckland, had organised this specific celebration I was attending, as they saw this as a day of bringing everyone together to celebrate and remember the culture. However, what I noticed straight away was the integration between the Māoris and the white population. It was not as separated as other global ethnic communities. I was met by a member of the Ngati Whatua Orakei Community who explained to me the objectives of the event. I was quite astonished by the fact that they were trying to do so much more than just celebrate Waitangi Day.

I was immediately impressed by the recycling and sustainability plans. One of the main objectives was to have 100% recycling on site, with absolutely nothing from the event going to landfill. The representative explained that, in 2018, the recycling and sustainability plan successfully recycled 98% of all the rubbish that came from this event. Extremely impressive. I kind of wished every event had this commitment to our planet.

When the event kicked off and the main stage went live, the Master of Ceremonies constantly made announcements reminding everyone about single-use plastic, recycling procedures and refilling water. "We can do this together, with your help." At each recycling unit there were members of the Ngati Whatua Orakei Community who volunteered to take the rubbish and separate it into large plastic tubs. They tried to discourage people from buying plastic bottles, instead providing the attendees with refilling units. However, remember earlier I told you about the heat – well, there was a BIG PROBLEM. The small pipes transferring the water from the underwater supply to the machines were being set on fire – not literally, but by the sun. I saw the police take a teabag and boil, through the cold water tap, a fresh cup of tea. It was, for me, a great observation of site management, and understanding the challenges that can occur within events that have high temperatures and little shade. After that, the site manager, a member of the Ngati Whatua Orakei Community, taped large 'out of order' stickers on the taps while the police enjoyed their tea!

The event also focused on health, and there was a health village open to everyone from the Māori community. They all had the opportunity to have free eye tests, breast screening and general medical check-ups. My media contact explained that members of the community are nervous about going to health services. This initiative allowed people to feel comfortable in a place they know where they were surrounded and supported by friends.

Another interesting observation was the event security. The police, when introducing themselves to the security guards, gave each other a firm handshake and a traditional forehead to forehead embrace. Seeing this nose to nose contact was at first odd to me, but it's a cultural action called the Hongi, which is performed at important ceremonies. And it was one of the beautiful moments I witnessed. Can you imagine police and security at any other event going to nose to nose and smiling?

At the far corner, there was a silent protest calling for peace in Papua New Guinea. Flags were draped across the marquees. But this was a different event.

I watched as a large group of people walked towards the stage. A ceremony was about to commence. Members of the Māori community and visitors (white westerners) followed on. The sun was beating down, so a lot of the elders had umbrellas and they sat contently under them while the event was happening around them. No conversations across the grass; just firm stares from both sides. A small tremble shook the event site. A bang with feet and a large stick. A voice. It made my hair stand on end. It is called the *challenge*. A young member of the community approaches the awaiting crowd from the stage through the middle channel, chanting in the language of *te reo*, which is the Eastern Polynesian language spoken by the Māori community. Fun fact – the language of the Māori community is one of the recognised official languages of New Zealand. The raw emotion of those participating was unique, and I could feel myself being pulled in. Why was there such deep emotion? Firstly, it dates back to the oppression of this community. However, it is more than that. While there, I got speaking to a police officer who said sometimes the events can see violence because of perceived unfairness regarding the Waitangi Treaty. It is viewed to have played a huge part in creating relationships for political and social advancements – to the advantage of the white westerners. But some levels of respect have apparently now been lost and some of the points that chiefs signed on in the past are viewed to be unfair. Every year there are protests for change, usually at the grounds of Waitangi, but there was no such violence in Auckland. Politicians are usually – and have been in the past – the ones who are punched or egged.

The cultural performances included speeches from Māori and Pakeha (European) dignitaries. It was beautiful to witness and experience. I couldn't take my eyes off the performance in front of me – which lasted about 20 minutes, while about 1,000 people stood and watched in the soaring heat. Once the welcome had finished, it was time for the other activities. But I watched as the Pakeha members of the community – who were local members of parliament and other dignitaries – performed the Hongi. They really embraced it, and sometimes even finished with a hug. I sat on the grass capturing photos of a moment that really defines what events can create.

To have the opportunity to witness this was a strong start to my adventure. The celebrations are known for their importance in cultural education. What I witnessed was the use of the Māori community's land to welcome people and educate as well as celebrate their culture.

One thing to take away...

Community togetherness – from the police to the organisers. I spotted the police joining in and throwing a rugby ball with a few kids. There was no 'we are the law'... it was togetherness. The success of the event was based on the messages from the elders to younger members of the community and the outsiders.

It was symbolic. It was fascinating. It was the greatest event to begin the journey.

Auckland...

I was severely jetlagged. Really struggling to stay awake. But I had an adventure to continue. I would have to catch up with my sleep at a later date.

Event 2: Broderick Summer Swim Series

7th February

The next day I was introduced to this event by Charlotte, who I had worked alongside at the Gold Coast 2018 Commonwealth Games. The Broderick Summer Swim Series is a swimming event that happens during the summer every Thursday for 16 weeks. It was organised by a former triathlete called Hayden. The event had grown and everyone from children and older people to regular swimmers, professional athletes and everyone else in between now took part. Swimmers interrupted the waves of the rough seas of Kohimarama Beach as I stood watching on.

This event is billed as New Zealand's largest weekly swim series (during the summer). Although it was casual, it was also competitive. Five different distances were laid out with buoys in the sea: 250m, 500m, 1000m, 1500m and 2000m. It was a race for all – and literally everyone was doing it. I was impressed by the organisation because it was a community event that had grown pretty big. Marquees squared up on the grass with a first aid unit ready to collect any victims of the sea, who would be scooped up by the jet ski or the kayaks. There were even massage tables set up for the returning swimmers!

Charlotte introduced me to Hayden, who wore shiny black sunglasses even as the grey clouds covered any hope of a beautiful summer evening. Hayden had built an interesting product and everyone there was part of this family.

The races were very relaxed, and swimmers supported each other. Yes, there were medals, but over the years it had become a Thursday night of swimming, rather than a competition. The perfect example of this was as the evening was wrapping up and the swimming gantry was being taken down, Hayden popped up with a spot raffle. Some of the kids who had been swimming had dragged their parents back and were standing in the middle of the beach hoping to win big! Prizes included swimsuits worth over $250 donated by various sponsors. Sausages sizzled in the background at some of the stalls as the masseuses finished up for the night.

Events need people like Charlotte and her friends to keep them going. Yes, Hayden had built an epic brand, but events need supporters who want to be part of something rather than just onlookers. At times, events happen through groups of people who are invisible. They might not be the face of the event but, together, they create its beating heart, doing everything they can to make it a success. I was learning pretty early on that events really are not just what we all think. They are complex in every manner of the word.

I was in absolute love with the key message of the event: come and have a swim AND be part of a family. There was not a chance I would be donning my blue swimming bathers – because I would show everyone up with my doggy paddling skills. But it was clear that everyone who attended was having an amazing time and could continue to do so week after week during the summer. It was something to work on and be part of it. It created a sense of achievement, whether you were there to lose weight, to train or simply to have fun. This was a great second event to see and experience – from dry land, anyway.

One thing to take away…

Community wins. Togetherness wins. Sport brings together people with different motivations at times, but they are all getting something out of the same activity – which makes it so complex to appreciate and understand – but quite extraordinary.

Auckland...

Walking the streets of Auckland, bouncing from meeting to meeting, I had to weave my way around all the roadworks. I had only been here for 48 hours and already I was onto my second meeting. Absolutely shattered, that was for sure. Today I was meeting Jon. Jon works with the events team in a large networking events corporation. We met in the lobby and I brought out my notepad, but we just sat and spoke non-stop. I was impressed with what they do with network events, the impact they have on the events sector in New Zealand, and their understanding of event trends that might influence the sector. It was a great chat – and a great hot chocolate. We spoke about the future of events being all about the customer. We also talked about the city of Auckland and the quite curious but incredible future ahead. We agreed that events are more than just moments but actually memories that can benefit various facets of society. And now talking about society – let's go and see the cricket...

Event 3: White Ferns vs India and Black Caps vs India (Cricket)

8th February

"That means it's a six." Gerry was a large Samoan man who, for three hours, explained the rules of cricket to me, a Scotsman, who had no idea what cricket entailed.

To ensure I experienced as much cricket as I could, I walked through the turnstiles of Eden Park when they opened at 3pm. This was the home of New Zealand cricket and one of the most popular stadiums in the country. I was immediately intrigued to see large boards with the word NEIGHBOURHOOD on them with OUR in red. They were a tool used to ensure those who lived in the area knew this stadium was theirs. A bit of background – because of residential objections, the venue was limited to how many sporting days it could hold. In my opinion, this was also very political. In fact, Eden Park had become a political storm. In the past, the owners had been forced to fork out thousands of dollars to navigate the rules so they could host concerts and cricket games, day or night. However, at the same time, and probably due to the restrictions, Eden Park had been in real financial trouble. In turn, the community residential association was concerned that the stadium could be demolished and used for housing. Mindboggling. I kept thinking, "Well, let the stadium host as many events as they can!" I looked into the situation after asking a police officer why there were so many police there for a cricket match. He told me about the need to protect people's front gardens but then, as I looked behind him – literally no lie – all the neighbours were sitting or standing at their gates ushering people along the pavements. They were protecting their own gardens! I was totally confused by the whole situation. But it did show me – and this was my first stadium event – the true impact that big venues can have on residential areas.

When I walked in at first, I was met with the best customer experience from 'fan experience' volunteers. They wore orange tops and beside them were people in blue and yellow with 'ASK ME' on their shirts. They were utterly amazing! Immediately, I felt welcomed. Running up the stairs, I felt like a child excited to walk into a large arena where their favourite cricket team was playing. Large billboards plastered all around said 'Enjoy your Experience at Eden Park'. It was perfect in terms of the customer journey – and I was very impressed.

I got to experience the stadium as the wind whirled around and some fans started arriving. The men's cricket was not starting until 6:30pm. Before then, the White Ferns, the women's cricket team, played a one-day series tour; it was the first time they had played at Eden Park, and also the first time it had been televised. At the start of their match there were only around 100 people dotted around the stadium. As time progressed, the 100 turned into 1,000 and then turned into 10,000 as more people finished work and school and decided to head down for the big night of cricket.

Sitting in a stadium by yourself can be boring. But I always try and make appropriate and deliberate moments of conversation. This is how I made a friend in Gerry. Gerry was brilliant, he really was a great sport. Waving his hands, he explained: "So this means six..." I would tap his shoulder. "What about this?" He was the father of one of the kids who would be going on to wave flags on the pitch, but they'd been invited to come and chill and enjoy the women's cricket beforehand. The kids were more interested in the food vans than the cricket (as was I).

I looked at the cricket in a different way to any other event I had been to as yet. Cricket is a televised opportunity for selling the country. I was not there to look at the bat and balls. I was looking at billboards, fan engagement, televised pieces, technological advancements for fan engagement and so on. The TV audience was estimated at 200 million people – 200 million seeing a Scotsman look extremely bewildered in the middle of the crowd. What did this mean? Auckland was taking the opportunity to sell itself to the world! Never mind the cricket, it was a chance to show off the skylines of Auckland.

Let us take a step back and go outside the stadium. Outside the entrance gates were small marquees, which had been erected for Auckland Tourism to sell a story to those who had bought a ticket. 60% of the stadium was full of fans supporting India. Auckland Tourism wanted to capitalise on opportunities to sell Auckland. Members of a Dohl drumming group played along to a DJ who was dropping the beats. A large group of about 50 men decided to share their dance moves before they entered the stadium. Why was this important? Well, people take photos and videos and post online a moment that shows community and welcoming behaviour. Those moments create interest and attention and, potentially, sales. That is what the cricket was about – not just the bats and balls.

The sports presentation within the cricket itself left a bit to be desired. At times, the audience was totally disengaged and when the presenter did try to get them going, it was drowned out by the sound of the Dohl drums coming from the Indian fan zone. However, they did have an interesting piece of technology: an app where you could pretend to be playing cricket and swing when the ball was shown on the screen. It worked for the presenter, but the organisers hadn't thought about the time it would take to get the app downloaded, which was a shame. However, the giveaways were brilliant – towels with the New Zealand and India badges on them.

As the day went on, I emailed the security company to express how professional and very forward-thinking I thought they were.

But back to the cricket! The cricket score was extremely tight – I believe it was all within one run and a wicket. I made friends with Sam and Elliot, a couple from Christchurch who explained everything and laughed at the relationship I had developed with Gerry. The atmosphere reminded me of being at a carnival. Very loud and lots of fun; such a positive place to be. It was sad, however, when a fight broke out in the middle of our section. Gerry was ready to jump in because a poor Indian fan was being heckled by a New Zealand fan, which is rare. But before you knew it the New Zealand fan was being booed out of the stadium. There was literally no place for this in the sport – which I applaud the fans for.

One thing to take away…

The key point here was about making the event a perfect experience so the fans will love it. The Indian fan zones were electric. The noise was deafening. The TV audience was watching and listening to a sheer spectacle – but nothing like I would experience in India itself. But the bigger picture is what is sometimes missed. Imagine if the stadium audience held up signs saying: "Hello India… See you soon… from New Zealand!" followed up with targeted adverts or a hashtag to follow. Something orchestrated like that would have an impact like no other – just food for thought!

More Meetings…

A friend introduced me to Matt and a company called Blerter, a new app that was being used to centralize communication, operation and safety processes. The app was just being launched into the events world when I met Matt, and the whole team were very enthusiastic about their product. I applauded their energy and their work so far; they were mixing technology with event experience and trying to connect the two like never before. I wish them all the best – I even got a hat – which I lost… Sorry!

Event 4: Bean Rock Swim, Auckland

9th February

So, it's Saturday morning and I am back on the bus, this time to Mission Bay. I can feel the jetlag in my legs; they feel like lead being dragged through the mud. The event today was for professional swimmers. As I arrived, I was met by a wall of athletes all wearing black suits and white hats. It was the turn of the professional swimmers to complete a 3.2km swim to the Bean Rock tower and back. Except there was one quite turbulent problem. The waves were high. The wind was up. The surf was swirling, and the conditions were worse than it had been on Thursday evening. There was tension in the air. (Cue dramatic music.) Swimmers wore a look that said... 'No chance am I going into the water.' A very different atmosphere surrounded this event.

Around about 300 people had dumped and left their bags under gazebos while the swimming event happened. I was in awe at the level of trust as no one was watching the bags – and I know this because for five minutes I stood next to the gazebo and no one came over. Even better, the trophies were all on display – everything was completely unsupervised. I had to get used to different cultures that had different levels of trust and confidence in the community. Also, apparently the area we were in was not at all an area of crime – so that made 'everything fine'.

Looking up, I observed the grey clouds rolling together. The sea was choppy. The lifeguards and those out on jet skis and in kayaks were up and down like they were on a shipping vessel in the Atlantic Ocean. I really didn't know why anyone would think, "This is a great idea... I am about to walk into a sea that might swallow me up." Even the buoys in the distance were moving and had to be rescued by some of the team who were out at the Bean Rock life tower, a warning signal for ships coming in and today the halfway point for the adventurous swimmers. I mean, I was scared just watching the tide.

At 10:30am the hooter went, and a sea of black swimsuits walked or ran into the water for their 3,200m swim. I felt cold just watching them. I could now understand why everyone was advised to wear black suits and white caps. It was easy to locate swimmers with the white hats. As soon as the swimming began, it was clear something was wrong. The current was sweeping them to the right. The route was straight but now everyone was being taken off course. There was a flurry of activity on the shore as a few swimmers managed to get back to the beach, but others had their hands up and the jet ski was plucking them up one by one from the water. As I stood watching, at one point four people were gripping onto the back of the jet ski. Thankfully, the lifesavers and lifeguards were on it, so it was safe. I saw some people getting back to the shore and sitting down after not even swimming 100 metres. I imagined they were thinking, "Why the hell did I walk in there?!" At the same time, others were keeping going, progressing towards the buoy and then turning around and heading back to shore.

I now understood the importance of the safety briefing that everyone had before the start. I could understand why, if someone was stretching at the back, they were pulled up and called out to listen. Each swimmer had a responsibility to ensure their own safety and that of those around them. Through the lens of my camera, I watched a swimmer assist another who had decided they'd had enough, halfway through the swim. They were about 200 metres off course. One swimmer raised his right arm while his left was holding up the one who needed desperate help.

On the horizon, I spotted a surprise visitor – one that was arriving into Auckland Port. As the main group of swimmers reached Bean Rock, they began their swim back to shore. In the distance – well, probably only a kilometre from the Bean Rock tower – a cruise liner was making its way into port. Some of the folk on board were glancing over their balconies to see what was going on. At first, I was fascinated by the size of the cruise ship. Then, my brain switched on to the fact that big ships make big waves. About two minutes after the ship had appeared, the waves had increased by about a foot. Of course, the swimmers were nowhere near the ship or in any danger. But it's funny how some factors that might never have crossed your mind can really affect an event.

Generally, New Zealand's weather means that the majority of events can happen with no issues outdoors. But, like Scotland, Auckland can have four seasons in a day!

One thing to take away…

Sport and lifestyle go hand in hand. A growth in lifestyle events sees hobbies become monetised. This event benefits those who love swimming and being competitive – and at times they use this for professional training. For me, I am scared to jump straight into a pool wearing my arm bands, even with a lifeguard on duty, but for them, they had no issues in the rolling seas.

Back on the bus…

I was back on a bus by midday and it was time to attend my first event as a volunteer. I was constantly on the go – I was pretty tired, that's for sure. So far, I had been to four events and had five meetings, yet I hadn't really discovered or experienced Auckland.

Event 5: Pride #ourmarch

9th February

"As we dream lesbian, gay, trans – all of those other ones; I am 57, I can't remember them all – the identity we choose is to be yourself and be you and who you are – I stand proud to be with you…" The opening lines of the welcome to #ourmarch.

Where do I even start with this event? Short story. In November 2018, the Pride event hit national news because of the decision by the Pride Organising Board not to allow the police of Auckland to wear uniforms on their float during the Pride parade. This was because of historical police brutality towards the LGBTQ+ community. Up to that point, there had never been a problem as the 60 colourful floats took over the streets of Auckland and welcomed 60,000 people to the celebrations. The 2018 decision erupted into a massive internal argument, which in turn resulted in external sponsorship pulling out, media catching the story and other repercussions.

Pride organisers did not want the police to be wearing uniform as part of the parade – point blank. This had major consequences with sponsorship withdrawal, cancellation of floats and other activities that were usually part of the event. The story was headline news for weeks. Now, instead of a parade, Pride 2019 was going to be a protest, a march, #ourmarch. But before we get to that, let's look at the history of Pride.

It has been reported that, in 1969, police in New York City raided a gay bar in Greenwich Village. These types of raids were really not unusual. Police brutality towards the gay community was common. After some resistance from the people in the bar, a brawl kicked off and police officers barricaded themselves in at the Stonewall Inn until backup arrived. The next night, the protest got bigger and the word spread. This wasn't the start of the Stonewall movement – LGBTQ activists had been demonstrating since the 1920s – but it was the turning point, the change that caused the media to relay the message, which in turn began demonstrations around the USA. Celebrations were mixed with political pressure and a call for marriage equality and other rights to be given to those in the LGBTQ community. These days, parades and celebrations are global… and now here I stand at Pride in Auckland.

I arrived at the allocated park and was met by a kilt-wearing pink-mohawk-styled male called Ricky. "You're Scottish," he said, as soon as I opened my mouth. Through sheer national pride, I celebrated at his observation! I explained what I was doing, and he said he had already seen my blurb on the emails I'd sent, and he was grateful I wanted to be part of the event. Ricky was not part of the LGBTQ+ community but was brought in as a freelance event manager. He was very well known around the event.

As I stood with him, I began to notice the amount of colour and some serious bondage that went with it, all around me. I admired the sheer beauty that was starting to grace Albert Park. Next to the fountain was a statue of Queen Victoria, who was now wearing a glittery bra. As some of the drag queens arrived with more glam than a fashion magazine, I felt like I was at a beauty pageant. More volunteers started to arrive, and I began to make friends. A woman called Lynn introduced me to all her ex-girlfriends and then went on to tell me what she thought about what had happened in the lead up to the event. "Basically, this is going to be a protest," she said. Great, I thought. I've just arrived in the country and I'm about to get arrested.

Lynn was right – it was a protest. But it was all official, with the police stopping the traffic and protecting the marchers from any anti-Pride protesters. Just think about that… that's right – four police officers were given the duty of protecting the march that didn't want them in the first place. By 2pm, 2,000 people had arrived. There were heels, glitter, drums, transgender flags and a carnival atmosphere.

As the heterosexual man of the volunteer group, I was of course put at the front of the parade alongside Lynn – and two police officers – to lead the march. Ironic. After what was not really an induction, we began. I met Jim, who was carrying the banner at the front. "Don't worry, you won't get hit," Lynn said. Umm... thanks Lynn! A few people weren't happy with the positions of some flags and I was right in the middle of it all. Lynn really did protect me while she was doing her thing and flirting. She got three new numbers on the parade while I had to stop a drunk man grabbing the banner – I'm not sure who had the better day!

Walking along the streets was fun. The chanting. The voices. The people. Of course, this all resulted from the issues back in the 70s. But there was something quite interesting about meandering along the streets. This was the type of event I wanted to experience – a protest. A constructed and manufactured protest from a small group of people who had an opinion – which was something that completely changed the scope of the whole event.

We arrived at the site where the programme had started, and it was pretty good. Food trucks and other expenditure opportunities. I was volunteering at the information stand. The questions ranged from "Why is he getting to sing on the stage?" to "Can I get your number... " But once I explained it was international, they walked away! There were also a few first aid incidents.

I loved getting to know Ken, who had volunteered with Pride for five years prior. He was a prolific volunteer who loved to be part of events. Married to Sue, he had recently completed the gruelling, year-long, around the world boat race.

Some people were friendly and some wary of me, which I can understand. After all, I was a Scottish guy standing around asking questions and telling them I was writing a book. "Are you a journalist? We don't like journalists." No, I'm not, I told them. Soon, though, everyone was chatting and telling me their story. *"I'm going to get an operation... Pride helped me come out... No one understands me... I want equal rights for my sister who is gay."*

This was more than an event. I witnessed what brands, who for years had sent large floats to the event, had missed – the people's stories.

I really started to feel for the pressures associated with what Pride really is and has become. This event, of course, was stripped back. But my observation was that commercialisation was absolutely ruining the objectives of the event. Instead, businesses have spotted an opportunity, in my opinion, to jump on the bandwagon and use it to promote themselves as 'LGBTQ+ friendly' – but sometimes just for that weekend.

I felt like, in Auckland, a statement by the few thousand people in attendance was more powerful than a radio station putting glitter and flags on a wagon and tweeting they were part of Pride.

One thing to take away…

Events can be used to make voices heard and this choreographed march really signalled the need for change, with the message that this was more than a commercial opportunity to sell your brand. This is why Pride 2019 in Auckland became the talking point for the whole global Pride community. It changed the position of Pride and for me it showed that Pride should be about fighting for rights for the community rather than selling more rainbow-coloured cakes in a café.

A run to a pub…

On the night of Pride, I had arranged to meet a great friend. Nick works in events and was in Auckland for one night. Meeting in a local pub, we spoke about my project, the world of events and how it was changing. We even played the piano – all over a few beers and a fresh orange juice. It was a great night! After less than five days in Auckland, jet lag was finally stowed in my luggage!

Event 6: Auckland Vegan Food Festival

10th February

Auckland was giving me ALLLLLLL the events. Only five days in and I'm already at event number six. Madness. Now it was time to go to a 'trendy' event that reflected the current popularity of veganism. However, I was met with something very commercial.

I was driven by Annette, a friend from the Commonwealth Games, who took me across to North Auckland. This event was in North Auckland for two specific reasons: wealth; and because the people were all over the latest lifestyle trend. Tickets were being sold from a small booth connected to the leisure centre, with the main event held in their park. It cost $10 just to walk in. I laughed. I was starting to see a different side to events. This was the 'tap into the trend' market and people were flocking to it. As I walked around, I saw display boards advertising talks titled *'What makes the best vegan...'* Well, for $20 I could buy an avocado burger – all it told me was that I didn't have the bank account to become the best vegan!

The car park was full of an array of food and drink outlets, all very pastel-coloured and all with a very authentic 'food truck' look and feel. Walking around, I saw a crowd that, demographically, met the profile the company was targeting: those in 'active wear', driving fancy cars, not scared to 'tap' their bank cards and buying all the protein shakes there were to buy.

The yoga classes were full, with pre-booked spaces for an authentic yoga experience. I mean, okay... but we're in a car park. Of course, they had put some plants around the traffic bollards to make it more like an oasis. Clever! A DJ had all the latest relaxing trance music coming from the iPad, jamming like he was the main act at a famous UK music festival in front of 60,000 people. Instead, the active wearers were more interested in the free samples of nuts or the 'vegan sausage' stall. Ten years ago, never would the events programme of a city or any event promoter be organising a Vegan Food Festival. But things have changed. People are looking for sustainable, trendy and, to a degree, 'Instagrammable' events. And this was one of them.

Veganism was a huge thing that New Zealanders were embracing and the appetite for more events like this was growing. It was about a movement. And the event tapped into that trend. But, as I sat at the lunch benches eating my avocado burger and watching the other attendees, all I saw was people taking photos to show people on social media that they were at the event. Great for promotion, but maybe less about embracing the lifestyle.

I just didn't see the value away from 'making money...'

One thing to take away...

In a way, I was a bit annoyed to see something that was about being a vegan made so commercial. The event seemed to encourage a dilution of the lifestyle – by active-wearing, Instagram-posting people jumping on the trendy bandwagon.

Event 7: Shakespeare Pop-up Globe, Auckland

<u>10th February</u>

I was met by the wonderful Liesl at the gates of a racing course in the outskirts of Auckland, who introduced me to the world of the 'Pop-up Globe'. I was taken backstage and to the costume department – which was just amazing, especially when I met an award-winning costume designer who has many TV credits from around the world to her name.

I walked through the grounds of Ascot Hospital to the site where the Pop-up Globe Theatre had been based for the past three years. It was quite a special building. The theatre was about replicating the London Globe and allowing Shakespeare to be seen in Auckland at affordable prices, and accessible to all. In theory, events are for everyone. But by the time all the costs are taken into account – tickets, travel, food and drink, merchandise – there are many who can't attend. Here at the Pop-up Globe, the organisers had made it very cheap. Standing tickets (not advised with those with bad backs or sore feet) were just $5. You were literally at the front of the stage. It was a theatre experience for all, literally for the cost of two coffees. I liked the approach. Yes, the food and drink were a bit pricey, but no more so than at other events.

Inside the theatre, I was introduced to the truly devoted fans of this run. For every performance, the group of devotees stood at the front of the stage, saying the script at the same time as the actors and fully decked out in merchandise that they were either gifted by the company or had bought themselves. They were all known to the theatre company and had their very own place to stand; you didn't dare go into that patch of land! The marketing manager explained that they have used their feedback to make sure the audience gets an experience like nothing before. Even better, they were invited by the director to the wrap party because they were all so well-liked and known.

Sometimes the arts and theatre can seem like a closed shop. But what tonight showed as I looked around was that a new audience was dawning. Those who may not have grown up with access to the theatre because of expensive tickets or a lack of interest were turning up. Shakespeare Pop-up Globe had a plan that was about breaking barriers. Walking in, the staff at the gates welcomed you to the performance with big smiles. The large, up-lit signs made the whole thing really welcoming – and a great Instagram photo. The gardens were very pretty. And the bar was built into a shipping container, which I don't think was originally in the plans for Hamlet but, you know, 21st century revamp and all that, and it gave it a nice urban buzz.

Tonight's performance was the 'press and fan favourite' showing of Hamlet – the director's run through. The director jumped on the stage at the start and spoke. He was very personable and knew some of the devoted fans. I was very impressed with his friendly approach.

The play was rough around the edges, but it was a splendid piece of work. However, it was also very long, as the company spent the evening cutting and changing and running scenes again. And there I was thinking I was clever turning down the offer of the royal box in favour of standing… Fast forward to three hours later and I couldn't feel my legs. But I was also glad to be standing so close to the stage, for sure. I got to see the actors forget their lines and hear the laughter that was not in the dialogue. I got to feel the passion when the monologues were so intense. Did I understand any of it? Some. I hardly understand common-day English, never mind Shakespearean English. But this was why I went. I wanted to discover how something like this made such a positive impact. It was a great way of pushing the boundaries of cultural consumption. We should all have the opportunity to consume something we have not experienced before – and for $5, the whole of Auckland had a chance to do just that.

Everyone was really enjoying themselves. No one in the spectator standing area moaned or groaned. They all knew what they were getting into. The great thing was how the audience became part of the performance. Occasionally the actors would come down the steps and do their lines from the middle of the standing area. Audience members shuffled around as they got the blood back into their legs. I don't think those seated upstairs had as immersive an experience. I would say standing gave me something of a 'pure' experience. That, for me, was all I wanted – and what I got.

To have this piece of artwork played in front of me, all within a scaffolded pop-up theatre, was truly wonderful. It kind of cemented the fact that an experience can happen anywhere.

One thing to take away…

Theatre is not about dividing – it's about immersion. It's about being in a theatre and feeling lost but guided by the performance and that is exactly what I felt. I watched a performance that was sublime and beautiful. I watched something powerful. It was a great insight and a great night.

Auckland Farewell

I remember back in June 2018 searching on LinkedIn for 'Auckland Events Professionals' and seeing who came up in the searches. I began to message people and was honoured when one of the contacts shared my post about the trip – and that was Stu. Stu opened so many doors for me and what I learned very quickly was that Auckland is a very small events sector, and everyone knew everyone. Stu works in event insurance and he really did give me so much insight into the industry. Stu is originally from England and has absolutely smashed it since being in Auckland. I told him all about my trip and we had a great discussion about the future of the events industry in Auckland.

Auckland overall was such a special time and the perfect place to kick off my adventure.

Melbourne...

I flew over to Melbourne intending to simply relax!

I had booked this very impromptu visit because my friend Andrew (my old flatmate when I lived in Melbourne in 2015) and his beautiful wife Catherine were having a baby. After the adventure of Auckland, singing *Twinkle, Twinkle* sounded like the perfect way to spend three days.

I met some other amazing friends while I was in Melbourne – Sam, Trevor and many more. I also visited Melbourne Cricket Ground, which was quite special. I had worked with Josh indirectly at the Australian Open. Now he was responsible for the customer service delivery plan at this historic, iconic venue, where 75,000 people can come and enjoy spectacular performances ranging from music concerts to Australian Football League matches. He took me on a backstage tour and I even got to stand next to the pitch!

Melbourne was just what I needed – it was about meeting people rather than going to events. Thank you to my very good friends the Jacksons, my former flatmate from Melbourne, for the time we spent together getting me ready for the next leg of the trip! I caught up with great friends and I even spent Valentine's Day in Melbourne... by myself; I did plan to attend a speed dating night as one of my events but unfortunately they were all full!

Queenstown

It was time to board my flight for the second half of my trip to New Zealand. I had a feeling this was going to be different. The people I met in Auckland absolutely made the whole thing for me. While the city was mostly concrete and glass, the people really brought out its character. But now it was time to see the countryside. To see the mountains and to take in a deep breath of that fresh New Zealand air. This was flight five – and I had only been travelling for 12 days…

I arrived at a shed of an airport and waited for the luggage belt to kick into action. Bikes and surfboards came first and then the bags. I grabbed my large backpack and then approached a wall of airport customs officers and police officers. I don't know why I felt nervous, but I start to stutter. "Do you have anything on you that you shouldn't have?" they asked.

"Nope," I said, very quickly.

"To the right…" This was for further questioning.

Queenstown is the adventure capital of the whole of New Zealand; it's an area that is all about adventure sports. Bungee jumping, speed boating, parachuting – whatever you think would get your heartbeat going over 180 beats per minute is here. In a way, it was great research for me to see who was engaging with the town and in what way. However, I was only in Queenstown for two reasons – to run my first 10km run, as part of Shotover Mountain Marathon, and to meet with Queenstown Council.

I was staying in a hostel and one guy in the room had a bag containing a shell with a dead fish in it. He apologised so much – the smell was revolting. There was another gentleman, a South Korean, who was always up late on his laptop; one night I walked in at about half eleven to find him watching something that I could only describe as 'light porn'. I don't know who got more of a fright when he realised I was in the room as I climbed up to my top bunk. He slammed his laptop shut and shouted "WHATTTT…!"

Now I had to prepare…

Event 8: 10km Run, Shotover Mountain Marathon, Queenstown

16th February

On Friday morning it was time to pick up my racing pack for my first ever 10km run. YESSSS! I felt very excited as I strolled through the town centre. By chance, I bumped into a friend I hadn't seen in a year, who was working in Australia. He was running in one of the other races, competing with his running partner and very good friend Martin. They were seasoned runners and very experienced, and they both talked me through what to expect.

The organisers had arranged for everyone to collect their race bibs and numbers from a local shoe shop. It was a very clever approach by the organisers, to positively benefit the local economy. What a perfect introduction for a runner, who is likely to need new shoes or new running equipment.

The event was Shotover Mountain Marathon in Ben Lomond Station in Queenstown, New Zealand. Held in the middle of summer, in New Zealand's summer heat, there were several different races, including a 5km, 10km (the one I was doing), 21km, 30km and 43km.

I got up pretty early on Saturday morning. Most of the backpackers in the hostel were heading off to paraglide, jet ski or do other extreme activities. But nope – not me. I was away to run up and down a mountain.

I had never run 10km before – ever. So, when I told everyone I was going to be doing 10km runs around the world, they were like "Wow! Crazy." And "Have you got strong ankles?" My first one was going to be up a mountain. How hard could it be? As I approached the bus where I was going to be collected, I started to get butterflies. We drove through pothole-riddled roads and over metal cattle grids and arrived in the middle of nowhere. A gantry marking the race start literally sat alone in the middle of a field with a few marquees around.

When the starting hooter sounded, I felt a buzz and just ran. Some people were off. Like, sprinting. In my head, I screamed: "This ain't a race!" My brain struggled to engage with my legs, and I slowed down tremendously quickly. I couldn't help but stop occasionally to admire the view of the mountain towering over me. The rough edges of the face of the mountain were truly spectacular. The blue sky was brighter than the sun. Each step gave me a new perspective on this journey and this run. It gave me a view that was – well, what can only be described as simply beautiful. The trees looked so green – untouched. They'd probably never had as many observers or fans run past them as they did today. Everything smelled so fresh – no petrol from cars – and no noise pollution, apart from the scuff of shoes on the ground.

Three people were ahead of me and my strategic plan was to run at the same pace as the person in the middle, which meant I would get ahead of the third person but still use them as a backmarker, and that is what happened. For about 2km I was loving the pace. It worked. And then the uphill drag began. My legs started screaming and my strategic plan disappeared. I was gutted as I started to slow.

I ran for my life. I ran for the experience of being able to take part in my first ever 10km in the middle of a mountain range. Nothing could top this. I couldn't believe I was part of such an amazing event. Emotionally, I had so much adrenaline. So many positive thoughts were running through my mind. I had an energy I had never felt before. It was either that or the realisation that if I didn't get off the mountain in four hours the sun would set and I'd be stuck!

I had to slow down slightly after 5km. I did ask the volunteers on the route whether the bus service would be coming through but unfortunately weekend service didn't apply. I was absolutely outraged!

The best thing was that I was running into the complete unknown. I had literally not checked anything about the course. Suddenly I regretted that as I saw the river below. I came down a hill that was at a 45-degree decline and was stunned as I plunged into crystal clear, cold water. It reached my knees and was pretty fast flowing. As I reached the other side of the river I looked above to see some people still clambering through the valley, which was a very steep drop. No green screen needed for the perfection that was this setting.

My final 500 metres approached, and I met a new running partner, a guy called Darren. I was pushing this guy to finish, and he was pulling me. I said: "Right, Darren – I'm sprinting." And I sprinted like I was about to win the 100-metre final at the Olympics. I could see the stadium (finish gantry in the middle of a field) come into eye line. I could see the thousands (well, 50 people and a few vans) erupt as I approached the final 20 metres. I could feel each step bouncing through my bones. As I ran over the finish line, the roars of the 50 people standing at the gantry were overwhelming and quite emotional. "This is Matt Lamb, who is writing a book. Here he comes…"

I put my fist in the air, punched twice and bent over with a tear in my eye. I had just done something I'd never done before. I had just completed my first 10km run and I was absolutely overwhelmed. I wasn't sure if the tears came from the pain shooting through my body, the exhaustion or the fact I had just completed the 10km. This was event number eight and already I felt I had achieved so much, just from this run. My time was 1 hour and 13 minutes and 48 seconds – very respectable.

After the race, I stood and smiled as I realised I was now a tenth of the way through my journey. Unbelievable. My feet were in agony, but it was a great pain to have. High above, I could hear the sound of the helicopter as it approached a makeshift landing pad, dropping off people who had either pulled out of the marathon or had been injured on one of the other runs and required first aid. The logistics that went into this was quite phenomenal. A helicopter, a bus, the planning of the runs, the welfare, the sausage sizzles and so on. The whole thing was just beautifully organised. The race welcomed people from all over the world. It was a great boost for local tourism and a great use of the land.

As I lay on the grass relaxing, which I guess only a week before had sheep grazing on it, I saw Steve and Martin come across the line after a great half-marathon run. Absolutely amazing achievement. They were brilliant support for me prior to the race and now I was their personal welcoming party. It was a wonderful feeling. We sat on the grass and had a burger.

Back on the bus and off we went. A simple bit of paper bearing my race number was my medal. A cherished keepsake.

One thing to take away...

Next time you see a running event that's happening or being organised, look at who is organising it. If it's a local company, go out and support them. Go down to the finish site and support the runners. Clap each of them on.

Back from the mountains...

I had planned one meeting with Queenstown Council regarding the events they organise and the direction the town was taking. With a population of 15,850, Queenstown is very sparsely occupied, but during the peak tourist season the population can go up to 25,000 a week. The strain on medical provision, policing and other public services had been noted recently by local councillors as a problem. 'Over-tourism' had been discussed by the council and University of Otago, and it had been noted that there needs to be more direction given to slow down the number of people coming to the town and enjoying the natural beauty. The roads were plagued with campervans and buses. When I met with the council it was clear they had never had to deal with the problem of 'How do we get tourists here?' Instead, they were in dire straits and were trying to stop the high street becoming filled with pop-up shops for tourism adventures. Local businesses were being driven out.

And I understood why. Queenstown felt like a tacky town centre instead of the beautiful wealthy town it used to be, which was popular for its relaxed atmosphere and attractive neighbourhoods. Apparently house prices had decreased and, when sold, were becoming Airbnbs – which changed the population. For sure, they are in a very difficult position. However, the position is clear as you walk about the streets and see signs saying 'Please do not walk this way – we want privacy' or 'Not a tourist attraction'. What will the near future hold for Queenstown?

On my last night in Queenstown I was sitting in the kitchen area of the hostel when a young couple came in. I was like, "YESSSS, friends!" For two hours we chatted and played Jenga. They were lovely people – the woman worked for a jewellery design company and the guy worked for Adelaide Water. We sat, we laughed and then at 10:20pm we were thrown out of the kitchen. That was it; our friendship was over. But it's alright – I gave them some butter to use the next day!

Bus to Christchurch

Christchurch, the city that had been devastated following an earthquake, was going to be my final destination in New Zealand. I jumped on the bus and had an empty seat next to me – excellent. Off we went as I sat typing up some things I needed to do in Christchurch and then in Asia.

My focus was to understand the future of the events to benefit a city. Now I was about to assess and analyse the positive direction of the city. The Christchurch I saw was full of hope!

Event 9: Electric Avenue Music Festival, Christchurch

23rd February

Electric Avenue Music Festival is an annual event that began during the reconstruction of Christchurch and brings international artists to the city. I was given permission to visit the site before the event opened and meet the amazing Jane, who I had been messaging for the last six months. She told me what the festival was like and about the audience, and we talked about audience engagement. Everyone around us was busy, with forklifts beeping and stages still being built.

On festival day I walked to Hagley Park. The place was already busy, and I encountered several individuals along the routes scratching their noses – not sure what's going on there, possibly hay fever... It was 1pm and already you could tell a music festival was nearby. Groups of young people on electric scooters were whizzing past, falling off just before they entered the gates of the festival. The closer I got, the more I realized: "This is going to be *fun* – and challenging!"

"Oh, the music is so loud..." I feel like an old man as I venture around the site. But actually, although I was probably the oldest person on site for about four hours, that wasn't true by the time the event truly began, as there were plenty of parents in the crowd who had probably come to keep an eye on their 18-year-olds, who had been here all day after being dropped off by a fleet of buses from the university halls. The festival takes place during the orientation week (Freshers' Week) for the two main universities in the city – which meant that 75% of the student community had purchased a ticket for the event.

Each stage was blasting out a different genre of music through the hanging speakers, attracting its own audience. At one stage, the crowd had their eyes closed as they nodded along to the 'dum dum dum dum dum dum...' beats. Elsewhere, the crowd was singing "I need a dollar..." back at the stage while Aloe Blacc basked in the glory of the performance.

My best memory of the whole day was when I stood right at the front. The stage towered over me. I felt like an old father who had got lost and ended up at the festival. All around me were gatherings of friends: some had grown up in the 90s listening to Orbital, while others were youngsters appreciating and enjoying Aloe Blacc. The front of the stage was the perfect place to meet people as we were crammed in like sardines and had nothing else to do but talk to those around us. My new friend Adam (from Christchurch, studying Social Sciences) and I helped lift people to safety when there were some major crowd issues at the front of the stage. It was a very warm day, so the security guards started giving us water to pass around.

As I stood in the crowd I got a real sense of the reason why people attend festivals – that feeling, that emotional connection, the purpose. My pulse was racing as I threw my hands in the air, high volume music and the euphoric experience taking me on a journey. This was my first music festival of the adventure and I am not a festival goer but I was loving this. It was 4pm. Would this energy sustain me throughout the day? Well, let us see.

One thing I loved was the secret stage. I had been told by Jane to search everywhere for this stage. Everywhere. I couldn't think where it could be. Apparently it was a cave, but we were in the middle of a public park. I went to the toilet and realised there was something suspicious about two of the *portaloos*. For a start, a security guard was protecting them. And the doors were a different colour to the rest of the *portaloos* surrounding me. Cunningly, they had taken out the toilet and created the most unique entrance to a marquee, which was well hidden behind the toilets! In I went.

A DJ was dropping the tunes in a venue with toilet paper

draped over the ceiling. The heat was overwhelming. This was house music in all its glory. The marquee – which had about 100 people squeezed in – felt like a very different event to the festival that was happening outside. In here were the advanced ravers. They were experienced. No first-timers here. Technically, it was beautiful. Practically, it was clever.

A very interesting feature of the festival was the payment method. A unique cashless system meant no bar or food truck at all was accepting cash or cards (although at times I did see some sneaky dollars being passed over). When you arrived on site you went straight to the cabins where you could add on money – which was ironic, in that you had to pay in cash. From the event's point of view, it was clever in that whatever you didn't spend you could claim back – but only for a certain amount of time. I wonder how much they made through students forgetting to claim back a few dollars. At the end of the day, I had 30 cents left after putting 30 dollars on, the majority of which was spent at the coffee van.

Night was closing in and the headline acts appeared on stage. I had been standing in the park now for eight hours. I was cold, lonely and overwhelmed by the amount of information I had collected. At this point you're probably thinking: "Matt, why were you lonely?" Well, let's just think about that. Generally, when you go to events, you go in a group – especially to a music festival. No way would I usually go by myself. I was thinking about heading home.

I am probably one of only a few people to be able to say I was at Electric Avenue sober – with two hot chocolates and a belly full of local ribs. The 2018 festival had been overshadowed by drug incidents, and one of the major changes I witnessed was within the welfare area at the end of the night. It was staffed by police and first aiders who wanted to make sure everyone was looked after to the highest standards before either being picked up by family or friends or taken to hospital for further medical treatment.

Today, the festival had seen 25 artists perform in 11 hours.

However, it was more than a music festival. The residents of Christchurch had bought into the festival and fully immersed themselves in it. They looked forward to it, saved up for it and circled it in their diaries. This event was not just about having musicians in Christchurch, it was about putting Christchurch on the map so the citizens could love and enjoy their city. A tide of change was coming, and this event was part of that tide. The passion the organisers had for this event was the same energy I saw throughout the whole of Christchurch.

When I left the event, I managed to walk in the wrong direction. By this point it's pitch black, my phone has died, and I have no clue where I am or how to get back to my hostel. Thankfully, five youths from the city saw me and shouted: "Hello, are you okay?" They were so kind and they took me back to the street where the hostel was. Aasha, Brooke, Mika, Seth and Victoria are the beacons of this city. They are the future and will drive Christchurch back to competing as a global city.

One thing to take away…

What did this festival offer? A cashless system, musicians from around the world, sponsorship activations, surprise stages and much more. The friendships I made at this festival set the tone for my whole stay in Christchurch. Electric it really was…

The meetings

I was very fortunate that in Christchurch I was welcomed with open arms. ChristchurchNZ is the city's tourism agency and in my opinion, they were doing a really good job of marketing the city. Jemma was responsible for bidding for events to be held in Christchurch and had agreed to meet me and that is where everything positively spiralled. It was fantastic to have Jemma's time and we delved into so much regarding the future of Christchurch and the different events that were coming to the city.

Event 10: South Island Lantern Festival, Christchurch

"Hi, I am Matthew..." I was meeting a very energetic woman called Amanda who was the project manager for the South Island Lantern Festival. Today I would be shadowing her and volunteering with her team. I was excited by Amanda's energy already and I could tell we would get on. She was full of excitement for my project.

First port of call was the volunteer briefing. I stood at the back, with my notes on my phone, taking everything in. Before I knew it... "Right, let's go, Matt!" Out the door and onto the next task. Eighteen volunteers had just experienced the most detailed and fastest volunteer briefing they could have ever imagined.

For two days I was given the opportunity to learn from the very experienced event managers of ChristchurchNZ and Christchurch City Council. Obviously, they did not know who I was, but before I knew it, I was being asked to "...carry boxes, swap over that fence line..." and so on. I was introduced to some of the staff and they were like: "YOU'RE THE GUY GOING AROUND THE WORLD – CRAZY!" Instead of feeling like a volunteer, I felt part of the team of five, who really welcomed me with open arms. The South Island Lantern Festival is a celebration of Chinese culture that embraces the city centre of Christchurch. This was their last major event of the summer season and a nice way to finish.

On the Friday, it was all hands on deck before the event began. A few of the team and I went around on scooters stopping cars, moving signs and setting up marquees. Originally the plan was for me to sit in the control room but before I know it, it became: "Matt, can you give us a hand... you okay with this?!" Absolutely fine, no problem was my response as I grabbed my hoodie and my high vis.

Excellent.

The clock struck 5pm and it was time for all the lanterns to be lit. I went around with Amanda, who was introducing me to everyone as "...the guy going around the world."

I was particularly interested in understanding cultural events, and how national and local government agendas achieve community buy-in for more than just an event. This event was about celebrating the Chinese community with parades, community market stalls and authentic food. There was a sense of inclusion, a sense of breaking down any barriers. I did a lot of reading into cultural events before attending. One key thing is the packaging of authentic experiences. The South Island Lantern Festival had:

✓ **The right food stalls** – culinary experiences and stalls that sold a unique Chinese food experience.

✓ **Language appreciation** – The information stall was staffed by students who spoke both English and Mandarin. This gave the students the opportunity to get involved in the community.

✓ **Performances** – Dance is a key part of Chinese tradition and culture. Even the band, who played a lovely version of *Country Roads,* were accompanied by large Chinese dragons – quite unique.

✓ **Lanterns** – The static lights are visual spectacles.

Cultural identity is important in a globalized society because some cultures lose their authenticity, whatever we believe it is! We live in a world where the question being asked is: "Is culture actually important anymore?" Well, I saw that question being answered. I would argue that events such as this allow culture to be brought to the forefront of people's engagement with society. It gives a level of emotional satisfaction and an identity of belonging.

"Matt, can you head across and bring some sandbags...?" I hadn't worked this hard in a while and suddenly I was sweating as I went from one side of the town centre to the other. An hour in, I had started to learn the shortcuts but I kept getting stopped and asked for directions. Before I knew it, I was being asked about the whereabouts of the bus station and the time of the last bus!

The crowd really did enjoy the event. But I kept wondering whether they were here because it was something to do or because they care about the culture and story that goes into the making of each illuminated light. Or was it because Christchurch was quite a tight community and every event needs to be supported?

One of the most important features was the food area. The spring rolls were lovely! The food queues on the Friday were just mad – in a good way. People were very patient as they waited their turn. Many people kept their bellies empty the whole day so they could eat at the festival. As we walked – me, and the team that I was now fully a part of – through the markets, everyone had a dish of something. People were sharing bits: "You want some of this and can I have that?" I really was seeing the relationships that events create between people. We were part of orchestrating that and creating a space that allowed togetherness, socialising and trying new things! The Friday was so full of activity that I was struggling to take it all in.

Creating something like this takes a lot of planning but one thing can completely throw all plans... the weather. Friday had been roasting; a great Christchurch summer's evening. Now on Sunday – it was pouring with rain. I arrived at 11am; call time wasn't until 2pm, but I knew I had to get down early to help out. The place was just wet. A lot of the beautiful lanterns were being protected with plastic sheets and cables were wrapped in anything that would protect them from this sudden storm. The traders' stalls were slightly flooded but the event was still going ahead – in a very restricted way.

Because of the weather all the entertainment had been cancelled so really this was now a food festival. But for me that was ideal because I got to experience something new. I got first-hand experience of the sustainability and trader checks that ChristchurchNZ and the council had in place. I was allocated to a team member of Christchurch City Council and off we went. I was promised it would not be exciting. "Oh yes, it will!" I said. "To be able to see the measures you are putting in place for sustainability on a local government level - I'm excited!" There was a moment of laughter before we set off.

"This is not the correct food packaging – you have a plastic coating on this." And so it began. The first trader was getting (politely) ripped apart by Shanti, the team member I was shadowing for the day. She was brilliant with the traders and knew them all. She produced the guidelines that all traders must adhere to. I watched as the traders, who knew they were in the wrong, would for about 30 seconds deny any errors and then realise their mistake.

As we walked around the car park, which was now the trading area, I found a used needle. After the call was made by Shanti on the radio everyone was laughing. "Trust you to find this..." The needle needed to be fully disposed of because it was a drug use needle. And I share this information because when you are working in the middle of a city centre environment the space is not fully closed – so you just never know. Events often use spaces that are used by others in ways that are of course drastically challenging.

The measures that were in place were part of a bigger picture. They were beacons of possibilities, trying to push forward sustainability around all the events that occur in Christchurch. Shanti also explained that she is the one who measures events' sustainability strategies. She attends the event and evaluates the use of bins, carbon emissions and other factors involved in compressing the impact the event can have on society. The only problem I noted in the sustainability strategy for South Island Lantern Festival was that one of the main sponsors was an airline company. This was having a huge impact on what they were trying to achieve. But partnerships are partnerships. Money is money. It is refreshing to meet someone who cares so much about sustainability; it's through people like Shanti that change happens. She was tremendous. It took a lot of hard work but all the vendors listened and respected exactly what she was saying. I was so impressed by the sustainability direction at this event.

Sunday was a hard day. As someone who wanted to write a story about the events industry, this was the perfect opportunity to see what happens when it doesn't go to plan. Unfortunately, the weather really did impact the numbers. Heads were down and everyone seemed a bit disheartened – including the traders, and the team who work tirelessly on the planning of every possibility.

At 11pm the final task was to move the bell that had been on display throughout the festival. The bell was called the 'Wuhan Bell'. I learned prior and post and also when researching and writing this book that Wuhan and Christchurch have had a Friendship City Agreement since 2006. The bell was heavy. Drew, Mark, Andy and I were knackered after three extremely intense days but now we pushed this special bell through the very quiet streets of Christchurch.

Finally, at just past midnight, I said farewell and goodnight. I was never meant to be at the heart of operations, but the team took me under their wing. I loved being part of the team and learned a lot. Although the weather dampened some of the celebrations, it was overall a success, with great press captured and happy memories for all those who attended on the Friday and Saturday.

One thing to take away…

Cultural celebrations are constructed in an authentic method to ensure community buy-in. Bright lanterns and a well-packaged event were truly spectacular to witness. I was also introduced to Pineapple Lumps (my new addiction). The organising team has massive ambition and I fully believe this city will benefit from generating ideas and putting them into conception. Christchurch will be a global name for events – I put my name on it and say it will happen. Be ready, world, they're coming to get you!

So, thank you to ChristchurchNZ – Jemma for first answering my email and Jen for the Skype chat – and thank you to Christchurch City Council – Amanda, Drew, Shanti, Mark, Paul, Andrew, Vanessa... Stu from P4G and I know I have missed people out, I am sorry. But you made my weekend absolutely fantastic!

Event 11: Christchurch Town Hall Opening

In the midst of Electric Avenue Music Festival and South Island Lantern Festival, I attended another event. Before I went to the music festival on the Saturday, I headed off for the opening of Christchurch Town Hall. Eight years after the city was devastated by an earthquake, the new town hall was about to reopen for all to witness. This central landmark's aim was to bring the community together even more. The sun was shining, the birds were tweeting and, as an outsider, maybe I was not fully grasping the true emotional significance of what was happening.

By 10:30am, around 150 people were queueing up outside the building. They were a completely different demographic to the people I'd been spending time with at the festivals. Even though the town hall wasn't yet officially open, you could sense the excitement in the air.

Compared to some of the events I attended during this adventure, the opening of a town hall might seem quite boring. However, my trip was about more than attending happy, fluffy events and this was an occasion that would be cemented into Christchurch's history forever. This was part of the vision for the city. A place of new possibilities and unity. It was a giant step towards getting back to normality. In 2011 the city was not just flattened; it was completely ruined – and there was no fast fix. Now, as I glanced around, over 500 people were standing outside the town hall. As the local police stopped to assist, the crowd grew. Security, I could tell, was not really ready for the numbers. Logistically, a lot had not been thought through. Maybe that was just the norm here – a very relaxed approach!

The crowd was welcomed from the podium by the leader of the local Māori community, a well-dressed giant of an elder. He was very well-spoken and delivered his speech like he was accepting an Oscar. The mayor spoke next. I'd been in Christchurch for five days now and had heard the mayor speak three times. It made me laugh because some of the local people I met had told me: "I ain't heard the mayor speak once and I've lived here all my life!"

The mayor was very proud of her city and, just like me, she had attended everything that was going on that weekend in an attempt to get as many locals as possible to explore the new city. She opened her speech with the words: "This is a dream come true."

At its heart, Christchurch was aiming to become a city for all. The red ribbon hanging in front of the doors was a gesture of welcome rather than anything symbolic. This was no big spectacle, but it was a unique event that will never be repeated – hopefully. I fully believe the state-of-the-art facilities being built will put Christchurch on the global stage and help them compete with Auckland, Tokyo, Paris... Crazy?

The city of Christchurch can go wherever it wants. The ribbon being cut did not only symbolise the opening of the town hall but the city opening a new chapter in a story the world should be excited to read!

One thing to take away...

The future is more than just bright, it's wonderful, just like the new town hall. Oh, I didn't get in – I was too busy going to a festival!

Christchurch Earthquake Memorial

Friday 22nd February was the 8th anniversary of the disaster. I was told there was going to be a memorial event to remember those who tragically lost their lives in the earthquake. For a lot of reasons, I didn't write about it while I was travelling. I didn't want to use a city's sorrow as part of my tale about attending events. However, after a lot of thought, I realised that Christchurch meant so much to me that I had to share, briefly, this show of unity.

As I waited for the memorial service to begin, I sat on the grass, far away from the main area where everyone was gathering. However, as more and more people arrived, I found myself now in the middle, with staff from the nearby office blocks and businesses surrounding me. Some people were linking up with family and friends and comforting each other. Firefighters who had been part of the rescue arrived in their trucks to a very subtle and quite touching welcome from those around them. I wasn't here as part of *Around the World in 80 Events;* I was here as someone who had been truly welcomed into the city and seen first-hand the spirit of the people.

Everyone looked towards the memorial wall, which sat on the banks of the Ōtākaro/Avon River. Everyone had a story from that awful day. I won't write any more, but believe me, this event, this whole experience – from the words of the mayor to the community leaders, and the names being spoken of those who tragically passed away – it stayed with me throughout the rest of my journey.

Thank you, Christchurch

Every time I spoke to anyone back home during the eight months and two weeks of my trip, I always said that I wished I could have stayed in Christchurch. Whenever I am asked, "Where was your favourite place?" Christchurch is always my answer. I fell in love with a city that was rebuilding its way to becoming, globally, even more competitive. Yes, it's on the corner of the world map – but it's not in the corner of my heart and it should be somewhere people watch and want to visit. Every time I walked along the roads and saw the new paving, the construction signs, the recycled shipping containers now used as art and much more – I fell even more in love.

With events galore and smiling hearts, Christchurch will

always stay with me. Thank you!

The bustle of Jakarta…

I deliberately hadn't looked at any travel books! I didn't have any expectations. Instead, I went with eyes and ears open – but eventually, because of the noise, I had to close them! The capital city of Indonesia would be a barrage of noise and an array of something never seen by me before.

"Be careful!" Those were the words of the police, security, hotel night manager and everyone else I met when they found out I was going somewhere. I think they were scared for me – but I wasn't scared at all.

I came out of the airport and caught a train heading downtown to Sudirman Baru station, in Central Jakarta. The time was 22:30pm. The streets were packed. The buzz and constant noise of scooters was the first thing that hit me, the noise engulfing me. With the sweat dripping down me I had two choices – get a taxi and probably get ripped off, or walk. Guess which crazy decision I took? I walked the 3.2km. With a total of 24kg of luggage on my back and 7kg in my front bag. The streets were full of dogs. The current temperature was 33 degrees and by now it was 23:35pm. As I got to a four-way interchange a security guard jumped out. I handed him a printed bit of paper and showed him the name and address of the hotel. After some pointing and gesticulating from the guard, off I went. Suddenly, in the middle of a street of houses, a marble walkway appeared with lights leading to a glass door. I walked through the doors of the five-star hotel. The manager looked at me. "Sir, water?"

Jakarta, be ready for chaos. I could tell you all about the noise, the scooters, the fun I had on the scooters, the porters warning me about certain food places – but I was in Jakarta for one reason only: the Jakarta Java Jazz Festival…

Event 12: Jakarta Java Jazz Festival

<u>1st–3rd March</u>

"Where you go today, Mr Lamb?" The porter investigated my movements as I jumped onto the back of a scooter.

"I'm off to the Jazz Festival."

The porter smiled brightly as I showed him my ticket. "Have a time amazing!"

Off I went for round one. I arrived at 12pm to collect my ticket and wristband. An email had been sent through with 16 points listed, highlighting the requirements for picking up your ticket. Stage by stage you had to follow. It outlined everything you needed to bring and said to ensure you had printed out the ticket on a piece of white paper with the specific dimensions of the print-out – which was A4. In exchange for the bit of paper, I would be given my three-day wristband, which cost £75 – Wow.

The sign for QUEUE currently read QUE as the other bit was being adjusted into place by two joiners, who were balancing on a fence holding the U in place.

Now, I was ready to enter the event. As I walked into the festival I was surrounded by ticket touts, and I learned something that astounded me. Most of the touts had bought tickets for the full amount and were selling them off at less than face value. I couldn't get my head around it. I spoke to a police officer who explained it was part of a bigger picture. "These men are here to prove to others," he said. It was like 'Look what I can sell!' and then move onto the next wheeling and dealing project.

As I walked through the fried chicken, popcorn and chocolate vendors I was met with the most amazing welcome at the festival gates – big smiles from the volunteers, who stood proudly in their clean uniforms. Such a contrast to what lay outside – literally. Jakarta is a very poor country and outside there were children with no clothes on, lying on mattresses. The excitement coming from the volunteers was infectious, yet I was on an emotional rollercoaster. I couldn't get my head around the difference within 100 metres. Many of those who were coming through the gates were well-dressed foreigners – basically, the event had global appeal rather than local appeal. I got my wristband checked and was welcomed in. I felt like a piece of machinery going along a conveyor belt. "Sir, welcome…"

This was day one. Friday night. I walked into the sight of a neon sign as bright as could be. This was the beginning of a festival I never thought I would experience. Everyone was getting a photo in front of the sign so of course, me being the solo traveller, I had to ask someone. First, you had to suss out who would be capable of taking a good photo. Second, you had to build up the confidence to approach them. Third, you had to ensure they knew how to hold the phone correctly. Then – smile and hope for the best.

This was not only a jazz festival; global brands had jumped onto the sponsorship bandwagon. I remember thinking: "The world NEEDS to see this festival." I had properly researched the event, but I don't think I was fully prepared as I walked through the doors of the Expo Centre and music began playing from every direction possible. The hustle and bustle in the entrance area was intense. Different notes and rhythms bounced around in my head as I tried to take in the colours, noise, exuberant staff, brands and freebies. My eyes and ears were drowning. I encountered way more than my senses anticipated. I was going to be in the festival for 36 hours – 12 hours a day.

Friday night was the night I was going to meet The Lucky Chops – but before that, let's talk about the brand activations. These are when brands bring people in to show them their brand, give them an experience and allow them to feel part of something – while of course taking something away. Kit Kat, Jack Daniels and other brands were dotted around the boundaries of the festival selling their brand and products. In some areas musical instruments were on display, like Yamaha showing off pianos; Jack Daniels was giving away freebies everywhere. Each activation had a target to get as many people as possible to sign up for a newsletter, enter a competition – and the rest. Before I knew it, I was entering a competition with Citilink for a flight around Indonesia. Then I was buying a Kit Kat pencil case full of chocolate and singing on the karaoke. Sorted. Brand after brand – it was like an advertising executive had got loads of crayons and decided to scribble a branding dream. Each brand activation had about ten PR girls wandering around in extremely tight clothing. Then there were the main sponsors of the event – tobacco companies. Sponsorship regulations in Indonesia are completely different to some of the countries I had visited. The tobacco company Djarum had PR girls wearing extremely revealing clothing and in high heels that were literally crippling their feet. For 40p I could get 10 cigarettes. I was constantly being pressured to buy. I was quite confused because I was here to watch music and instead, I could win cigarettes through playing a game that was being promoted like I was at a seaside resort. I don't know I felt about this side of the festival – a bit confused, and I had been here less than two hours.

The Jakarta Jazz Festival involved 150 artists playing over three days on six different stages. This was a huge event and its popularity had grown over the 15 years since its birth. The musical genres were extremely varied and there was a great mix of international and national performers. Tonight, I had planned to meet one of the international groups, The Lucky Chops. The band went viral when they played their brass instruments in New York subway station in 2011. Everywhere they went, they created such an amazing atmosphere. And now they were playing at Asia's top jazz festival.

I watched them perform on the main stage. They began with an introduction, long notes that suddenly captured the audience. I wept in excitement. I couldn't believe that, after four years of watching them online, I was now seeing them live, experiencing their energy first hand. I mean, I don't know how to describe on paper how amazing it was. The speakers were bouncing, as was the whole front of the stage as we engaged in that moment. That moment. An event creating that moment. The band gave it their all. Josh and the rest of the band had sweat dripping down their faces as the current temperature was now 39 degrees and humidity was 100%.

After the show I ran backstage. "Hello, Josh. My name is Matt Lamb," I said.

"Matt from *Around the World*?" And that was it. For an hour we chatted. This was my first ever real interview as part of my trip. I started recording the conversation and Josh gave me all the information I needed. We talked about what performing at an event was like because I wanted to understand what it was like to be on stage. What did it feel to be a performer? It was a fascinating discussion and I can't repeat all of it in this book, but here's a snippet...

"What we want to do is give everyone the opportunity to enter the performance. I like to start the show that way. I like to get to know everyone and everyone get to know each other. We can get out of our comfortable boxes and truly enter the event....

This simple insight was really interesting to hear. 'Comfortable boxes' are things events can sometimes break down and it was amazing to listen for an hour to a performer who is so passionate about creating memorable moments. I could not have thanked Josh enough. I walked away on the first day with the biggest smile on my face.

Now, it was Saturday. Saturday's main focus would be to experience and understand the activations even more. This whole festival is an events manager's and commercial director's dream. It had everything. It had purpose. The creative aspect was so extravagant and commercialised but so exceptional.

Fastron was one of the other activations with a quite incredible unit. It had two floors, including a performing space inside the unit, which was about 20 metres long by 20 metres wide with colourful bright neon lights, and a well-furnished lounge with a bar and anything you wanted to eat. Fastron operates large sheet metal production for precision metal enclosures and I was very confused about why they would choose to be part of a jazz festival. I realised the founder of the event was a successful business person himself – so of course a lot of the sponsors were involved through business interest. Molecool was another one. This is an app that allows people to get free CCTV in Indonesia and check out the CCTV of Jakarta's traffic jams. They had an Instagram photo catwalk. I mean – I don't know whether people would download their app because of their activation, but the broad spectrum of companies was truly eye-opening. I didn't sign up to them, but I did enter competitions with the airlines and an insurance company – which was all draped in pink and handing out festival survival kits.

Karaoke was a big thing. The person would sing (good or bad) and then have it sent to their phone – the company then collected that data. Perfect. The bigger picture there was database management. This was not a jazz festival. It was a brand festival with music. Huge opportunities for the brands to engage with 15,000 people throughout the weekend. People with money. Attendees had paid £75 for a three-day ticket (1,600,000 Indonesian rupiahs) and were throwing money at anything they could. I watched Yamaha selling electronic drumkits, and people enquiring about holidays with the travel companies. Yes, the festival drew music enthusiasts, but it also drew people who wanted to sit in the Jack Daniels activation all day and be treated to live music in the VIP room.

I was across in the food area when I suddenly heard a large bang. The rain dropped. It felt like someone got a large bucket of water and poured it directly onto the festival. Lights were going out, men with tools running through the puddles, everyone grabbing the outside umbrellas and trying to find cover. Electricity boxes were being fixed and covered with plastic bags and some of the event crew had climbed up the bamboo scaffolding to get to the fuse boxes – I was speechless while I watched. I covered my shoes with plastic bags and tried to wade through the water out of a kitchen I had jumped into for shelter. The water was at least two inches deep. It was madness. Some of the stages were being swept, only to be flooded again. Some of the electricians obviously hadn't read their health and safety manuals as they lit up a cigarette while fixing the fuse boxes that not only had water pouring onto them, but out of them.

But the show must go on, and go on it did. The four indoor stages were packed – mainly because people were hiding from the rain. I decided to try and get some great photos and I really did. The reflections of the neon lights in the puddles were amazing. Funnily enough, it seemed this storm was really proving the impact this event was having – no one was leaving. It was a magnet. Not that they could if they tried Indonesian rupiahs. For me, it was brilliant to watch the chaos of the electricians running about in their flip flops.

The weather was also causing havoc with the traffic. For two hours I battled with my *Go Jek* app – a bit like Uber – to try and get a scooter back to the hotel. I was freezing cold and soaked through. But I was better off than the stall holders, who were still trying to sell everything on their snack stalls. They were rain-soaked. No shoes. Umbrellas ruined. Mattresses soaked. But they were still smiling and waiting for the rain to pass. This put things into perspective. I was absolutely fine.

This event was not only one of my favourite events of the whole trip because of the production values, but also because of the life-changing perspective it gave me of the contrast between 'inside' and 'outside'. I was on the inside. I could afford to buy a ticket, to go and enjoy and appreciate what I was seeing. I could afford the scooter. I could afford snacks. I could buy merchandise. I could rent a hotel room. Those outside had nothing – but, with families surrounding them, they had everything. At the moment I was really confused with what was happening. Events should do that – they should change your perspective on things. However, this was not just a change or a moment of thought – it was confusing, and it was getting to me.

On day two my takeaway message was that Jakarta Jazz Festival is not about Gucci-wearing tourists from Malaysia, or the Instagram models who live in Bali – who were everywhere. The festival was about making changes to the lifestyles of the citizens of Jakarta – well, it should be. It should be a chance to give back. The festival had opportunities to engage with the local community to enhance opportunities and give them a vision of possibilities. Or to create a shoe drive for those who walk the streets barefoot. When I got home that night I scribbled on a bit of paper 'What if...' The festival has a lot of 'what if...' questions that could deliver lots of 'here you go...' answers.

I couldn't help but reflect on the night before. I was very much lost in my emotions. Overall, the event was spectacular. My senses had been punched in every direction. But I was exhausted. The weather was hot, but it was pouring huge drops of rain. In my mind, I was going back and forth over how the event was about social class. One positive was the legacy environmental impact. 'Less waste, more jazz.' This was printed on all the domestic workers' T-shirts. Recycling was a big agenda! Bins were positioned everywhere and sometimes someone would suddenly appear and give you clear instructions directing you to the right bin – green, black, red or orange. Jakarta Jazz Festival, I think, was going to stay with me forever. It just had so much – probably too much – and I could not keep up with the pace.

This was it. The last scooter ride along the Jalan Benyamin Suaeb was superb. As I entered the arena, I recognised some faces I had seen during the first two days – staff and spectators. I got talking to a few and they asked me if I had enjoyed the event. Yes but no but yes... I couldn't give an answer. I loved the event, but I think the neon lights were getting to my head. This event presents

64

more than meets the eye. It also gave me the opportunity to ask not "Where is this stage?" but more "Why is a tobacco company the main sponsor?" Indonesia has an epidemic of children smoking – and is apparently the only country in the Asian region to allow tobacco companies to sponsor events and have direct advertising. It was all glitz and glamour, but this was something that didn't need to be there.

For me today, the programme was full of music. Toto was playing – you know, the band that sings about the rains in Africa – but I wasn't following the crowds to see them; I was going to see a Jakarta jazz singer at the Signature Stage. Today was by far the quietest in terms of crowd engagement and PR staff. A lot of the brands were even calling it quits. They were handing out goody bags without me even giving them my email address. One staff member even said to me: "You have been here for three days – have three bags!" Absolutely no room in my luggage – but I took them for the hotel staff.

Wandering around, I had no problem getting photographs at all the photo opportunities. By about 7pm I was starving, and I had seen six bands already. You could walk in, sit on the floor at the back of the large arena and just be lost in your thoughts as a trumpet player took you somewhere you never knew you could go. I decided I would soak up the atmosphere for the last time at the food area, which was its own small festival with a stage and 40 stalls. I had put £60 on my cashless wristband and, with only four hours of the festival left and after eating and buying a lot of things I didn't need, I still had £25 left – this was over three days. The merchandise stall was out of everything – but I didn't have room in my bags anyway. Instead, I bought enough food to last me my whole trip.

Everything at the festival was overwhelmingly questionable for so many reasons. The world could learn from this. Each activation could be transported to another city and used in exactly the same way as it was in Jakarta. My experience was what I made it. I got to appreciate the look, the layout, the artists, the programming, the festival feel, the emotional connection, the food, the technology usage, the sponsors, the brand activations – and none of it impacted on each other. The whole thing was truly bonkers. The stages and the music were outstanding – even though I have kind of focused on the brand activations here.

I don't think I can get across my excitement of experiencing Jakarta Java Jazz Festival. After the final musician took a bow and the President of Indonesia was escorted through the site by men on bikes with AK47s, the event was done – and so was I!

One thing to take away...

To understand someone else's vision is difficult. It is sometimes a complex beast to pull apart. The jazz festival was just that. But I experienced it. I lived it. I consumed and immersed the journey.

I wrote this in my diary the next day...

'Never judge something in life until you stand with your eyes and ears wide open – then you can judge...'

Jakarta...

As I said, I wanted to see the impact that events made on Jakarta. I wanted to understand the power events can have on a place that has just short of 10 million people. This was probably my only chance to soak in such a diverse city and fully immerse myself in it.

Event 13: Go Jek Food Festival

<u>4th March</u>

I walked through the city one last time. I had done everything I needed to experience in Jakarta. The time had come to buy a postcard and a fridge magnet. After doing that, I stumbled across a food festival. I was so tired, but I couldn't walk past it. Red shipping containers took up most of the public park – 140, all lined up, some open and some closed. I meandered through the stalls as a few people stared at me. At that moment I was the only non-vendor/tourist in the area. I decided it was time for a ham and pineapple pizza, so I went to an 'Italian Indonesian restaurant' and, through Google Translate, ordered my pizza from a chef called Dani. I asked Dani why most of the containers were closed. At this point, a man called Trevor appeared. He spoke very good English and started translating for Dani. Trevor explained the Go Jek Food Festival was sponsored by the scooter taxi company. The event had been on for six months already and it had another six to go. I looked around. The place looked very tired and a bit run down.

"Every day we come here, set up, food prepared... but no one comes," Dani said. He owned a restaurant outside Jakarta and every day he rode for an hour and a half to the festival on his scooter with his supplies (I didn't ask how). He was determined to see it through. He said business was booming for four months. Every day and night, thousands of people would cram in and enjoy food demonstrations and different world cuisines. But now it was very quiet. The place felt slightly abandoned. Some of the vendors had pleaded with the organisers to close the festival but unfortunately no one was listening. "A hundred stalls have closed for good – they lost a lot of money... but me, I stay," Dani told me. The location – in the middle of the city at Gelora Bung Complex – was perfect and it was busy outside the park, but not many people walked through.

The staff who were managing the festival – all sitting around a makeshift campfire in the middle of a park when it was 35 degrees – were smiling as I walked around while I waited for my pizza. I asked Trevor where the staff came from and he explained that many were university students, and some were event managers. For them, this was a large contract, an important event to be part of. The financial implications of cancelling would be felt everywhere. Instead, they were focusing on trying to remarket the festival and they planned to bring in chefs from all over Indonesia to do cooking demonstrations. The marquees, decorated with lanterns, bunting and bean bags, were great; it was well thought through. At this point, I must add I was very surprised and somewhat in awe at how visionary Jakarta is when it comes to events. I was amazed by what the food festival organisers had achieved in the past and still aimed to do. Hats off.

I headed back to Dani for my pizza. It cost the equivalent of £3 but there was a problem. I had to have an app and an Indonesian bank account to pay for it. The event was cashless, which is fine when there is the opportunity to top up. The system was called Go Pay. Each vendor was provided with a scanner and they scanned customers' phones for payment; customers topped up the app at an on-site 'bank'. But they hadn't opened the bank because, well, there was no one here. And the vendors were not allowed to take cash. So we had to devise a plan while my pizza kept warm in a non-pizza oven. Like, literally, a white oven you would find in a university dorm. Trevor showed me his phone and demonstrated the app that I couldn't use. He showed me all the features, which was great but useless. It was a complete waste of his breath for him to show me the personalized touches he had made to his app. So I asked Trevor if he would pay for my pizza and I'd give him the money. Perfect. In events terms, this was a barrier for tourists to be able to come and enjoy the festival. It was a restriction for anyone who didn't have a phone connection or an Indonesian bank account. But for me, it was now time to enjoy my ham and pineapple pizza, sitting on one of the hundred benches that I had to myself.

As I was finishing off the well-burnt pizza a few of the students came over with Trevor. "Are you from England?" they asked. I said I was from Scotland. "You Glasgow Celtic or Glasgow Rangers?" Now, let's just give some context here. I was in the middle of Jakarta, 7,200 miles away from home, and I was having a conversation at a food festival about the manager situation at a Glasgow football team. Football is, quite literally, the language of the world – but the conversation also demonstrated the impact social media has. It was quite incredible.

So, what was my impression of this carnival-themed festival? The red shipping containers were positioned in a way to welcome thousands, but thousands had disappeared. This wasn't the fault of the vendors. It was the fault of greed. I later found out, after a lot of research, that within the Jakarta metro area there were 24 of these festivals. It would probably cover about 4 million people in terms of the local population. I could understand why many of the vendors had walked away. The supply in so many different places simply outweighed the demand.

One thing to take away…

The circus theme was brilliant. The colours were brilliant. The lanterns and stage were incredible. I could have been in London or New York. But no – I was in the city centre of Jakarta, thinking a lot about why western countries don't look to Asia for inspiration in events.

Farewell Jakarta…

Jakarta was a mosaic of beautiful chaos. I did not know what to expect. But I fell in love with the place as I found a city trying to move forward despite the challenges. I walked pavements and roads that I could never ever have imagined I would ever walk. I immersed myself in what a music festival is and experienced a story that forever will be entrenched in my mind. I reflected on a storm that was not only on the outside of the festival but inside too. As I sat in the departure lounge, I thought – a lot. To everyone I met in Jakarta. From the Irish couple who were on their honeymoon and came from Singapore to enjoy the festival, to Lucky Chops, the Rasuna Icon hotel staff...the whole Jakarta experience was AMAZING.

Bangkok

Where do I start? Globally, Bangkok is known to be a backpacker's dream. From the beginning, it was a bit of a nightmare for me. I got on the 10-pence bus from the airport to the centre of Bangkok. The city was dirty, it was dark, and I was just not feeling it. Maybe I was still flying high from Jakarta. I arrived at my hotel. The area was seedy. Instead, I was feeling a bit like – why am I here? Instead of going out, I locked my hotel room and got a Mars Bar from the hotel vending machine.

I was here to attend a Maroon 5 concert and visit Max at the IMPACT Arena – very exciting.

Max was from the communications department within IMPACT Arena and for four hours he took me around this complex. It was an AMAZING place. Each year they host 490 events and it's not only an arena but has a convention centre, outdoor events venues, go-kart race track, shopping centres, outlet malls, music venues, hotels, sports stadium and so on. In one day they can have nine events on the go at the same time.

We spent at least three hours just walking – not in circles – literally straight, stopping so Max could explain where everything was. He had weddings on today, conferences, casting agent calls and a furniture exposition, all on one side of the complex. Max explained the vision for IMPACT Arena, which was not in the central Bangkok area but strategically closer to the airport. I was interested in the vision. It was clear – IMPACT Arena intended to control the Bangkok events and leisure markets. They had hotels for those coming to the events to stay. They had shopping districts. They had plans for transport links directly from the airport.

Max suddenly grabbed me and we ran across the road to a car, which he approached with a bow. Out came an elder, to whom Max said "Sir," before speaking in Thai. Before I knew it, I was being introduced to the general manager, who was being greeted by all the staff surrounding him. And then there was me. "Hello, I'm Matt, and I am going in for a handshake."

The elder laughed and said: "You're from Scotland." He had been to the Highlands many years ago and he talked about Edinburgh – to my dismay. "I didn't get a chance to get to Glasgow," he said. "One day…!" We both laughed and I got a quick photo. He was very interested in my project and wanted to understand why I'd chosen to visit IMPACT Arena. I explained I was trying to discover places that were more than events venues but leisure destinations, with a focus on impacting people's lives.

It was great to meet him, and Max was very nervous as the general manager and I hugged farewell. "I've never seen him hug someone!" he said, laughing.

Event 14: Furniture Galore

8th March

The furniture expo Max was overseeing was called Furniture Galore. I got my photo taken at the large welcoming gantry. Max was a great tour guide and pretty good photographer. The place was very fancy. Max explained that this event was held at this venue every year and was very popular with those in the furniture, textile and wedding industries. As we walked in, Max explained it was predominantly a trade show but some independent consumers would also visit. This free event was appealing to anyone who was buying a flat or house or fancied starting up in the furniture business. I didn't fit into any of those categories.

It was really bright in the hall. Max was very kind to walk around with me – I don't think he had anything better to do that day! The place was full of tables and TVs and washing machines. The vendors kept coming up to us but as soon as Max explained who I was, they retreated. One aisle was full of wedding dresses. A catwalk was in place and I was told there were shows throughout the day over the four days of the event. It was a very interactive exposition – but today it was very quiet.

Six different functions halls were being used. The venue's role was to make sure they kept the organisers happy so the show would return year on year. The blurb about Furniture Galore on the World Fair Company website said it offered the 'most variety of public consumer products to meet the needs of the audience…' And it was right. If I wasn't travelling the world, I could have purchased everything I needed to have a clean home, clean clothes, a wedding ceremony… I could even purchase a trolley for my shopping adventures!

The whole relationship engagement as part of the fair was brilliant. Consumers could purchase directly from brands, stall holders and suppliers rather than through a website with no personal touch. I watched people engaging with each other in ways that only happen at events. You don't get laughter and human connection through a screen.

Interactive consumer events such as trade shows and exhibitions are key to support. They bring money into the economy, they create event opportunities, they rent space from venues and give jobs – to name just a few. Online companies are different. Online shopping is convenient but it's also not an emotional memory. Remember when you were a child and you walked into a toy shop? You would see the demonstrators demonstrating toys you had never seen before. You would experience and be part of the journey in the shop. Something would happen to you as you discovered a new product or saw your next favourite character on the third shelf. Online – what does online do? What do you remember about a five-minute transaction? Absolutely nothing. This fair demonstrated exactly what I'm talking about – it was an event with purpose, and I came away with memories. I even got a picture of me next to a washing machine!

One thing to take away…

Interactive experiences are what our world is about. We should live to make memories.

Event 15: Maroon 5, Bangkok

9th March

In the same venue the next night, I saw Maroon 5. It was an absolute dream. I had only booked the ticket the week before when I suddenly saw they would be playing. For £60 I was able to enjoy a night of music and thousands of Thai locals screaming in my ear. Max had advised me to get there early as there were seven events happening in the space of six hours, including 25,000 people at a football (soccer) match. So, I arrived at 2pm – only to discover I wasn't able to get into the venue until 7pm, so I had a lot of time to relax.

The place was busy, with taxis, scooters and private cars arriving, dropping off and then quickly leaving through the one-way system. It all felt very chaotic, but the traffic marshals and police had it under control.

I had printed off my confirmation A4 piece of paper at the hotel. A large snaking queue had formed, which was a meet and greet for the band for 100 devoted fans. I was just here to collect my standard ticket. The tables were all laid out and the tickets spread everywhere. It wasn't the most secure or organised procedure. My name was on an envelope in a white box. It seemed like a very informal way of doing it – like a dodgy drug deal, to be honest. Or even a music event 30 years ago.

Outside the room, the local security team, who had been contracted in for the show, were being briefed. Wearing black armour and stab-proof vests, it was not the most welcoming sight at a concert like Maroon 5. It felt slightly intimidating. The most interesting aspect of the security team were the cable ties they had for handcuffs. Personally, I didn't think the event was going to be full of drunken revellers or troublemakers. Instead, when the queue began, which, funnily enough, I was at the front of, it was mainly teenagers and their parents who had been dragged along. I think the security guards were prepared for the wrong event.

As well as the card (ticket) that I was given, I also had a blue wristband. It was a real operation to get everyone to show two pieces of accreditation, just to get into the concert. Once I got through the tightest security I had ever experienced, I was met with a Maroon 5 cardboard cut-out. The queues were 45 minutes long just to get a photo with it!

Before Maroon 5 came on stage, the national anthem was played. Everyone stood to attention – including the security team. Even though there were no seats, everyone took that patriotic stance. After being at music festivals, I don't think I had ever experienced a crowd of screaming uncontrollable teenagers be totally silenced with the beginning of the national anthem. It was very humbling to see the level of respect they had for their country. After this, we watched a venue evacuation video. "Please exit by the nearest exit if there is a fire…" Excellent.

After those two interesting moments, Maroon 5 came onto the stage. The noise was ear-piercing as we went from a serious atmosphere of patriotism and safety concerns to "OMG, Maroon 5 are here!!!" On came the three-time Grammy-winning band. I could not believe I was here in Bangkok watching one of the greatest bands of the 21st century. *Move Like Jagger, Sugar, She Will Be Loved…* all the classics were played during the show. The sweat was pouring off Adam Levine. He was just an amazing singer. Although I was about 150 metres away from the stage, he was singing to me!

Despite the screaming fans, one thing that was lacking in the venue was atmosphere. The concert was in Challenger Hall 1. Large black curtains had created a square with a gap of about 50 metres to the external walls. The square in the middle was the concert venue. But as I watched the area beyond the curtains, there were cleaners and security guards literally sitting at the back of the concourse on their break, eating sandwiches. The place felt a bit lost; there was no real sense of you being at an amazing venue. The light coming from the bars and concession units was blocked out by the curtains but the way it was constructed all seemed a bit amateur.

But I guess with 10,000 people packed into the black curtained-off area, it seemed quite a set-up. Budweiser had a bar activation with PR models dressed in very little clothing giving away freebies (no ID required to collect – strange). A photobooth was set up next to the bar and even when Maroon 5 was on, there was a queue. But this is what I question. Did the level of ticket prices reflect the level of interest and engagement? I was in the cheaper section at the very back, which cost 3,000 Thai bhats. At the front it was way more expensive. Where I was standing, people were going in and out all evening, but at the front hardly anyone came out of the side gates to go to the bar or merch stands. Did this mean those at the back were just looking for something to do that night? Were they actually fans?

Two screens positioned either side of the stage could be seen by all. The performance was not full of high-tech effects; it was about the music. It was all about the songs, from four different albums, that everyone knew and loved. This was part of the band's Red Pill Blues Tour. Maroon 5 had been on the road since the end of May 2018 after literally finishing their Maroon V tour two weeks earlier. In general, they were flying every two days. Being on the road and delivering so many shows would take its toll, not only on the band and musicians but also on the crew. Production-wise, the logistic management of this tour would be probably similar to organising *Around the World in 80 Events* – a tricky challenging nightmare.

Other Maroon 5 concerts on this tour had colour-changing cubes and a 75ft triangle walkway as part of the show. Everything was, of course, down to the city and what was able to be used. This show in Bangkok was more stripped back. But Maroon 5 – and Adam Levine specifically – used the whole stage to make everyone feel included. Even those still queueing at the cardboard cut-out!

The overall experience is not only about the show – it's about everything surrounding the production. It was and is about the event attendees and the performers. It's about something you can take away in your heart – but also in the form of merchandise. A story that comes from the stage is hard to retell through a phone. Live performing is not only about singing and dancing; it's about engaging with the crowd. Music concerts are about more than music – it's a story to the heart from a performer you love.

I decided to leave 10 minutes before the concert finished. The whole of the IMPACT Arena complex was going to be coming out at the same time. The only way of getting home was a shambles, to say the least. Then this happened...

I was a bit unsure about who to listen to and who I should allow to give me information, as you would be anywhere you didn't know. I was worried about getting home and not being stung by the taxi drivers at the rank. I was actually running out of money pretty quickly in Bangkok. Suddenly I felt a hand on my arm and a security guard said, "English?" I nodded. "Come!"

I felt a bit wary, but he had a high vis jacket and a gun. I mean, what could possibly go wrong? I understood what was happening once we joined three other people standing at the road by the main information point. "English?" said a girl and her mother, who were standing with another security guard. "Are you trying to get a taxi home?" I explained where I was going and the amount they had asked for. "No, you cannot pay that. Come with us," the girl said.

Before I knew it, I was being told to get on the back of a scooter, with the daughter and mother on another scooter. The security guards all high fived me – they still had guns, so I was not disagreeing and not *not* high fiving them back. The scooters were waiting up an alleyway and being filtered down as more people came over to the guards. It felt like they were dodgy dealers doing a bit of bad business, but it wasn't at all like that. We flew through the streets, but I didn't understand what was happening because we came to a stop about 2km away from the arena.

The mother and daughter explained that the procedure was

that the scooter drivers get 50 bhats (£2) to transport people back and forth to the outer ring. Then taxis come in and charge less than those sitting at the ranks within the complex. Excellent! I loved this plan. They were being picked up by their husband/father, but they knew this secret from previous shows. One of the drivers grabbed a taxi for me and in I went. It felt like it was all too good to be true. But really it wasn't – there are some amazing people out there – so thank you!

One thing to take away...

It's a show. It's a music concert. Sometimes so much emphasis is placed on the importance of music concerts. Well, they are important in the context of employment, opportunities for learning, emotional engagement with crowds, a boost to city local economies and so much more. I think sometimes not enough is done to think through every stage that makes the event a special and even more memorable experience.

Back to Bangkok...

Now, I had to enjoy Bangkok. No point not enjoying it! I had to make sure I soaked up some of the culture. Bangkok is a city of 8.2 million people. The city is known as the 'City of Angels'. I wanted to buy some fruit and engage with the fruit vendors (I bought pineapple every day for 15 days in three different countries). It was fresh and for sure worth 50p each time. The fruit vendors sat on plastic chairs awaiting their next customer.

I went on a river boat trip. I had to grab my ticket from a small window with white blinds in front and a set of eyes peering out of the room. It was all so dodgy. And also a very authentic experience. The river was, how can I put it, slightly murky. I remember thinking, "Okay, well, if I go under, I'll experience a new sense of diving into murky water." The engine spluttered out oil. The boat sat lower on the river than I wanted it to. It seemed to have reached capacity very quickly and, after five minutes, I decided to walk instead.

At times I felt I was chasing pavements simply for the sake of walking. On my last night I remembered I knew someone who was working out here as a teacher. We caught up and spent the evening laughing and reminiscing. James is a great guy and he and his friends really welcomed me to Bangkok. Such a shame we never got to spend more time together. It was fantastic!

It was time to fly to Chiang Mai.

Chiang Mai

As I walked out of the airport, it was very quiet. My ears were having a holiday. So now, Chiang Mai. I kid you not – I fell in love again. I had not even been in the city five minutes and the contrast was already so different from Bangkok. The difference was what I needed. No constant whistling of over polluted street traffic. No hustle and bustle of markets – not to the extent of Bangkok, anyway. No pushing of authority on the roads. It was calm. The sun was setting, and the place was beautiful.

My driver asked me where I was from and when I told him, he said: "GLASGOW CELTIC!" Brilliant. Again, the power of globalisation. We were in the middle of the north of Thailand and I was being educated about a team that train four miles from where I was born.

Chiang Mai was the perfect destination for a holiday. I cannot explain in words how calm, peaceful and beautiful the place is. The plan was to have a break. In short, this included hiring a scooter, being stopped by the police (That wasn't planned…), being ripped off for 1,000 Thai bhats (Neither was that!) and finding myself in the middle of the most beautiful mountain range as the sun set.

Event 16: Muay Thai

<u>12th March</u>

Tourist traps... Literally every hotel had 'professional photos' of Muay Thai matches. I organised a trip through the hotel reception. I would be picked up at 8pm by a bus that collected tourists from all the different hotels, and taken to the fight, which began at 8:30pm. I didn't really want to go – I'm not a fan of fighting – but let's go for the experience!

By 8:15pm there was no sign of the bus. The hotel phoned. "No, we've been to your hotel!" was the response. The receptionist was getting angry – 'No you haven't!' was what I translated from the shouting. Suddenly a bright pink neon-lit tuk-tuk arrived and in I went. We arrived at the gym, which was across the road from a very busy shopping area. From the outside, the arena looked pretty professional. But the opposite was true as I walked through the turnstile. It was tacky. It was a gym by day; at night it was throwing rave tunes and a very basic light show from the 'DJ booth'. I was in the cheap seats – but actually they were the best seats for observing the matches. Before it began, I noticed there were about 100 people in this gym, sitting on wooden bleachers. Most of them were tourists; about 20 were elderly locals who sat smoking in the bleachers and gambling away.

Suddenly, to my amazement, a tour guide walked through with a group of *proper* backpackers. Hands in the air to the music and typical backpacker clothing – singlets, colourful shorts and sandals they had purchased from Primark before coming to Thailand. And then I heard their accents. They were British. I felt the cringe come over me. The phones were out as they started to capture selfies of themselves walking around the ring. One of them decided to go for it and jumped into the ring. A few locals jumped in after them and pushed them out. Before the first bout had even begun, the British backpackers with their bumbags were being laughed at by the rest of the tourists sitting in the general seating – and were about to be knocked out by the locals.

They sat down in the VIP seats. It was like they had been allowed out for the weekend by their parents and decided to rave at a local gym in Thailand. Or they had been to a supermarket in the UK and purchased the 'British Backpacker Starter Kit'. They had immediately got themselves into trouble and lost the respect of everyone around – and the event had not even begun! It's so important to always respect the culture and the rules of the place you are in – but I suppose that wasn't in the starter kit…

Muay Thai is steeped in religious meaning and ceremonial procedures. I was fascinated by everything, from the bow to the ritual of *'wai khru ram muay'.* This was a warm-up completed to protect the fighters, which, in turn, would give each fighter power and strength. Compared to other sports, Muay Thai is very much about rituals and traditions.

Before the event began the thundering dance beats stopped and the atmosphere changed from nightclub to church. Everyone stood – well, the fighters, the trainers, the locals and then eventually the tourists understood what was happening. It was time for the national anthem – of course it was! The anthem could be heard very faintly through the PA system connected to the gym USB port behind the bar (the DJ had his own surround sound system). We all sat down, and the thundering beats began once again to welcome the first fighter to the room. All the fighters came out of the same changing room. Most of them were 18, but some were children. I, along with some of the tourists, was a bit shocked about this. This was not in the promotional materials and unfortunately you couldn't leave – I will explain why in a moment.

The 20 locals sitting in bleachers nearest the ring had a small betting ring going. As the fighters walked in, a man wearing a red jumper would stand up and shout a few things. Money would be passed between the 20 of them and the match would begin. I even noticed a few of the trainers going over and talking to them. Not at all would I ever suggest there may have been 'fixed betting' going on... Muay Thai is known for having a dark past. Under the table betting was part of this world and child trafficking was also common. I was so confused about what I was seeing. This event had been sold as an 'authentic Muay Thai experience' but instead it felt like an organised tourist trap with dark undertones. I had a feeling the gym was more than just a gym.

About 20 of the tourists who had been sitting near me – all from different groups – decided to try and leave early. I joined them and we were told to wait another 10 minutes. But as soon as a few Americans began to use their charm, a bus was organised. The reason we couldn't leave earlier was because the owner of the gym controlled all the tuk-tuks and buses that were sitting outside the gym. No one was allowed to take anyone until he said so. I was astounded by his level of control and quite angry because this was not what we had signed up for. The fact was I don't think every hotel knew what was going on, to be honest.

I realised I needed to go to more events I didn't like because that makes the story more interesting. I got to experience the Boxing Stadium. I got to see how tourists, including me, bought into 'authentic' packaged experiences that were the complete opposite. What is an 'authentic experience' anyway when demand is higher than the real supply? I got to explain to the hotel manager my observations and they were shocked. Next day, the manager explained that it is all part of a bigger picture... I didn't ask anything else.

One thing to take away...

Tourism is based upon trust. It's based upon experiences being delivered to the highest of standards. But instead, this event really did not do the reputation of the sport any good. On the whole, Muay Thai is not like this and it does have a really exciting part to play in the sporting world. I, unfortunately, had been caught up in a tourist experience.

Farewell Chiang Mai...

Beautiful. Absolutely beautiful. Chiang Mai was truly special. I cannot explain how amazing it was to relax in this city. The temples in Chiang Mai were incredible, whether it was the golden rooftop of the Wat Phra That Doi Suthep that dates back to the 14th century or the Buddhist temple of Wat Chedi Luang built by King Saen Muang Ma. Chiang Mai – I will return one day, but for now I depart.

Ho Chi Minh

I started my time in Vietnam arguing with the taxi driver, who was demanding I pay him 10 times what the guides on the website and the meter in his cab said. He locked the car and demanded my wallet. For the first time on my journey, I was scared. I had no choice but to pay and that literally burnt my budget before I had even got into Ho Chi Minh.

I was in Ho Chi Minh purely as a stopover and sadly I had no events arranged. I sat in a restaurant on my second night and ate the best EVER spag bol. I don't know whether this was maybe just because I hadn't eaten properly in a few days.

At Le Lai, just around the corner from me, were about 20 bars in the space of 200 metres. All extremely loud and all full of tourists and locals. The noise of the strip was not only overwhelming but quite frightening. At some points it was so loud your feet lifted off the ground and you would glide 50 metres down the street. Overall, this street was something of an attack on the senses.

Now to China...

Shanghai

The first thing that surprised me in Shanghai was finding warm water dispensers everywhere. Literally, I couldn't find cold water anywhere. I learned it was about balancing the internal yin and yang and the belief that hot water would ensure any toxic bugs would be flushed out and restore balance to a person's health. Everyone I met in China had a flask and in went the hot water. Apart from me.

Shanghai was electric in atmosphere and electric with scooters with no engines; all electric. With bright lights down at the Huangpu River and all the buildings illuminated, it is the brightest city you will ever see. And then there was the noise of construction and the very modern walkways, pedestrian areas and shopping complexes. It was strict, of course. The police would stop anyone walking across the road after the red man had appeared. IDs were taken off them and a ticket written.

Getting from the airport to the hostel was a doddle. Well, only because I noticed out of the corner of my eye that a Chinese girl was logging onto Facebook on the train. The only way she would have been able to sign on to Facebook was through a VPN and if she went to an English-speaking university. And she did. After I'd asked her for directions, she told me she had studied for a year in Newcastle in the UK. Her Chinese accent had a Geordie twang – although I think she was probably just putting it on because she was talking to me. She said in Newcastle "they like to party." I don't know how she survived a year of that but well done!

Unfortunately, there were no shows on at the Shanghai Grand Theatre while I was in the city. However, I did shelter from a rainstorm for about an hour on the padded seats in the box office area. The venue had some really interesting free exhibitions, but unfortunately, they were closed. There was one really cool exhibition along the corridor exiting the venue, called *Artists Talk*. Hanging on the walls were photographs of famous musicians, and audio came through small speakers underneath. Instead of pressing buttons, the user scanned a QR code under each photograph to continue to listen to the audio later. I was so impressed – I loved that concept. The theatre collected data from the user and the user got an app full of stories of performers who have performed at the theatre. Clever!

Shanghai has some brilliant cultural arts facilities. In 2005, the Shanghai Creative Industry Research Centre was formed with the aim of growing the country's cultural and creative output. It led to the development and implementation of policy for Shanghai's creative industry, in a bid to become somewhere of international influence. It is estimated that by 2016 the creative industries in Shanghai accounted for 12% of GDP. In 2018, Shanghai decided to package culture and encourage as many international productions to come and perform; it also promoted the growth of Shanghai's creative industries.

Event 17: Masterclass, Sino-British College

20th March

With the help of a contact, I had arranged to deliver a masterclass about *Around the World in 80 Events* at the Sino-British College in Shanghai. We organised the marketing and I was told the event was all in hand. Leaflets had been printed and it was advertised on the college website. I was being promoted as a 'visiting expert', which made me laugh! All the events management students studying at the college were expected to attend – around 300 people – and I was very excited. Standing in front of the students, telling them my story would be an honour. The hall was going to be full!

As I stood in the hall awaiting my audience, a few university professors came through to say hello – but there was another big event on today so they couldn't stay. The lecture was to begin at 4pm. I waited nervously for 300 people to arrive – I hoped. Even 30 would be great. My adventure was going to be the main topic of the masterclass, but the focus would be on the students living their own dreams. I was very excited to tell my story and to ask them what their dreams were.

With five minutes to go, 14 students sat in front of me. Okay… 14 people were going to get a show like no other. Suddenly two walked up to the lecturer and asked him, "Is this…?" I knew immediately that they were here for the other event. Then another six students stood up and walked out. They were all at the wrong event too. I was gutted – but six people were better than none.

Sometimes it's important to think not about a venue being full but about it not being empty. So, instead of three hundred, there were six… but I managed to angle the camera to make the photos look as though the hall was packed! This is what events are all about. You can plan, as I did, an engaging event and offer everything on a plate – but sometimes people won't take anything from that plate. But that's okay. That's expected. Events are very unpredictable, especially when they are free. Today, I learned the art of presenting to a small group and still giving the same energy as I would to a large audience. And hopefully at least one person walked away having heard an anecdote that would affect their life in a positive way.

One thing to take away…

To speak about this adventure is great. To do it on a global scale is an absolute honour. Sharing my journey was a dream of mine, and yes, it was to a few, but they still left knowing more about my story than they did an hour ago!

Beijing

On the train from Shanghai to Beijing I got some sleep, and relaxed. I also wrote a lot about my thoughts and feelings on this trip. Tiredness was certainly one of the top emotions up there at the moment.

Beijing has a thriving tourism and events sector. I mean, honestly, I was shocked by the amount going on and excited about what the future holds. The National Centre for Performing Arts and the Zhengyici Peking Opera Theatre had become extremely popular with both Chinese nationals and international visitors. Beijing is also popular for its historical shrines, parks and, of course, the Great Wall of China. When I arrived, I was struck by how modern the city was. A few years earlier I had lived near Peking station at Peking South Hostel, and the modern Beijing I was introduced to now was very different than I had expected – but on every street corner I was watched by soldiers. Beijing wants to be viewed as a city that is opening up even more to international visitors. I saw it. I felt it. It is only since the 1970s that international tourism has existed in China; in 2019, over 400 million international visitors came. I can promise I felt a warm welcome.

Event 18: Earth Hour, Beijing

30th March

It was 30th March and I had been in Beijing for three days and had another four to go. Tonight at 8:30pm the world would turn off its lights. Earth Hour was not Beijing specific, but joining in demonstrated that China wanted to show commitment to resolving the environmental factors that are crippling our world. Earth Hour originated from the World Wildlife Foundation. The movement is seen as a powerful opportunity to show world leaders that people want to stop and reverse the effects of climate change. Everywhere from Edinburgh, London, Paris and New York to Beijing and even the International Space Station were taking part in some way. More than ever, in 2019, climate change had really come to the forefront of politics. Friday afternoon protests by children and young adults had propelled climate change discussion to a new level, and this pressure from the future generations of this world had put the environment firmly on political agendas. In 2019, individuals, organisations and cities in 188 countries had registered to take part in Earth Hour.

In Beijing, Earth Hour would see the lights turned off in the Olympic Park, including the Bird's Nest, which is the national stadium. I arrived at the park at 6:30pm. It was so cold my toes were literally about to fall off. After an hour I decided there was no way I could stand outside anymore; I could feel the frostbite. Funnily enough, the park was deserted. I jumped into a supermarket that was outside the perimeter. The place was absolutely packed. This was not a tourist attraction or anywhere that tourists would go; it was just a shopping centre full of locals. I needed a hot drink and a snack, and I wondered how many people in here were taking part in Earth Hour – or even knew it existed.

It was 8:28pm and I had my cameras in place and the perfect

view. Suddenly, two tourists decided to stand in my way. I quickly switched to plan B, grabbed the cameras and moved my whole 'set-up studio'. 8:29pm. I knew I had to capture the moment that this iconic global landmark was switched off or else the opportunity would be wasted. Just before I pressed record, the tourists strolled away, giggling at their photo. I hope they enjoyed posting it on Instagram.

I'd rehearsed a voiceover to do at the moment the lights began to go off. I'd practised over and over: "Ladies and gentlemen, good evening and welcome from the Bird's Nest..." I am not claiming to be a broadcaster, or even attempting to be one, but for this historic moment I needed to get it right. What I didn't expect was that the lights in the Bird's Nest would go out right as I said it. I'd captured the moment! I could have cried with excitement, but my tears would probably have frozen.

All around me I could hear a lot of "OHHHH! WHAT'S HAPPENING...?" as people realised that the stadium was beginning to go dark. However, there were no signs around, nothing to say 'This is part of Earth Hour'. This meant some people did not understand the purpose of this moment. Even online, there was a lack of information regarding Beijing's involvement.

I watched some of the online coverage and saw the impact these events had in other countries. In China it was broadcast live on TV, with an online stream that included the Olympic Park – probably with me somewhere below, jumping up and down after the completion of my video. Overall, in all the different time zones, it was reported that over two billion impressions were recorded on social media channels to do with Earth Hour.

Globally, there is a lot of negativity towards events because of the amount of waste generated. But this event was the complete opposite. It was an opportunity to change people's mindsets and make them more aware of environmental issues. As well as raising awareness, action also comes as a result of Earth Hour. For example, in the Russian region of Kyrgyzstan, 17 million trees were planted as part of the Earth Hour commitment. In Vietnam in 2019, it was estimated 910 million Vietnamese dollars were saved in energy costs over that hour – which shows the usage of those who took part in the mission.

The only problem is, even when everyone does turn off the lights, even with billions taking part in this project globally, it doesn't solve the problem. But education is at the forefront of Earth Hour, and raising awareness and making commitments to change our daily lives can benefit the world of the future.

One thing to take away...

Earth Hour is about more than the lights going off; it tells a story about the importance of understanding our impact on climate change. In Beijing there was no merchandise on sale, although some events in other parts of the world handed out lanterns for people to turn off. Events can have a global impact if they are positioned correctly and have the correct messaging and this one was certainly the biggest so far. Together we can brighten our future.

Beijing...

My adventure was not solely about going to events. Tourist sites are popular attractions that can evoke emotion and create memories. In Beijing, the management of these places is strict. As I was meandering towards Tiananmen Square, I was aware of a high presence of security – police and army. I entered a cabin and handed over my identification, which was scanned through a computer, and my photo was taken. Some locals aren't able to get through security; apparently, this is often because of political differences and historic involvement in protests.

Tiananmen Square was the location of the 1989 student-led protests against censorship and corruption, which were beamed globally and shifted the world's perspective of China. The most memorable moment was when the tanks arrived and martial law was declared by the government. These days, the square is about more than statues and images of the Premier of China. Being there was quite surreal. The place was a tourist hub! There were even opportunities to have a photo with 'Chairman Mao'.

One of the biggest symbols of China is the Great Wall. I woke up at 4:30am to conquer it. That day I walked 36km, bought fresh pineapple from the mountain villages, and watched some tourists appreciate the land and some completely miss the significance of the place.

Tourists from all over China were packed on the train. The ticket cost £20, but it was cheaper and a more authentic experience than going on a tour bus, sitting with westerners who couldn't face the challenge of doing something the harder way. I won't go into the history of the wall, but when I saw American tourists sitting on it to eat their lunch and leaving rubbish at their feet... Did they actually understand the significance of this place? It really annoyed me. It's like events – sometimes they are not fully respected the way they should be; their value is not appreciated. Money can buy you a ticket to an event or to walk along the Great Wall of China (20 Yuan, or £2.30) but respect and connection are priceless.

Never in my life have I felt the way I felt in Beijing walking the wall. I literally felt drained, not only physically but also mentally, through learning about the history and appreciating what the Great Wall of China is. Next time you go to something that is organised, built, deemed a place of cultural importance – respect it and give it your utmost attention. Walk out of the experience drained of energy. Standing on the north side of the wall and just admiring it and taking it all in was truly a privilege.

Beijing was outstanding. Standing outside the Apple store to get WiFi to phone home was an experience in itself. Yes, in China I didn't go to many events, but I did come to appreciate a whole new level of culture and a world of possibilities.

Now for Seoul.

Seoul

It is 9:30pm and I am on the AREX – the cleanest train I have ever been on. I arrive in Seoul, where the current temperature is -3 degrees. I have come here for the Seoul Motor Show, but I suppose I can squeeze in some tourist stuff. My hotel room is windowless, the smallest box I have ever stayed in. But I wasn't here to rate the room.

Event 19: Seoul Motor Show

2nd April

I wouldn't classify myself as an engine nerd – I'm an event geek, and I couldn't miss the Seoul Motor Show. It's the fourth largest motor show in Asia and the only motor show in South Korea recognised by the International Organisation of Motor Vehicle Manufacturers, the global alliance of car makers founded back in 1919 in Paris. With electric cars dominating the motor industry and 700,000 people expected through the doors, this event was going to be interesting.

Lights, girls, cameras, flashy activations and money. A bit like Jakarta Jazz Festival. And then there was me, walking around in my worn-out baggy jeans and my *Around the World in 80 Events* hoodie. A day pass was 10,000 South Korean won. Expensive, eh? Nope – it cost £6.70 to walk around the seven halls of the Kintex Arena, which was in Seo Daehwa, 13km outside the city and close to the airport.

So let's get talking cars... well, car events.

Jaguar, Toyota, Range Rover, McLaren, Mercedes, Kia – all featured, with some of them making their debut in Asia. Even motorparts companies and automobile suppliers like Shell Helix Ultra were on display. This was not just a place to show cars. Deals were to be done on 'investor day', which was closed to the general public. The event was vast but once I'd seen the layout and what there was to experience, I understood why it was so huge. All the car brands I mentioned (and another 20 more on top of that) had their own objectives and had built their own personalised activations. I introduced myself to a crew member for the Jaguar stand, who spoke very good English. He explained that the car manufacturers used external event production companies to produce their stand. It was a big deal for the events industry in

Seoul to bid and win the contracts. Even some international brand experience companies apparently bid – and won. The stages featured everything from spinning cars and light shows to eye-catching illusions and staged Q and A sessions with engineers.

And there were girls everywhere. Most of the cars had models draped across them wearing very close to nothing, and each stand that had girls modelling had 80% more of the audience than the few stands that had no girls. On the BMW stand, Korean girls were being instructed on how to stand and when to change the pose. Everything was choreographed. It was all structured to be a show within the show. I was interested that car companies needed girls to sell their brand. However, this was apparently common for the South Korean market. I didn't think it added value – but apparently it did for all the men with professional cameras.

I noticed that Mini, a very classy British company, had used their history to deliver a stylish activation. No over the top music here; it was all about class. They were representing exactly what Mini is, which is an elegant experience. On the walls of their fake living room space hung photos of Minis from around the UK, showcasing the life that can be had when you own one. It was clever. It was creative. But not only that, Mini was one of only two car manufacturers to use male models – interesting.

Tucked away in a corner of the first hall I walked through were stands signposted 'Education and Research'. As you can imagine, there was no one here asking questions – apart from me! I got talking to four young Korean researchers and their professor. They had been eating lunch – but in South Korea the level of respect is quite phenomenal, as they all threw their sandwiches on the table and came running over with a bow as soon as they saw me express interest in the stand. The job they were doing was actually the most important role of the whole show. Each car that was brought to the show had to be tested against car safety regulations; no car would be allowed to be displayed unless it had certification from these research experts. I was intrigued. With all the different parts, models and companies coming from all over the world, at different times and using different modes of transport – this would be a logistical nightmare! The researchers told me they had been really busy for weeks. There was no glitz, no glam, no lights and no music here – it was all reports and testing and really interesting information to move car safety forwards. Throughout the event, car regulation experts from around the world came along for networking and discussion about regulations. This was the most intriguing stall and I stayed here for an hour, just soaking up all the research, while behind me a constant buzz and a pounding bass assaulted my ears.

If you are a brand event activation lover, you must go and check out the Seoul Motor Show. *Nissan Intelligent Mobility* allowed people to test how accurate their driving reactions are – I was below average. *Playboy* had a basketball ring where you could win prizes (absolutely nothing to do with cars, but I suppose it was fun). Porsche had *Sound of Porsche*, where everyone wore very expensive, top of the range headphones and listened to the different roars of the engines. There were long queues at the stations where you could practise your drone skills. *Let's Go Eat* was a food festival within the motor show, where you could try different world cuisines. Each activation was using hashtags to become events in their own right, like #meetgenesis, which was a light show you could stand in the middle of. You could sit in cars. You could sit on tractors. I even stood next to cars that had not yet been released. Seoul Motor Show had taken the manual for how to display cars and ripped it apart.

And then there was the *GREAT BRITAIN* marketing campaign by the International Trade Department of the UK Government. Where do I begin? The whole thing was boring – let me just come straight to the point. The atmosphere was flat and no one was engaging with what they had developed. There was a *Touch and Discover* light-up map of the UK, which showed all the UK car manufacturing companies. Interesting, maybe. Boring, certainly.

There were 22 companies on the map and they had some brilliant products, but there was absolutely no engagement. At all the other activations you were able to sit in the seats, feel the car and envision yourself driving it. On this stall – not a chance. Being British, everything was locked up. There were even signs saying 'do not touch' and barriers around the vehicles so people couldn't even take good photos. The staff were sitting behind the reception desk, playing on their phones. That night I wrote an email to the British Embassy in Seoul, who had organised the stand. I told them what I thought and offered a few recommendations. I got a response a few days later, which was lovely, but all they offered was a giant excuse that there were budget constraints. The most important part of this was understanding the product and how it is delivered – and they failed. They didn't, in my opinion, just fail with the campaign; they failed every UK manufacturing company that had put their trust in the government to represent them.

Seoul Motor Show, to conclude, was not just a motor show. It was an opportunity for global companies, a marketing platform and the key to the Asian market. I loved the brand of the show. I loved the organisation. I loved the activations.

One thing to take away…

The event was for sure eye-opening. It gave me an appreciation for cars that I never knew I had. But it also showed me what can be done with cars to create amazing emotive experiences. Queueing up and seeing the excitement for a Jaguar has made me appreciate my Astra even more.

Bye-bye, Seoul

I was only in this beautiful city for three days and, after the motor show, I did a lot of walking. I went up the hill known as Seoul Tower, or Namsan Tower. This observation deck is extremely popular. Padlocks had been chained to all the fences – apparently to symbolise love. In one area were rubber ducks – I'm not sure what they symbolised, but I could write on them and leave a message. I grabbed a pen from the local shop.

When I'd arrived in Seoul I'd flown into Incheon International Airport – a big airport, with lots of international flights. As I jumped on the train now, by chance I glanced at my ticket for the flight to Tokyo and noticed it had GMP on it. But my inbound ticket definitely said ICN... Ahhhh. Sugar. Luckily, both airports are next to each other and I was on the right train heading in the right direction. Very lucky! I grabbed my bags and off I went. Considering the amount I'd had to plan in advance, I really was doing okay. No flights missed – yet!

Japan... First stop: Tokyo

Japan is a country where respect oozes from every person and is taught as part of a child's education. It also has the most amazing toilets. They sing to you when you pee! AMAZING! As soon as I arrived in Tokyo I immediately saw a very unique culture. The way people talk to each other – no shaking of hands here, it's all to do with the bow. Although the pace they do it at is as if they've been fast-forwarded through a DVD player. I was not just impressed; I was actually in awe.

When I came out of Narita International Airport at 6pm, I jumped onto the train for the city. WORST TIME TO GO ON A TRAIN IN TOKYO WITH BACKPACKS! I tried to blend in as a local, but it's a bit difficult when your luggage is absolutely killing your back and you ain't got a clue where you're going. Fortunately, I would be staying with a dear friend of mine Sam.

Tokyo is known globally as being quite advanced. It is, and it isn't. Many places do not accept credit/debit cards. Cash is king. People can smoke inside cafes and in some areas in restaurants because of the good air ventilation – but it is illegal to smoke on the street. Yes – you read that right. You can only smoke at designated shelters, which are actually simply large boards signposted 'smoking area'. These shelters are not covered and you are still very much standing on the street. Confused? Me too.

Let's crack on and discover the events industry in Japan.

The plan was that Japan would be hosting the Rugby World Cup in autumn 2019 and Tokyo would then host the Olympics in summer 2020. (Of course, this was prior to the coronavirus pandemic which would see the Olympics being postponed until 2021). To be chosen to stage both events shows the desire Japan has to jump into every opportunity they can. The whole country would benefit, economically and socially. You could also argue that this would cause disruption to normal culture. However, events are about adapting into a culture and culture being celebrated… so let's bloom with this one.

Event 20: Cherry Blossom Festival, Tokyo

<u>4th April</u>

The Cherry Blossom Festival (Hanami, or Flower Viewing) is held every spring and it's estimated to bring in 63 million extra visitors and an additional 301 billion yen (£2.3 billion) to the economy. The festival, celebrating the beautiful trees so synonymous with Japan, is an example of a natural event that has been jumped on and made commercial. But it's important to understand what the cherry blossoms represent within Japanese culture – it is viewed as the season of renewal. I knew I would be arriving just at the end of the flowering of the cherry blossoms and hoped I would grab a glimpse – and I did.

I was in Kudanzaka Park in the Kudanminam area of Tokyo, a very popular spot. The blossoms were 'blooming brilliant' and a great reminder of how beautiful nature can be. Japanese people naturally do not show fear or cause anger. Instead, they take photos. Cameras everywhere. 'Click click click' was all I could hear as the cameras captured the beauty of the blossoming trees along the river bank, where fencing had been erected to stop people falling into the water. Really, we could have been in an art gallery or museum by the way people were reacting. I watched as, every 45 seconds, the next person shuffled forward to take their perfect Instagram photo.

Operationally, you would have thought you were at a football match with the number of information stalls, security, trained staff, police, road closures and thick dense crowds walking to and from the park. Street vendors were all around selling potato chips, Oreos and Hiyoko sweets.

The branches bled with the absolute beauty of the full blossoms as they met the horizon of the Tokyo skyline. Every guidebook outlines the key things to see in Tokyo and the cherry blossom festival is always up there. For once, I was in agreement with the guidebooks – this event was truly spectacular, and one not to miss. I walked around and around for two hours. There were crowds as far as my eyes could see.

From an operations perspective, the event was very secure. It was, of course, a target for trouble, but culturally the event was not plagued with any issues of aggressive behaviour. Instead, it was a festival of hope. In Tokyo alone there were 26 organised events like this, with trees at the heart of the celebration. All the public parks and some private ones had been transformed into carefully controlled areas for exploration. I loved watching mothers and fathers pass on generations of appreciation for the event. I loved the mixture of old and new beliefs. I guess you could argue this was a pilgrimage: a pilgrimage of culture; a pilgrimage of beliefs.

In contrast, commercial brands including Nestle, Starbucks, Lawson and Family Mart had jumped on the bandwagon and created specific themed promotions during Cherry Blossom season. In Starbucks I could buy blossom-scented tea. Interesting; I didn't know blossoms had a scent! KitKat wrappers were light pink, the same colour as the blossoms. Nestle was also selling chocolate specifically made for the festival. Lawson shops were selling everything a festival attendee could need, including flowery umbrellas and snacks. Family Mart had posters in the windows welcoming everyone to the Cherry Blossom Festival. Commercial opportunities everywhere. The commercial drive was impacting the economy positively… but there was another problem that was threatening the future of this event.

Due to meteorological changes, unusually high temperatures in the autumn and winter meant the trees were starting to blossom early. This could mean an economic loss in tourist income as Japan would be busier for a shorter span of time. Every spring when the Cherry Blossom Festival happens, it is very much a gamble when the blossoms will fully bloom. Each park I went to – five in total –

had noticeboards with the weather predictions for the next four days. By the time I left Tokyo, the events, vendors and lighting production companies had packed up and gone home. It was all over for another year.

The Cherry Blossom Festival was majorly affected by the pandemic. Cleverly though, instead of just letting the event go a virtual event, Cherry Blossoms 2020, was launched, which allowed people to experience the wonders of the blossoms from their own homes. I applaud this effort to achieve some sort of normality in an event that, if entirely cancelled, would put millions of people out of work. It's all about getting the balance right for the future.

One thing to take away...

The lights. The trees. The nature. The impact the event has. It's not only about the parks coming alive. This event turns natural beauty into an economic beast. Tokyo, and Japan, really needs this and without it – no economic benefits mean no investment...

Still in Tokyo

As I experienced Tokyo, I started to learn more about the culture, the city and the people. Going out for a drink in Tokyo was always a great learning opportunity. I went with my friend who was working here in Japan. We went to an extremely busy street and it was packed – on a Thursday. The story goes that if the office boss says "Drink," all the junior staff must go. It is not negotiable. The pub uniform was black suit, white shirt and black tie. Even on a weeknight the karaoke bars were packed. The next day the trains are full of a lot of tired people, with some even sleeping.

But now... bring on the Penis Festival...!

Event 21: Kanamara Matsuri (Penis Festival)

<u>7th April</u>

When I began the planning for the Japanese leg of my trip 18 months ago, I decided I had to get to the Penis Festival. Be prepared for Event 21 – the event that is not about that giggle you just made when you read the word 'penis', but about the symbolism of the penis as a shrine. Welcome to the sight of pink and black penises moving through the streets of a suburb outside Tokyo.

I had researched this event – a lot – and I wanted to be in the best place. Locals would be eclipsed by tourists, with approximately 50,000 people from all over the world attending what is now known as a global bucket list event. Many people go for the opportunity to have their photo taken with a penis – literally. Others come as part of an Australian or American backpacking experience. But as the streets filled with Buddhist priests, I realised the event had a larger purpose than to fill someone's camera roll or be a story at a university reunion party after the summer holidays. I wanted to appreciate what people gave to and took from the event. It was actually one of the main reasons I had come to Tokyo.

I arrived at 7:30am. Some locals were preparing the shrine. By 8:30am a buzz was rising from the small groups of people gathered within the shrine's boundary. About 200 people were milling around, mostly locals. The large mikoshi (the penis statues – portable shrines) were positioned with ropes around them. Locals were jumping in and out to get a quick photo, and some tourists were chancing their arm.

Shrine elders, wearing long white Japanese kimonos, stood with their arms folded. Looking around, I asked a local resident to take a photo of me at the rope line. As he ushered me in, the elders shouted to him: "He can come and hug it...!" Now – this was 8ish in the morning and I was staring at a two-metre tall pink penis. I had my photo taken with one of the elders and I thanked them and then stood at the front, watching in awe. It was a hive of activity. Busy. I was squeezed up against the barrier as more people arrived. But I was being protected by my new local friend and a Dutch photographer, Ryan, who lived in Tokyo. I was so excited to have new friends, especially as they could translate and give me top tips on how to best experience this unique event.

It wasn't even 9am and already the place was packed, with thousands of people surrounding what was globally recognised as a penis. Suddenly, from the side road, groups of locals arrived and were greeted by the same elders I had spoken to earlier. All wearing traditional kimonos in different colours, each person was welcomed with a bow. They moved into the shrine for a briefing, leaving behind the flocks of tourists who had come to see these special shrines be paraded through the streets. However, before I start describing what happened at this bizarre and fascinating festival, let's talk about its history.

The festival began in 1969 to celebrate the history of the Kanayama Shrine. Legend has it that, way back in the 17th century, the shrine was seen as a safe space by prostitutes, who would visit and pray for protection from sexually transmitted diseases. And still to this day it is a safe space. Nearly 50 years on, the festival attracts crowds of thousands. Nowadays, its focus is on raising awareness of safe sex practices and fundraising for HIV prevention, and the impact is positively immense.

The Kanayama Shrine is part of the Shinto religion and the event is organised by the priests and elders. The priests wore wooden clogs and had their faces completely covered with white cloth. They walked behind the mikoshis – the penises – blessing them as they progressed. Coverage on social media, newspapers, internet, travel blogs and so on means interest in this event has grown sharply. Today, thousands of people flock to what is now deemed one of the 10 best festivals in the world – in the 'unique and weird festival' category. I don't really know how they rate all these festivals, which, of course, are all different, but this one is certainly up there.

Etiquette was extremely important at the event as, firstly, we were all guests to the shrine and, secondly, the event really has a serious side to it that must be enjoyed in a respectable manner – it's not just about the penis lollies on sale.

Standing for three hours was not a problem because watching the excitement of the locals and listening to the music took me to a peaceful place. The music was called 'kagura'. Occasionally, a vocal opera-style 'scream' would come from the upper level of the shrine where the musicians were sitting. As I began to focus on the details, I looked behind me. The place was crammed. There was no room on the pavement, and police were whistling at people as they ducked under the ropes to try and get to a space on the road.

Out came the first group, who were carrying a black mikoshi. A woman dressed in duck blue directed them into position. Well, when I say directed, I mean she shouted and demanded everyone take three steps back. Her next argument was with the self-entitled American/British TV crew (which we will discuss in a moment) who she told to get out of the way. I loved the authority she had. She glanced behind. After a blessing from the Shinto priest, the men and women lifted the portable shrine… and we were off.

The Shinto priest was treated like a saviour. I found it very humbling, but all around I could hear giggles from those who were not appreciating that this was a sacred moment, mostly backpackers who were not aware of the religious significance. On command, 20 people began to walk forwards. But just as the shrine was about to leave the grounds, there was a problem. The penis was being held high in the air and it wasn't going to fit through the entrance/exit gate to the shrine grounds. Suddenly everyone shouted: "Aahhhhh…" which translated as "STOP!" Everyone stopped, while still holding tightly onto the heavy wooden structure. The boss, the elders and the police all tried to protect the gates and the statue. A gasp could be heard. It all got a bit serious for a moment. They had to get the structure through, but it wasn't as easy as it sounded. It was heart-stopping to watch 20 people, huddled up, holding a giant penis and trying to dip it at the same time. After about 10 seconds the rhythm returned, along with the sounds and energy. Through the gates the penis went, and the parade began.

The flocking tourists were driving me slightly insane. "Look at that huge penis... not as big as mine!" said a short, large, well-gelled backpacker next to me, iPhone raised and bumbag across his chest. As he played up to his group of frat brotherhood friends like he was at a music festival in a field, he seemed to think this was acceptable behaviour. *No, you don't. Don't behave like that.* My friend the photographer had to stop me from saying something. Thousands of backpackers choose to come here because of the draw of the uniqueness of the event – a penis. And you know what? In a way that's why this area still hosts this event – because of the boost to the local economy, and so on. But it's about so much more. This is the reason some events have lost their origins – the unappreciative tourists.

Every event has commercialisation opportunities and this was not exempt – except it wasn't companies but locals who had created as much penis-related merchandise as they could. Lollies. Magnets. Tea towels. Keyrings. Everything was there to be bought, shaped like a penis. I walked away from the event with three penis lollies, two keyrings and four fridge magnets. Not sure why. But I suppose I was caught in the moment and I was okay with having penis magnets in my bag, even though they would have to go through the airport scanners, which did cause some questions at times. Did this mean I was fully immersed in the experience? Yes.

So, with my tourist tat and new keyrings, it was time to go and see the mikoshi be carried back from one shrine ground to the other. Because of my photographer friend Ryan's Japanese and English skills, we were learning loads and getting to really engage with the elders. I wanted to know about some of the people who were carrying the shrine through the streets. When we got a chance, I asked Ryan to find out why some of the men carrying the pink penis were in drag. It tuned out that this year they were raising awareness and money for the LGBT movement. Considering Japan is not very 'out there' with LGBT rights in everyday culture, it was quite a thing to have this at the forefront of the event.

Many people think the Penis Festival is about male domination but actually the opposite is true. We learned that the pink penis was called Elizabeth. I have absolutely no idea why. The people walking with the penis were elders and locals but also some 'celebs', one of whom was Japan's most famous porn star. Wearing a yellow jacket and accompanied by his mate from *PornHub*, who was filming, he was invited to be part of the carrying. He lasted about 10 minutes while others, with smaller frames and builds, held on for longer. Their shoulders were bouncing to the rhythm while he… well – he just didn't have it in him!

I want to tell you a story about the British camera crew who suddenly appeared. With 15 minutes to go, they rolled in (around about 15 of them) and began to move local elders out of the way in order to get their 'perfect shots'. As they weren't wearing traditional clothing and were all very tall, they stood out in many ways, not least through their arrogance. The executive producer's family was standing past the barrier and in the middle of the main cultural site. It was slightly embarrassing and not at all welcomed by the locals. However, they had a local fixer who translated everything. I was questioning this for days and here is what I concluded. As I watched, the main female organiser pushed them behind the ropes and into the crowd, only to be told: "We are a British camera crew." But that means nothing when it comes to respecting culture. You must always respect the rules.

When the documentary was produced and broadcast on TV, it showed the Penis Festival to be some kind of a joke. But it wasn't a joke to me, or to many who were there; it was a spiritual event.

When you are a guest in someone else's country, it is important to respect the elders' requests and remember you are in their home. Even if you are a TV producer... you must understand your place. And the presenter... well, without naming names, he was just a puppet who had misunderstood the whole thing. He even carried the penis statue for about two minutes before collapsing onto the pavement.

For many, the word 'festival' means party, but in some religions and cultures it means 'celebration' – but within certain boundaries of behaviour. The noise you heard from those carrying the mikoshi was deafening and I will always hear that rhythm anywhere I go. One thing that was clear was the Japanese locals loved to party. Once they got to the park and the shrines were covered with white cloths, it was beer all round – though not, of course, for the priests, who were guided away by their commander. This was not just a 'tourist event', it was a chance for the locals to have a party. And party they did.

With the parade finished and the partying continuing, at about 3:30pm I headed back to the train station. But before I did, I decided to walk around the ward area I was in. Now, there were over 55,000 people just three streets from where I stood – but you would never know there was an event happening. I saw locals doing their washing in buckets outside their flats and laundry hung between buildings. A man sat on a blue plastic chair reading his newspaper. There was no traffic and no people walking past. I was quite amazed by the contrast.

After 18 months of planning and researching, I went to the world's most interesting event. I got to understand and truly appreciate how culture has a local impact on a global audience. Not only did I experience a bucket list event but I went to an event with charm, character and so much more than the British TV crew and backpackers could see.

One thing to take away…

The Penis Festival combined myths, religion, tourism strategies and globalisation to create a beautiful event. The key point is that cultural celebrations often have a long and important history. We should appreciate and enjoy these events, but always remember we are just visitors.

Tokyo

In Tokyo I was glad to see familiar faces. Great to have a bit of normality and go to the pub with friends. Great to chat about the adventure with people who understand me. Great to be able to be open and honest about how the trip was going.

Tokyo has really made a shift towards focusing more on the visitor economy. Prior to COVID-19, they predicted they would have 20 million visitors in 2020. Standing in the middle of Tokyo, it felt like any more people here would make it absolutely chaotic. The streets were already crammed at rush hour. Pavements with no space to breathe. I had visited shrines, palaces and other attractions with wall-to-wall crowds crammed into small areas. Popular places like Shibuya Crossing, Senso-ji and Tokyo Disney were always going to be busy.

Event 22: Tokyo Disney

9th April

Tokyo Disney – a destination thousands immerse themselves in on a daily basis. It is a picture of perfection, with numerous constructed moments for all to enjoy. I was there on 9th April. The Easter season had just begun and a beautiful sun shone down from the crisp blue sky.

Tokyo Disney is just outside Tokyo and, built in 1983, was the first Disney Resort constructed outside the United States of America. The park, however, is owned by The Oriental Land Company. It is the only park that is not wholly or partly owned by The Walt Disney Company; however, they do have creative control. Yes, I am sure people who go to Tokyo Disney would not care about this but for me it was very important! After spending a day there, it was evident that the park was very run down and losing touch with technological advancements. Paint was coming off the walls, buildings were crumbling and some of the activations looked tired.

The reason I included Tokyo Disney as part of my adventure was because everything at Disney is an event. The gates opened at 9am; I arrived at 8.20 after taking two trains and already the queues went right back around the car park. My printed ticket (which was called a passport, because obviously Disneyland is a destination). The ticket cost £55 and with the amount of entertainment I would experience throughout the day, it was going to be well worth it. The queue was a mix of tourists and locals, many of whom were wearing full-on Disney memorabilia. I didn't have a Donald Duck or Goofy hat and felt I was missing out. But it was brilliant to see so many excited people waiting to enter. The gates opened – not really to a big fanfare, more of an *'I need to get to that ride!'* Unfortunately for me, I wasn't so prepared. Instead, I just walked around looking at everything shiny. I wasted time getting to some of the rides, but that is the art of Disney – there is so much to take in. Where to start?

The rides. The shops. The diners. The parades. The character appearances. I actually do not like fast rides. Literally, you would not see me going anywhere near fast rides. But as soon as I arrived, I went straight for one ride. Space Mountain. But instead of dwelling on the fact that I had to hold the hand of the poor guy next to me throughout the whole rollercoasting experience – let's talk about the journey getting to the ride. Activation engagement is what Disney is known for. Delivering a dream and giving an unforgettable experience. The queue was long but I had a queue skip. Great. Along that queue there was music. The queue zigzagged through a space just 20 metres by 15 metres. Just as you got to the end of the line and felt you were close, you had to turn back again. As I got closer, I wished I was in the diner instead. The darkness reminded me of when I was a child and it was pitch black on a winter's night, with the rain pouring, and I was scared. This was a very similar feeling.

Each stand-alone themed ride was its own event, with its own unique uniform and staff badges. After the ride, which can be described as a life-changing experience, I entered the gift shop – clever. The perfect place to buy a photo of me about to faint while thundering down the plastic-coated mountain. Everything about the ride was exactly what an event is. Over a fixed period of time you are taken through a set of emotions and then offered the chance to take something of that experience away with you.

Between Japan being recognised globally as a leader in technology advancement and Disneyland for just being Disney, you would think technology would be at the forefront of everything they do. But I found it was the opposite. The timing boards were marked up with numbered wooden blocks by an employee (cast member) who was given the ride waiting times over a radio. However, when they went on their break the board would be empty. The board was also dirty; in fact, the overall look and feel of the park was just a bit dated.

Some areas of the park had been thought through, step by step. Disney themes everything at every opportunity. I was there at Easter and everywhere was draped with brilliant Easter egg-themed décor. Even Monsters Inc characters Sully and Mike were shaped like eggs. Clever. There was an interesting array of things to buy. Actually, you could buy anything and everything you wanted, from jewellery and watches to stationery, toys and homewares (just to name a few of the 52 different retail shops). Oh, and I could get my hair done too – why not? The home store was certainly my favourite. Baking equipment, table décor, Christmas decorations and so on. Everything with a Disney logo on it – and slightly more expensive. Unfortunately, there was no room in my bag for a Tokyo Disneyland-shaped cookie cutter.

For sure, Disney knows how to put on parades. Parades as a concept are interesting to observe. For a certain amount of time they shut down normal activities while people watch a choreographed experience within the boundaries of the park. In Tokyo, the behaviour of those waiting for the parade was exemplary. Sitting on the ground, they waited at least two hours before the parade began to ensure they got the best spot. I watched everyone be instructed with signals from the Disney cast members, who would blow the whistle and point to tell the person to sit. There was no pushing and when the cast members said: "Please put your feet behind the imaginary line," or "Back from the kerb," no problem, it was done – and no one shuffled back later. Forced smiling and lots of waving at what was coming down the road. Lots of people around me knew the dance moves to the parade songs; it felt slightly brainwashing. The floats, all in Easter colours, were bright and colourful. Very pastel. Everything was constructed perfectly. Characters ran back and forth, waving to grown adults who sat waving identical stuffed characters back at them. I was a bit confused. After the first parade, the wind had picked up a bit. Goofy was struggling to hold on to the top of the podium. So let's skip and conclude that the 1pm parade was just that – a parade.

The 4pm was cancelled because of the wind. So, let's get to the night parade – known as the Tokyo Disneyland Electrical Parade. Now, this parade was fascinating. Over 25 floats at least two storeys high with every Disney character you could imagine. This time, I took a seat on a bench an hour before it was due to begin. I didn't fancy sitting on the kerb, especially when it was cold. It was 7:30pm when the procession lights came through the Magic Castle. The brightness of the floats was truly magnificent. Special does not even cover it. I was amazed. The lights dazzled everything and everyone around them. The floats were all going at the same speed and the characters, harnessed to the top of the floats, were all lit up, and waving and dancing to the thousands lined along the road. I saw the Genie, Aladdin, Beauty and the Beast, the Chipmunks and more. I loved the detail on each float and enjoyed the music blasting through the speakers along the route. Beauty and the Beast stood on a golden podium with a life-size chandelier hanging over them. It brought back childhood memories; 'Be our guest... be our guest...' kept playing on repeat in my head. The electrical parade was truly pulling the nostalgic heartstrings. It was absolutely freezing, and I only had my jumper on, but I was at Disney – so everything was perfect. I had managed to sit next to two teachers from England. They were Disney obsessed and had been all over the world visiting Disney. They even had their own Disney Instagram. I loved talking to them and learning what it is like to be a fan.

The food and drink options in Disney were just epic! The top product was popcorn. It was not only popcorn – oh no – it was popcorn in a character plastic bucket. Everyone wanted their favourite character or the limited editions. I watched people stand in popcorn cart queues for 20 minutes just to get their favourite character. Everyone wanted Dumbo (it was just out in the cinema) or Mickey Mouse ('cos it was Mickey); the Chipmunks weren't as popular, but they were quite cute. Even the flavours were different. Milk chocolate, plain or even curry popcorn (because of course – why not?). Hats off to Disney for this plan. Obviously, following my extremely healthy diet, I ate a few slices of pizza and a few crepes.

As an event, it was a long day of taking in as much as I could. I was overwhelmed and tired and soaked. Here is some deep thinking on everything I saw that day. Everything was psychologically controlled with a passport. Each area was a stamp from Disney I could take away with me. On top of the passport, I could take home merchandise and other consumable memories – tangible. I was dragged around the resort by my interest but also by the fact it was Disney and everything in Disney needs to be seen. You might miss some of the magical experience and your life would forever be boring if this was the case. Oh, and I even got to hug Woody! However, Tokyo's park is slowly falling asleep. It is tired. It needs a new lease of life. Disney needs to enter and take back overall control.

One thing to take away…

Twenty years ago, Disney was the absolute best in everything to do with immersion, event engagement, customer experience and so on. However, in my opinion and in comparison with the events I have attended so far on this adventure, Disney is falling behind. Disney cannot risk not keeping in touch with trends. To stay current and magical, it needs to keep the hat-wearing, T-shirt-buying, cookie template-buying customers and give them even more – things they never expected.

Back to Tokyo…

On the train home, children were napping on their parents' laps and everyone was wearing their Disney T-shirts. A lot of international visitors were figuring out their best route home. It was quite lovely to just sit back and watch the packed train in silence after the frantic euphoria of the day.

On the Sunday, Sam let me know we were going to a drumming festival – so here we go.

Event 23: Narita Drumming Festival

13th April

Sam and I left Tokyo Central Station at 10am to travel to Narita International Airport, which was 70km away. We weren't able to take the fast train to the airport, so we knew it was going to be a long journey, and then Sam realised we had picked the wrong train anyway! Thankfully we could switch to another one, which saved us an extra hour of travelling.

The festival was just seven minutes from the airport. We stopped in a hut-like shop to look at the food they were selling. We were instructed to come towards the back of the shop – not suspicious at all. On a small black box was the Narita Drumming Festival, broadcasting live from the festival site one mile down the road. It was great to see how excited this elderly couple were to show us the festival we were about to witness. We waved goodbye and left them to their small-screen TV.

Narita is famous for a few things. Firstly, it is best known as a hub for airline crew. Hotels – lined the streets with vacancy signs written in pencil, sellotaped to the windows. The shops all sold cheap duty-free items, cut-price cabin bags and other necessities for an overnight stay. The second thing Narita is famous for is eels. There were 300 shops in the village and they all sold eels. In fact, eels had even been incorporated into the drumming festival map, which was quite bizarre, but I liked that they were taking advantage of this local theme.

With 1,500 performers and 800 drummers, the noise was constant. Drummers from all over Japan had descended onto this town for the festival. The atmosphere was pulsing. The rhythms were thunderous. Narita Drumming Festival had eight different zones, with performances going on throughout the day. The type of drum used was a taiko. The term comes from Chinese and Korean folklore in the 6th century. There were up-and-coming drummers as young as four, right through to more experienced elders, all wearing traditional costume or band uniforms. The clothing was not just about being identified as a band member but about having pride in your culture.

I was already impressed by the various stages – and we were only at the first zone on the eel map. The route led up to Naritasan Shinsho-ji Temple and each zone and stage along the route was packed with tourists and locals from neighbouring villages. It was a truly magnificent sight.

Each zone was sponsored. This small local event offered real commercial value for major sponsors. At times you would see 'commercial partners' being ushered out of restaurants, escorted through the streets and treated to the full VIP experience. So, we had a cultural event being commercially driven. Company logos were plastered around, which changed the direction of the event – but for the companies it was important. Despite the commercialisation, people came to this festival because they felt an emotional connection to what they understand and identify as their culture. I could really appreciate why drumming groups from all over the country wanted to be part of something that was so special and unique. It gave them a sense of identity.

Across from zone one were vendors selling taiko drums. Being the active tourist and researcher, I wanted to discover what it was like to hit one. *'Be the drummer and feel the rhythm,'* I thought. I held a beat. I gave it a wee shot. The wooden blocks you hold are extremely heavy. To then strike them in a certain downward stroke was tricky and hard to figure out at first. But after 30 seconds, I felt accomplished. It was a great engagement piece for the audience and for anyone who drums, and I gained a new respect for the energy and talent a drummer possesses.

When I jumped off, two teenagers jumped on. Standing either side of the drum, the beat started off gently and then became a controlled rhythm that got louder and louder. They were outstanding. Even the vendor, smiling as a crowd formed around his stall, was surprised. As the vendor ran around trying to give out leaflets, it was like an online viral moment. The boys were utterly breath-taking. They weren't with a band – they were just drummers here to enjoy the event. I was happy with my 30 seconds – bang bang bang – but they were able to showcase their talent. With a bow, they mingled back into the crowd. Strolling further along, I could feel the buzz. I was very much interested in the why? Why do drummers perform at this festival? Why do taiko drummers love what they do? Drumming does bring with it a real energy.

The purpose of each zone was to lead everyone to the Naritasan Shinsho-ji Temple Omoto Domae special stage where, on the second day, the scene was set for what was called the 'Night of 1,000 Drummers'. Throughout the day there were no performances on this stage. So, the plan was – and I liked their thinking – that everyone attending would travel along the eel route through the different zones, which had performances going on all day. When you reached the end of the eel, you had arrived at the ultimate performance.

A leading group were on the special stage, which towered over the 3,000 audience members. Our mouths were open in awe. I say 3,000 because it was rammed – you couldn't move. Some local VIP guests were ushered to the very front. The grounds of the temple shook to the thundering rhythm. As the sun set in Tokyo, the shrine was lit up and the thunder of the drumming continued. I was really not expecting what I saw. The lights were flashing, but in a pre-set computerised pattern to the beat of the music, a bit like an electronic dance festival. At the side of the stage, a team was huddled around computers, controlling the light show. They were super excited about the beaming lights – you could see them truly loving each moment. Standing stage left, they gazed upon the ever-changing lights, the drums and the audience.

The surroundings gave the whole event such a unique feel. A real moment for me was staring at the temple as I took it all in. The temple grounds were at the summit of a very steep hill and the Buddhist shrine was important to all members of the religious community. But today, music was used to awaken the land. The culture here was so rich. The traditions were so spectacular. Over the two days of the festival, 200,000 people are estimated to have experienced the spectacular event.

One thing to take away...

A drum. A beat that some people hate. They say it's too loud; it's not music – it's just noise. But this wasn't noise. This was culture. This was a part of tradition and celebration and was being held to the highest heights in Narita. It was splendid.

Back to Tokyo...

Tokyo was a very interesting place. From Sam's flat, I watched the sunset over the city six nights in a row. Each time I spotted a different part of the city. The city was ever-changing, ever marvellous and mysterious. I was told to always look up for restaurants, which confused me – but then I started to understand. Some restaurants were literally in the middle of apartment blocks or on the second floor of an office block! This wasn't just to be trendy; this was the way it was. Tokyo was full. The only way to open somewhere was often to go up. It was such an interesting thing to experience. You would be walking along and suddenly there would be a restaurant in the basement of an apartment block, or a shop in the middle of a housing estate. Or you could go into a stairwell and find a beauty salon, a sushi place and Starbucks, along with a woman who had lived there for 50 years.

During my time in Tokyo, I visited the Rugby World Cup offices to discuss the forthcoming 2019 World Cup. There, I met a friend, Ross from my days volunteering for organisations in Glasgow. I loved learning about the impact Japan would have on rugby (and mega events) and rugby would have on Japan.

Event 24: TeamLab Presents: Borderless

15th April

Interactive art is not just interesting; it's the future. Imagine walking into a room with water up to your knees and light projecting onto the walls – what does it do to your body? How does it make you feel? Art installations are not just about 'something occurring'; they are about creating a change in the participants' minds. Think of art as a way of expression and immersion. People read the image differently. They see things from different perspectives. Interactive art gives people a sense of emotional control.

It was the day after the Narita Drumming Festival – this is how full-on my trip was. Tonight was all about experiencing *TeamLab presents: Borderless.* TeamLab was founded in 2001 and brings together an interdisciplinary group of self-named ultratechnologists (people who understand design, computer science, engineers and so on), production companies and other creative bodies to produce an experience that is unique, immersive and spellbinding. I needed to visit things that were revolutionary to show the possibilities of the future, and this was a world first. It was digital art on a scale I never knew possible.

The TeamLab plan was created to give a step-by-step experience, with 15 people at a time going in every 15 minutes. Online reviews say it is the 'most Instagrammable place in the world'. A big reputation to live up to. On arrival, we were arranged into three lines and instructed to watch a TV. Perfect start. I was about to be welcomed into a set engagement with set rules that I had to abide by. Standing on the footprints on the floor, I watched as the video guided us, but didn't give anything away. The instructions – both in Japanese and English – were very clear.

We had free lockers to put our belongings in. A member of the team, who spoke Japanese and English, stood at the entrance to the first room. I was totally in the dark about what was going to happen. It was all about the element of surprise. It was the unknown. The staff member checked my trousers were rolled up to my knees – as per the instructions – and that I only had my phone with me, nothing else.

Walking into the first room, I saw beanbags. The lights were very dim; it was almost pitch black. I needed to reach the other side of the room. In front of me were about 10 people, most of whom were just lying on the beanbags, laughing as they tried to balance. This was not an Instagrammable room.

The next room was a water room. Wait? What? The water room was quite intriguing. *'Make sure your trousers are rolled up...'* I took a step across a metal board and my feet dipped into the warm water. Looking below, I saw fish. FISH? Really? No – it was a light show that was being beamed around everyone's feet. The whole process was quite extraordinary. All around me, water sounds were plumbed into the room and playing around the walls. It was very relaxing.

After leaving the water room, we dried our legs with the provided brown towels and moved on. The next room was the brightest of all the rooms. It was a mirrored light room with dangling lamps, light being reflected all over the place. This was the room that was all over Instagram. It was the perfect room for an influencer trying to be cool. I watched as people tried to strike the best pose at the best moment. But I think this room had deeper meaning than simply an Instagram opportunity. It had mirrors with reflections. It had colour-changing lights that represented something.

Everything was manufactured so exquisitely. Everything was about the connection. The connection to water, the connection to the ground, the connection with your reflection. We walked barefoot the whole way. We were literally engaging with the event with every sense of our body. Interaction between the person and art was important here. It was about the person becoming *part* of the artwork. I can absolutely confirm that was the case.

In the second-to-last room were large white balls that moved whenever you walked; you could push them wherever you wanted – like into random people, who would dodge them or push them around. We know technology as a way of communication but tonight I saw the capacity of technology in delivering an art event. Lying on the floor in the final room was quite special. A moment to stop and reflect. I think watching flowers projected onto the ceiling and zooming towards your face is how art may connect with people's senses in the future. This was a famous painting that had been magically broken down and transformed into a video projection show. Now, I was getting to see it in a way never seen before.

Social media is key to the success of TeamLab. People share images, but do not give away the whole experience. Those attending are saying: "Look, I am part of this very well-known event – I am trendy." They make their friends jealous and create a desire in others to want to know more. *Borderless* has become so popular that models often use it as a backdrop for photoshoots. At the time of writing, TeamLab has been tagged in over 700,000 posts on Instagram. TeamLab is not just delivering a sensory experience but creating the sensation of a futuristic lifestyle that you can be part of and share with your followers.

This is not a norm in people's lives. They buy into the product because of the value of what the experience can give them: an orchestrated production, mind mapped emotional engagement and the deliberate feeling of a departure from normality. Here, I was well and truly departed from reality. I felt disconnected, not only from global issues but also from all my personal problems and worries I had about my trip.

Attending an event like this is not just for the novelty value; it's also for the bigger picture it brings about our unique perspective. I loved that each room gave me a different sense to enjoy and consume. Art galleries are one way of experiencing and engaging with art. But this is a different way. It put the consumers in the driving seat for engagement. Walls of lights. Mirrors on floors and walls. Beanbags. Soft floors. Barefooted. Textures that, together, gave an experience like no other. Human interactional behaviour and the combination of art created a perfect process to be enjoyed by all.

One thing to take away...

The whole point of travelling and experiencing activities like this is to get a sense of escapism before we return to our very boring, routine lives – that sometimes feel as if they have zero purpose.

Events can be sometimes stuck in the ways they do things. But this is not the case for TeamLab. A photo taken here would set your Instagram or Facebook notifications on fire.

Time for trains...

Over the last couple of weeks, I could tell my body was getting tired. I was going from event to event, place to place, dealing with different weather patterns and different paces to keep up with the citizens of each city. My luggage was heavy and I felt tired after doing the easiest of tasks. Mentally, I was exhausted and a bit overwhelmed. What was my next move?

Tomorrow I was going to Kyoto, on the way to experiencing something special – but my body was telling me I had to slow down. My back was giving in and carrying over 30 kilos for the next six months was going to be a struggle. Maybe I needed to see a doctor...

Have you ever been scared about a situation? Have you ever had to make a decision that could alter everything? This was exactly the situation I was in. I spoke to a very good friend. We always give each other a hard time when we don't listen to advice. This would be the person to tell me straight.

The hospital... well, I went. I won't bore you with the details, but I left with a small back brace and some straight-to-the-point advice.

This incident was a reminder of the fragility of health when travelling. I had to listen to and appreciate my body. I had to sense when I needed to take a step back and slow down. At the moment I had been going fast (although not as fast as I was about to go...) but I was going to be knackered if I carried on. So I listened!

Pod Hotels... WOW! Everything was laid out for what I considered to be one of my best accommodation experiences. I was given a locker for my bags and in the locker was everything I needed for my bed, which was in a room with 25 other pods. Pyjamas were laid out, towels... it was a five-star experience. I was on the lower level of the pods – it was so simple, yet so spacious and peaceful.

With only two evenings planned in the city and one whole day spent in the hospital, my time in Kyoto was brief. But this was just a pit stop to get me to the bottom of Japan.

The train to Nagasaki...

Nagasaki is situated at the bottom of Japan on the island of Kyushu. Bridges connect the city to the mainland, but it still takes two days to get there from Tokyo. Nagasaki is known as the place that was bombed by the United States of America during World War II, devastating the entire harbour town. Not just devastated – between 60,000–80,000 people were reported to have been killed. Since that day in 1945, everything has been rebuilt – there are very few historic buildings – and because everything is new and due to its geography, it's not really a tourist attraction. The malls were busy, of course, and there were plenty of people buying what seems to be the only brand of coffee in the world – Starbucks. But I was here to attend Japan's only annual sailing festival.

Event 25: Nagasaki Tall Ship Festival

18th–22nd April

The 19th anniversary of the Nagasaki Tall Ship Festival took place from the 18th to 22nd April, and it was a truly special event. Nagasaki is known globally as a leader in the maritime community and its extremely busy harbour feeds Japan with cargo from all over the world. It is also the base for the Nagasaki Naval Training Center. The event meant a lot to the people of Nagasaki – and to me – and it was a local event in every way. Every signpost, map and publicity poster was in Japanese only. This was not aimed at tourists.

First, let's talk about the 'blue economy' (events that are based around the water). Globally, sea and ocean events have increased significantly. It has been noted on maritime websites and in news articles that this increase is due to the public wanting more unique things to attend. Cities have begun to utilize natural resources more, which, in turn, has seen harbours become a hustle and bustle of regeneration, welcoming more people to experience these beautiful areas by the sea. And Nagasaki was no different. Restaurants, cafes, bars and shopping centres lined the seafront, and new cultural centres, a sports centre and library had been built directly next to the regenerated harbour.

The highlight of the first day was the arrival of the tall elegant ships, which spanned between 48 and 101 metres in height. As they glided into the bay from the East China Sea, the sight was breathtaking. For two hours, thousands of people stood watching in awe. The first ship to arrive – as tradition had it – was the Japanese tall ship. I did a double-take as I realised that the sailors were all standing on the masts! On three levels, sailors were harnessed onto each beam. As more ships arrived, each 300 metres from the next, they were brought in by patrol boats from the Japanese Coastguard, with pilots on each vessel communicating via radio. Along with the thundering music coming from the Japanese Army's brass band right behind me, I didn't know where to look.

The MC was enthusiastically presenting, fully in Japanese, the programme for the day. One by one, the ships were introduced as their sailors waved to those waiting on shore. Without any police guidance or security, we all stood behind the imaginary safety line as the crowd waved frantically. School groups, elders and everyone in between were obviously extremely excited about the arrival of 1,500 sailors on the brigs, barquentines and brigantines (I learned all about tall ships that week!). Paper fans were handed out from the market stalls for you to wave as hard as you could to welcome the world to the harbour. Apparently, some offices had closed earlier than scheduled to allow staff to welcome the ships to shore. Each time a ship docked properly and the gangway was attached, a group of elders – aged between 75 and 90 – from the Nagasaki Tall Ship organising committee would approach and bow at 90 degrees. The whole process of docking the ships in harbour took about five hours. I think by the end there were probably only about a hundred of us still watching. The main festival started tomorrow; today was the 'boring' part. As each ship arrived, procedures were followed and then I watched the sailors beginning to sort out the deck and start their duties onboard. As the sun set, I decided tomorrow was going to be a huge day. Bedtime!

On the second day, the tall ships were open for all to visit. Set hours were advertised outside each ship along with information on the history of the vessel. Each ship had a crewmate welcoming everyone on board. I was happy just to see how excited people were to explore these ships, so rarely encountered, and have their picture taken with the sailors. Or to be able to walk along the deck and pretend to be ship's captain for a few seconds. Imagine being a child and being able to walk the decks of a tall ship that has sailed from Russia on the Seven Seas! The Russian boats were run by cadets from the Russian Army and had been part of their training programme for the last 30 years. The cadets were young lads out to experience the world and they were managed by retired Russian Navy captains. I went on board and got to experience the living quarters, where six males lay their heads at night. It was extremely dark and very cramped. Exploring the tall ship was educational more than anything. A ship like this has many stories to tell each time it goes to sea – and today I got to experience my own story aboard the ship. I got to feel like the captain of my own ship.

Every day for four days I went to a market stall run by a family and by the end of the festival they were calling me 'Mr Scotland'. I bought popcorn chicken in a soda cup. It was brilliant – about 20 bits for £1.50. The reason I mention food was because there were food demonstrations going on all weekend and they were always packed with people wanting to learn new techniques and appreciate different local cuisines of the area – as well as get some free treats. Top chefs from all over Japan had flown in. There was something quite special about the tall ships but something even more special about Nagasaki's positioning of this festival. Under a clear blue sky, it could not be any more perfect.

The locals loved the festival because 1,500 sailors came on land after being at sea (sometimes for up to six weeks) prepared to spend money. All of a sudden, coffee shops and food outlets had special offers on. Everyone everywhere welcomed the sailors. And the local girls were there, waiting for their dream sailor on shore. The Russians were the biggest hit. They'd wander off into the sunset and then you would see them, two hours later, sprinting back to their ship.

On the last day I headed into Starbucks. As I ordered my soy hot chocolate from the same server I had seen over the last few days, she asked me, in broken English and using the wrong grammar, "Matthew, do *I* speak Russian?" When I said I didn't, the employee looked a bit upset, as if I was her last hope for having something translated. I looked around. It was 9:25am and there were over a hundred sailors in the café, all sitting at tables or standing. Every chair was taken – but no one was actually drinking anything. She said to me, in very good English, "We are trying to tell them that they need to buy something or not sit."

"No problem. Leave it with me..." I said. Taking a quick breath, I turned around and marched over to the main group of sailors like I was the captain of Starbucks. You couldn't write the next bit. "Attention sailors!" No one reacted. Now all the Starbucks staff were staring at me and smiling, including the manager, who had ducked out of the office at the side. "All understand English..." I shouted. "You either buy something or you get up right now and leave. No more sitting here using the WiFi – bye bye – be gone!" Within 30 seconds the rough translations were being whispered around, at which point 80 of the 100 sailors started to filter out. Suddenly the staff were bowing to me! The sailors' captain, who was drinking coffee, then apologised to me and to the staff. He hugged them to say sorry – they looked awkward – and I laughed as he patted my back with a whack.

This was a learning point about events rolling into destinations. Economic investment is critical to towns like Nagasaki, but it's always important to understand that the locals are still trying to go about their day-to-day lives. Coffee shops host weekly book clubs or welcome a meeting of new parents – so it is important to feel the rhythm of the city before disrupting it. Nagasaki had a tight community – even Starbucks was a cathedral of engagement. Once I'd cleared out the sailors, before you knew it nearly every seat was full of locals who had been waiting.

There were lots of lovely touches to the festival. Each ship had a uniquely designed stamp that participants could walk around and collect in a souvenir booklet. A team of volunteers – all students from the local university – had been brought in to manage the marquees and the stamping process, and it was constantly busy. Some stamps, such as the Russian and South Korean stamps for two of the ships – were deemed quite special. It was such a simple idea, and it maybe seemed old-fashioned, but it was a joy to experience. I felt like I was 10 years old and collecting Pokémon cards again – such a cool personal keepsake.

The Nagasaki Tall Ship Festival Committee had two divisions of organisers. The first section was the elders, who 'managed' the boats and the history of the festival. They wore blue hats and had a table for them set up, and most people who walked past it would bow to them. The second team was the festival organisers, who managed the land programme and also had some responsibility for sea safety. They wore a white sash with words written in Japanese. Their headquarters was a blue marquee and on the back – I kid you not – was a picture of the Scottish Rugby Team! Apparently, it was because the team would be based in Nagasaki during the Rugby World Cup in 2019. It was a surprise to see, but a real nice treat to get a picture next to it and remember home while I was at the bottom of Japan.

On both Saturday and Sunday evenings, a huge firework display on the harbour took over the skies. I took some great photos after sitting on cold concrete for three hours. The tall ships were all lit up in amazing colours. The firework display pulled in close to 50,000 people each night, who were perfectly managed by the local police. With traffic management, barrier patrols and the control of the sailors, it can't have been easy, yet it was a slick and amazing production.

On the last day it was time for both the tall ships and me to depart. I had planned to be in the harbour until the last possible moment of the event. At 11am the last of the official programmed events kicked off. Using my translation app, I worked out this was called 'The Farewell'. I could have cried. I was upset to be leaving. But that's the point of events. They happen for a set amount of time and at the end you take away something, whether that's materialistic or emotional. You grow as a person. You have a wider understanding of something you never knew before. I had experienced the inside of these cramped but well-aged tall ships. And I saw the positive effects of this event on the town.

Standing in the seaside park, I watched as the market stalls started to pack up – including my popcorn chicken stall. I was even sad saying goodbye to them. We all bowed at each other and honestly, I had a tear in my eye just at the fact that I was saying goodbye to a popcorn chicken stall! (I would never do this or get emotional at other events – well, maybe.) As I turned to walk away, they grabbed some leftover chicken that was destined for the bin and instead gave it to me as a parting gift.

The official farewell was about to begin. Six schools had arrived with brass bands and flag bearers. Suddenly, from the bridge, I saw 20 sailors sprinting back to their ship. Awaiting them stood their not-so-happy captains – you could sense the anger in the air. The organisers, unaware of this, were frantically trying to get the ships' captains and senior staff into line. Time constraints were a factor and language barriers were causing some amusing mass panic at times. The tug boats were all parked alongside the ships, ready to go – but not until Nagasaki had given the tall ships the biggest farewell.

The parade began with all the sailors in formation. It was actually the first time I'd seen all the crews together as one. With thousands watching – surprising given it was a Monday – it was a huge operation to manage. The bands were playing music like *I Love You, Baby* and the *James Bond* theme song. The mayor of the town, Tomihisa Taue, led the tributes – all in Japanese. By now I was an expert at guessing what was being said. He started with thanks to the crews and the ships. Everyone cheered – including the sailors. Gifts, including beautiful plaques, were given from the city to all the captains. Then he thanked the organisers and sponsors (of course – very important). And he thanked the people who were sitting and waiting for the ships to depart. Around me I saw no tourists. It was all locals, wishing the sailing community good luck and goodbye. That shows how much this tall ship festival means to the town. It was a really well-positioned event with subtle objectives but beautiful outcomes. I was gutted to see it end.

Ceremonial duties all done, now the tug boats started their engines and smoke bellowed over the harbour. The ropes were released but suddenly there was one final panicky moment – which I captured on film. The Russian boat was starting to be tugged but the blue-hatted harbour masters couldn't unhook the rope from the shore. The Russians were screaming and the Blue Hats were panicking as the boat, still attached, was pulled along. Watching in horror, everyone held their hands to their faces. I looked along the dock and saw 10 Blue Hats sprinting to lift up the rope. The police were running, the Blue Hats were grappling and the public was standing in silence. And suddenly, with 20 pairs of hands, the rope was thrown over. With disaster averted, everyone bowed to each other.

As the masts disappeared into the distance, I ran to the train station. For me, Nagasaki was just glorious. The town. The atmosphere. The character. The potential. And the fact that a tall ship festival had just delivered both social and economic impact – but also so much more. Have you ever been to an event and seen yourself not as an attendee but as a guest? If you have, you'll understand you get so much more from that moment...

One thing to take away...

We live in a world where sometimes we are scared to come out of our comfortable bubbles and discover new things, so we just attend events that are popular. Nagasaki Tall Ship Festival was way out of my way. Logistically, it was kind of a daft decision. But decisions are never about the easy option – they are about taking risks. And this risk completely paid off. A Tall Ship Festival is just extraordinary with the amount of impact it can have. And this event did that.

More trains...

I got talking to a lot of people on the trains back to Tokyo – I was in a talkative mood. I meet four teachers from England who had decided to come to Japan for their two-week Easter holiday. They had planned everything out and had a set agenda. They laughed at my global planning; I was becoming used to it now, but for others it was quite a challenge to follow.

The next day I met an American family. There were six of them: the parents, and four children from the ages of three to eighteen. The man was from San Francisco and was involved in the tech industry – he was quite a big deal. The family had everything – every gadget, every ounce of privilege they could have. "Why are we not in first class...?" the children kept asking.

The dad and I really hit it off. His partner, who he had been with for four years, was, I think, jealous of our relationship! We chatted and laughed for a good three hours. Eventually I noticed that all his family had fallen asleep, except for the 18-year-old who had joined our conversation. I dared to ask him what the kids kept asking: "Why did you choose not to sit in first class?"

"I never had what they have had," he said. "I never got five-star luxury accommodation everywhere I went. I always had to work to get what I had. When I was 14, my parents made me work. By the time I was 18, I was a manager. I began my college education – but still worked. Some people think I was born into these shoes... but these shoes are worn because I walked far to get into them."

I really appreciated his honesty – but I will never forget what he said next. "First class means what? What does it show? What does it represent? What do the kids see in first class, and what do they begin to think? That everything comes in crystal glasses and we receive meals everywhere and food is always warm? No – this trip is about educating them to walk in their own shoes..."

Wow. I wrote that just after he said it – word for word – and he laughed and said, "I guess that will make the book?" And I nodded.

When our train arrived in Tokyo, we exchanged emails, said our goodbyes – and off we went. It was time for the baseball!

Event 26: Baseball in Tokyo

<u>23rd April</u>

Have you ever thought about why sport transcends borders like nothing else? There's an emotional attachment to sport and it can create a community like no other. Sport is sometimes adored by the most surprising of communities. To experience a baseball match in Japan was a must.

Baseball was introduced to Japan in the 1870s. The Nippon Professional Baseball Organisation – the NPB League – is the highest level of the sport, and tonight I was going to see the Tokyo Swallows play at home against the Tokyo Giants. Big rivals. But both teams were completely different – one team had a brilliant record, the other not so much. Baseball is considered one of the top sports in Japan and I could tell by the packed stadium and fan engagement that everyone consumes the sport. The Meiji Jingu Stadium can hold over 37,000 spectators and was opened in 1926. The Tokyo Giants, who were the away team and more established, had a stadium with a capacity of 55,000. Quite a difference, for sure. There were 25,000 people on the night I was there, all cheering and chanting.

Japanese baseball culture is slightly different to American baseball. I met Sam and some of her friends after work and they were dressed very casually and appropriately for the game. However, Tokyo residents literally wear suits and ties to baseball matches, with a baseball top worn over their workwear. We'd see them with briefcases at their feet and two full pints of beer in their hands. Groups met outside and bowed to each other.

In we went to what I can only describe as a frenzy of noise and excitement – and the Swallows were losing. The stadium was like any other stadium in the world with commercial opportunities everywhere. Merchandise was thrown onto makeshift tables:

keyrings in the shapes of penguins, gum, pencil cases and much more. But the merchandise was not the only 'buy in' opportunity. The team had a membership programme, the Swallows Crew, which created a real sense of belonging. On the wall at section J were screens where members could collect points by scanning a QR code. It was brilliant to see first-hand the opportunities for fans.

Considering we were in Japan (an expensive country), and considering I was at an event (which usually increases prices considerably), the food and drink were pretty cheap. It was only £3.50 for half a pizza – which was fresh out of the greasy oven tray and actually looked good. Down each stairwell came young women with large heavy kegs strapped to their backs. They entered the stadium with a bow to the thousands of fans. Suddenly, hands were going up everywhere, clutching folded yen notes. A wave indicated you wanted beer. I had a few issues with this – it was quite evident that they were using the female body to sell beer. Outdated, but any complaint would probably be thrown back to me that it is part of the culture and part of the sporting experience…

The baseball clubs were great at manufacturing fan engagement. Every so often an American accent would come over the speakers: "GO GO SWALLOWS!" Three times this would be repeated. Two bands were there, one either side in the stands, and everyone sang along. People wanted to be part of every element of the event, as much as they could. If they could not swing the bat, they would make noise. There was also the Swallow Umbrella Dance. I was warned: "Get ready for this – you will want to write about it…!" Suddenly, the music blaring from the stadium PA signalled the moment I was waiting for. Everyone took out small plastic umbrellas from their pockets, briefcases and jackets. Everyone sang. They waved their umbrellas to the right and to the left. I was so confused. I did not have an umbrella, so obviously I wasn't fully part of it. With umbrellas raised and the right music, the PA announcer could tell everyone with one signal what it was time for. The whole place was alive.

It's a shame the game did not reflect fan engagement so much. My argument here is that those people arriving in their work gear, enjoying a beer (or five), having a membership card, buying chicken and chips are actually purchasing the experience rather than the sport. It's all controlled. I hate to say it, but the match was honestly boring – but the way the event was delivered was truly captivating.

As I was leaving, I noticed spectators pulling small bags from their pockets and picking up litter. Everyone was cleaning up. I knew what was going on because I had read about how this was an important part of Japanese culture. Waiting at the exit doors, two stadium staff stood with larger bags and everyone bowed and dropped in their rubbish bags. I mean, I was stunned. This behaviour is usually not what you see when thousands of spectators leave a stadium. Japan had intertwined culture with sport. Win, lose or draw, there is always a group of fans who will stay behind and clean the stadium. In fact, Japan had already been recognised globally for this sort of behaviour during the Men's FIFA World Cup. My thoughts? Why can't other countries see this behaviour and copy it? Why can't stadiums enforce policies to ensure those attending clear up after themselves? Events need to do all they can to limit the environmental impact they have.

One thing to take away...

Tokyo Swallows on the field... well, they got beat. But what won that night for me was Japanese culture, which was fascinating to observe and enjoy – and be part of. It was not the baseball that excited me – it was all about the culture.

Goodbye, Japan

Japan was a tremendous country to explore and I loved understanding a refreshing culture. Refreshing, because we live in a globalised world where everything can merge into one, but Japan has an individual personality and is very much a place that will stay with me forever. From meeting friends to exploring different destinations, I visited some beautiful places in Japan – and I experienced a fascinating world that has a big future in events.

Now... India

From one culture to another... The oven door opened as I walked out of the plane. Arriving in India was an experience I will remember forever. I got into a white minibus. With his flip phone in one hand and a cigarette in the other, my driver balanced the wheel on his knee as he dodged through thousands of cars and blocked scooters from trying to whizz past him. My hands were on my head. He laughed – as did the other six people in the minibus, who were locals. I was ready to die. I knew this was it. I kid you not, at one point the rosary beads tied to the rear-view mirror began praying for me – it was that scary.

Each street in Delhi had what felt like 100,000 people milling around. Arriving at my accommodation, Hotel Sunstar – where, for seven nights, I was 'Mr Sir' – I dropped my bags into my windowless, non-air-conditioned room and headed out to adventure. The city was a haze of culture, smog and character. The markets were busy until midnight every night. The humans ran the streets from 5am until midnight and the wild dogs ran the streets from midnight until 5am. Believe me, it was scary at times in the streets of Karol Bagh, where I stayed. The wild dogs were literally wild – wild and aggressive. Delhi has an economy that relies on technology, telecommunications, media, banking and tourism. Some manufacturing does exist, but mainly outside the city – which is why the smog sometimes floats in when the wind is blowing in the right (wrong) direction. Residents rely a lot on the Delhi Metro to get around. A journey through Delhi was always busy. No matter what time you ventured out, there were either 20 people huddled around an umbrella selling ice lollies, or a bar – well, a hole in the wall – where everyone was huddled around drinking nimbu pani (lemonade) or tea.

I spent a lot of time in Connaught Place, because the Starbucks there had great WiFi and air conditioning. The last thing I wanted to do was walk around the city in 43-degree heat. But the history of Connaught Place was fascinating. As I walked out of Rajiv Chowk Station, I would be dazzled by the brightness of the marble and the white chalk, which shone brightly in the sun. The area was named after Prince Arthur, the 1st Duke of Connaught, who was the third son of Queen Victoria. It was built between 1767 and 1774, modelled on some areas of Bath, in England – and it was wealthy.

Let me tell you a story about my experience in Starbucks. It was busy there every day. I would find a table, nest my head into my laptop and type. Sometimes I would be typing that much I would forget how long I had been sitting there for. One day, one of the employees walked over to me. "Hello Mr Sir, what do you do?" We got chatting. She explained that all the staff wondered what I was typing whenever I came in – which I found an interesting observation in itself. I told her about my journey and why I was in Delhi. She asked me how I could afford the trip and I explained I had saved so much for seven years and worked hard to try and make my dream come true. She then said: "I have saved for so long time too, but we are not paid well." I asked her what she was saving for and she said she really wanted to go to the cinema but couldn't afford it. I did a double-take. As she stood in front of me, so tall and so proud in her extremely clean Starbucks uniform, and with the biggest smile, she had literally rendered me speechless.

I was kind of taken aback and the only response I could think of was: "What movie?" She wanted to see *Avengers*; shame, because if her answer had been *Sister Act* or *Cool Runnings* I would have taken her myself! She was working to survive but also trying to save to see a movie that I and most people reading this book could probably go and see any time we wanted. So… that was the difference.

After she left, I put down my pen, closed my laptop and

thought about what she had said to me. She had a dream: to go and see a movie that cost the same as three Starbucks drinks. A cinema ticket was 1,000 Indian rupees, which is roughly £10. We take so much for granted. We don't realise how privileged we are within this world. I am so fortunate to be able to do what I do. Fortune, for us, is about wealth at times – but of course health fits into this discussion as well. I was completely changed after this moment. I was in a different mindset. I messaged Starbucks India and told them this story. I got a response to say they would contact the area manager – whether anything was done was another thing, but you never know.

On to my first meeting in Delhi. I had thought outside the box and wanted to try and get into a nightclub to find out how nightlife is consumed in India. Located in the basement of the five-star LaLit Hotel, Kitty Su is very well-known in Delhi. In September 2018, the Supreme Court of India decriminalized being gay in India; although it's not accepted by all, it is very much legal. Later that year, the club became front-page news globally when its owner, a gay Indian businessman, decided Kitty Su would host LGBTQ+ nights, thereby becoming a pioneer in moving India forwards in its human rights. However, I didn't know any of this until I met the manager.

To be honest, I wasn't expecting to find a nightclub like Kitty Su in the middle of a five-star hotel (it costs, on average, £400 a night to stay here). But I wanted to try and appreciate different aspects of the leisure industry. The walls were leather. The décor… The look was 'provocateur'. Very sexually stimulating. Chains. Floor shows. The hidden rooms for only VIP guests. Yet this was a nightclub for everyone – open to the public. Akal, the manager, was an interesting character. Very confident and very focused on the nightclub's inclusivity. He gave me a tour of the three-room premises and we talked about how people consume the establishment. "It's for the elite of Delhi," Akal told me. And I could tell that was the case. It was about the luxury. We sat drinking water from crystal glasses and discussing how luxury consumption of nightclubs was on the increase. "Everyone wants to say they were here," Akal said. "They want their photo taken here…" But at the same time, it was about discretion. Whatever happens in the club stays in the club. All the staff understand that it's about allowing the customer to feel that this is a safe space and anything is acceptable. (Ah, that's what the showers are for then.) We talked for three hours, although Akal did keep getting calls or being called away. Posters screaming "Go F**k your #selfie" were plastered on some walls; other walls displayed pimp masks. #IAMFREAK was the official hashtag of the club. It was all about escaping. It was a place of 'anything goes – as long as it is luxury'. The theme continued into the toilets, with luxury products and plaster busts in sexually explicit poses. This club was not about music; it was about freedom of the mind and body. Escapism – complete and utter escapism. Drugs. Sex. (Actually, not sex – but the suggestion was clear.) Being a freak. Freedom.

I was invited to come along to a very special evening featuring two DJs who were the first lesbian DJs to play in Kitty Su since being gay was decriminalised. The ticket cost double what it was to go and see *Avengers* – I was now comparing everything to a cinema ticket. The nightclub was a place of consumption for the middle classes – and, tonight, for one night only, I would be hitting the dancefloor in my one shirt and un-ironed trousers. So this wasn't a scheduled event, but it was an opportunity to immerse myself in a nightclub environment that had been created to give people a safe space within a country steeped in culture and religion – and, historically, disapproving of this behaviour.

The night was fun. Full of antics. It wasn't the busiest evening, but it had its moments. Bottles with sparklers were common through the dance floor, which is a status thing that happens all over; it's all about '*Who is getting the £300 bottle of vodka? Are they famous?*' But this club felt like it was about more than just status. This was a club not scared to disrupt the norms of nightclub engagement. At 3am, I headed home. No chips and cheese here.

Event 27: Hindu Wedding

1st May

The next day was huge for me – and an even bigger day for my friend, who was getting married. Actually, he wasn't really my friend; I just briefly gate-crashed his wedding. I'd been due to watch cricket in Delhi, but the dates had changed because of the Indian political elections. So, I had to find something else to do... and I did.

I really wanted to go to a Hindu wedding in India. My plan was to blend in and enjoy it, while understanding more about the different elements that made the whole thing work. Weddings are one thing we all have in common that are interpreted so differently around the globe. I had asked a few friends who have family in India whether there would be any weddings I could attend, but unfortunately I wouldn't be travelling during wedding season. But I was not deterred.

One evening I was out for dinner with a friend I had met at the hotel who was here on business and happy to take me around the city. We had just finished sampling some of Delhi's finest cuisine when we heard fireworks. "That's a wedding," he said.

Immediately I shouted: "Let's go!" and we ran towards it, dodging tuk-tuks. We clambered over the concrete reserve in the middle of the most unstable road I had ever seen, to be met with an array of colours. This was what I wanted to see. The bright colours and noise. I wanted to know how love was celebrated in other countries. When two hearts fall in love, how do they say, "I do"?

I was in an area called Janapura West in Delhi. A nice area with a few wedding complexes – like small convention centres. There was constant hustle and bustle. Traffic and building rubble was everywhere. I watched the wedding procession and saw a few guests dancing at the front. At the rear, sitting on a horse, was a man wearing an extremely large pink turban with gold embroidery.

"That's the groom," my friend said. As the horse made its way along the streets, fireworks were thrown into the air by some of the staff and guests. This was the beginning of the parade towards the man's new married life.

He looked over the moon to be getting married. I joke. He was sitting on the horse like he had just picked up his weekly shopping. No excitement. Of course, he was probably wondering why there was a guy in grey shorts and grey t-shirt smiling at him. That was me. My friend jumped over and explained that I would like a photo.

"Hello, I am from Scotland – congratulations!" I said.

"Ah, I'm from London – Brixton!" The guy laughed. As we exchanged words while he trotted on the horse, his whole family and everyone around us just stared. He had lived in London his whole life and was now back in India and remarrying. I did wonder because I had been advised the wedding season hadn't kicked off yet – he was doing it on the cheap. "Get me off of this!" he said, eventually. "I hate being up here." As we walked along the busy road, we discussed his marriage. He was carrying his son, who had also been on the horse, and was wishing he could be somewhere different. I asked him what he thought about the culture and tradition. In summary, he was doing this for his family. He understood the symbolism and the importance to an extent, but his body language told me he was not interested one bit. It turned out his sister had told him he had to get married in India, and that was it. He was planning to move back to London – but he was not sure about his wife.

Indian weddings are sold as being loud and colourful. Traditions can include the introduction of families over the three-day celebrations, and the performance of the *saptapadi*, which translates as 'seven steps'. The bride and groom take seven steps and after the seventh step they are married. Traditional foods are served, including *saag paneer* and *muttar paneer*. Music is a big thing. Drums – loud and constant. My new friend invited us to the wedding. I was just happy that for 45 minutes I got to watch the parade and his entrance – the wedding should be his and his bride's, but I did promise it would be my book. I gave him my card, but he might have lost it. Did he look like he was having fun? Nope, not one bit.

The horse handler was equally full of enthusiasm: his face looked like he was dragging the horse to a funeral instead of a wedding. I was a bit confused because everything felt so forced. My focus was on everyone's body language. The groom really didn't want to have this celebration. The horse handler – part of the events team that had been hired in – did not want to be here. At the front of the parade was a band marching under a banner advertising for future business: 'Titar Pur – Master Band'. The band were wearing orange garments and red hats. Yellow slippers covered their trainers and when they could be bothered, they would lift their instruments. They didn't want to be here. So why was it so important to have the wedding? Culture. Tradition. Keeping people happy.

We approached the venue, which was called Casa Royal Banquet: Pure Vegetarian and had gold streamers from roof to floor. Its electricity supply seemed to come from the array of cables dangling outside the building. Underneath them was a sign for G.K. Singh Valet Parking and a car wash area. I didn't think the horse would be going in for a valet, but you never know, he might have had a quick once over. As we arrived at the front of the banqueting centre, men carrying large red fabric umbrellas waited for the parade to arrive. They smiled at me as if to say, "Look at the tourist standing watching us – photo?" Yep, I was the tourist. It was truly quite mindboggling.

At the end of the day, weddings are basically the moment two people officially become married in the eye of the law and/or religion. What I wanted to experience was the atmosphere and energy that makes weddings in India be known globally as celebrations that are a sight to behold. This wedding was held in the middle of a street and fortunately the groom was kind enough to chat with me. However, his whole attitude towards it was one of dismay. He would rather be watching Arsenal on the TV or jumping down to the local council's registry office. So here is a question that could be its own book – do we push cultural tradition too much?

One thing to take away...

Weddings are moments to celebrate and party. The story being told here is how wild fireworks, out-of-tune bands, grumpy horse handlers and so on all are all part of the package of getting married in Delhi. It's interesting, for sure. Hopefully I have sold you the dream wedding package.

Back to Delhi

Delhi is home to ruins, temples and historic sites. The beauty was everywhere. The Red Fort is one of the tourist attractions that was popular with both international visitors and locals. However, there were two significantly different ticket prices. For locals to go in, it was the equivalent of £1. For international visitors it was £12 – and tickets were bought at a separate window where it said, 'INTERNATIONAL VISITORS – MONEY ONLY'. Because of the heat, I wasn't in the mood to ask why. Instead, I paid the money and in I went.

Apart from the obvious 'corruption' I was falling into, the fort was quite special. Inside there weren't 10,000 people milling around on one street – it was quiet, structured and a million miles away from what was outside the fort walls. But one thing stuck with me, and probably always will. As I walked around, I saw an unfinished path. On the side of the path was an AK47 balanced on sandbags, with a young Indian soldier literally staring down the barrel of his gun at everyone coming past. His finger was about two inches away from the trigger. I wasn't scared. I was petrified. This was the first welcome you got at this very well-known tourist attraction...

And then… well, at the end of the path was what I can only describe as a heart-breaking sight. I watched a man place stones one by one to finish the path. The path was part of the main route for tourists to walk along. At first, I noticed that the man's feet were bare. Then I looked higher and realised he was not wearing trousers or a top. Dressed in pants that were very dirty, he was almost completely naked. The pathway around him was closed off and he smashed stones on the ground to make them smaller. I didn't know what to think. But the worst was still to come. Next to him were two children, both completely naked and sitting in the dirt. One of them was no more than 8 or 10 months old, lying on a blanket. The other was smashing stones for his father to collect. I was speechless. I had paid £12 to see what I thought was a tourist attraction but inside was a man who was working in the soaring heat, obviously in slave conditions, and looking after his children. Their bare bodies were open to the elements and there was no water anywhere near them. I just could not understand what was going on. This was the most perfect example of the stark contrasts of life in Delhi. I'll leave it there.

Next, I went to the Gurudwara Sis Ganj Sahib. I wanted to experience the heart of a bustling temple. Outside the temple were three transit vans. Members of the Gurudwara were unloading food from the van for the local community, who queued up. Some also required medical treatment and again there was a van with supplies and help. I asked someone if I was allowed to cross the road and enter the temple. "Yes sir, head across," the man said, looking at me as I looked at the traffic. Suddenly I was being dragged across the road, through the weaving motorcycles and cars, by a man on his way to pray. Top tip: if you ever go to Vietnam, India or Indonesia, shut your eyes and walk. It is always the best way to get across the road.

Having survived the crossing, in I went past large barriers. The white marble was breath-taking, stairs glimmering in the Delhi sunshine – slightly ruined by the sight of a man climbing 40 feet in the air to fix electricity cables. I continued along and met the older gentleman who had escorted me across the road. He told me about the kitchens, which were huge. In one sitting alone 500 people would squeeze into the hall, and every day they fed approximately 5,000 people. I mean... WOW. On top of that, the Gurudwara had vans that went out into the community. I was amazed by the size of the operation.

I'd now reached one of the praying areas and I was the only tourist. No photos in certain areas – I completely respected this and had put my cameras away already. I washed my feet and put an orange hairnet across my head. I was ready now to watch the band and observe the worshippers, who sat and chanted. I sat in the temple for about an hour, sometimes praying myself. I was welcomed into different groups as people dashed in during a work lunch break, jumped across from a restaurant or came out of the underground parking complex. We were in the middle of Chandi Chowk in Old Delhi, but life definitely slowed down in this temple. No noise. No scooters whizzing through. Just chanting and music. My tour guide never did introduce himself and he disappeared into the crowds when I tried to find him to thank him. This was a compelling part of travelling – when sudden moments of kindness came from nowhere and disappeared just as quickly without accepting my thanks.

At 3am the next day, I was picked up by a taxi driver for a three-hour drive to Agra and the Taj Mahal. He drove, I slept and suddenly the orange ball in the sun was rising from behind the flat farmlands surrounding the Yamuna Expressway. The highlight of our 180km drive was stopping at a service station at 5am and talking to a father and his two children, who could not speak a word of English. I drew a picture (well, a scribble) of the Taj Mahal and pointed at me, and they laughed and nodded.

At 6:07am I was dropped off in the car park, where the police had blocked the road to all traffic heading towards the Taj Mahal. "Stay as long as you want!" my driver told me. The temperature was 49 degrees and the sun was rising fast. Walking down was daunting. All the shops were already open, and the owners were screaming at me to buy things I could not take into the temple. When I say shops – they were actually homes; they'd simply thrown the mattresses behind the till before any customers arrived, grabbed a bottle of water from the display next to the postcard stand, had a quick wash and checked themselves out in mirrors decorated with tourist keyrings.

The earlier you go to the Taj Mahal, the more likely you are to be able to see it. Buses, crowds and everyone in between filtered in. The security was extremely tight – highly trained soldiers with AK47s staring and shouting at everyone. Being from a culture where gun carrying isn't a normality, it was quite a sight to adjust to. But then, the Taj Mahal is a global icon that would be an easy target. Some buggies arrived with tourists from five-star luxury hotels and they were driven through. For me, that would be a waste of money because they were missing out on the full experience.

Inside the Taj Mahal village were a few houses and their residents, part of the small team that lives within the complex. Through a gap between the buildings I glimpsed the Taj Mahal over the heads of those scrambling to reach the temple. It literally took my breath away. The white marble sparkled in the hot sun. Everyone was taking photos at the iconic bench near the water feature, about 200 metres from the temple. A few official photographers were trying to make some money. I ended up helping a Russian couple take some photos. They were wearing traditional Indian attire. I was kind of conflicted about their gestures and the clothing. Was it cultural appropriation?

After taking the required photo at the bench (because society has its expectations…), I took a walk around. It was a peaceful and beautiful experience. At the back of the Taj I saw people farming marshland; oxen were pulling large blades to cultivate the ground. On one side was the Taj Mahal, one of the most visited tourist attractions in the world. On the other, small gatherings of barefoot farmers were burning the stubble fields in the shadow of this icon. What a complete contrast. My visit to India was reinforcing the fact that we are all lucky to have what we have in our lives. Travelling was not only opening my eyes but also my heart, my emotions and my overall appreciation for life. Yet I was also questioning why this distinct difference exists.

The Taj Mahal – it was special. When we arrived back, the driver said he'd never done such a quick trip to Agra. I decided it was time to get out when the thermometer hit 51 degrees. Back at the hotel the manager even said, "Mr Sir Matthew, that was quick!" I enjoyed it, I really did, but there is only so much heat you can take. Also, what else are you meant to do once you've looked at the building a few times from different angles?

While I was in Delhi, I visited the Ministry of Sport Library Archive. As I walked in underneath Jawaharlal Nehru Stadium, I met an older gentleman who asked to see my bag. Established by the Indian Government, the Sports Library is part of the Sport Authority of India and security was tight. The library had a vast collection of sports disciplines and academic subjects from all over the world. The green metal storage containers housed books on every sport going.

I was introduced to the general manager and the deputy sports administrator for the Sports Ministry, who came through the doors, across from the sports offices, after a call to let them know I was in the library. Hilarious really but gaining access to people like this was important for my adventure. We spoke in depth about what sport means to India: "Culture, identity and social," and they explained the impact sport has on the country. "Well, with over a billion people, India looks to cities to try and calculate through engagement... Sport is what India uses as a tool to combat poverty and ensures, through sport, people get fed. Not many people go unfed in India, especially if they are within a sports programme." I asked them about the library. "We have been here since 1984 and our mission is to be used as a central part of furthering sports education and appreciation for global sport. We need more money and a better location, but we have many schools come and visit and spend time using the books for learning." We sat chatting like we were best friends for an hour. "*Sport is central to allowing physical, educational and social progression in this country – whatever we will do we will make it work*". Job done.

Here's what I learned. India has a mandate to make sport an integral part of society that brings benefits to the community. Educating the masses about sport is inspiring and I appreciate that India is now creating a platform for other sports to enter the market. Yes, it might be (most certainly is) for commercialisation purposes, but it's also to do with opening the horizons so people in India can learn about the different sports they can participate in – such as introducing them to the NBA, but also demonstrating how cricket welcomes international players, who then have an Indian following when they return to their own club and country.

I really did enjoy my seven days in Delhi. I learned so much about Delhi through reading the local and national newspapers, like the Hindustan Times, Mail Today and the Times of India. The main things I took from Delhi were the noise, the beauty, the mess, the poverty, the richness, the metro, Starbucks... It would be fair to say that Delhi was an eruption of chaos. I loved its character and I loved the complete madness – including the baboons running up pipes and along cables across roads at 7am for their morning commute, and scooters with fridges and rugs on the back. It was a unique experience.

From Delhi to Mumbai... It was time to fly on to my next Indian city. How would they compare?

Mumbai...

Welcome to Mumbai. It felt very British. The buildings were beautiful, with remnants of the British Empire everywhere. Mumbai is a magnet for tourists but still a functional port. Fishing boats were coming in and out and I heard shouts from the harbour walls as ropes were thrown over. Riding on the trains in Mumbai was exactly like all those viral videos and Hollywood movies: holding onto the hand rail with legs swinging while the train propels forwards at 40 miles an hour.

On my first day, I took the train from Juhu Beach to somewhere near the Gateway of India. The arch-shaped monument was built to commemorate the arrival of King George V and Queen Mary, who were the first monarchs to venture to India. However, when they arrived in 1911 the archway had not yet been built and instead, they were met with a cardboard model. The building was eventually completed in 1924 and is 26 metres high and very palatial.

I squeezed into what I thought looked like a standing area on the train. However, this was the luggage storage and it was packed. I was offered the only seat in the compartment about five times, but I really wanted to stand and be crammed in with all my new friends. Suddenly, a man threw a box in from the platform. Everyone grabbed it and put it in the middle of the carriage. Then the man was dragged on just as the train started moving. Apparently, this was normal. As he sat on top of his box, I smiled at him. It was quite impressive to see India's way of boarding a train. I looked away and he stood up, revealing the box. I realised he was commuting with what must be what he sold in the markets. Yes, staring at me were the eyes of dead fish. I did a double-take as about 50 fish gazed at me. There was nowhere else for me to look, and it was a moment that stayed with me. When we reached our destination, he chuckled as he grabbed his box and went off to the market.

Royal Opera House

The Royal Opera House in Mumbai is the only opera house in the whole of India. The impact this venue had on me was quite unique. Although I disagree with forced culture, I was emotionally moved by the fact that India had really embraced something as British as opera. They had taken on board something they are now proud of. I went in as a tourist and after 30 minutes of chatting at the ticket office, I was now talking with two of the general managers. They were so pleased I had chosen to visit them as part of my adventure.

Built in 1909, the opera house became financially unstable during the 1980s; the iconic building was losing more money than it was making, and in 1993 it closed its doors. The building was left in disarray until 2008, when Maharashtra State Government gave an order for renovation to begin to 'bring it back to life'. The doors reopened in 2016, much to the excitement of the world's cultural audiences. As I stood in the red-seated, high-ceilinged, beautifully painted building, I realised this extraordinary place was not only full of character, it was full of hope for the city.

The opera house hosts a huge variety of acts, from ABBA tribute bands to Indian fashion shows and theatre productions. The Royal Boxes, situated either side above the stage, all include original features from the 1910s. The chandeliers, the archways, the look and feel – including the small box office with its one window – were exactly how the opera house was in 1910, and exactly how it would remain. The one change was in the technical elements, which were obviously much more advanced. I was taken on stage by the management, who were delighted to show me the wings and the hoists, speakers and backdrops. All this was fascinating to see but not just that – I had the opportunity to hear the enthusiasm those that worked here had for the venue. It was all truly beautiful.

Some ushers arrived ahead of their shift, wearing full uniform, and took me around for a bit. They were fascinated to hear where I had been and was going. I showed them my camera and for 10 minutes we sat on the seats, which were comfortable but quite short on leg space, and talked about our dreams. "New York, New York," said one of them, obviously a Sinatra fan. He wanted to work on Broadway. "I go!" he kept saying, with the biggest of smiles. India was teaching me that many of the young people had huge dreams and were not scared to tell the world about them. I loved their passion. As I left the opera house I was applauded and hugged by the team. I was a bit confused about why I left through a tunnel of claps – and too polite to ask – but it was a lovely way to end a memorable cultural experience.

Tonight it's time for six or four or two... it's time for the cricket!

Event 28: Mumbai Indians vs Sunrisers

2nd May

"This was not a ticket to cricket – this was a ticket to culture."

I checked where I'd put my ticket for the tenth time. It was 2nd May and I was going to see the Mumbai Indians vs Sunrisers as part of the Indian Premier League; this was game number 51. Tickets were like gold dust.

Before I left the hotel, I had been briefed by six bell boys and the manager about protocol at the cricket. "Take nothing with you, sir," they said, explaining that security is extremely tight and "they will shoot." Excellent – good inside information. I was able to take my phone, my wallet and my ticket – and that was it. No bags. Women were allowed a bag, but it had to be smaller than a purse. Even as I was walking out of the hotel door the bellboys were warning me: "Sir, you cannot take that water – they will not be happy and you will not get in." As I write this, I can still hear the concerned tone in their voices. Oh, and I also remember them all taking a shot at holding my ticket. "This, sir… you are going to the cricket, sir. You are so lucky!" They all loved cricket, they were all Mumbai Indians fans and for them this was an absolute treat. They would do absolutely anything to get to see the cricket, and this really intrigued me. Cricket is the sport that unites, divides and sells India, yet a vast majority of the population who play, watch and love cricket cannot afford to walk into the Wankhede Stadium, home of Mumbai Indians.

I came to India with an agenda of experiencing, talking about and attending a cricket match. Purchasing a ticket was a two-day process because I was not in India at the time of purchase and did not have an Indian credit card. I tried five different cards from different friends, two specifically from a friend who had family in India. I won't explain how I eventually bought the ticket, but it was a long process.

I arrived at the station closest to the stadium and walked along Marine Drive. The noise was piercing both my ears: horns, chants and the usual hustle and bustle of the area. I was looking for gate five (of twenty-one) and there was no signage to help me get there. As I joined the flocks marching up the stairs into the stadium, a lot of people were staring at me. My ticket was securely in my pocket. There was a heavy security presence, including men with machine guns. When I eventually reached the gate I realised the staff at the hotel were spot on – people were being turned back because they'd brought more than they should have. I had received an email about the restrictions prior to the event and there was plenty of signage about prohibited items. Once searched, I walked through and realised a couple of things. Firstly, I was the only tourist walking through, and secondly, just as at the Red Fort, there were soldiers sitting with AK47s on sandbags and their fingers on the triggers. It's not something I've experienced at a sports event before. Quite a unique fan engagement piece...

The reason I wanted to experience the cricket was about exploring the story of how sport and culture fit together. Here in India, it is part of life. The Mumbai Indians had a great slogan, 'One Family'; their supporters were not a fanbase, they were family. Everyone was part of this sporting family – including fans, players, and team and stadium staff. I headed in through turnstile 16 at gate 5 and looked for my seat, A42. An older man was sitting there, next to his wife, but they looked at me and said it would be fine. I knew they hadn't skipped the barrier to get in – because you would most likely be shot! So I sat in A44, next to them, and nodded at everyone around me as they just stared back at me. '*A westerner at our cricke*t.' I could feel the eyes drilling through the back of my head. So I decided there was only one way to combat this and show I was one of them. I headed to the merchandise unit intending to buy a hat or a scarf – perfect, it's 42 degrees, let's melt! Instead, I bought a cricket shirt and pulled it on over my t-shirt. As I walked back to my seat the crowd started clapping.

The older man sitting in my seat introduced himself as Raj. He and his wife lived two hours away and had decided to treat themselves and buy tickets for this special match. Raj was an absolute godsend when it came to cricketing knowledge. "So over there…" Before I knew it, everyone around me was part of an initiative to 'teach Matt everything about cricket'. I had Khash and his girlfriend, his boss and his friend welcome me to the match. We chatted and then I was introducing Raj and Khash to each other. I was beginning to bring all the rows together. By the end of the evening, everyone was saying goodbye to everyone else. But I was really interested in Raj. He was a prominent figure, with a structured beard. He had spent 30 years on the seas in the merchant navy and had visited the UK many times. He had been to Greenock in Scotland several times and would always have haggis there. I was loving meeting everyone in the A Section.

Before the game began, a video was played as part of Mumbai's policy to help reduce or eradicate the use of plastic. Ironically, the point they were making was waiting for me when I arrived at my seat: a nylon flag on a plastic flagpole, part of the fan engagement piece for Mumbai Indians. Not ideal when they were trying to stamp out single-use plastic. But a very nice souvenir. After the video, we all stood for the national anthem as the players came out to a full-on sports presentation production. Fireworks and cheerleaders – it was truly a spectacle. The Indian Premier League was organised by a UK/USA company, IMG, which brought a very British/American feel to the proceedings.

In the tier below us in this 33,108-capacity stadium (it was 45,000 until 2010) was the over-exuberant DJ, who got everyone rocking while cheerleaders danced along to the music – he did an amazing job. Raj told me that the cheerleaders came from either the UK, USA, Russia or Spain. Interesting – I was sure India would have some superb cheerleaders of its own.

The place was absolutely packed and bouncing. On the field, the pace was a bit slower. However, every time the cricket ball went over the boundary I grabbed Raj and we celebrated. It was like being at the cricket with an uncle and celebrating as one. We all high-fived each other whenever there was a six. Remember, I had a team shirt on – I was now part of the family. However, most of the time I had absolutely no idea what was going on. I just loved watching everyone else engaging. I was a bit disappointed that the ushers and security were standing there using their phones and looking bored. It was a contrast to those who were begging to get in.

A lot of Indian-specific companies like Vivo and hotstarVIP were present. However, global companies like Subway were very popular in the stadium. Of course companies wanted to be in the stadium – not only was there the crowd inside to sell to, but the watching audience for the IPL was estimated to be 411 million people – each match. Eye-watering figures. The TV audience was bigger than most countries in terms of population. Opportunities were vast. The Mumbai Indians' stadium is old and needs to be knocked down and rebuilt, yet the team was valued at $114 million in 2019. The IPL itself is worth $6.8 billion. This league is way bigger than the bat and ball we see at the wicket. In 2010, IPL was the first sport ever to broadcast live on YouTube in an attempt to grow its international audience.

I talked to everyone around me and found out they all had good jobs or owned their own companies. They had disposable income. I began to see a trend: affordability. It allows people to access entertainment and experiences like this. It's a global trend but in India specifically it was quite apparent. "It's pricing a lot of people out," said one of my new friends in Zone A. "Outside, kids are barefoot while trying to sell the flags for tonight's match, just to get some income. It's embarrassing." I totally understood where they came from. I saw it too.

Sport is art. It gives people the chance to express themselves. It allows people to enjoy a moment and cherish it. And it offers a learning opportunity. At one point the DJ and MC announced that the PA systems were being turned off at 10pm. At 9:57pm I looked down to see two men standing next to the DJ section. The MC got everyone rocking and bouncing for the last time. At 9:59pm the men stepped closer and at 10pm (literally on the dot) they forced the DJ to stop. The MC had his microphone taken away and that was it. I learned there is a rule that no amplified noise is allowed in the stadium after 10pm – because of the surrounding residential homes. This meant the crowd had nothing to engage with and the cheerleaders were just dancing in silence. It was very surreal to watch. Considering I could now hear the traffic and the hustle and bustle outside the stadium, I was confused about the ruling and confused about what I was now to focus on. But I got it. I understood, because there were some blocks of flats visible through the gaps in the stadium. The change in the dynamics of the atmosphere was quite interesting. It allowed the crowd to create their own chants and if the players performed badly, they soon knew it! I kept on saying to Raj, "This is bonkers." But Raj just smiled at me, shrugged his shoulders and kept eating his popcorn. He was used to it. It really is the fans that make the sport what it is.

The focus on sustainability is important for the IPL. With the emotional film about the planet played at the beginning of the match – they were taking it seriously. Food packaging was paper, not plastic. The effort they were making was apparent; sustainability was at the forefront of everything they were doing. 'Green Operations' was an aim and I saw it being implemented. Yes, they gave out flags, freebie signs and a lot of other merchandise, but it was positive to see the attempt. Cricket might be the biggest and most popular sport in India, but they certainly were aiming to have the smallest possible footprint. They were trying everything they could. Now it's up to the 411 million people watching to make the change.

At 11:30pm there was still a long way to go until the match

would be over. As I was staying 25km away at Juhu Beach, on the other side of Mumbai, I decided it was time to leave the stadium. I was gutted to be leaving Raj, but before we left his wife said: "You need to get a photo," so we did, and we exchanged details. The friendship I created at the cricket with Raj and Khash and the crew was truly special. Sport brings people together and when you're travelling and have your guard down, you can open up even more to sharing stories and learning.

One thing to take away...

The consumption of cricket is complex – not only the purchase of tickets, the class division and the poverty, which is unimaginable, but the scale of it all. Indians associate cricket with life and this produces an adoration to the sport that's unique compared with any other sport I've witnessed. A barefoot boy swinging a bat on the beach and dreaming of becoming the next great sportsman is something that happens all across the world. But in Mumbai, for some reason, it made more of an impression on me because it shows growth and it propels the future of India.

Farewell, Mumbai

I was only in Mumbai for three days in total – literally for the cricket, for the atmosphere and then to get out. But leaving – well, I was gutted. Everything I witnessed, both events-wise and culturally, made me take stock of my life. People need to ignore the stories of what India was like 20 years ago and focus on the country's future and everything that goes with it. A few things are questionable – specifically, gender inequality and safety – but times are changing, admittedly very slowly. A visit to India is breathtaking. I loved the welcome, the people, the feeling, the madness and the deafening sounds – it was priceless. It can take a while to get used to, but I'd fully immersed myself in the experience.

Thank you to the tuk-tuk drivers for driving so carefully while I was gripping onto the handlebars at the back, and to the hotel staff, who welcomed me better than any other hotel anywhere. I salute their commitment to guest services. Some major hotel chains would do well to take a look at Hotel Sunstar and Raju in Mumbai (one chain in particular – but we will get to that later…).

Thank you, India, for showing me the true beauty of your country.

Dubai

The tourism and events industry in the United Arab Emirates is estimated to be worth $133.4 billion. These are mind-blowing figures for an area that was mostly desert as recently as the 1970s. Sports stadiums, exhibitions halls and venues have all seen a major footfall increase because of the attraction of holding an event in Dubai. Over the last three years, Dubai and the UAE had been gearing up for Dubai Expo 2020, which was going to bring in an estimated five million extra people during the event. However, for me visiting Dubai was about seeing my best friend and attending event number 29, the beginning of Ramadan.

I was intrigued to experience a location that has grown over the last 40 years into a buzz of overpriced experiences, towering skyscrapers and marine animal and water parks in the middle of supermarkets. In the 1970s, Dubai was a modest port, and while they had visions of becoming bigger, I don't think anyone, including the western powers, could have envisioned Dubai today. The marinas, the boats and the skyscrapers – everything was Instagram-ready.

But Dubai is about more than fashion. It is a place for financial opportunities and it holds a unique position culturally. Dubai Mall took two days to navigate and everywhere was air-conditioned!

Event 29: Iftar

<u>6th May</u>

In 2019, Ramadan in Dubai began on May 6th. The date of the start of this extremely sacred celebration is all dependent on the moon. This year, for the first time, daytime fasting would be less than 15 hours because of the movements of the moon. I was about to see the difference in Dubai when Ramadan begins. Because of tourism, many places stay open – however, these tend to be allocated 'non-Muslim areas' in the shopping centre food courts, and signage makes it clear that only those not fasting can enter. Most shops do not open until nearer sunset. The idea of foreigners going to attractions or even visiting a country that is partaking in Ramadan would have been unthinkable 10 years ago. But now they accommodate tourists.

Ramadan, the ninth month of the Muslim Islamic calendar, is an annual period of religious observance. It's thought to be a time to feel closer to God. It's about spending time to pray, spending time with loved ones, but also supporting charities and remembering those who are less fortunate. During Ramadan, accommodation prices in Dubai drop significantly; it's actually noted as the best and cheapest time to go. I stood watching areas that had been extremely busy the day before Ramadan; now they were deserted. It was quite mind-boggling.

Tonight, I would be attending Iftar – the breaking of fast – with my friend, who lives in Dubai. Daily fasting begins at sunrise and concludes at sunset when, after final prayers, family and friends come together to breakfast. My experience of Iftar in Dubai in a five-star hotel were macaroon-shaped camels and a dream buffet awaited me.

The Iftar was being held in the hotel car park due to the size of the event. The whole thing – kitchens, catering staff rooms, dining area, smoking areas (for when fast was broken) and so on – had all been built from scratch. Staff took attendees' coats and were responsible for ensuring guests reached their allocated seats. There were very strict procedures in place, because around 400 people would be seated and then when we left, another sitting would begin for those coming in to party until sunrise.

White drapes surrounded the seating area. Everything was lush. Most people were dressed traditionally in black and white, *abayas* for women and *kandoras* for men, who also covered their heads with a *ghutra,* which was held in place with an *agal.* The table was set with a range of cutlery; after the first knife and fork, I was confused by the cutlery selection. The food selection for breaking fast ranged from fruit, vegetables and potatoes to ice cream...

As it got closer to sunset, more people rushed in to get ready for the moment when those who are fasting are allowed to break fast. I watched in apprehension to see what people would do first. And remember, half the staff serving the food and even making the food were fasting. As the sun set, everyone geared up. Traditionally, goat's milk and dates are the first things eaten and drunk at Iftar. In Dubai, the tradition is to wait for the Iftar Cannon (*Midfa Al Iftar*) to be let off. This has been the rule since the time of the founding father of the UAE, the late Sheikh Zayed. All around us, televisions were turned on at full volume just as the cannon was fired. And then we were off. Many people embraced, but a few men ran out to the smoking area and lit up.

Glamour and exuberance were so evident in both the delivery and the structural construction of this experience. The symbols of the importance of this special moment were everywhere. I saw friendship and togetherness while celebrating Ramadan.

As a whole, Dubai does embrace some changes during Ramadan, and it's important to appreciate that. Important respect towards the observance of Ramadan, even for those who are not fasting.

One thing to take away…

Iftar reminded me that it is important to spend time together with family and friends – and, ultimately, that is what events do. Whether cultural, historical, sporting or religious, events bring people together. It's the sole reason why they happen.

Ramadan Kareem!

Dubai…

Dubai was gearing up for Dubai Expo 2020, which was going to be an event the likes of which had never been seen before. The venue size was to be the equivalent of 614 football pitches and the dedicated metro station being built would be capable of carrying 24,000 people per hour – crazy. It was a World Expo and the whole world was coming. All around Dubai, everything was plastered with logos to remind both locals and international visitors that the Expo was happening. It was bigger than any other event marketing campaign I had ever witnessed – and the Expo was still 18 months away. The event – due to take place from October 2020 until April 2021 – had been dubbed the 'World's Greatest Show'. Sadly, Coronavirus put the World's Greatest Show on hold…

The older part of Dubai, an area that reminded me of Aladdin, was full of markets and passages, all easy to get lost in. Each step you walked along the alleyways took you past shops selling emeralds, diamonds, scarves and fridge magnets. It was a community in itself, the clay bricks home to businesses and residents. The pavements were cracked but the community heart was full.

Seeing friends was the best part of this very short three-day visit. I got to catch up with Nick, who I had met in Auckland at the very start of my adventure, literally on the third day, when I was extremely tired.

Dubai is a city with its own hope. Fishermen on one side and skyscrapers on the other - a spirited journey towards a future that will, for sure be a determined bright future.

Istanbul

Here is a funny story. Boarding my flight to Istanbul, a thought crossed my mind. "Do I have a Turkish visa?" This was ten minutes before boarding the plane. My brain went into mass panic as I realised that I didn't have a visa and even though I was British, and even though the UK was still part of Europe at the time, a visa was required.

"FLIGHT DELAYED..." I don't know why, but suddenly I had bought myself more time. Using the WiFi at the airport, I jumped onto a website to begin my eVisa application.

Then an announcement came that my flight was due to board. "NO NO NO! ... email address ... @ ..." I was not finished; I was still scrambling with the application. I let everyone in front of me board while I kept typing. No one around me realised that I was in an absolute rush but more than happy to take my time getting on the plane.

"Ladies and gentlemen, we are now having to rest boarding." Rest? EXCELLENT! After an hour of frantic purchasing, we finally boarded the flight and in I went with my Turkish visa approved and screenshot in my phone's photo album. When we arrived at Istanbul airport, I walked over to the border police, who were standing there in polo t-shirts and with guns on their belts. I waited for the clearance bell to ring and dreamed of heading straight to the pub. It was the most relaxed but secure border check.

Suddenly I heard a cry of: "What do I need a visa for? I'm a British citizen!" Should have checked the website! While I was welcomed in with a comment of "You just got this two hours ago... That was close. Have a nice stay."

Turkey was a stopover before I experienced Europe fully. Istanbul city is very interesting. The airport is on the Asian side but the bus that took me into the darkness of Istanbul on May 7th was in Europe. I arrived at midnight and the light was dim. The bus, IST-19, dropped me off in Taksim Square. Immediately, I noticed police barriers and vans sitting at the entrance to Gezi Park in the square. Civil unrest had taken off in the area in 2013 and during the protests, which resulted in over 4,900 arrests, 22 people died. In the square the night before I arrived there had been a mini protest, mainly Turkish and Eastern Asian men, and tonight there was a large police presence. Brilliant.

Due to Ramadan, the city was slightly different to how the tourist books sold it, but it was still an array of noise and sound. It's home to Besiktas JK, Turkey's most successful football team, and I aimed to go on a tour of Vodafone Park. The stadium has a capacity of 41,903 and the team has never been relegated to a lower division. I imagined the trophy room full, every wall gleaming with silverware.

The stadium, built in 2016, had an energetic atmosphere but overall, the tour was dated. Vodafone Park (obviously selling the naming rights for such a lucrative team was a no brainer) was built on the site of BJK Inonu Stadium, the former home for the team. Today I was on a tour that cost 8 euros (60 Turkish liras) and would last an hour – some of it was alright, and I learned some interesting facts. I actually thought the start of the tour was okay. After a short wait in the closed café area, where the seats were stacked on tables, we went through to have our photographs taken against a green screen. The backdrops included first-team players in various poses. Then we waited for our tour guide, who stood chatting while we all sat in the awkward silence like we were in a doctor's waiting room. It should have felt more exciting – especially for those who had come wearing the previous season's home strips; one couple were here as a birthday treat. The briefing was short and boring. Oh, and in Turkish.

The stadium was pretty interesting – artwork on the cement walls, and the stairwells covered with vinyl giving results from previous matches and seasons. We ducked our heads into a space and before we knew it – out again. The tour felt a bit rushed but luckily I made friends with someone else who was travelling, and they translated what was being said. After an hour of the tour we had visited the press room (cool), the stadium (very cool), the dugout (extremely cool) and outside the main gate (average). I began to question why we were in such a rush, but my friend explained in a few words: "It's his lunch in twenty minutes…" Ah.

Tours are about setting the emotions on fire – I mean, this one did to an extent, but with the tour guide's cigarettes in his pocket and his phone in his hand while he replied to messages and occasionally chatted to other staff, the fire was dwindling. At the end I collected the three photos I had chosen to keep as a souvenir, which cost around 15 euros, and the tour guide waved goodbye – as he lit up his tenth cigarette.

Stadiums are all about telling a story. The lighting, the trophies, the tour guide and so on. Here, some of it worked and some of it didn't. The atmosphere created by the tour guide was 'Oh well, this is just another tour…' Yet there is a huge market for stadium tours and the opportunity to go behind the scenes. Maybe I'll find another one that can light up my senses.

Back to Istanbul…

I could sense in the air a feeling of animosity between the police and the Turkish men, who were standing in small groups drinking coffee. Food stalls were everywhere. Ice cream vendors. Kebabs. Each sizzling kebab pole was surrounded by men, usually smoking. Every corner and every street sold some type of kebab, all traditionally wrapped and garnished. Every 100 metres I would be stopped by the sound of men with guitars, singing with some amazing voice control in tune with the guitars. I can't even explain; it was kind of yodelling but in its own majestic manner. They would usher the crowds away from blocking the doors of Body Shop or Starbucks and continue singing. In a way, they seemed like a gang that was controlling the streets – the yodelling yobs – but they weren't. Dressed in light denim and with the cleanest of hair, they owned the streets.

Also, during my 56 hours in the city, I got to experience a more culturally observed Iftar. Community mosques with marquees outside prepared for the moment fast was broken. Streets were closed to allow for prayer areas and food to be served. It was a beautiful moment that showed me the true meaning of Ramadan.

Istanbul, it was a pleasure. Now to get into the beating heart of Europe.

Brussels

Welcome to Brussels. And for me, country number 12. I really do have a soft spot for Belgium. I wanted to explore Brussels and understand the very exciting 'alternative music video industry' – because of course that is what Brussels is known for. Arriving in Brussels was exciting as there was a lot going on this weekend. Also, it was Mother Lamb's birthday on 9th May – happy birthday! – so I sent her a postcard.

Every year in January the Brussels Motor Show welcomes 540,000 people through the doors for a 10-day event. The impact on the economy is beyond imaginable. The Brussels Tourism presentation I managed to find online had a real sense of 'we are showing we are a big fish here and have a huge impact'. I'd contacted some of the big events organisers to arrange a meeting but sadly, none of them got back to me. Never mind. I was only here for a short visit, with a late evening, one full day and a midday departure. Let's see how much I could squeeze in.

Event 30: Music Video Festival – VKRS #1

9th May

Have you ever been to an event, unsure of what to expect? Invited yourself to a party created by cultural legends and creative geniuses? And stood on your own, in a wet North Face jacket?

Welcome to my world.

From 9th–11th May, Brussels was hosting the first ever VKRS #1 Music Video Festival across two theatres, and I was talking to the barman in one of the venues – it's always a safe bet to talk to the barman. The event was about combining art and music and spearheading a campaign to put this type of art at the forefront of the Belgian cultural agenda. It was all about art of the visual senses. Understanding that art is more than just paintings. Music and videos coming together to create a representation of visual arts that provides enjoyment for all. I was in the midst of the elite of cultural specialists from all over the country. Over the weekend there would be video viewings, workshops, conferences and competitions. The barman explained that everyone who is 'known' in the industry would be attending tonight: cultural funders, creative directors, cultural bodies and so on. Basically, very influential people in the arts world in Belgium. Everyone wanted to experience an event like this because it was the first time an event like this had been given a platform.

The attendees arrived wearing alternative arts clothing – faux leather jackets, circular glasses with clear glass – and then there was me in my North Face raincoat and blue trainers, looking so very out of place. I completely didn't belong here – but this is what public events are about. Being given the opportunity to experience something new. It's important for the event organisers to attract a new audience and it's important for an audience – like me – to go and discover new things and soak it all in – quite literally.

The doors to the theatre opened and in we went. Before I entered, I got a glass of water. The photographer, who obviously didn't know I was an esteemed event critic, stopped me, quite aggressively: "No glass in the theatre," but in French. Quick gulp down – I was in. The two volunteers at the door smiled and said: "Thank you, sir – welcome." Their English was perfect, and they were much more welcoming than the photographer, who knew everyone – but no one knew him (oh, the irony). Feeling more comfortable, I sat – once again, all alone – in the middle of the theatre to allow everyone to filter in at the sides. Once everyone had arrived, silence came over the theatre as we were all handed a piece of paper. The paper listed all the music videos we would see during the three-hour screening. The audience was going to rate and record feedback for each video. The overall winner of the festival would win something – sadly they said it in French, and I didn't catch what it was. Maybe a DVD player or a toaster.

Max, the festival director, was wearing a brilliant shirt and I could feel the passion he had for music videos and this industry. The crowd erupted when he appeared like he was on a Saturday night TV show. If there was a king of music videos in Brussels, I guess he was it. After 10 minutes of discussion, the event began. The auditorium had about 220 people in it – a mixture of art creators, critics and funders – and they were ready. And then there was me.

Art is about telling stories. But music videos are about telling stories that challenge thoughts and get people going – with a physical and verbal presence. Stories that include creative out-of-the-box thinking. Some of the locations used in the videos were slightly bizarre – like bathtubs, and other extremely weird places to film a sad song – but that's what being creative is about, to an extent. Each video was around four minutes long. Some had been created specifically to be shown at the festival. Some were outstanding and some were okay… and some I closed my eyes during and mentally skipped.

Let's discuss what a music video is. We can use the band OK GO as an example – a band whose videos were not included in this festival, but who would probably have loved it. They are well known for their outrageous ideas and making obscure things work, whether it's playing on a zero-gravity plane, driving a customised car towards a thousand pianos and playing the song with a beater on each keyboard as they pass, or the famous treadmill video. Do we know the music? No, but they captured us with the story they were telling. The video captured our attention more than the song did. That is why music videos are so powerful.

The leaflets, graphics and staging for this event was brilliant. Thought had been put into intertwining the look of 90s music videos with a futuristic modern-day approach. Sadly, leaflets were left all over the venues and around the city – it could have been slightly more environmentally sustainable. However, it was the quirkiest event I have ever experienced, and considering it was the first time it was held, I'm sure there is more to be done.

Music videos really have broken societal boundaries. Whether it's Gangnam Style, which attracted over a billion views in three years, or Despacito's billion views in less than a year, music videos have an important part to play in allowing self-expression within society. People engage with music videos, and now I was sitting at a festival that was trying to bring Belgian and global artists to the forefront of art and bring a focus back to something that has been lost.

One thing to take away…

This was quirky. This was celebratory – but this was about the future. Learnings could be shared globally. The organisers are now friends of mine, as I reached out after the festival and they were honoured that I included the event in my adventure. But really, sitting on a stool in the bar area of the venue – the honour was mine. Especially when I was then told after the event: "We did wonder who the man in the North Face jacket was...?"

Back to Brussels

It's the 10th May and my only full day in Brussels. But to another event I go!

Event 31: George Ezra

George Ezra rose to fame after the number one hit *Budapest* and was now a global star with two albums to his name – and I was going to see him perform in Brussels. I planned to head to the venue using the free train ticket that came with my concert ticket (clever!). However, a freight train had just derailed so sadly it wasn't to be... Instead I made it to a station four miles from the arena and meandered through the streets of Brussels. I arrived at the Forest National Multi-Purpose Arena feeling quite exhausted. On the outside, it looked very fresh and quite a modern arena... but in reality, it wasn't.

This show wasn't designed to bring people into Brussels, but it allowed 5,500 of George Ezra's fans based in Belgium to have fun. It was a Friday night so of course it was date night. I donned my best shirt (last worn in Dubai), picked up my ticket from the box office window and went in to watch... well, not a performance but a story.

I had no expectations about this event. I didn't know what the show would look like. Instead, I was going to be focused on understanding the crowd. Everyone joined the entrance queues with their tickets in hand. All tickets had to be printed – no barcode scanning on phones. The reason for this was simple: the scanners didn't pick up the barcodes with the glare of the phone screens – that's what I was told by one of the security guards. I was kind of puzzled.

The demographic for the event was mixed. Mainly, it was couples. I fitted right in. It's funny – going to all these events by myself, by now I'd become accustomed to standing alone with everyone thinking: "Oh, he must be waiting on someone." The arena was pretty run down inside. No food stalls or anything that was safe to eat – but there was a Haribo sweetie stand. Randomly, I was now eating Gummy Bears and marshmallow flumps while I waited to watch a pop star. As I walked down the stairs, I was chatting on the phone to a good friend back in the UK. I had my earphones in and was looking around to try and get a sense of the arena. Signage was nowhere to be seen. The paint was coming off the walls and the staff – well, they weren't really up for engaging.

5,500 people were now arriving to watch The Hot 8 Brass Band, who were the support act. The Grammy-nominated band blended hip-hop, jazz and some very funky beats. Based in New Orleans, they were bringing funk to the stage and warming everyone up for George Ezra's music, which would be a bit slower than the beat The Hot 8 Brass Band were playing.

The energy they gave was electrifying. Warm-up acts are a bit hit and miss, because people aren't there to see them. Usually they are also unknown, so the crowd doesn't get too excited. I mean, don't get me wrong, I wasn't that excited. But after five minutes the brass trumpets, French horns and tubas got me going as a great melody came from the stage. I looked around to see only a few heads bobbing along; not everyone was focused on the stage. It was a shame because the band was absolutely outstanding. My head was bobbing so much. "Hands in the air – clap clap clap!" The band's efforts to engage with the audience were brilliant. The last song was *Sexual Healing* by Marvin Gaye and this band brought it. By the end of their set, the whole arena was up dancing. Good luck, George!

"Welcome to my living room…" Twenty minutes after The Hot 8 Brass Band left the stage, George Ezra walked on and gave a welcome that was more than just a "Hello, Brussels." He went straight into singing *Don't Matter Now* and the lights on the lampshades and the lighting chandeliers swaying made it so homely. The spotlight was solely on George. On stage were purple couches and the backdrop was formed like window frames, which created a sense of us being in his home, like we were all family. I thought it was so clever. I appreciated this setting. It was constructed yet it was fun, enlightening and enjoyable. I'm not sure whether most people would be thinking this deep or if it was just me – the solo guy standing in a sea of couples. I decided to phone a few friends, and my mum and dad. They laughed at me doing this, but events are all about sharing the moment of being together – and for me, the only people that were with me were a thousand miles away. So close, yet so far.

George took an approach I quite enjoyed. He was storytelling throughout the show. Not only did he sing, he explained how he wrote the songs. He gave the history. He gave more than people were expecting. I enjoyed listening to his approach of "going away, staying somewhere for three months, grabbing a notepad and writing about everything I saw around me." Sounded very similar. A lot of musicians wouldn't take that approach to explain the stories behind the songs. It really felt like George was in a large armchair and we were all sitting on the living room carpet, drinking cocoa and becoming friends. His singing abilities threw me; I was not ready for the husky voice and the way he was so powerful at controlling the space.

His overall performance was one that can only be explained through his songs. He transported me to *Paradise*. Along the way, he took me to *Barcelona* and *Budapest*. He tried to *Blame It on Me* while he also told me to *Hold My Girl*. I tried to *Listen to The Man* but there were too many *Pretty Shiny People...*

His voice well and truly could melt butter.

One thing to take away...

George performed from the heart. He immersed the crowd in his show. The performance was amazing, but the place the performance was held was questionable... More needs to be done by artists to understand the venues and the journey taken by those who are paying to attend.

Back to Brussels...

Posters for events were draped, stapled and plastered on boards all over the city. Short Film Festival, Gay Pride Festival, Park Surpriz, Kunstenfestivaldesarts and a local election – all happening over the next week. I was really excited about the future of the Brussels events scene. I was only here for 48 hours and not only did I get to feel the effects of the cobbled streets on my knees, I saw a bustling city. I experienced an events sector that was really booming. Brussels is popular with day-trippers from France, the Netherlands and the UK – and it is the capital of alternative events. The day-trippers are how they could keep tourism going while trying to penetrate new markets. As I checked out of the city, I was sad to leave. I was going to miss the Brussels energy. Bye-bye...

Amsterdam

I took a train ride across the border. Sunday was the final Ajax FC football match of the 2018/2019 season. Ajax was known to have a challenging group of home fans – I was like YESSS, EXCELLENT! Buying a ticket, however, was very difficult. So, instead of going to the game, I spent two days just wandering around Amsterdam. Actually, I didn't feel too well, anyway.

Amsterdam began in the 13th century as a fishing village and its old-fashioned charm is enjoyed by millions of tourists who come to discover the buildings and canals – and, of course, the red-light district and the 'organic' growth of drugs.

Amsterdam's tourism board put together some fun facts. In the city there are 2,500 houseboats, 1,281 bridges, 75 museums and 1,515 cafes and bars (which include coffee shops). Coffee shops are where the smell of weed spews from the air vents. The excitement in the 'youngsters' faces as they head into the coffee shops... Unfortunately, it had been reported in newspapers globally that Amsterdam has lost its identity as a place of beautiful buildings, canals, bridges and bikes. Sex, drugs and puke were now the common features of the city. Seeing the place during the day, and then at night, I felt like I had been transported to a completely different location. Amsterdam just felt a bit – lost. And sadly, due to my tight schedule, I was not able to do anything particularly 'eventy' while I was there – plus I really was not feeling great.

However, some observations for you. Amsterdam has a booming music, ballet and dance culture, epic nightlife and an urban art scene that is a magnet for artists (of all types) from all over the world to connect with. Johan Cruijff Arena, Olympic Stadium Amsterdam and Bimhuis are just some of the venues that host events, and concerts and sporting fixtures are very popular. But due to me feeling a bit ich… That's all, folks.

Amsterdam – thanks for having me, briefly. But now, attempting to sit on a train for eight hours was a huge concern.

Dresden

Dresden is a beautiful town with a population of over half a million. It is far from sleepy and has an array of opportunities that add to the hustle and bustle – and a lot of tourists! Like A LOT! Buses every day bring in more people to reflect on the history. Dresden was bombed heavily during World War II and approximately 25,000 people were killed. The entire city centre was completely flattened. Even today areas are being rebuilt, but a lot of buildings are very 'different' in style and era. However, some of the buildings left standing, including Dresden Castle, Semperoper Dresden and Zwinger, really were eye-catching. But for the next three nights I WAS STAYING ON A BOAT… So exciting! My hotel was literally a boat moored two kilometres from the city centre. It was authentic!

Dresden was beautiful – a really amazing city. Bikes constantly weave in and out of the tourists walking around the bridges. However, Dresden also has a very dark side. I began to see graffiti that showed a racist element to the city. Isolated, but present. Ethnic communities were not prominent or visibly represented anywhere in the city centre. Symbols painted on the walls portrayed some interesting 'views.'

I had worked for the last four months to try and get a media pass for my next event – and, with support from the lovely Nicole, who worked in the media department, I gained a pass – PERFECT! Strap in, turn on Spotify and listen to Mozart while I tell you the melodic story of the Dresden Music Festival.

Event 32: Dresden Music Festival (Dresdner Musikfestspiele)

<u>16th–19th May</u>

'The crescendos raise the hairs off of my arms.'

Everyone was wearing a dickie bow. Sadly, I didn't – but I suppose I didn't fit into the age bracket or the social class. In many circumstances, the classical music genre is linked with those who have a high level of disposable income. However, Dresden was trying their best – and I do applaud them for trying – to tap into the younger market. They were trying to understand the next wave by tapping into music influencers.

Dresden Music Festival began on 16th May 2019 and lasted until the 10th June. A long haul for a festival. It was a huge operation to organise. This annual festival featured over 1,500 international artists in more than 20 venues – and they didn't all arrive at the same time. I ain't a fan of classical music, but when I researched events in Germany and found Dresden Music Festival, I decided I wanted to gain some insight into the world of classical music. After all, the objective of my *80 Events* adventure was to experience contrasting events – like visiting this festival and comparing it with Jakarta Jazz Festival or even the Rock Festival I would be attending in Chicago. Were there any similarities? I had never been to a classical music event – ever. I'd have to get used to a few differences.

Although I had been given a press pass, I really wanted to get a perspective of the audience journey. On the first night I sat slap bang in the middle next to lots of journalists. They all had notepads and pens and scribbled notes throughout the evening – and then there was me. I ripped a bit of paper out of the festival brochure and used the free pencil I'd been given. *'The crescendos raise the hairs off of my arms.'* That was it. That was my critique. But really, the festival surroundings, within the Kulurpalast that was Dresden's Concert Hall, were very typical of my perception of a classical music concert. Beige walls, red chairs and bright lights. As it was the opening night, it was full of VIPs and local politicians – and everyone had an umbrella, because it was protocol that no jackets or bags were taken into the venue.

So I had a brochure, and then I was given another programme but in a different format, and then I was given an opening night one-sheet document and, on top of that, some sponsorship materials. Sustainability literally was not something that had been considered. Paper was everywhere. I calculated that every person – around 1,500 – would be given five bits of promotional material that night, as well as a goody bag when we departed. Paper. Why paper? Well, it's clear. A lot of those attending didn't have phones that were suitable for browsing the world wide web. And they were used to paper. How do they change their ways? How do event organisers get people to engage with their phones instead of taking home five bits of paper each? Although I did see some people taking photos with iPads...

Tonight, was very much about formalities. Being able to get this insight into what for me was the unknown world of classical music was great. It was all about the clapping. All about the bowing. Each time anyone from the orchestra stood, departed or entered the stage or asked to go to the toilet, there was an eruption of applause. Some people were squinting while looking through rented binoculars – though we weren't too far from the stage.

One thing I couldn't understand was the rubbish left behind. By the end of the performance on the first night, every seat was surrounded by chocolate wrappers and glassware – everywhere. People were deliberately stepping over the glass with absolutely no thoughts of taking any of it back to the bar. 'That's not my job... I am the customer' kind of thinking. The more I was discovering about the different cultures and behaviours attached to events, the more I spotted the differences and changes that needed to be shared and implemented – and behaviour around rubbish was one of them. Never leave your rubbish under a seat if you can take it with you – but in western countries, it appears this is totally acceptable.

I liked the outlook the festival had. 'Visionen' was the theme and the motto. But the motto was more than a clever marketing logo. Dresden Music Festival wanted to reinforce the importance of using vision for the evolution of humanity and how important it is for artistic inspiration. Intertwining past centuries of work, the artistic director, Jan Vogler – who we will discuss shortly – said it was important to use work that was "inspiring of the great founders of the culture of modernism". Incorporating works from current 'visions' from various genres allowed a programme that would not only tickle the taste buds of classical music fans but delve into other genres, while maintaining the roots of the festival. I loved the whole idea of an event using its platform to subtly shape and carve out personal growth engagement as well as musical engagement. Interesting.

Who is Jan Vogler? Billed as a world-renowned cellist, he was a well-connected musician who had built quite a reputation in the global world of music. Jan was a member of the classical world who had broken through into popular culture, even collaborating with the likes of Bill Murray (yes, the American actor). It left me wondering what the vision he had implemented as Artistic Director for the Dresden Music Festival was really all about. At the core was, of course, classical music – but he was opening it up to a wider audience. Past performances included the Royal Scottish National Orchestra and Nicola Benedetti, Danilil Trifonov, Jose Cura and the Birmingham Symphony Orchestra, who I got to see – which was very exciting! In 2019, the Rock and Roll Hall of Fame and former Cream member Eric Clapton closed the festival. This was a huge move and probably goes back to the idea of 'visions'. I really admired what Jan had done. It was different and could actually challenge how people engage with the festival. The product needs to be diversified. As the artistic director, he was really bringing the festival to a new audience. Slowly, change was coming because of the themes he was introducing. Exciting times, for sure! Jan was so honest when I got 10 minutes to speak to him. He knew his festival and also knew that without change, the festival would lose potential future attendees.

I attended the festival for two days and although I only visited the Kulurplast venue, I absolutely loved the experience. Dresden Music Festival has an audience that is very much stuck in its ways. But the vision set out by the artistic director means change is coming, and I could see it. Outside the main concert hall was a seaside-like information booth with deck chairs and a great interactive approach. Changing perspectives was important and implementing structures like that was the materialistic way of getting the ball rolling. One quite interesting point was the relationship that Dresden had with South Korea – and the impact this has on the festival. In 2011, Jan Vogler performed in the residence of the German Ambassador to Seoul to launch the 2011 festival. In 2019, the impact of that relationship with South Korea meant Korean musicians coming for the festival, and also studying here in Dresden because of the high-profile music schools in the city.

To summarise the festival... Demographics need to change. The use of Eric Clapton was clever and opened the festival to even more people. Identifying opportunities is critical for Jan and the team. But it was still a classical music festival – and that was it. No light shows. No engaging interactive activations around Dresden. This means those who follow this sort of genre of event will just keep attending. Until they try something different, I suppose they will never know how successful it could be.

One thing to take away...

Dresden Music Festival has the potential to be a catalyst of change for the genre and for the area. Use diverse successful artists who absolutely belong at this prestigious festival.

Back to Dresden...

The tour guides, interpreting into English, German, French and Italian, echoed through the streets. Softei's ice cream stalls were everywhere in Dresden. A beautiful array of buildings captured my imagination. One of the most amazing sights was a sculpture of King August II, which was covered in gold leaf. The sculpture, dating back to the 18th century, was in the middle of the Kulturplast so I saw it every day. I feel like we got to know each other pretty well. Each time I walked past, we saw each other from a different angle. It was truly beautiful. Dresden was beautiful. But even more special was that, on May 15th, I celebrated being 100 days into my adventure.

A hundred days. HA HA HA....

Can you actually believe it? I had survived on plain pasta and every type of chicken imaginable in Asia. I had flown around the globe and back (kind of). I had seen some of the greatest events in the world. I had stood in the middle of fields and activation stands, walked through crowds, and felt the excitement of more than just the event. I had listened to music I would never have thought of listening to ever before. I had even discovered the excitement of standing in an airport and watching the departure boards, and grabbing my bag from an ever-changing baggage belt. I had posted constantly about #comeonthejourney. I was questioning people as much as I could about events. I was challenging the norms of why events occur. A hundred days in – and I was very much on it. I was missing home but, considering everything about this project was down to me, I felt proud. A hundred days in, and I had learned so much about the events industry that, for others, was just something that happened. And I was in awe at it. Here are the top three things I'd learned so far:

1. Gatherings – events are about people gathering together to enjoy a common theme.
2. Recycling – We must start respecting how much waste events create.
3. Fan activations – Fan engagement is key to the success of the customer journey.

So let's dabble briefly in a market...

Event 33: Dresden Spring Market

16th May

German markets are a staple of society – globally. They're about a sense of tradition and culture, a sense of belonging to a community. The ability to purchase whatever you want from the authentic German market is what is expected when they roll into cities. No clinical superstore can compare to the magnificent experience of a market – and in Germany. Perfecto! In another respect, market stalls sell things you really don't need. Like toilet roll holder covers or wooden shaped elephants. Or plant pot covers. They're a place where disposable income just disappears down the nearest drain.

Saturday 18th May was the fifth day of the Dresden Spring Market. For the next six weeks the market would be in full swing. I visited during the day, before I attended a concert at the Dresden Music Festival. The market was reasonably busy, with people buying crepes and beers, browsing the 40 market stalls, and enjoying the children's funfair. In the middle of the market was a stage. The stage was Easter themed – bunnies, eggs, flowers; everything painted in bright pink and yellow colours.

Dresden's German Christmas Market dates back to the 15th century. It takes over the streets from Altmarkt Square towards the train station and along to the Albertplatz. This Spring Market had been designed along the same lines as the Christmas one, and log cabins lined the square, although they were much smaller than at Christmas. However, the Christmas theme of the products on sale was slightly misguided. No one really needs 'make your own snow' in spring.

Stall holders sat with their feet up, chilling behind their merchandise as they dreamed about what they could be doing today. And that's why most people were just meandering along. Nothing was standing out to enhance the visitor experience. Shout.

Engage. Entice! Bring a flavour of your product to the floor. Of course, I didn't need any kitchen appliances, Easter bonnets, coins or anything extra baggage.

The most important section of the whole market, and the busiest, was the picket-fenced food and drink area. It was mobbed with people grabbing a light bite or eating a full dinner with a beer or four. Markets can turn an alternative venue into a socialising heaven – and Dresden, with its world-renowned reputation, knew how to do it. However, seven euros for a German sausage that I could buy for three just around the corner – I suppose you're buying into the experience.

Did I just wander around a market and consider it an event? Kind of. But the key observation here was the effort put into ensuring these Spring Markets did not affect the overall satisfaction and reputation of the Christmas ones. No one can dispute the successful impact they have – so it is crucial to appreciate the art of running a market. Understand the packaging and understanding the benefit.

One thing to take away...

Markets make up such an important part of the events industry. Dresden Spring Festival is a nice addition to the city during the springtime. It needs to be more engaging, but meandering was fun, and it was for sure a nice addition to the beautiful experience here in Dresden.

Farewell from Dresden...

Exiting my cabin at 5am, it was time to leave the boat and walk back to the railway station. Tourists boost cities' economies and Dresden really does depend on tourism. I loved the city, with its bridges and buildings; although they are from many different eras, they manage to complement each other. I'd happily attend Dresden Music Festival again!

Vienna

The train from Dresden to Vienna started moving. Vienna has 23 sub-divided districts and a population of 1.8 million (a fun fact I learned on a free map). The main language is German, and it is a popular city, with over 22 million passengers arriving at Vienna International Airport each year. It's also home to one of the four UN Global Headquarters. Vienna introduced the Tourism Concept in 2009, which brought more attention to delivering tourism experiences. In 2013, the city recorded 12.7 million one-night stays – fascinating, eh! I was here in Vienna to experience two cultural music events.

Event 34: Open Air Performance at Vienna State Opera

<u>21st May</u>

The building I was walking towards, the Vienna State Opera, was built in the Renaissance Revival architecture style and opened on 25th May 1869. I was in Vienna from the 19th to 24th May 2019. I only realised the significance of the date once I arrived – good one, eh! Yes, that meant there would be a HUGE celebration on May 25th – and I was missing it by a day. But the opera in Vienna was something that I wouldn't get to walk through the gates to see, simply because I didn't have hundreds of euros to pay for a ticket. Instead, I experienced the 'working-class approach' that meant those who can't afford tickets still get a sense of what the opera is like. A live feed of the performance, which was being beamed around the world, was also played to the crowds outside the opera house on a large screen. Around 180 black chairs were lined up at the side and as soon as they were set out, they were full.

Inside the building were a few thousand people dressed in the compulsory suits and cocktail dresses, enjoying a very luxurious evening – while outside we were wrapped up in rain jackets, jeans and tracksuit bottoms. Today's performance was *The Barber of Seville* by Gioachino Rossini, which was an absolute gem of an opera. It's also the song that begins *Mrs Doubtfire* – yes, that one! Opportunities to allow people to enjoy the opera have been cleverly devised by Vienna Tourism. In my opinion, it's an absolute gem of a strategy.

Vienna (Wien) Tourism calls this *Opera For All.* The video wall was open April, May, June and September and on New Year's Eve. Everything streamed to the wall was enjoyed free of charge. Of course, not being in the venue brings a sense of disengagement –

but the strategy does make tourists feel like the city wants them to get a glimpse into what Vienna is best known for.

Outside the opera house, the stage had been set up and fence lines in and around the grounds were ready for large crowds. This was a huge occasion. The production was orchestrated by the internal director of photography and used five cameras and two sound systems outside to give the best experience for all watching. I stood for two hours in the pouring rain observing how everyone else engaged with the event. There was no sense of excitement. No real 'OMG, I am watching an opera.' No one was taking photos. No one was eating snacks or drinking anything. Arms folded. Hoods up. Legs crossed. Eyes glued to the screen. Most of the people in front of the 50m^2 LED video wall sat and listened in silence. I was really missing the Penis Festival, or even the cricket – where the audience was immersed and engaged with the event.

One thing to take away...

Vienna is trying hard to connect the upper classes with the lower classes. Unfortunately, I missed out on buying a fridge magnet or a tea towel printed with '*I was there at the big screen'*.

Back to Vienna...

According to various sources, every day in Vienna there are, on average, 20 classical musical performances at a range of scales and levels of 'talent'. This was very much diluting the market and apparently many of the concerts would be half empty, or full of seniors – which meant less profit for the venue and the concert organisers. I needed to get into one of these events. I needed to see it for myself. And I did...

Event 35: Wiener Festwochen (Vienna Festival)

<u>20th May</u>

The Vienna Festival was on from 10th May until the middle of June. Vienna has an abundance of theatres and performance arenas; in total, there are approximately 120 different venues for music consumption. Because of its location and facilities, Vienna is also one of the top three destinations for international conventions. This results in a certain type of person being attracted to the musical performances. The festival organisers are trying to embrace variety through the artists and art disciplines they book. The festival is constructed with different components, including lectures, guest speaking slots, workshops, performances and other elements that make it extremely diverse. 'Edgy' was how I would describe the aims of the festival – although I couldn't see anything edgy about the gold-leafed room I found myself in for a five-musician recital of Beethoven and Mozart. I probably brought the average age of the audience down by 30 years.

And then it began. Musicians walked from stage right. Bowed in silence. Took a seat. Finished a piece of music. Stopped. No applause. My hands were clasped, ready to clap – until those around me didn't. We were sitting on banqueting-type chairs and the venue was half empty. The ceiling was dusted with golden flakes and the whole venue was extravagantly decorated. I glanced at those around me. It looked like my grandparents had arrived and brought lots of their friends. There was absolutely no way these types of events could be sustained.

The music was emotionally moving – but unfortunately that was not how it was marketed. Even the venue didn't seem to want young people to attend. I was asked, "Are you not with an elder?" I checked on my ticket, the website, the programme, but nothing suggested it was a performance for an older crowd. Possibly this could have been part of a 'retirement ticket' special deal. But that was not in any of the promotional materials. I didn't walk away with a WOW. The cellos – yes, they did stay in my ears; what a beautiful sound – but the festival didn't capture my heart.

One thing to take away...

I cannot judge the whole festival, because I was not there for the entire six weeks. I really think the edgy element of the festival could push it forward. In fact, I think Vienna needs to push forward as a city. It is trying to, for sure, and this festival could be at the forefront of the battle.

Farewell Vienna...

Vienna is a visitor magnet. A busy city. A lot of tourists. From 9am to 8pm the place was mobbed with wandering, map-holding sightseers. They rolled out of the tour buses and waited for their tour guide to take them to the next destination. McDonalds was constantly packed. Spanish tourists waved their umbrellas in the air as the tour guide announced: "Senors and senoritas..." They also always wore bold coloured jackets.

Time now to stop off in Prague.

Prague

For me, Prague was so much better than Vienna – and I had only been here 30 minutes. The balconies. The art. The gothic-style buildings. Modern-day Prague is on one side of the river; on the other is the old city, filled with cobbled streets. I love Prague, but there is a tainted side to the tourism industry: the stag dos and hen parties, mainly British, who think cheap beer and direct flights from the UK make for a perfect weekend away. Thankfully, I wasn't there to watch them. Instead, I was here for three days of full-on events. Here's to the first of them.

Event 36: Night of Churches

<u>24th May</u>

The Night of Churches on 24th May was abbreviated to NOC on the front of the bright red brochures that were being distributed around the city. The brochure was the 'bible' for the event and would help you to weave around the various locations in Prague and delve into some extremely amazing and unique sights. NOC was the main reason I had taken an earlier train from Vienna. I wanted to make sure I arrived here on time. Starting on the Friday evening, this annual event was opening doors in Prague and all around the country. Dating back to 2005, this event was launched by complete accident and had now spread across Germany, Austria and Czech Republic. A church in Austria was left open one night with a candle lit outside. The community, curious about the light, came to see why the doors had been left open and became part of the first ever Night of Churches. Offering a glimpse inside the church was about welcoming people and inviting them into a maybe unfamiliar setting. It was a way for the priest to ensure the community knew the church was always open. The following year, more churches and religious temples stayed open at night. In 2019, over 1,650 churches took part; in Prague alone, 450 religious buildings were open for the night.

The objective was to allow the public to meet members of the congregation – whether it was those who attend mass, or those who are celebrants. I spent some time reading the brochure and discovered there was a mixture of music, fine art, theatre and dance encounters happening. Activities including bible readings, creative competitions, puppet shows and book readings were all being held in the unique setting of religious buildings on this special evening.

An annual event – but one with a long-lasting impact on Prague, in terms of both the economic benefits and positive tourism experience and for the social aspect of opening religion to those who may not have been in an orthodox building before. The free event created so many wonderful moments, like walking through the choir lofts and seeing the inside of roofs, places that would normally be off limits. Now, you may be wondering why I've categorised this as an event. Well, it takes you behind the scenes and in a way you are able to experience religions you have never discovered before. Also, it allows you, with permission, to walk through otherwise closed doors. It gives you permitted boundaries of consumption. It makes you want to wander around and not only see things you may not have seen before, but hear things, and feel things. Many people around the world view religion as a chance to connect, so if this event can connect people – excellent.

I stood at the first chapel in Prague Nove Mesto. My focus tonight was on avoiding the stags of *Snow White and the Seven Dwarfs* rolling around the street and follow the amazing route of churches all open this evening. This was special. These were moments to cherish. This was not only about religion; it was about enjoying, celebrating and appreciating the beautiful buildings. In total, I went to seven buildings. In the first church, I stood and admired the beauty while people at the front laughed and talked at the altar. It felt a bit weird just wandering about the building and talking. It felt disrespectful in a way – but NOC was about breaking down boundaries and exploring the buildings. I couldn't help but watch everyone wandering around and looking up – something we sometimes forget to do.

From Nove Mesto, I walked to the next venue. I was heading to Prague Square, Namesti Republiky, for my next visit. The way you navigated was by using the online map or the brochure, which had a very good map to follow. There was no signage on the roads; it was all about following the map. I stood outside the chapel, which had bells ringing. There was a high gated wall in front of me with high archways and a large wooden door with cast iron handles. It was a spectacle to behold. An a cappella choir harmonised in the sweet sounds of a hymn while people gazed up at the art on the high ceilings. It was quite extraordinary. Did I know where to look? Nope! I was looking up, to the left, watching everyone else reading about the history of the church and enjoying the experience. Literally, popping in and out of the church doors were curious tourists and locals interested in learning about the beauty of this building. NOC was all about discovery and my ears were being treated to some unique sounds. As time progressed, I would learn that NOC was so simple yet so complex.

I walked through Prague Square. The event was only halfway through, but I was knackered after the train ride and dumping my bags and running to the event – I was nearly done. NOC started at 6pm and some buildings were open until 4am, but most closed at 1am – to ensure that the stag dos and hen parties didn't think they could go to confession after a wild night in Prague. I was actually surprised not to have seen any around the buildings I visited.

I loved the uniqueness of each building and the special moments I experienced. This event was pure genius. As I stepped into the next church, a 12-pedal bike with a bar in the middle went past with a "Wheeeeeeeeeeewwwwww!" while its intoxicated riders missed the absolute gold that Prague had to offer. I just didn't get it. They could have been walking into a church where a 54-member orchestra was seated at the altar. Every pew was full. The church was probably more full tonight than it was during a regular Sunday service. NOC really was pulling at my heartstrings.

Even though NOC had grown in scale since 2005, it had kept some of the traditions from the first year. Each building of worship had a candle outside to signify they were part of the event, and banners were draped from the roofs of the churches. It was beautiful and so simple. On tourism websites it was classed as an 'unprecedented experience'. I loved the idea being demonstrated here that events can have hidden meaning. The meaning here was inclusion. Religion is something that is quite topical and at times can build barriers to engagement. By opening doors, holding concerts, standing at the entrance to a church and welcoming everyone in with free cake and coffee – this was more than just an event. No one was passing around the collection basket. NOC was a tool of the future, enabling people to experience the spectacular beauty of the buildings but also have topical conversations in a safe space. I saw people question Catholic priests about out of date views or challenge the ministers of other religious buildings – but they were listening. And listening is so important.

From an event geek point of view, I noticed that each church had a welcome desk with lots of programmes and lots of paper – but they were also out there engaging with the community. I met monks, priests and church volunteers. Each had a badge saying, 'ASK ME'. The message was very clear: 'I can talk to you about this building, this community and my church. Welcome.' Sometimes organisers miss the point that events bring people together more than we expect. We can put up a building, but it's those who look after it and have an association with it that create unity. Do we in the western world – and the UK specifically – sometimes not realise the importance of events like these and what they can bring? Tourism boosted, with thousands of people descending to see, for free, some of Prague's best-kept secrets. Appreciation of cultural and religious differences – bringing unity as one.

One thing to take away...

Events can build, create and open communities. That is exactly what this growing event achieves every year. So here is the message I have for you reading this today. Go and explore somewhere you have never been before. And I hope that one day the stag dos will go back to Prague and see the true beauty of the city – though it's probably unlikely.

Back to the cobbles of Prague...

I walked down to the Vltava River and meandered towards the

Prague Fringe. On one side of the river was the Old Town and on the other, the New Town, with bridges connecting the two halves of this beautiful city. As I walked back towards Prague Square, I saw a bit of a ruckus kicking off. I was on the phone to my mate Ajay in the UK and he could hear something happening in the background. "What's that?" he said. I watched a young British guy being pushed aggressively out of an Italian restaurant by two waiters and two chefs. After one swift punch he was about to land on the ground and there was no one around to help him. He was obviously out on a stag do and his mates had ditched him. He was being screamed at by the restaurant staff, so I walked over and grabbed this guy by his shirt and dragged him back.

"You don't know me," I said, "but if you don't come with me right now these three guys to your left and the four guys in front of you are about to kick your ass." Cut a long story short – we ran. We got back to his mates and he bought me a Starbucks chocolate muffin to say thanks. He'd basically told the restaurant the food was s***...

To the fringe!

Event 37: Prague Fringe

<u>25th May</u>

Prague Fringe is a cultural event that is alternative and edgy, not least because it takes over some unusual venues, like hotel basements. Prague Fringe was set up 18 years ago and is extremely small still in comparison to the global fringe festivals of Adelaide and Edinburgh. It is, however, an established arts festival and has a growing array of performers who use this platform to test materials for future shows. Due to time constraints, I was only able to make one show, *How to Make Friends in Hollywood*, in the basement of the Golden Key Hotel.

The concept of a 'fringe' festival dates back to Edinburgh in the 1940s and it is viewed as an 'alternative event' offering a unique artistic experience. These days, fringe events take place globally and very much have their own identity and character. Prague Fringe, modelled on Edinburgh Fringe, welcomes 200 artists and 45 productions over 8 days and in 8 venues ranging from basements to theatres. The financial impact that fringe festivals have on the local economy is crucial. In 2018, Edinburgh Fringe brought £200 million of direct financial economic benefits to Scotland; tourism in Adelaide increased by 24% and resulted in a direct $90 million (AUD) economic boom during the Fringe Festival there. And then there's the impact fringe events have on the arts world. Providing a platform for new and expressive arts has a direct impact on the audience, with people becoming emotionally connected.

I walked to the Golden Key Hotel and was met outside by a sandwich board. It had the Prague Fringe banner stapled all over and, in chalk, screamed 'TONIGHT!' It felt very Fringe. As I looked around it felt like I could be in the middle of Edinburgh (but without the crowds and constant bombarding with leaflets); the cobbled streets reminded me of the Royal Mile. Arches on

Nerudova Street, which I could see in the near distance, really did remind me of the backdrop of Edinburgh's old town. I went into the hotel but there were no signs sending me to the basement. However, without speaking a single word the receptionist signalled me downstairs to what must have been the breakfast area. I went down into a basement with a marble floor and a brick archway, and imagined that this basement, one floor beneath the hotel, must have been used for smuggling, or hiding out during the war.

As I walked in, I heard an Australian accent in conversation with an English accent. It was the first night, so obviously everything was being set up. "You done this before…?" The staff were still getting to know each other. "I was in Perth and then went travelling and got this gig, before I go to Edinburgh." The conveyor belt of fringe work is a lifestyle for many. In a way, therefore, I was not really at the Prague Fringe, with Czech nationals welcoming me. It was part of a global fringe series (although not officially).

Fifteen seats were laid out under the brick archway and two white sidelights beamed up to the very low roof. I was quite excited and very intrigued about the layout. If you hated closed spaces, there's not a chance you would survive. It was all very tight.

Although I'd read up about the Fringe, I didn't know anything about this show, other than it was called *How to Make Friends in Hollywood.* I totally had no idea what to expect. But that's the point of the Fringe. It's about going along to unknown shows and enjoying them. The ticket cost me the equivalent of £6, and the majority of other shows here were just as cheap. I mean, I don't know what to say about that. Did it devalue the arts, with tickets being so inexpensive? Did the performer actually make anything? (No.) But on the other side of the coin, taking the GDP of the Czech Republic into account, the ticket price was affordable. Thinking about this, the festival gives locals a chance to come to shows they might never otherwise see. It's a chance to go out for a luxury experience. Of course, in Edinburgh, if a show was £6 the performer would most probably make a loss. But the Prague Fringe, now in its

18th year, is building momentum and those performing were here to entertain, demonstrate their skills and begin their careers.

A well-written, one-woman play with a great performer. The actor was from England and the play was written by a man also from England, who was in the crowd. I really appreciated the fact that they were putting themselves out there. They had written a show, punched their hand in the air, booked a flight to Prague, taken a risk, skipped past the stag dos and said, "Let's do it!"

The actor's interaction with the crowd was outstanding. It was a small audience, but she was such an engaging performer. The content was also quite special. The whole performance was great work – but not just that, it was inspiring that two kids from Brighton had written such a wonderful piece. It was a shame there were only 15 seats, but one day they will sell out a full theatre, maybe an arena – you never know. You certainly never know what can be achieved until you try – and this show was doing just that. After the show I bumped into them as I was taking some 'artistic' photos with the programme. They were so delighted that I enjoyed the show. Sometimes, as consumers, we never get a chance to thank performers, and performers never find out what emotions they evoked for the audience. This was the perfect opportunity for us both. We even hugged like new best friends. They were studying performance arts and took a punt at coming over. If my memory is right, they were even missing classes for this. Such dedication!

The Fringe event really does fulfil a void in beautiful Prague. It enhances the cultural offering. It enhances the image of Prague. The audience demographics for most of the events were between 15–34 years. This shows that the direction of the Fringe can only be enhanced even further.

One thing to take away…

A Fringe brings so much to a city and, over the last 18 years, Prague has begun to see the impact. The play in the brick archway basement venue was only a small representation of the Fringe – but the event has a wider impact in a city that has a tourism problem. It's a cultural event with a bigger purpose – and it can have a positive impact.

Back to Prague...

Prague was a beautiful city. The trams. The streets. The sounds. Everything was amazing. The problem was the negativity associated with stag do and hen party tourism. Walking through the city, men graced the streets with t-shirts showing their 'to do lists'. Unfortunately, this was a dark norm. The town hall was also up against it with the negative effect that Airbnbs were having on the town's accommodation services. Buildings were being overrun by large all-male or all-female groups here for the weekend who didn't mind if a microwave was thrown out of a balcony. (True story.) Prague was battling a plague of issues – but couldn't say no. Change was needed because the police and tourism boards are sick of it; you can see it pretty clearly. News articles brand the incomers as 'the tourists that no one wants...'

Event 38: Czech Republic vs Canada Ice Hockey – Prague Live Zone

<u>25th May</u>

Prague Square is the home of the extremely famous Prague astronomical clock but tonight it was the centre of the Ice Hockey World Championships' Fan Zone. The championships, held in Slovakia, were on for 16 days and tonight the Czech Republic were playing Canada – and by chance I was in Prague. This was the night after the NOC, the same weekend as Prague Fringe, and my third event in Prague – so far. Tonight was the semi-final and tensions were high. This was a huge deal for the Czech Republic and as I watched the crowds, I could see the national pride oozing through.

Police and firefighters were sitting on top of their vehicles – not watching the crowd but enjoying the beauty that was ice hockey on the big screen! This live zone, organised by the council, was in the middle of the city where tourists would normally be meandering around, but tonight it was overtaken by locals. The volume of people coming through was really surprising and by the time the match began the place was full.

The evening painted a perfect picture of patriotism. What really astonished me was the volume of fans who had immersed themselves in red, white and blue – the colours of the Czech Republic. Everyone was draped in scarves and flags. Face stickers in the Czech colours were being handed out by PR staff from a local radio station. Everyone was grabbing a £1.50 beer (yes – that's right… cheap) and getting in place to watch with pride. This was a Czech experience. The stage to the right of the screen was covered with flags and dancing mascots. Songs and chants assailed my senses. It was delightfully patriotic. I also loved that it was completely to everything I had witnessed over the last 24 hours.

The pride that comes from these types of events can transform communities. But it is also about appreciating and understanding the celebration of national identity. As an aside, it is sometimes evident that patriotic behaviour is more popular in countries that have dealt with war. The Czech Republic has had its fair share of situations – but now, with direction and opportunities, the gates are opening to possibilities. Tonight I stood in the middle of a large crowd, chanting, loving it and showing my affection for a country that, for one hour and thirty minutes, I felt truly part of. I thought about my homeland of Scotland – sometimes we don't flare our kilts, strike up our bagpipes and shout freedom loud enough. Sometimes it takes outsiders to show adoration for our country before we react and express our patriotism. Often, it's only when we are away on holiday in bars in Tenerife that we say we're from Scotland with absolute pride.

The city had created a space for people to come out and be as one instead of sitting watching the game in their home or local bar. Hosting the fan zone in the centre of Prague could be translated as a chance to say to each other, 'We are in this together. We are one. We are more than just Prague, the party town.' It was loud. It was festive.

Sometimes live zones are seen as wagons of global mobility with realms of possibility. They are enshrined into the organisation of mega events, located in dynamic urban spaces and branded in a way that disrupts day to day life. A fan zone allows people to be at the event, but nowhere near it. Make sense? Nope. But then the whole concept of a fan zone makes no sense. We were in a different country but, through a screen, we could be at the game. But the true success of a fan zone is dependent on whether the integration of food, drink, merchandise and entertainment touches a sweet spot with those present.

Beer went all over me... When the Czech Republic scored, you would have thought they had won the championship. I struggled to breathe for 10 seconds when I was swept off the floor and hugged by a group of three very tall, well-built men who were adamant I was part of their gang. However, the atmosphere quickly went from one of euphoria and excitement to sheer devastation for these proud sports fans. It was sad – but it was also interesting to still see them chanting and the happiness continue even as the crowd watched their team lose the match. The Czech nationals really do love their country. Even the police were high-fiving fans (well, some of them – others looked as though they would sooner shoot them!).

As soon as the game finished, the boundary and the fence lines were gone. And this analogy is quite interesting. We put up boundaries for events to invoke a fixed period of emotion, love and, above all, joy and happiness. Then it's gone, and those people who chose to come, leave.

One thing to take away...

A celebration about national identity in this country was not about politics or divisions or history (even though the EU elections were on that weekend). It was about the colours, the pride and the feeling of what it is to be Czech. As one.

Back to Prague...

I decided to go to another event because I might as well do as much as I could in my three days in Prague! I was living on no sleep as it was...

Event 39: Khamoro Festival

26th May

The Roma is an ethnic minority with a global population of 12 million, and Prague was hosting the world's largest festival for the Roma community. This adventure was all about attending events I would never experience at home – and this was just such an opportunity.

The Khamoro Festival took place that year in Prague from 26th May until 1st June; it is the largest global celebration in the world of Roma culture. As the website states, the Khamoro Festival has been organised since 1999 and has become a unique gathering in Prague. The festival aims to bring people together to celebrate the richness and depth of Roma culture and traditions; at the heart of the event was Roma music. Each year the festival attracts around 10,000 people. On the website they state the festival's aims to be 'improving relations between major society and the Roma community through presentation of Roma culture' and I really appreciated that they were being so honest. This ethnic minority is believed to have a high concentration in Europe, with 10 out of the 12 million people living here. However, because of previous altercations, the community has to deal with hostility in modern society. The festival was an opportunity to say: 'We know we are not liked – so come to our festival and we will show you our culture'.

The festival was being held within Kasarna Karlin, a renovated square that was quite spectacular. It's surrounded by buildings dating back to the times of the Soviet Union and they still bear the scars, with bullet holes in the brickwork and smashed windows – but that adds to the beauty. The venue was actually a very active cultural hub with galleries, an outdoor cinema, bar, café and areas used for art and sport. I was impressed by the history of this place and the surrounding buildings. The venue website states it's an outdoor venue for people to meet within a 'cultural oasis'.

Because I had a flight booked on the 27th May, I was only fortunate enough to get a glimpse of the festival, the opening night's open-air concert. Looking around, I would say there were about 600 people here. A stage had been built in the middle of the square and picnic tables set out. Piles of bricks, designed to give an authentic feel to the venue, were placed in stacks and seemed quite appropriate.

Pure pride oozed from each member of the Roma community who walked through the gates. I'll be honest, I was the minority here. I was the outsider. I could only imagine what being a member of this community felt like. Some people turned up covered in 'bling'. Others were literally sharing one bit of bread between five people. I couldn't get my head around the interactions between those attending – but I was for sure seeing a divide within a divided culture. I really was trying to understand the event – but it was difficult. The festival programme was diverse, but it also intended to break the boundaries about what the Roma community represents. Photograph exhibitions, gipsy jazz, theatre – venues right across the city held events associated with the festival. It was huge. It was a big party.

Events are very much about putting yourself in a situation where you can develop knowledge and see new things. I think events fill a gap in our education of the unknown. I fully believe events have a purpose that is stronger and bigger than we understand. I was just the tourist here. There was absolutely no need for me to be here – but every need to attend. For me, it gave me the opportunity to delve into a community that I knew nothing about. But I couldn't help but feel the eyes peering at me from every angle. I suppose that was always going to be the case.

Discrimination is something the Roma community battles with every day. I could see it here. However, I could also see, even within the Roma community themselves, discrimination and division between the different groups. Some people were throwing shade at others, giving them looks that said, 'Why are you here?' It was evident the way everyone was split. And not just that – add some alcohol and the festival was all go. I guess this is why the bouncers were very large. The MC on the stage was evidently the 'grandfather' of the event. He passed around bottles of wine to the performers and even some of the crew, and everyone took a full glass. To start the event, he required everyone to make a toast. That started a transformation in the audience, who were becoming more 'ready' for the event. They were awakening to the moment it was about to happen. He was the hype man, while all the men standing at the barriers cheered like fan girls for a famous pop star, watched him in awe and did everything he commanded.

Apart from the obvious divisions within the community, the event was great, and I really loved the idea of an ethnic minority group wanting to bring its culture to the forefront. I stayed for two hours and watched the production crew, stage management and security team. The production was very good. Lights strobed around the facades of the buildings, the main stage was well lit, and the sound was brilliant. At one point there were 12 musicians all linked up to microphones – and I felt as though I was in the middle of a large music festival in a major city. But then, I was. I was at a world-leading festival. It may not have been an event on my agenda, but it turned into a lovely reminder. A reminder that ethnic minorities who are very much suppressed in mainstream society have a strong voice. A voice that they want to share. A voice they want to entertain people with. A voice that can widen and broaden cultural reach and share the positivity that comes from the Roma community. I think it needs more mainstream support – and, hopefully, me writing a few pages about it will open your eyes and encourage you to find out more.

One thing to take away...

The Roma culture is an interesting one. For me, events are undoubtedly a great way to convey, enjoy and continue to spread the word about cultures. This festival was not just about walking into a four-wall square but about leaving the space with a deeper understanding of the people.

Goodbye, Prague...

Prague went from being a weekend with just one date in the diary to a packed few days where I attended four events. Culture is the biggest and most important identity many people have. A sense of belonging is achieved. I really think Prague has so much potential. It's a shame that a large proportion of the tourists here are drunk British stag and hen parties. Both these groups are important to European tourism – but by changing their behaviour and attitudes, they could ensure that the beautiful streets of Prague keep their beauty throughout the year.

Hello, Bilbao...

Flying to Bilbao began with the most amazing conversation with Bert and Paulina, a couple from a village in the Netherlands. The plane was very quiet – except for row 23, seats A, B and C. We discussed some really in-depth subjects and we laughed a lot. It was a masterpiece of conversation. We talked about their family. We talked about travelling – the good times and the difficult. It was like chatting with my parents and having an honest conversation about how hard life was.

I collected my 26 kilos of weight from the baggage claims area and left the airport. "One way to Bilbao please..." On the bus I went and ended up in an area that was described by the police as "the area no one walks into if they don't want to be mugged."

I decided to go on the Athletic Bilbao Stadium Tour.

"The best stadium tour I have ever experienced!" I cried when I came out – because everything was so well constructed within the museum. The escalators, the toilets, the screens, the lights, the fan sounds, the welcome – ABSOLUTELY EVERYTHING! I was fully immersed.

Let's start at the beginning. I walked along a short corridor and came to a red tunnel leading to an escalator. As soon as my left foot was on the escalator, the cheers began. It got louder and louder and suddenly I felt like a football player! I could envision myself in my shorts and new football boots, ready to warm up before taking the winning penalty. Upon my chest was the top I would grab when I scored. Of course, all of this was just a dramatized fantasy – but still... I felt it.

Spanish commentary turned into English commentary that turned into German commentary and then we were in – it was all very clever. The museum had black walls and black flooring and each display of pictures and memorabilia was lit up against the dark background. But the most special thing, the thing that caught me off guard, was the split in content across the walls. On the left was the history of Athletic Bilbao. On the right were global events.

We were taken through some of the most heart-breaking situations, like 9/11, the death of famous iconic people and so on, while at the same time the history of the football club was playing out on the opposite wall. An amazing idea, for sure. It used graphics and wording and also had sensory activations that started videos playing as you walked past (SO CLEVER).

The tour inside the stadium was just as cool. As we walked onto the pitch there was crowd noise each time the doors opened. It was about allowing us '*fans*' – or '*not fans*' – to have the most memorable experience that was as close as possible to what it is actually like to walk on the pitch for a game.

Athletic Bilbao not only had a modern and innovative museum that used interactive systems and playrooms with lights and sounds, they have put serious thinking into the whole experience.

Overall, it was simply beautiful. This museum and tour left me with more than just a ticket stub and an overpriced shirt. I was educated in life and sport, and I remembered a few milestones that none of us should ever forget.

Glorious! I even emailed them to say how amazing it was.

WELL, READERS! Ready. READY!

We are halfway there...

EXCITING! Can you believe it? But we have no time to stop. Let's keep going... it is time for Madrid!

Madrid

It was 6am and I was sitting in a very dodgy bus station in Bilbao, waiting for the right bus to arrive. It was chaotic. As each bus rolled in, the grumpy Spanish drivers were saying: "No, this is not you..."

Today I was travelling to Madrid and I would be there while the Champions League Final was happening. For football (soccer) fans, this was the holy grail of European football. And although I was not going to the actual match, I would be in the city with thousands of Liverpool and Tottenham fans who had flown over.

Because guess what? There was a cultural event happening just for the Champions League Final...

Event 40: Champions League Final Festival

1st June

Liverpool FC and Tottenham Hotspur (Spurs) FC, both English teams, had reached the Champions League Final and the multi-million-pound game was about to kick off in the Athletico Madrid stadium.

I was in the centre of Madrid city and focused on immersing myself in the activations and fan zones that were designed to unite fans and celebrate their passion for football, even if they didn't have a ticket to the game. Plaza Mayor was taken over by the UEFA Champions League and the activations were part of a bigger objective. I was stunned by the scale of what was being delivered. Hats, pencils, notepads, t-shirts, Mastercard footballs... it was the best place to get free stuff. Okay, they were giving away things that, let's be honest, would never be used ever again – but it's all about the feeling of being given a pencil with 'Champions League Final' on it. The live activation sites aimed not only to attract those going to the match but also to encourage local people to enjoy the spirit of the competition. It was about partying. It was about celebrating. And it was about the journey of a fan – well, supposedly. It was actually about the long queue to have your photo taken with the Champions League trophy before it was police-escorted through the streets of Madrid to the stadium.

Let me tell you a bit about the layout of the Plaza Mayor. In the middle of the square was a Heineken-themed bar. Mastercard had a computerised football 3D camera set-up. Around the square were shipping containers, converted into hospitality units or mobilized into fancy cocktail bars.

The festival stage had an interesting variety of entertainment.

The headline act was a group of 14 dancers from all over the world – even countries that aren't involved in the European Champions League, like Brazil and America. I found it interesting because when they spoke, they sounded like a Disney-manufactured pop band. "Hello Madrid, we are so excited to be here! We would love you to sing along – will you sing along for us?" Now, I am not being cynical at all here – but when a Liverpool or Spurs fan has come all the way to Madrid for a football match, the last thing I think they want to do is to sing along with *High School Musical* auditionees. Instead, the Liverpool fans were at a different plaza – and boy, did they know how to party!

Madrid was not a welcoming place, and nothing was done to create a welcoming atmosphere outside the manufactured Playa Mayor. The city didn't want the Champions League final. The only businesses in Madrid that did seem keen for the event were the restaurants – although even some of them had signage up saying 'Do not enter' – and the Spanish bars, which were quiet, had bouncers on the doors who were not allowing any Brits inside. I can understand, but this was a chance to take a share of the 128-million-euro investment and economic impact that the event brought to the city.

Liverpool FC's official fan zone, in Felipe II Square, was where you wanted to be. Suddenly, I was met with baton-drawn armoured police officers – lovely when I arrived. Madrid really did know how to welcome everyone. Then my eyes were drawn to the sea of red. Literally. Approximately 50,000 Liverpool fans were standing in this area holding flares, banging drums and singing songs associated with their team. It was an absolutely electric atmosphere – and so much better than the official Champions League Fan Zone. The fans just took control – and this was before the match. It was quite spectacular to see the crowd. The locals, watching from their balconies, were loving it. Tea towels in the air, swinging to songs they had no idea about. Smiling down and watching the pure joy on the faces of the visitors. Proposals from Liverpool fans to Spanish grandmothers in their *pinnies*. Balls were thrown up to them and it was all banter.

But the police were ready to riot. To enforce the law, police were dotted in different corners of the city. Vans full of baton-wielding officers. The police in Spain is comprised of three different forces – the Guardia Civil, Policia Nacional and the Policia Local – and they each have different levels of responsibility. However, for the Champions League final it was all as one. And unfortunately, in my neutral opinion, their responsibility was to create trouble. I watched as police started screaming at groups who were causing no trouble at all. I saw batons being deployed, which caused a response from the fans – but honestly, they'd done nothing except try to figure out which way to go. Later that evening, I watched the police stand in their riot gear every 100 metres, just waiting. Luckily, I was not wearing football colours, but after the match I witnessed what I knew could have become an episode of tragedy – if it had escalated any further.

Liverpool fans outside restaurants were singing and embracing after the match had finished with the score in their team's favour. A mixture of children and older fans were in the middle of this group. The fans were taken by surprise as the police charged. I honestly could not understand what was happening. Sirens sounded from all over as police came flying down the alleyways. I'd been standing on the steps of a closed shop, watching three guys singing and the waiters smiling. Then it became 10 singing and embracing. Now police officers were charging in. The atmosphere had changed dramatically. People were being targeted simply for being football fans. Finding myself in the middle of this chaos, I was scared. I ran away and skipped through a few alleyways – all absolutely packed – only to be met by another brawl. This time it ended with some fans gushing with blood.

At 5pm in Plaza De Mayo, the big screens had messages in large font saying, 'The Match Will Not Be Shown Here – Please Leave The Area Immediately'. Very welcoming. It was a sweltering

30 degrees in the city and everyone was drinking as much fluid as they could. The majority, of course, were not on the water, but with this increase in plastic and glass a recycling plan had been adopted. Whether it was fully implemented – well, I saw it all being put into the same truck and, post-event, I couldn't find any reports to tell me otherwise. Every area had a sweeping crew and some of them had police protection (a bit of heavy-handed policing there), but the city was clearing up before the final whistle had even blown. There were also recycling bins dotted all over the various festival fan zones. On the top of each, along with the UEFA sponsor logos, was a question: "Who do you think will win?" Each bin had two holes, marked 'Liverpool' and 'Spurs'. Of course, it failed. It just wasn't a way of getting people engaged – because the majority of fans didn't care when they put their rubbish in the bins.

So, Champions League Festival. You know what? Overall, it was exciting. I got photos with all the different activations; I even went down to the Plaza De Oriente to a Giant Trophy Selfie Point. The four venues – Plaza Mayor, Puerta del Sol, Plaza del Callao and Plaza de Oriente – all historical venues, were changed for the weekend. The white palaces and statues were brought to life with chanting fans – who really were well behaved. Bands, DJs and dance groups provided a great cultural programme – but for me it wasn't a display of Madrid's culture, it was a display of what UEFA wanted to present. For example, the night before I arrived UEFA had brought in Dimitri Vegas and Like Mike – Belgian DJs.

It felt like Madrid was a landing pad for UEFA, yet the city missed so many opportunities (or maybe had their hands tied). Instead of the festival adding value to the city, it felt as if it was simply causing road closures and disruption. Economically, of course, there was a benefit – but as a festival attendee I didn't feel I understood what the benefits would look like. Major events should always have an approach that ensures the community integration is 100% throughout. Having observed events around the world, some arrive and deliver a change in the city, and others don't. The priority for Madrid was to put enough police out there to deal with the fans – who were not, in the majority, causing any trouble. I absolutely applaud the fans for their exemplary behaviour.

One thing to take away…

Did I enjoy the festival and what the Champions League brought to Madrid? Yes, because it was not a normal day in the city. But I feel that Madrid did itself no favours with streets packed with police in vans, waiting to jump – and jump they did. I witnessed an atmosphere that would be admired by millions globally, but was damaged by the police presence which, of course, was not at all reported. But thousands of fans passionately singing *You'll Never Walk Alone* is something to remember forever.

Back to Madrid…

For many, the next day was spent sleeping in a café before rushing to the airport. I had one more full day to go in Madrid. My whole trip was about discovery but also about understanding why certain events happen. Tonight, I was about to see something I couldn't watch…

Please be aware you may find this next part distressing. If you think you might be affected, please skip to event 42.

Event 41: Bullfighting

<u>2nd June</u>

Where do I begin? My heart was ripped apart. Tears streamed from my eyes and steamed up my glasses, making it hard for me to see. I was experiencing a middle-class/upper-class Spain that believes bullfighting is acceptable. I chose to come to this event because I wanted to write about things that in some countries are seen as culturally acceptable – but for outsiders, like me, they are not. I had a choice – and my choice was to buy an 11-euro ticket in the sol (sun) area. It was the first event I walked out of. Yet I want to describe this event exactly as if we were standing there...so let it begin.

I am standing outside an oval amphitheatre in Las Ventas, a middle-class area of Madrid. My heart is anxious. The bars are full of well-dressed Spaniards drinking small beers with their families. Everyone is wearing Lacoste – interesting. *'Bullfighting, sponsored by Lacoste-wearing Spaniards?'* For two hours I have been standing across the road, just watching the build-up of the event. Stalls are set up outside. Traditional Spanish treats like flans, olive oil cakes and, most importantly, Pick 'n' Mix are being laid out. Everyone is getting Pick 'n' Mix. I watch horse carts arrive on the far right and then I see large gates moving back and a thunderous sound suddenly occurs. It's the bulls transferring from the bull pens to the arena. My stomach has just flipped. Ok...ay. Yeah. I'm not sure how I am feeling at the moment. I think I'll go for a walk.

So, I'm now about a mile away from the arena. There are 45 minutes to go. I am still not 100% sure whether I am going to go near or go in. What to do? Okay, I need to go in – think of the message I could write; if it's as bad as I think it will be, I can reflect on it. I have my paper ticket and now I am looking to go in Gate J. Families and friends are all meeting up. There's a celebratory mood here. The place is busy with people from all over Madrid. I am going upstairs, into the arena, and I immediately start to see a divide. The well-dressed, middle-class Spaniards, who have brought their own cushions and are draped in every Spanish fashion label going, are over in the higher priced seats (which can cost up to 400 euros each). On my side is a mixture of tourists and t-shirt-wearing teenagers, who are on their phones and waving at their parents on the other side of the arena.

I walk in. I gasp. Wow. The place is absolutely packed. Like, absolutely mobbed. The sound is overwhelming. Suddenly I have a Spanish usher take my ticket. "Let's go." I am taken up to the 21st row in the top tier. If I look over the wall behind me, I can see the skyline of Madrid – but there's quite a drop, so I'll focus on what is in front of me. I am sitting on solid concrete and each block is numbered. There's no room to walk along the concrete and no hand rails. I try to avoid standing on anyone's feet. It's a health and safety nightmare. As I look around at my surroundings, I ask myself: "What if there is a fire?" I kid you not – it's an absolute mess and the event hasn't even started yet.

Okay… Suddenly music sounds and everyone rises. Up I go. It's time for the arrival of the matadors. Three black horses drag a trailer into the middle of the bullring. I wonder what it is for. The matadors are on horseback and parading around with straight backs, their hats lifted high into the air as they applaud. The horses are also parading their talents – for them, this is their moment to shine. Individually, the matadors go into the centre after the parade has ended and take the applause for what seems like forever. Off they jump from their horses, grabbing flags from large boxes that are at the sides of the barriers of the bullring; I am guessing these large flags are to 'seduce' the bulls. Okay. It begins.

I won't go into details, because it will break your heart. I am watching animal cruelty. I'm watching thousands of Spaniards on a beautiful Sunday night go positively crazy for what is happening – and it is the opposite of anything positive. What the hell am I watching? Why is this still legal? And then I phone my mate and say, "I can't do this." I start to cry. I feel so angry. This is only seven minutes into a three-hour 'show'. I know I've made a mistake coming here. The exit doors are locked – I heard them being bolted when the bull entered the arena – and I am stuck with hundreds of people around me. Nah nah nah – screw this. I cannot watch this anymore. The large bulls are being absolutely... Mauled is the only way to describe this scene. It's devastating. I get up. I began to film me departing, literally climbing across people. I almost ended up falling. I also get booed by a few people as I film (which was not allowed, unsurprisingly). I am leaving. A security guard has opened the doors for another guard to enter and I just storm right through. I can't not do it. I am angry and I am absolutely disgusted that WE as humans think that THAT'S okay. Yes, tonight I purchased a ticket and I could have chosen not to go – and still written about it. Instead, I have witnessed the brutality with my own eyes.

After I stop recording, I lean against the wall, my body in shock. I think I'm going to collapse. An usher comes over to check I am alright. Apparently, each night around 30 people collapse as a result of what they witness. There was no prior warning given about what would be on show. Some would say, "Well, you should know!" but actually I didn't, not really. The type of 'show' that was put on here is illegal elsewhere. Las Ventas is one of the last standing temples of bullfighting. I feel a bit light-headed, but I am okay – and I am very pleased to be out of the Madrid heat as well as away from the scene that's playing out within the arena. The noise is deafening – for many reasons. I can't understand how someone could cheer what was happening. How can you cheer the torment?

I ask the usher why this is seen as entertainment. He explains that most of the people that work there don't actually agree with bullfighting. But the money is good, and they can just stand and watch the crowd. "This is a dying sport," he tells me. I'm shocked, because politically, this sport has the backing of so many parties; it's usually something that divides political elections. My heart is still crying as he explains, "One day this won't be here – but while it is, Spaniards will enjoy." Enjoy what, exactly? Enjoy a mindless – AN ABSOLUTE mindless activity. And do not say it's part of Spanish culture. That argument is so outdated. Give me a break.

Eventually I'm let out of a side door, like a smuggler's tunnel, or an escape route only visible to those who choose to escape. Immediately when I get out, I drop to the ground. I feel ill. Travelling by myself is great, but this is the one time that – for the wrong reasons – it would have been good to have someone with me.

I notice individuals standing around with cameras. They are from an anti-bullfighting political party. They stand outside and record the opinions of anyone who comes out early – or at least ask them to explain what they saw. They tell me they try and get people's views on camera but sometimes it's difficult because they are so upset. I am in agreement with them. And I agree to go on camera. I explain my position as someone who has travelled the world and is now in a country that is blaming historical culture for the reason this still happens every Sunday night. I tell them how difficult it was to watch. I'm finding it difficult to speak; I'm a bit overwhelmed. They are grateful for my honestly and input. Just as I finish, another couple comes out, absolutely in tears. They say that 20 people had already left through the 'get out door' – mainly tourists. Las Ventas is only surviving because the elite of Madrid still support the event.

So – tourists go because it's obviously part of Spanish tourism. It is part of culture, and holidays are meant to be about discovering culture. However, this culture is outdated and backwards. But Spain has a very traditional way of going about things – so to demolish the bullfighting industry, which in 2016 was worth 3.6 billion euros – it's hard for everyone to agree. Because, of course, money talks. It can ruin the career of a politician to go against the grain. This grotesque sport should be banned. Immediately. However, in 2013, it was voted in law to regulate bullfighting as 'cultural heritage'. So take the heritage, take the political divide, take the economic factors – this is a huge issue for the country.

The establishment of Spain will stand tall for what they love. I saw it. They love it. The cry of 24,000 people is a large voice. Yes, there's a voice of division, but also a voice of defiance, which, sadly, is winning – while the country and animal rights protestors are losing.

I felt sick. I felt really unbelievably moved by this. After the event, I decided to write a letter to the Prime Minister of Spain and the Minister of Culture and Sport in the UK. Of course, I got no response. But I bombarded them with emails and real passionate anger.

One thing to take away…

I was raging…

Farewell, Madrid…

So, a bullfight and a Champions League final – my weekend, you could say, was pretty varied and packed. But I was really tired. Budapest was next and, sitting at Madrid Airport, I kept dozing off. I can remember lying on the marble floor, thinking: "If this is what I am like after 41 events, what will I be like when I reach 80!"

Hello, Budapest!

Similar to Prague, Budapest is a city that has built a reputation it doesn't really deserve. It welcomes an astonishing 30 million tourists a year – WOW! Huge numbers – and it does really well in managing them. It is a beautiful place to visit, and very safe, but it is also cheap – so it attracts a certain clientele, with stag dos coming from other cities and causing 'noise'. And then there's the currency, the forint, which is all about the coinage – and confusing at times. But I was here for St Stephen's Basilica…

Event 42: Organ Concert

5th June

St Stephen's is a Roman Catholic basilica in Budapest. Tonight, I was about to witness the organ above the altar come alive. However, my key reason for choosing this event (other than it being the only thing on during my flying visit) was about experiencing the diversification of the 'product' of the basilica. During the daytime mass there were empty pews, but that night everyone, whether Catholic or non-Catholic, was making their way in to enjoy a beautiful performance like nothing else – and it was sold out!

That night, I spruced up. As I walked out of the hostel I looked pretty on point – if I do say so myself. I went up the stairs to the basilica and gave my ticket to the staff member sitting at the desk. On the ticket and website, it had said to ensure to dress accordingly. However, most of the people working here looked like they had been to the seaside. My ticket for the concert cost 3000 Hungarian forint, which is £7.54-ish, and the place was full to the gunnels, with not a spare seat to be found. I was at the back (because I am a cheap skate).

As I stepped into the basilica and looked up at the ceiling, I was awestruck. About 1,000 people were watching and waiting and each ticket holder was shuttled back and forth by an usher. *Nice customer journey,* I thought. It was a bit rushed, but I did like the approach. However, the best part was the instruction set out on laminated paper. A sign said, 'Tourists stop'. So I stopped, while all the other 'tourists' carried on through. The Hungarian usher got angry as he stopped them and told them to return to the imaginary line. Once I was the chosen one, I sat down, to the sound of my chair creaking – excellent. All the chairs were locked together so when I moved, so did the whole row. Although I was away up the back, I could see the altar, the roof, the organ and everything that made the venue the most amazing and unique place I had experienced. My trip was about discovery, and in Budapest I was fast discovering how mass one morning can become a concert at night!

I looked around me. This was a clever move by the church for bringing in more income. This concert was part of a unique programme that offers shows three times a week during April, May and June. Of course, I was probably the only person in the whole venue who was critically analysing consumer behaviour and the success of the event based upon engagement and storytelling. I was ready for something special, but I didn't know my heart was going to be lifted and squeezed by this musical performance.

The concert began at 8pm and it was due to last one hour and ten minutes. I was already smiling, but once the organ began... WOW. Show on. I watched as everyone statically sat and just listened. It was very different from the atmosphere at George Ezra or Electric Avenue, yet this was quite a melodic musical performance. So, what was making everyone so static? Why was everyone stationary? I could not see anyone engaging with the music. Well, it was simple – to an extent. You could say it was the demographic that had chosen to come here. Although the voices surrounding me were global, the owners of the voices were of a certain age. And, of course, it's not really possible to do any Night Fever-type dancing to Mozart anyway. A new audience appreciating this event would broaden its reach – which can only be a good thing!

The concert was truly a unique spectacle. The music was not my cup of tea, although an organ is always an exhilarating instrument to hear. But then there was everything that went with it – like the organist rising from his seat at the end of every piece to bow for 45 seconds while we applauded. *Why is he doing that?* I kept thinking. It was all very traditional – and traditional is beautiful, but traditional can also get boring. After five minutes of clapping with a bit of music in between, I was bored. Respectfully, they needed to encourage a more varied approach here to persuade a different crowd to engage with and attend events in the basilica.

When I was leaving, I overheard a lot of people give their honest opinions of the concert. Some people found it quite remarkable; however, one man commented: "I cannot believe we sat and listened to that. His performance was not worth an event here." Now, if they were regular consumers of organ music, then fair enough – that's their opinion. The key question to ask here is: what was the selling point of this event? It was probably 30% the music and 70% the venue. Believe me, with the echoes of everyone talking and the music playing, it was an absolutely beautiful place to enjoy.

One thing to take away…

Diversifying the product that venues offer is important – but understanding the impact of the event is even more important. Get it right and you will hit the right note!

Budapest…

I had met lots of people during my adventure, but it was always fleeting. But in Budapest, for the first time in my whole journey, I had made friends with fellow hostel travellers. Here's one story that will always stay with me.

I was given a sticker. A simple sticker. The sticker was given to me by someone I met in the hostel. They explained the story behind the sticker, which was linked to the death of a young family member. She always dreamt of travelling around the world. She had even drawn a boat travelling on the seas, with the masts full and the wind taking the boat on an adventure. Sadly, she was unable to make that adventure happen. She died young, but her legacy was now being carried on by her friends and family – and strangers.

The sticker had been distributed to many of her family members and friends and when they travelled around the world, they would stick it somewhere in the city. The sticker said: 'Let Her See The World'. So, I took five stickers – one in my hand luggage and four that I would take to some of the other cities I would visit. I looked at the sticker to remind me how lucky I was. I loved the sticker concept – but more than that it was now part of my adventure.

Goodbye, Budapest…

Berlin

The adventure in Berlin began with a 4am departure from Budapest.

Let's get straight to the main reason I was in Berlin…

Event 43 – Carnival of Culture

<u>7th–10th June</u>

One and a half million people over three days – the equivalent of the population of Estonia. Wild, eh. The world was literally descending on Berlin for a unique celebration of culture, something unknown until it's packaged and presented to be discovered by those who are intrigued. As millions arrived to celebrate the event, it was set to be a clash of noise and feelings.

Global events have a significant impact on our world. But this event does not, in my opinion, receive the status it thoroughly deserves. Carnival of Culture is exactly why a well-positioned TV documentary about events is needed. It happens as part of Pentecost Sunday, welcomes all cultures and creates beautiful moments of humanity. We all need to experience standing in the middle of the parade, immersing ourselves and enjoying it. Chicken from Jamaica, Greek Moussaka and so on – today I was tasting and smelling the world.

I arrived in Berlin on Friday evening, early enough to appreciate the celebrations. The festival began properly tomorrow; really, this evening was more about food and drink, with some stages becoming active. Each of the different zones around the festival had a different vibe – although the smell of weed permeated nearly every corner of this 5km site. I took a leisurely stroll while listening to music from the stages, which were brought alive with large amplification and had a true 'free spirit' feel to them. This was a modern-day urban attempt to cast freedom towards the handcuffs of society. However, a cloud of 'politics' from the officials hung over the festival, with security and police still controlling the event.

Carnival of Culture originated in the 1990s as a protest against xenophobia and racism, and today it has become a flowerbed of emotional connection with culture. However, I felt slightly scared as

I strolled in on that Friday night and was met by machine gun-wielding police staring at every single person, who then had to weave through the police trucks and large garbage trucks that were blocking the busy entrances. However, once through the gates, the free event welcomes you with open arms. Music could be heard everywhere – from the speakers on the sides of the food trucks, and from areas with names like 'Charlie's Beach' and 'Clave Latina' – every corner had sound. And the place was packed. The streets of Blucherstrasse, Waterloo-Ufer, Zossener Strasse and Blucherplatz were BOUNCING! The sunshine and relaxed atmosphere had encouraged people in, and I would say the green space had more sunbathers in it than a Spanish beach on a hot day! Berlin was really bringing it. I decided that evening to do something I had always wanted to do at an event. I stood in the middle, closed my eyes and opened my ears. The noise... I was lost for words. I really was listening to Berlin's beating heart – and it pulsed.

The beautiful sound was made up of conversation, laughter, food orders and more – all in German. This is what events bring – noise. But sometimes we miss the noise because we focus on *looking* at everything. Sometimes we forget to listen. Events are truly about bringing people together and leaving them with a whole new terrain of experience. This festival was about engagement and while I was probably standing in the most awkward place, I was listening to happiness and the pure joy an event brings.

On Saturday I arrived at the festival site at 12 noon. I walked about and listened to some music and found a completely new area to enjoy – welcome to the DJ booth. It was already packed but there was no trouble here; it was all about expression. To the right of the DJ booth was a very relaxed and somewhat 'hippy' area where you could chill on bean bags. I strolled around, watching people playing Jenga and relaxing. In the same area, thousands of people were chilling, smoking weed, having a beer and dancing – expressing their inner and outer souls.

At 2pm I was told to head to the green cabin at the red brick church to meet the organisers, Steffi and Nadja. This was a rare opportunity to talk with the organisers of an event while the event was happening. As I knocked on the door, I suddenly realised I didn't speak German. I panicked. Quickly, I Googled 'English to German...' A man, quite tall and well-built, spoke to me in German. Then, thinking I was a random tourist, he told me: "Wait, wait."

Steffi then appeared, after realising I was the Scottish guy from the emails, and introduced herself. Her involvement over the last 19 years has shaped this festival and parade into a really local event – even though the audience participation is in the millions. Steffi apologised for the delay and said there were a few issues. I was happy to wait all day for her colleague, Nadja, but then she suddenly arrived. "My English is not that good..." she said.

I laughed. "I can't say that in German!" Nadja was very busy and we would get five minutes into a discussion and something on site would happen, like the police would come to the door, and so on. Every time I said, "Look, please, this has been brilliant, but you can go back," but she'd insist on speaking more. And before you knew it, we'd got into the real point of the event. It wasn't just to close the streets and have a celebration. This was about culture, and it was put together by volunteers and community groups from all over Berlin and Germany for seven months prior to the event. Their mission was to represent the global community and this year 74 different cultures were represented by people who live in Berlin. The event was held in the middle of the city, a park in Kreuzberg, which was not the safest area, but it was a community that had been transformed positively thanks to the event.

The only things they had a challenge with were convincing the city about the location and demonstrating what the event could bring. The festival was about free spirit, and this ethos came from the organisers, who just oozed so much love. Yet the security measures for the event didn't fit the purpose. A welcome from a police officer with a machine gun was the opposite to what they were trying to achieve.

From sponsorship to security, policing to politics, we discussed it all. I couldn't argue with Steffi and Nadja's passion and commitment. How many other event organisers who were dealing with security concerns and planning a parade of 73 floats the next day would invite me in to sit and chat? The door would have been closed before I even knocked.

They were not trying to push the event online; that wasn't for them. They had some information on social media – but even then it wasn't updated or shiny; it was very basic. The stages were also not technologically fancy. There weren't even any screens; they were simply scaffolding with some lighting, and that was it. Quite literally, the stage was set for cultural entertainment, not something shown on a big screen. Different communities, cultures and families came together for this moment. With so many complexities this street festival could teach the world how to conduct an event, but really the participants themselves were creating it. If you don't want to buy jerk chicken, no problem – just dance down to the stage playing salsa music or head bang over to the stage with the rock band.

I'd been talking to Steffi and Nadja, who were fast becoming my new best friends, for 30 minutes. I was just about to say I'd head off when I was introduced to more of the team. Before I knew it, I'd been sitting there for over two hours talking about Carnival of Culture. We spoke about flow of people, the challenges of financial funding, about local government – and they showed me maps and booklets as evidence of everything they said. Some of the team spoke to me in German and Nadja and Steffi would translate. I hope they never change the way they run the festival because it was so beautiful and demonstrated such team spirit.

Just before I left for a seating area well away from the over one million people waiting to watch the parade, I was handed a VIP pass. I was honoured. As they gave me it, they said, "Tell us tomorrow what you think we are doing right and wrong," and I agreed. This was no longer just Matt from *Around the World in 80*

Events – I was with friends who love events! At 7pm I met up with two people I'd met earlier that day in the hostel, Anna and Lorcan. We got some food and I bamboozled them with my thoughts on how this festival was the ultimate in escapism. By the time I'd been talking non-stop for two hours, I think they were as tired as me...

The next morning, I watched as the police arrived on their bikes. They'd make a call and suddenly a pick-up truck was there towing away parked cars. The streets were empty but every so often a feathered man would appear, dragging his kit to the start of the parade. It was one of those moments where I kept thinking: "Is this happening?" The parade didn't start for another three hours but the preparation was exhausting just to watch.

From 8am until 10:30am I wandered around to get a feel for the parade, which would be made up of community groups representing different global cultures. At 9am I received my first gift, from a kilted German. He was part of the Jamaican/Scottish group, who were sponsored by a Jamaican Rum company and were handing out beautiful hip flasks from float number 31. I saw the kilts and got a tiny bit excited. I introduced myself, said I was from Scotland and asked if they were too. "No – we just drink whiskey!" was their reply. Excellent! Every year they travel to Scotland, and every year they take part in the parade to share their love of both Scotland and Jamaica.

Every five minutes, thousands more people arrived. The groups participating – 4,400 performers – were getting ready for the biggest show of their lives. How many events would be successful with a Scottish pipe band on the back of one lorry and a rock band playing *Sweet Child o' Mine* on another – not to mention floats representing so many other cultures? And yet despite the differences, it worked.

Before the parade began, I stood a slight distance away and watched *Love Korea* set up. The dancers wore beautiful white hanboks and those playing the traditional Korean drum, the buk, wore yellow. There were people accompanying the drummers who wore large hats with peacock feathers. This was a huge tourist push by *Love Korea*. The embassy had popped down to say hello. Although it was not officially part of any tourist campaign, it felt like they were selling their country.

Festival of Culture was the perfect antidote to all those traditional boring trade shows, because the dream was to sell countries and their cultures to thousands of young people who were really up for adventure. This was an active, live and purposeful show with an energy that would eclipse any other tourist trade show. A lot of the groups had actually been invested in by embassies and private sponsors, to enable them to have the best float. Because – surprise, surprise – the floats were judged at the central part of the parade. I'm not sure what the winner received, but it was more about pride and being able to say they had won here.

All the floats were different. India was showcasing five floats, from five different societies that had been set up by Indians who called Berlin their home. "Hands in the air!" A Bollywood DJ kept encouraging everyone to bounce and there was a lively atmosphere everywhere you looked. The Japan float offered something I had seen before: a mikoshi, a sacred religious shrine, very similar to the one at the Penis Festival. It was being carried by about 30 people who kept screaming what can only be translated as "Ahaaaiii Ahaaaiiii." The rhythm was quite catchy and reminded me of the sounds I'd heard in Tokyo.

As more participants arrived, I was stunned by the costumes, which were almost unbelievable. I felt as though I had been transported to a carnival in Rio. At the front of the float were banners and behind the banners stood Nadja and her team. 'Miteinander', the banners proclaimed, which translates as 'Together'. Remember, this festival originated as a protest; its whole purpose was outrage against inequality. Now being part of something was the whole philosophy. Inclusion was the pinnacle of success for this event. The banner that fronted the parade led not only a parade and its people; it led a movement of inclusion. It led to a purpose for this event that, for three days, had eclipsed a community and was embraced.

The parade began with a police convoy in front of the banner. About four police vans, with one commander calling the shots through his walkie talkie. His head popped out of the sun roof as he shouted at the young officers along the route. It was like Julius Caesar had returned to be the controller of the parade. But really, he was just a pace maker, and there was an officer by each float monitoring the speed the floats were moving. They were also telling people to stand behind the lines at the kerbs. I felt that was just them showing who was boss – but really, culture was the boss today, and the millions responsible for creating a peaceful and harmonious parade were in control.

I could write for days about every small part of this wonderful festival – but I will leave you with one thing. A parade with millions of people is not only about the organisation of operations. It is about the freedom you allow the participants to have. At the gates of the event there were no bag searches – and this was deliberate. Instead, people could be, bring and do whatever they wanted. Millions did – and being with them gave me such an exciting feeling. This was an event of complete escapism.

One thing to take away…

Festival of Culture was a place for cultural freedom and social interactions that in other places would be limited or quashed by rules and expense. It was a place of trust. This was cultural exchange in action. This was a way of life. It stood up for cultures and communities. And once each stage had been dismantled and each community group had packed up their drums, the one thing left was the sense of being together and the understanding of what they did for the future.

Goodbye, Berlin...

Berlin was short but so sweet! As I arrived at the railway station, I looked at the information board and noticed that the 5:30am train to Frankfurt was missing. The current time was 5:11am... Where was it? After investigation, I discovered that the train had left at 5am – but: "It's okay, sir, we didn't tell anyone so no problem, we will put you on the train at 6:30am," said the man in the customer service booth. Excellent. Anyway, goodbye, you left me with more culture than I had experienced so far!

Hello and goodbye, Frankfurt

I now had an overnight stop in Frankfurt...

Hello to Zurich

Welcome to the most expensive city I think I visited. Zurich's city centre has outlets for every high-end fashion label going. The city is busy with events during the summer, and tonight I was off to the circus.

Event 44: Cirque du Soleil

12th June

The sun was scorching on the day I was due to see *Cirque du Soleil: Toruk*. It was a beautiful day and it was also the day I was going to be meeting the CEO of the venue that the show was taken place tonight. I had emailed the venue ahead of my trip to request a meeting to ask some questions about the customer journey. They agreed, but then the day before the meeting they emailed me to say: *'We do not think there will be any benefit for us to meet with you...'* It hurt. It really hurt. Because firstly, they didn't see the value of my project (I mean, maybe I was biased because I'd been planning this for seven years), and now they were slamming the door on me with quite a rude remark. So, I sent them a reply.

"Dear....

Thank you for the email. It's a real shame that the CEO has decided after three months of communication that he is no longer available. It's a real shame also because this is a global project that is being picked up by many media outlets and also being read by thousands online, and it has a growing social media presence. In 2019, this project is the only – ONLY! – project of its kind and it will rock the events world."

Within five minutes of sending my email, I had a reply.

"Dear Matt,

Sorry for the confusion – please meet tomorrow at 3pm.

Kind regards,

... "

Wow – that was quick. And the meeting, shall we say, was interesting. First, the venue very kindly gave me a ticket to the event that was happening that night. I was then told the meeting would be 30 minutes and no more. No problem. However, the receptionist seemed more interested than the executive assistant and the CEO. The conversation went something like this.

Me: "What's the direction of the venue?"

Them: "To be the best."

Me: "What's your customer journey strategy?"

Them: "We don't have one."

Me: "What's your catering outlet like?"

Them: "World class."

I mean… Where do I even begin?

I felt like I was hovering over someone who was just throwing words at me and hoping I would back down and not ask any more awkward questions. I challenged him every time he gave an answer that had nothing to back it up. And when I went to the show that night, the venue was falling apart inside – literally, paint crumbling off – and the food prices were double everything outside.

So, I had a ticket for the event that night, a performance by Cirque du Soleil – and… well, brace yourself. This event was one of a four-night tour of Switzerland by Cirque du Soleil, the spectacular acrobatic brand that produces many different shows that are toured globally. As I walked into the venue, I was excited. My ticket didn't scan, but instead of calling a supervisor they just waved me in. Literally, "No problem, happens all the time." I was beginning to be proved right in my thinking about the venue. Posters for other events were dangling off the walls, with one bit of Blu Tack holding up a corner. I looked around at the spectator engagement stalls. *Camel Cigarette Company.* What? Wait – what? On the opposite side from them was a vaping company. So far, the only other event in the world where I had seen a cigarette company involved was in Indonesia. I was so confused – and this was before I'd even walked into the actual arena.

As I moved further into the crushed waiting area, screens were advertising future shows. The screens were very bright and you could not avoid them. In one way, it was fantastic. But they were missing an opportunity to create a fantastic interactive experience ahead of the show tonight. I didn't need to know what was happening here next year. This could have been a chance to share the show's hashtags and really build some excitement. And then, for the only time in my whole journey, I was given earplugs. The performance was 100db and apparently, to comply with local law, they had to give out earplugs – but it was your choice whether you wore them. Sound regulations had been introduced in February 2019 following a research group study that ordered that all performances were to limit volume to 100dB(A) through an hour of a show – with no sound to ever exceed 125dB(A) at any time.

I watched the flow of fellow fans of the show. Many of the attendees had just finished work or come straight from home and off they went, straight into the arena. With half an hour to go, I noticed a change. Food purchasing was slowing down and now it was mainly alcohol and ice cream. When it was quiet, I decided I'd have a purple vegetarian burger before I went in; the purple colouring was added to make it look 'fancy'. The burger was freezing cold and went straight into the bin.

At 7:20pm the bell went off and I got to my seat, which was exactly where I thought it would be after checking the map online. A couple were sitting to the left of me and another couple to the right. Instructions came through the PA: "Please download Toruk: The First Flight app to be part of the show, during the show." It all sounded very interesting. The app would allow in-show effects to be viewed through my phone. Intriguing. I was very much like, "This is exciting!" Unfortunately, the venue had no WiFi and my phone data didn't work in Switzerland, so I had no joy. But watching others…well, actually, no one really used the app. Everyone was struggling to download it because they couldn't get a signal in the venue. Not so clever. I could feel my positive energy disappearing very quickly.

The show began at 7:32pm. *Here we go*, I thought. I was about to see Cirque du Soleil; what an honour, so exciting. Ten minutes in I thought *What is this?* The first half of the performance had a lot of dance on the floor. Not much extreme Cirque excitement. Weird, I know, but honestly, it was a truly underwhelming experience. Not only that, the whole venue was just... bland. No atmosphere. The sound was disappearing into the metal beams of the venue structure. I was literally in one of the dullest venues I had ever experienced. Up to now I had visited, toured, seen or just gandered into over 50 multi-purpose arenas and this one was way down there – sadly.

So, the atmosphere didn't feel right and the actual production was flat. And then – I kid you not – people began to leave. Remember the couple to my right? Suddenly they rose. The husband glanced at me and gave me a nod and then they literally climbed over two rows, which were empty, and left. The venue had been half empty before the event and each section had only half of the allowance – so before you knew it, it was even quieter. I counted about 50 people walking out during the first half; they all had their jackets with them and no one came back in.

During the interval I went to the exit and watched probably 150 people walk out, never to return because there was a no re-entry policy. I watched as the security team tried to encourage people to stay and shall we say there was complete outrage? I'll admit I enjoyed some of the show, but other aspects, including the app not working, made me feel even more demotivated to watch the second half. In the end, I decided to leave because I had a bus to catch at 6am the next morning. So I was leaving the show early for a genuine reason.

It was not the performers' fault; all the performers were really pushing the limits. It was just that the show didn't meet the usual expectations of what Cirque delivers. And I think that's what happens when global brands become so huge. People begin to reach conclusions about the show before they actually see it. I thought it was a real shame. However, the overall impression I took away as I jumped back to the station was that this venue needs to get up with the times. No longer are venues just spaces for events; they are centres of engagement, enjoyment, attraction and escapism. Sadly, this one missed the spot. Hey, they can't be perfect all the time – but they can at least try.

One thing to take away…

It was intriguing to see consumer behaviour in a town where people obviously have money and are able to walk out of an event and make it seem as though they're not really bothered about losing the ticket price. The loudest part of the whole thing was the fact that the venue was half empty… Welcome to the complexity of events.

Goodbye, Zurich…

Zurich bus station for Flexibus destinations was madness. Literally, if you didn't ask the driver where the bus was going you would most likely miss yours. I was there at 5:30am and my bus hadn't arrived. I watched as a lot of people realised they'd missed the bus. It was sad – and there were a lot of tears.

Zurich – you know what? It was nice. I even made a great friend in Shaun, from Dublin, Ireland. The two of us are completely different in every single way but we laughed so much. That's why I love staying in hostels. It's an opportunity to meet people who are the opposite to you but for the amount of time you're there, you have everything in common.

Hello, Paris (and Mother Lamb, with my hay fever tablets and Scottish macaroon)

I decided to meet my mother for three nights in Paris. She was flying in from Glasgow and I was bussing it from Zurich. I arrived in Paris the night before my mother arrived.

Paris is the city that many have on their bucket list. According to the Paris tourist office, Paris Info, the city welcomes 30 million visitors a year. Thirty million! Wow! I think 10% of them were in attendance at the Eiffel Tower as I wandered around. Today was a

Saturday and over the last six months, Saturdays in Paris had become known as the day of the Yellow Vest Protests. As I wandered through the city, armoured police and water cannon trucks were awaiting directions – it was a weird experience. Originally, the protests were begun by motorists out in the rural regions protesting against fuel taxes and wanting economic justice. This turned into a protest against the government and before you knew it, an online petition had collected a million signatures and the protests began, with protestors calling themselves the Yellow Vests. It was a mini revolt against the political establishment – basically, an event. However, when it becomes violent, does it lose its impact?

Today it was very much a dying trend. Two billion euros had been wiped from the Paris economy because of the Yellow Vest protests. Many people had felt the economic impact and had now dropped their support. Today there were only about 100 people there – and me, watching from a distance. It was a shame.

Event 45: La Nuit du Handicap (The Night for the Disabled)

<u>12th June</u>

I stumbled across event number 45 because I came out of the wrong railway station. Without doubt, it was one of the most heart-warming events I have ever experienced. I'm smiling as I write this story, which will give you an insight into something more than just an event – it was about hope.

When anyone draws up an event plan or idea, it's always about trying to be different – and this certainly was. Some events are for commercial purposes, sometimes it's for city planning purposes and sometimes it's just someone thinking outside the box. But this was a night designed to enable people who are outsiders in society (as it says on the event's website) to become part of society – for one night. The event is organised annually by the Catholic Church in association with many other organisations. The objective was to allow those who felt locked up at times, with nowhere to go on a Saturday evening, to come together to showcase their talents and be free. Just to be free. Those who have disabilities may not find it easy to socialise in town. Think about that before I tell you anything else. This event was being used as a way of enabling others to be free. It didn't have any major sponsors. It wasn't about commercialisation. It was about acceptance. This is what I had been searching for throughout my journey.

In previous years, the event had been held at Notre Dame. However, after the fire that destroyed the iconic building a few months earlier, the event had been moved. They had decided to set up in a square called *Republique*. When I spoke to the staff at the information desk, they explained the change but also talked about the improvement it had brought, because the event could now be held in the city centre and be very inclusive. Although the Catholic Church is the main organiser, there were no religious symbols anywhere in the square. The flat surfaces were important, as many people were in wheelchairs or had mobility requirements. All the toilets were fully accessible. The stage was also fully accessible and every 30 minutes a new choir appeared. By changing the location, the organisers allowed more passers-by to appreciate (and donate to) the wonderful meaning behind the event.

That Saturday evening I stood and watched as people glided through bubbles in their electric wheelchairs. It was so simple, yet so important to many. I also heard a choir whose members were deaf but who expressed and sang louder than anyone could ever have imagined. The bubbles were in an area called Bubble Corner. What a sensory overload! It was amazing. Blow bubbles and burst them immediately, or whizz through them in your wheelchair. Or, even better, experience the Fragile Express. Just think about that. The word 'fragile' being used to explain who was on board – but oh, the freedom this train was giving! The 'choo choo' noise was chanted as it looped around within the event space. Laughter and positive energy brought a wave of happiness to everyone. I watched as the train went past, some of its passengers feeling the wind in their hair for the first time as they waved at strangers and smiled. I cried. I literally cried. Why did other events not see the beauty of something like this? It was all so simple. It was all so magical. Bubbles in the air were met with sheer joy. Bubble wrap had been laid out for children and adults to burst. Paint and paper were set up on the floor so people could create magic with handprints. It was so messy, but so beautiful. You could even create wheelprint art for children who were unable to get on the floor – I mean, YES to the world of inclusive fun.

A large banner was draped over the fountain – a welcome sign, with two hands shaking each other. Bright colourful bunting hung all over the event site. It was a haven of peace and love in a minority. The visuals were designed to deliver excitement, the opportunity for expressive freedom and inclusivity for those celebrating.

In practical terms, I was met at the gate by ushers and event staff, all of whom were volunteers. The first people I met were a blind man and another man who was signing in French. Security personnel checked all the bags (because of the Yellow Vest protestors in the area; there was pretty tight security to protect those at the event) yet I had never seen a more amazing welcome. The two men were loving life. They couldn't communicate – but they could. They really did. Then I watched them leave for their break. The man who was deaf took the blind man's arm and placed it upon his shoulder. The guide dog followed. It was quite extraordinary, so amazing. Now, just think about this. These two men were both volunteers and their smiles were worth more than any salary for that role. It was just breathtaking to watch. And I knew as soon as I saw it happen… *This will be in the book!*

I got talking to a few volunteers who told me that the event was about education and awareness, but also an opportunity to come together. The disability-positive space was something I didn't expect. Anyone, with any level of ability, could come and have the time of their life, whether this was laughter therapy or noise creation. The more I lapped up the event, the more I began to question why all events cannot be like this. The event space must have been about 100 metres by 75 metres – it wasn't huge. But it was huge. The impact was huge. It wasn't busy. But it was busy with hope. The stages were packed with people who possibly don't go on a stage or have a chance to perform normally. It was their opportunity to wave to family and friends and allow their voices to be as loud as they wanted. Many of those participating wore noise cancellation headphones and many had supporters around to guide them on and off the stage. I ask you now: when would you ever decide to go to an event like this? Most probably not. Because it's not flashy or attractive or backed by major sponsors. Some may disagree and say it's appealing because it's different. But it's not,

not really. What it is – is exactly what the world needs. Inclusion and togetherness. Remember the banner in Berlin: 'Together'? This was it, but on a much smaller scale. Next time an event is happening, ask yourself what effect it will have, not just on you but on the wider world.

One thing to take away…

My heart cried. My eyes opened. My message from today is simple. No barriers should be put up to prevent someone smiling on the Fragile Express or in Bubble Corner. Moments from this event stayed with me the whole trip. I am so glad I got off at the wrong station.

Mother Lamb arrives!

With my bags by my side, I jumped on the metro and it was time! Mother Lamb was arriving and it was a huge deal. For the next three nights I would be able to switch off and have a proper meal. I thought I would treat my mum to something special and bought us tickets to see Elton John. Very exciting! Mother Lamb didn't know anything about it. Brilliant! I picked her up from the airport. My sign simply said 'Mother Lamb – who has my macaroons and hay fever tablets…' Basically, my mum's case was full of everything I needed for the next part of the trip – clothes, a new shaver, sweets, a new belt and a new notepad (a special one I had bought prior to my adventure). I was super excited about everything in the case – oh, and about seeing my mum, for sure; she was a close second.

We spent one day exploring Paris and chatting about my trip – and I reassured Mum that I had eaten everything I could. I mean, she didn't believe me. But she did say, "You're looking well…" Must have been all those ham and pineapple pizzas.

Then I had to tell my mum about the surprise – but I had realised two days before that I made a HUGE mistake. I had booked tickets to see Elton John in Lille instead of Paris (mind you, he wasn't playing Paris until the following week). I had to book trains, find another hotel and get ready, because we were off to Lille. My mum was both annoyed and excited by my usual 'oops' approach. So, here is the story of Elton.

Event 46: Elton John in Lille

18th June

This was one from my personal bucket list. I have appreciated Elton John's character and music for as long as I can remember. The *Goodbye Yellow Brick Road* tour was travelling around the globe and landing in hundreds of arenas worldwide. At 8:07pm in the Stade Pierre Murrouy in Lille on the 18th of June, it was time to see the showman himself. But instead of a showman, I saw a musician. As he walked on stage, there were no fancy flares as at previous performances – it was one man and his piano.

Obviously, because I wanted to soak everything in and experience the security, the welcome, the food concessions and the merchandise, we arrived at the stadium even before the police briefing had happened. "We are far too early, Matthew," my mother gently reminded me after I had dragged her from the station. I'd forgotten what it was like to travel with someone. About 10 people got off the train with us and now all 12 of us were walking up to the Stade. I was in event mode and I laughed. "Switch off, you're with me," Mum said. "I am not sitting here if you're going to be like this." My mum hates it when I am in event mode, when I am constantly analysing everything – but that was the trip. I had to. I needed to. *Did they say hello to you back there? What was the food concession unit like? Could you read the menu board?*

The welcome was… okay. And, thanks to my mum, I got to see a different perspective of the whole adventure. Outside were all the concessions and because we were early, we bought coffee and some delicious cold chips (all I ever wanted) while we waited. We'd had dinner already but fancied a wee snack. I bought a 20-euro programme because why not? And we took photos next to the different photo opportunity walls. It was a dream. It was special to spend the time with my mum. The customer service was amazing and the show began.

The show itself was emotional. I have listened to Elton John's music for years and never did I think I would be able to listen to him sing live with my mum by my side. We have reasons for engaging with events and tonight it was about engaging with a performer who I had grown up with. Meanwhile, my mother was still going on about the weight I was losing. "Here, go get yourself more chips…"

Everyone has different reasons for going to events and my reason was to spend time with my mum and tick Elton John off my bucket list. The piano. The voice. The overall performance. The use of the screens. The artwork. The stories. Throughout the show (and also in the programme) Elton was very honest about how he almost didn't survive addiction. It was a great experience.

But there were some event operations that didn't go so well. Obviously, being up in the gods, we could see everything. The rows of seats started about 15 feet from the front of the elevated staged, which was about 8 feet in the air. Great stage, great screen content – visually perfect. All the 'on the pitch' seating was in zones. Each zone had a letter and at the beginning of the show everyone was seated correctly by security guards. However, once the show began most of the security guards were deployed to other areas – actually, all of them. Not one guard was in the area. I am sure you will be able to guess what happened next. About 20 minutes in, a group of five people came running down and sat in the middle aisle to watch the show. The way they were seated, the security sitting stage left didn't clock them and people around didn't really bother complaining. But three minutes later that group of five had become forty. And then people standing on the balcony noticed, and started coming down the stairs to the main arena. Suddenly you had chaos. About 500 people were running around and blocking the views of everyone in the seats – some of whom had paid around 300 euros a ticket – and also blocking the fire exits and causing congestion. And then the 500 people doubled. Every aisle was blocked. Suddenly, security appeared from backstage and started removing people from the aisles. I was trying to tell my mother about everything that was going wrong but her response was just "Shut up – I am trying to enjoy the show."

The music stopped. But it wasn't because of the crowd; it was Elton's water break. For 30 seconds you could see the security guards trying to disperse everyone – but no one moved. Elton was literally sitting at his piano with the stage manager pointing at what was going on. And then the show went on. Those sitting in the seats at the front had totally lost their view and the ultimate VIP experience they had paid for.

We loved the show. The most amazing thing was how stripped back it was. No massive fireworks; it was all about Elton John's voice. *Goodbye Yellow Brick Road* was exactly the song it was. The videos being played behind had been created to fit with the songs and the mood. Videos included some of his past work with the AIDS Foundation. Some showed black roses being broken, bit by bit. Some were of the original music videos – including *Tiny Dancer*, for which the video was only released for the first time two years ago. Elton mentioned that this was his 50th year of touring. He had been on a blessed and incredible journey. Although he says it in every city he tours, you could tell that this speech has an impact on him. Touring was and is a big part of the success he has had. However, in the programme he highlighted that he will not stop writing music but he will not be touring ever again – after he has finished this three-year tour. Retirement fund.

Ten minutes before the end, I said to Mum, "We either leave now or we wait for the feather boas to be in front of us on the train and for 70,000 people to leave at the same time." I knew there were only two routes away from this stadium: the railway station or the car park. Nothing else. This meant we were going to be trampled getting out. So we left the stadium via the ground floor, with Mum poking her head in to see from a distance the last song. I would say we had the best seats. Yes, miles up – but the true scope of the spectacle could be enjoyed.

As we crossed the bridge, we looked behind and saw the audience descend. I watched people running from the stadium and then others following – because of course that is what you do. "Come on, Mother, we can do it. Run!" I said.

"I swear, Matthew, I am not going to another event with you again…" she said, laughing.

Thousands upon thousands of people were heading towards the station. It was a small station but the priority was not the safety of the passengers. Oh no. It was ticket checks. Everyone had to have the right ticket or go to the machine. I mean – okay, I get it. Some events I had been to included your transport ticket with the event ticket, but this was a money maker for the train company – and they made sure of it. The police (who had large machine guns) and security were the most delightfully cheery bunch of humans I had ever come across and were very focused on catching a 3-euro fare dodger. As we headed up the stairs you could hear the wave of people getting closer and closer. "You just dragged me from the stadium," my mum said, laughing, as she found a seat. The carriage was empty. I laughed too, because sometimes you can have the perfect evening and then all it takes is a delayed train on your journey home to derail your happiness.

However, our journey had almost been derailed before the concert. A police officer brandishing a machine gun had spun around and lost control of his weapon. Yes. Fear eclipsed Mother Lamb and I felt as though we were in a *Die Hard* movie. The gun swung around and then dropped to the ground – all in slow motion. Time stopped – as well as my mother's heart. The officer had just laughed it off as if it was a normal thing.

Overall, the production, the management of the stadium, the expectations, the food and so on – everything was there and was above averagely good. It was a great opportunity to see a musician of his class and era – but also to tick Elton off my bucket list.

One thing to take away...

Music adds value to our life. It adds joy. It can represent the good or the bad times. We can see music as not only a commodity but also an opportunity for expression. People will pay good money to consume something special to them. For thousands tonight, it was an opportunity to say farewell to Elton and thank him for his music – and Mother Lamb and I were part of that.

Lille...

We only stayed for one night but that one night was truly spectacular and not enough time to experience such a glorious city. Lille is so much more beautiful than Paris. Paris may be steeped in history and has developed a better tourism strategy, but Lille has some golden nuggets. From 27th April to 1st December 2019, Lille hosted an event called *Lille3000 – Eldorado and Mexico Mio*. Over 700 events took place, with art displays of the US Mexico borders and exhibitions in a gallery in the town centre of Lille. Part of it was also about 'displaying global migration issues'.

Farewell, Mother Lamb...

Oh no... It was the time that I was dreading. I now understood how my parents felt and how heart-wrenching farewells can be. I was given my instructions. We flipped everything in my suitcase. I took all my Scottish macaroon with me and my mum took my dirty washing and some event memorabilia. And off she went.

Literally no time to cry. I was back on it for another event. Tonight was Scotland vs Argentina in the Women's World Cup. Would it be sorrow – or surprising success?

Event 47: Women's World Cup – Scotland vs Argentina

20th June

With my Scotland top, on I stood in Zone J watching a 3 – 0 lead by the Scotland women's football team disappear from the nation's hands. I was gutted. I had about 50 French people around me, all obviously supporting Argentina and laughing at me as excitement plummeted to despair – and it was all FIFA's fault. But we will get to that in a moment.

I arrived six hours early for the match – mainly because I was missing my mum already, but also because I wanted to get in early enough to check out the fan activations and see how much effort FIFA had put into creating such an amazing experience. I wanted to understand the FIFA Women's World Cup objectives in terms of fan engagement and the overall difference between this and the men's competition; although I have never been to the Men's World Cup, the event is for sure more engaged with by the global football audience. I was ready. I was excited. But my days, I was far too early! The ticket office, where I had to pick up my pre-purchased ticket, opened in four hours and the activations – well, there was nothing here. The security and police hadn't even shut down the roads yet. So, let me set the scene for the Women's World Cup 2019.

Held in France from 7th June to 7th July, a total of 52 matches were being staged in nine cities across France. In total, the global TV audience was approximately 993.5 million people. The competing teams represented 24 nations in what was being billed as the biggest women's football tournament ever. In the past, the Women's World Cup had been laughed at, but this was not a joke – actually, it was the opposite. It created role models and opportunities for women's inclusion in sport. Women's football may have become a trend, but it was also making a statement, mainly on social media, which included a push forward in gender equality pay rights. The conversation was loud and continuous throughout the tournament and it began to gain a huge media and social media presence. It was reported the total financial gap between the men's and women's tournaments was $370 million! Let's break this down.

Men's World Cup

- Prize money – $400 million
- Preparation costs – $48 million
- Club compensation – $209 million

Women's World Cup

- Prize money – $30 million
- Preparation costs – $11.5 million
- Club compensation – $8.4 million

(All estimations, and discovered through various channels.)

Could it be any more obvious? However, FIFA released a statement that the pay imbalance reflected the revenue produced by both competitions globally. So, in my esteemed and well-read opinion: this is a load of crap. At the end of the final on Sunday 7th July, chants for "Equal pay!" broke out around the stadium. This was not only a message to FIFA – although it was needed. It was a message to the world. And it was loud. And there is absolutely no excuse for there to be such a wide gender pay gap.

Back to the empty car park…I was standing at the stadium. As time progressed, I began to see the lack of attention that was being paid to the set-up of the activations. What we saw was… well, still nothing. It was 6pm and the match was kicking off at 7:45pm.

Scotland fans arrived with noise and great energy – really creating their own spectacular atmosphere. The ticket office was due to open at 6:15pm and the gates at 6:30pm. The Kia car sat – idle. Nothing was happening. It literally felt like a Sunday after the night before. But it wasn't – this was a big night

The quality of football during the tournament had surprised many locals, which meant tickets were being touted (in events terms, the demand was higher than supply). The queues for the box office were huge and Scottish fans were arriving en masse – like they were up for invasion by song. Outside the venue it was heavily policed but really – as with most major sports events – there is and was no real trouble. France, however, is always on high alert.

The fans were full of energy. But it was such a shame FIFA didn't deliver the standard of activation I would expect from an organisation like them. Instead, we saw activations that were poor. By 6:45pm everything was happening. One solid card frame was placed for people to stand behind and get a photo on. Great. It was like we had stepped five years back in fan management. Stickers were handed out by four PR staff – and that was it. Nothing really spectacular. I was disappointed – and this was before a ball had been kicked.

Women's football had really exploded in 2019 – and yet the stadium environment and the effort put in by FIFA and the activations were lacklustre. There was nothing here to say: "BE PART OF THE BEST EVENT!" Instead it was more like, "We had to be here to fulfil an obliged contract." It felt defeated. I know FIFA is one of those organisations whose public image is at times about money or sometimes even about controversy, but I was hoping to be blown away. It's easy to welcome fans with a "Hello, welcome to the best tournament in the world" and an organisation like FIFA has the resources to make that happen. Hey, FIFA, give me a ring and I'll explain what should have occurred!

The stadium was full, absolutely packed with large groups and lots of Scottish fans dotted around. The Women's World Cup slogan was #daretoinspire. Instead of being simply a game of football, this was an opportunity to inspire – but unfortunately the lack of attention paid to deliver even a basic welcome was totally uninspiring. And when it came to the local security company – I don't know where to begin. It may seem like I am being really critical but when the staff are away from position and in the hotdog queue with their supervisor joining them while lighting up a cigarette in the venue – when the whole place is at its busiest – well, I just don't know what I can say. I was lost (although I did get to my seat despite there being no signage in the stadium).

I was sitting in the front row next to a French family who were part of a larger group. I talked to the leader of the group, who spoke extremely good English, and she explained the event had given local community groups 50 tickets each. So, the stadium was full – but a vast amount of tickets had been given out for free – including the ones I was sitting next to. I could argue about what is better – empty seats, or devaluing the price of a ticket by giving them away for free? I worry about the product appreciation...

However, I was absolutely blown away by the noise, which was not at all driven by anything in the stadium but solely by the behaviour and passion of the fans. This was an opportunity to give women's football a position in the world and here in the stadium I felt the wave coming fast. Outside was boring, but inside was anything but. For years the phrase "the standard of women's football" was always followed with "...is not that great" – but the women's football I saw here was extraordinary. The speed of play and the fearlessness of launching in for tackles was brilliant to watch. There were no complaints. There was no diving. It was a beautiful game of football and I was getting right into it. I – along with a quarter of the stadium – was screaming every time Scotland got the ball and when a goal went in for Scotland... well, you would have thought we had just won the World Cup. After the third goal, I was on cloud nine.

However, this moment was not to last. The players on the pitch did nothing wrong. It was the referee. The decisions going against us were absolutely ridiculous (us… see what I did there? I am now part of the team – clever in terms of psychological belonging). My enjoyment of the game was being affected by the referee. The score was being affected by the referee. And before long, the boos began from Scotland fans. The screen said 90 minutes, but the 5 minutes of additional time was never played. Scotland had one last chance, but the referee didn't give it. Instead there was sadness; a real crash to the ground for athletes who didn't deserve to have lost.

The Scottish players were running about, pleading with the referee. I couldn't believe it. I just couldn't understand what was going on. But this is the point of professional sport: the audience is so engrossed that emotions can get in the way of understanding the game. The Mexican waves going around the stadium at the end were a great way to finish but I could only sit and think… what if? What if we had actually won?

FIFA had well and truly really shown their true colours. I actually sat next to someone on the train home who worked for FIFA. They said they agreed that during the last 10 minutes the performance of the referee was not ideal. The MC even joined our carriage and before you knew it we were all in agreement that the whole thing was chaos. Absolute chaos. I really felt for the team – they had played so hard and the referee's decisions had changed everything. Welcome to football…

Overall, my experience of one match in the Women's World Cup was interesting. It did a lot for women's football – it showed how epic it is – and I loved knowing that Scotland was part of this change. I had an emotional connection. As for the host country, France, you could argue they didn't take it as seriously or create as much impact as they could have.

One thing to take away…

If you are ever 3-0 up, never think you have won…

Au revoir, Paris...

Paris, thank you. You were where I got to spend time with my mum, and see Elton John, yellow vest protests, a night of inclusivity in action and Scotland play their hearts out. Paris gave me a lot. Oh… and I went up the Eiffel Tower. A lot was done! Now to Charles De Gaulle for my flight to Minsk…

Minsk...

Welcome to Belarus, known as 'Europe's last dictatorship' (the leader refer's to himself as Europe's last dictator)… and getting out of the doors of the airport was proving difficult. The sweat was dripping down my head as the army checked each page of my passport. I was literally shivering inside with fear. I was here for the European Games and because I had a ticket and was visiting for less than five days, I was visa-exempt. "Okay…" The three army staff passed my passport on to someone higher than them, but before they even gave her the passport they saluted her. I felt like I was going to salute too. "Make sure you have your ticket," they told me, as I heard the almighty sound that I love to hear at an airport – CLUNK – the stamp being crashed onto your passport.

I spotted a huge well-branded desk between an ice hockey table and a glass-box taxi office in the middle of the airport, which had smoke billowing from the middle-aged woman who looked as though she had never left the box. (Literally, it was a weird glass box with curtains!) Sitting at the desk were about 10 volunteers. "Are you with the games?" they asked, as they rushed at me like I was a quarterback at an American football match. I think they were just desperate to be doing something. Some of the young students wanted to practise their English; others were more focused on collecting pin badges.

I went outside and found a 12-seater minibus heading to the railway station. Brown curtains draped on each side, and the seats were brown with orange patterns weaving through. It cost £2 for the 45-minute ride. I recognised some of the faces. Four of the military women from border control were on the bus – all now in civilian clothing as they had finished their shift. They were glammed up to the max, laughing and joking. I sat there in silence at the back of the bus, slightly awkwardly. On came Tom and Jerry! Wait, what? Am I dreaming right now? Nope, I am not. The couple next to me said "I guess you're not from here..." and I laughed.

I got off the train at Plosca Pieramohi station and tried to find the gate to leave. The problem was there were 12 exits and I was going around in circles. I felt a tap on my shoulder. "Are you here for the games?" Kind of... Suddenly, this person, Kat, was saying they would now take me to my hostel. It a genuine gesture!

So now to the games!

Event 48: Minsk 2nd European Games Opening Ceremony

22nd June

I had purchased a ticket for the Opening Ceremony of the 2nd European Games, the first multi-sport competition Minsk had ever held. Minsk was draped in every colour of Europe and the slogan *Bright Year, Bright You* was clever. Every event I went to had a different slogan, and I liked Minsk's approach and what they were trying to achieve. They were opening Minsk up to the world. Fifty countries were represented – and it was a big deal for Belarus to allow so many people into the country from so many different nationalities.

The Minsk 2nd European Games lasted for nine days and saw over 3,500 athletes come to the city to compete in 23 disciplines across 15 sports, including 200 medal events. The opening ceremony was the opportunity to showcase a different side of Minsk and I was ready for a spectacular show. The tickets were translated into both Belarusian and English. Considering nothing else was in English around the city, I was pleased to see this event had spotted the opportunities it could tap into. On the last mile up to the Dinamo National Olympic Stadium, I was met with volunteers. Forced high fives. Foam hands in the air. Waving flags. It was very similar to most mega sporting events; the same model of engagement, just in a different country.

"Let's together make this evening unforgettable..."

And with that, it began. On each seat around the 30,000-plus stadium was a yellow bag. In the bag were programmes, leaflets, a wristband (for active use during the event) and a fan. I loved watching the big screen and seeing the montage that played, the camera whizzing through the countryside of Belarus. It really was showing a side to the country that many didn't know about – including me. It's a modern country with pockets that are hidden and discreet. The people in the stadium were erupting with energy. The noise was penetrating my ears. The emotion I felt... I wasn't here for the whole competition but I absolutely wanted to stay. In a way, it felt like this was a chance for Belarus to establish itself within the world. The announcements were in Belarusian, some in Russian and all translated into English. Surrounding me in the seating bowl were many Belarusian citizens, the majority of them middle class. Most people were dressed extremely well.

The ticket said the ceremony began at 8pm. I went at 7pm to experience the welcome and by 8:30pm we were still on the warm-up. The actual ceremony didn't start until 9pm, and for that hour everyone sat there kind of bored. There was no real "Let's get going!" like when I arrived. Instead, it was quite dull. And then, just as we were about to go live on television, it began and the ceremony came alive. Ablaze with noise. A production that you would see at any other major sporting competition – and it was here. It was huge. It was bright. White lights beamed through the sky and across the stadium. The music was loud. The story of the ceremony was based on Belarusian folklore; stories about mythical characters. The event was building up to a big finish with 'the flame of peace' being lit in a cauldron. Interesting. A flame of peace – which, post this event, we would find out would be quickly extinguished and was immediately pointless. This was Belarus offering a handshake to the world. But, prior to the lighting of the cauldron, the Belarus president spoke, and it caused a standing ovation from the spectators. It was a proper rousing call. Some of the speech was ad hoc – with no English subtitles – but some of the on-script and official lines are below.

"Such moments unite nations, which means the great Olympic mission of presenting an arena for peaceful and honest rivalry of athletes and countries will always be of current interest and in demand...

"Let's work together to move all the modern political battles to sport venues for the benefit of mankind. Let's fight for the title of the most powerful country only through sport."

To be fair, it didn't rouse me but it certainly was a welcoming hug. And I felt it. The European Games felt like a cheaper version of the Olympics but world leaders from other governments were present and there was an apparent sense of unity, a spirit of togetherness. The Russian Prime Minister was also there (a huge political message being sent here).

Back to the ceremony. It was draped in culture and really was a platform for Belarus. Over 1,300 people were involved, including 500 artists who created the art and made the digital plans come alive. Volunteers – about 300 – ushered people to their seats. Some spoke English and some would state, "I do not speak English, I am sorry," and that in itself was more English than I could speak Belarusian. I really did admire the desire to be so welcoming – although the government was being very cautious. Government officials were in the stadium, wearing armbands and checking that everyone was in their allocated seat – including me.

It was now 9:30pm and time for the arrival of the teams. Never have I experienced the roars from the crowds like I did in Minsk. Nationalism and patriotic behaviour – cheering for your country and waving your home nation's flag – is a common output of these type of events. I was in my Scotland top – even though Scotland were part of the United Kingdom at the event. Everyone around me – even those who were well-dressed and there alone, like me – got up and cheered as loud as they could for the home nation. The flag was waved with uncontrollable energy by the athlete, who was obviously being carried by the spectators in the arena – but also, in my opinion, politically. It was electric. Completely electric and completely manic. Each spectator was oozing pure pride. It was amazing. I wish more events had this powerful energy, which sometimes they lack. Instead what we appreciated here was citizens able to show the world the pride they have in their country – and the freedom.

The Games' programme only cost £5, which seemed very reasonable for a collectable mega-event programme. It wasn't really up to the standards of an Olympics or Commonwealth Games programme, but it did include an illustrative retelling of the story of the ceremony. Minsk 2019 really did understand the consumer experience and had put effort into delivering things powerfully. The music (way loud) and the production were all extremely thought-provoking and created an everlasting memory.

The production on the large screens was good. The pyrotechnics went off in succession as fireworks fired into the sky over Minsk. Everything was in sync, including the lip-syncing by the musicians at the end. A production like this always comes across better on the TV and the large inflated bull all to do with folklore. *Preset FX* were part of the special effects team for the ceremony and I must congratulate them on the implementation of the flame lighting up the final cauldron. The silver cauldron itself was quite spectacular craftsmanship, with bells and olive leaves twisted around it. Then the torchbearer lit a flame, triggering rockets to fire towards the cauldron (most certainly a health and safety nightmare) – but it worked and was successful in lighting the flame for the 2nd European Games.

Large screens, mascots doing handstands, incredible choreography, intense waving by the volunteers in the arena and that big bull... The bull actually featured in the UK newspaper *The Times* as a top 10 photo from around the world in sport that week. It was a visually amazing experience – and I was there.

Overall, I had a really enjoyable time. To sit through an opening or closing ceremony at a huge sporting event is always special. It gives you a different type of emotion. It gives you a feeling that is hard to explain. For me, it gave me an experience like no other, which I shared with 35,000 people. And I was excited to be in Minsk for two more days and hopefully to see some sport.

One thing to take away…

I couldn't mention everything. From the stickers to getting a photo next to the volunteers in the Spectator Services Umpire Chair holding a microphone… but I'll leave it there. I do wish, though, they'd told me when I went in at 7pm that I wouldn't get out until 12:45am and home until 1:50am… It was a long show!

Minsk… it's not what you expect

Kat took me to the most amazing places in Minsk. If it wasn't for her knowledge of Minsk and willingness to share her city, I would have missed it all. From a random tap on the shoulder to now me seeing Minsk!

I was in a country that was secretive to the outside world, but while standing on top of a pile of rubble, drinking lemonade and waiting on my fish and chips, which were being served from a recycled army van, I was falling in love with Minsk. You could argue that modern countries in the western world have more traits of dictatorship than those countries with known dictators. Yet I had walked through the streets of Minsk with no worry or stress. I jumped on and off the Minsk Metro like I was born in the city. DJs wearing fashionable clothing were performing on top of wooden pallets. It was warm. It was enjoyable. And it was constantly evolving.

It was time to depart Minsk. I was gutted, absolutely gutted to be leaving. Memories of this destination will stay with me forever. Off to the airport I go. Thanks, Minsk. And thanks, Kat – you star. I'll be back, Belarus.

As I was writing this chapter in 2020, Belarus was revolting against the political regime following a political election. The country is trying to change – but the politicians are refusing. It's become a very dangerous place and I feel sorry because I know the country has so much potential. Violence has escalated and the streets are no longer safe. Sadly, I watch, helpless. I really feel sad for Belarus.

Now to Riga...

Riga was a turning point in the whole trip – for a short time, anyway. It allowed me to take a step back but also a step forward. The streets are very narrow and cobbled and many of the buildings are pastel in colour. I saw this quite a lot in Europe, but in Riga it was more common. Riga is known to be super cheap – which again means the weekend city hoppers arrive on a Friday and leave on a Sunday. I was here for a Latvian festival and then I was out of here... Well, so I thought.

I was staying in quite a rough area of Riga. At first, I couldn't understand why the accommodation was so expensive. But then I realised I had deliberately picked a week when there was a national holiday. I walked into the hostel, unpacked my bags and left. Because today was Ligo Festival...

Event 49: Ligo Festival

<u>23rd June</u>

"You couldn't have chosen something more Latvian if you tried," said the older gentleman who was with me on the plane from Minsk to Riga. He was heading back for the night to go to the Ligo Festival. As we flew over Riga, all I saw were marquees dotted everywhere. This was a huge celebration, but for many it was also an important rite of passage.

What is Ligo Festival? Well, this question was something I had asked myself and I still didn't really understand until I got talking to people. Ligo Festival is the celebration the summer solstice. Taking place in mid-June each year, the greatest holiday in Latvia is known to be an ancient fertility festival that is part of midsummer celebrations. It originated in farming villages during the start of the harvesting season, when pagan farmers held celebrations. Crowns of flowers were placed on the women's heads and men wore crowns of oak leaves. Every city in Latvia celebrates and in Riga it begins at 6pm. I had arrived at 5:30pm and knew I needed to get straight down there. The actual programme began at 7pm, with the last performance scheduled for 5am.

The festival was open to all and anyone could come in through the gates – guarded by police, who also wore crown oak leaves and flowers. Many traditional elements were still in play, even within the large city environment. Usually people would go to the farms and countryside but instead the cities were the place to be. Burning of the bonfires was happening right in the city centre, on the banks of the River Duagava, were two huge wooden structures that were going to be burnt to the ground as a symbol of cultural representation. These wooden structures were set alight at sunset.

To my mind, the place was alive with this unique festival. And it was televised on Latvian TV live. Culture was represented through traditional bread making, flower arranging, beer tents, food tasting – the whole thing was extraordinary busy, but it worked. Actually, what I saw here was the majority of the festival being shaped by locals – which doesn't happen regularly at outdoor festivals. It was all very charming.

Lines of wooden pallets were spaced out throughout the site. Suddenly, just as the sun set, a fire was lit in the middle of them and up they went. Traditional singing of Ligo folk songs echoed around as people began dancing. In the 1980s, songs and poems were a strong part of the resistance movement during the years of Soviet rule. Now, 40 years later, these melodies are used as part of a celebration; they are still symbolic of some type of gentle resistance against the regime, but they are also part of the Latvian identity.

It was about 12:45am and I was starting to get pretty tired. There were long queues for food, and beetroot soup and potato pancakes, the national dishes of Latvia, were being scoffed at picket tables. Everywhere was packed. Inside the marquee there was a different feel to the outside areas. It was quite family-oriented. The entire site was about 1km long and there were at least 70,000 people packed in. All around the countryside similar celebrations were happening. This was a time when the country united and came together – not for tourist purposes, but for their own national pride. What a wonderful thing.

This wasn't a commercially driven event. It was all about peace and culture. I had tried to contact the council for a meeting but as I watched council vans and lorries stop for their drivers to grab a bite to eat while being dragged along by party-goers through the streets, I realised why they were too busy. By 3am the wooden pallets were still alight. A rota had obviously been created because every hour another man wearing fire gloves would take charge of observing the giant burning towers. I mean, if one collapsed, a lot of people would be hurt. Still the music played. The bands on the stage were dancing non-stop. And I noticed that no one had their phone out, recording. I felt it was something to capture – but for many it was about enjoying the moment together. This was a festival about being with each other – and being together was exactly what was happening. That was quite humbling.

This festival dates back to the 17th century and, apart from the master-engineered stage and the high-tech cameras, everything was very much like it's always been. Games earlier in the day, fire, flower arranging and so on. There was no major drinks company sponsoring the festival; it was simply a community integrating during the darkness of the night and waiting for the sun to reappear for the summer solstice.

Eventually it was time to leave. I was knackered. Police and fire crews stood at the gates. Toilets overflowing. People still arriving. The streets busy. And everyone was just waiting for the moment when the sun rose. It is believed that those who stay up all night and wash their faces in the morning dew are guaranteed beauty all year. Unfortunately, I was not going to have this luck.

Overall, I did not just go to a party – I went to a Latvian celebration that was the heartbeat of the Latvian summer. It was the biggest and best event I could have experienced, and I am so glad I did.

One thing to take away...

I have never seen the embracing of cultural events as I have in Europe. There is something quite special about European culture. Some countries are unbelievably outdated but still part of modern-day society and that is the reason the tourism industry in those areas exists and survives. Riga was literally on fire with this offering.

Riga...

Riga was a real treat. I loved the atmosphere. And I had my photo taken next to the famous clock tower at the town hall.

It was the night before I was due to move on to Bologna, and then to Sienna.

But that was never to occur.

Instead of having a good night's sleep in Riga, I was ill. So ill that, the next morning, the hostel phoned for an ambulance. I couldn't stand. I had a fever. My temperature was over 39 degrees and I was not at all well. The hostel looked after my bags and I was taken to hospital. I left the hostel on a drip, helped down the stairs by two paramedics with another two ready to catch me. It was surreal. I was scared for the first time on my trip. And I also didn't have my phone charger – OH OH. Apparently, I had some type of poisoning – and it was serious. I was put on meds in one hospital and then transferred to a specialist unit on the outskirts of Riga. For three nights I was with four other people in a room in an infectious diseases unit in the middle of what I can only describe as a forest. Three nights with no telecommunications or friends or visitors. I wasn't allowed to walk along the corridors but my surroundings were very weird. The building had been an infectious diseases unit for more than 50 years and had an obvious Soviet Union design. The doctors and nurses spoke zero English. Luckily Lucas, who had swallowed half of the Black Sea in Lithuania, spoke perfect English and translated for me. "You're not going anywhere for a while," he said, after listening to the doctor check me out.

Have you ever just sat and thought, *was this meant to happen*? For me, maybe it was. By the end of my time in hospital I had taken everyone on a journey. They knew all about cricket in India, swimming in New Zealand and even the Penis Festival. To my biggest surprise, my phone survived three days without being charged – a miracle! On the last day Lucas' girlfriend brought in a charger and I was able to charge it up and call home.

"You must rest. Your body needs to recover," said Rita, the doctor, in broken English.

"Okay, so what if I fly home tonight?" I asked. The doctor laughed and shook her head. But I knew that was the only way I would rest. So, I booked a flight home and made my way to the airport, after going back to the amazing hostel to pick up my packed bags (thank you!).

While I was sitting for two hours waiting for my plane to be called, I heard crying. In front of me was a table where a girl of about 17 was sitting with a man I found out later was her father. Tears were pouring from their tired faces and the father was drinking. Shot after shot. Whiskey and then beer, like he was a machine. Yet it had no effect. It was obvious something was wrong. For an hour they sat, and I sat. We didn't speak. We didn't need to speak for me to feel the anger and emotion that was coming from table seven. They were constantly on the phone – sometimes on loudspeaker. The girl was in charge; the father was more focused on his next drink. Occasionally she would leave the table with the phone and walk briskly to the sales desk while he just stared through the television. They left with literally no luggage. The girl had a handbag and the man had a wallet. That was it.

The barman knew I had been listening. He spoke good English and he glanced at me as they left. "They are having to go home as his wife has died suddenly." I stopped. The girl's mum and his wife had died. Imagine being in that situation and having no control over how fast you could get home. Imagine being stuck at the hands of other people's judgements. Just think about that next time you're on a plane – everyone on it has a completely different reason for being there and sometimes it can be the most heart-breaking...

Back home, I relaxed. I breathed in the pure Scottish air as my mother treated me like a king – and then I booked my flight to get back onto my trip. It was time to experience more events. Edinburgh to Bologna – here I come!

Bologna...

After arriving in Bologna two hours late, I headed to the taxi queue. As I waited, I got talking to two people behind me. "That flight, what was it like...?" We had literally bounced into Bologna. Denise and Stephen were the nicest couple I could have wished to meet. We exchanged numbers and for three days we were travelling friends – it was superb!

Bologna is in the Emilia-Romagna region of northern Italy. Beautiful iconic buildings stand tall over the terracotta rooftops of the abundance of flats. The towers, Basilica di San Petronio, the Fountain of Neptune within the Piazza Maggiore – all are beautiful places for visitors to enjoy. In terms of population, the city boasts 388,000 proud residents who really do meander the streets. Bologna's tourist board was running a very successful campaign, *Be Bologna*. All around the streets were colourful squares with large bold writing proclaiming 'Be food...', 'Be cinema...', 'Be music...', 'Be Bologna...' Clever. Such a clever marketing plan. But this wasn't intended for international visitors – it was for locals.

Event 50: Bologna Outdoor Cinema

2nd July

Thousands of white plastic chairs were laid out in Piazza Maggiore. This free activity took over the public square. Coffee and cigarettes were the only consumables being consumed in the cinema. For a whole month, the programming was brilliant. Each night the free Cinema Ritrovato Festival was full. The outdoor area held 2,500 people seated on white poolside-type bucket chairs. Any spare space around the chairs was also taken. The festival lasted from June until late July and I was there on the 2nd and 3rd July.

With a comfortable 25-degree heat bouncing off the marble, I felt a bit sweaty as I stood at the side. I sensed a real forward-thinking approach to events in Bologna. An opportunity to see a different way of inclusion through events that mean something directly to Bologna's residents. The movie was presented and curated by cinema lovers, culture groups, the City of Bologna and Camera Di Commercio, Industria, Agricoltura e Artigianato – an official group of some type. It was evidently a great partnership, bringing possibilities and opportunities.

At the entrance to the site was a large board, roughly 10 metres high and 30 metres wide, showing the programme of movies for the duration of the festival. Crowds of people were checking out what was on tonight and next week – before it was all over for another year. I loved listening to a language I had no way of understanding – but whatever they were saying, I knew they were excited. Excitement sounds the same in any language. I expect they were arranging with friends to attend the cinema and make sure they were part of this city event. The plain white chairs positioned in the square were full of a community that brought love to the city streets.

On the first night the movie was a French film with English and

Italian subtitles. No spare seats here – it was a full house. But it was not ticketed. First come, first served. I watched families descend with picnics into the rows. People meandered from restaurants and grabbed seats at the edges, and would either leave when they were bored or do the opposite and stay the whole time. I watched first dates and those married for forty years take their seats to enjoy the spectacle. I watched the conversations turn to silence as the movie took over their evening.

The first night opened with a welcome speech from the festival director, who spoke for an astonishing 12 minutes. Even I was getting a bit yawny and the crowd had completely switched off. All they wanted was to watch a movie. Some would say this gave it more depth than just any old outdoor cinema. Watching different generations sit row after row and watch movies they hadn't seen before – well, there was something really nice about that. I loved just seeing everyone sit in silence while they read the subtitles. Many couldn't understand French, so it meant we were all in the same boat. The first night was beautiful. No one can take away the fact that the seats, the cinema screen, the lighting and the silence from thousands was charming.

But on the second night the event descended into chaos. I was sitting on the marble steps of the Basilica of Bologna, waiting for my two new best friends Denise and Stephen and watching people enjoying the film. Bologna seemed to be a city that looked after its people. I observed the red bricks, the bell tower, the street names engraved onto the walls, the basilica towering over the white chairs in the square – the whole thing was charming.

And then I saw a thunderstorm rolling in. Lightning bolts could be seen over the terracotta tiled roofs and the wind picked up vigorously. Panic set in. There was no rain as yet – but then it began. An announcement was made by the event's spokesperson and suddenly everyone watching the film stood up. Police were on patrol each night, and there was always an ambulance in attendance, but tonight it was late arriving. As it pulled into its usual spot, about 2,000 people were briskly walking towards it. You could see the confusion. The police were totally caught off guard as they sat in their cars and watched everyone leaving with no prior warning. The staff seemed a bit lost. The wind was strengthening and the lightning bolts becoming ever so close. I actually did fear slightly for our safety because above me were electrical cables and metal fencing. However well organised this event was, it was clear that emergency planning wasn't thought through. The outdoor cinema had been constructed to give the city something special, and health and safety in Italy – well, you could argue it was left at the door.

I was very impressed by the *Be Bologna* campaign and couldn't have felt more welcomed if I tried. It was bright in colour, it seemed diverse in the free activities it offered, and it was bold and innovative. The question I know you are no doubt asking is – what do we actually gain from free events? Why didn't they charge? The answer is it allowed locals to have a bond and a connection with their town. Why should a public space always be used for commercial income? Why not use it to benefit the local people? The campaign was different and clever. These events may be forward-thinking and yes, there's a cost – but actually the return is tenfold through the satisfaction of the residents.

One thing to take away...

Anywhere around the world has the ability to create a strategy such as *Be Bologna*. Introducing this type of plan takes guts – but guts pay off when a city is aiming to be different, engaging and bright. It's a vision of community brought together. A vision of a city with purpose.

Bye Bologna...

Obviously, I was meant to be taking it easy. I was extremely tired. Bologna should have been the perfect place to rest –but to be fair, it was constantly a succession of activities, because I was in a city whose first objective was for the people. So for two hours I sat in the shade on a ledge in a street far from the tourist route, eating grapes, drinking water and writing in my journal…

Wow. The heat. Europe has switched on the radiator. What am I doing? I am sweating and I have not even walked much today. I am excited for a good sleep tonight. But I am also looking forward to getting to the next destination. As I sit under this archway, I think about its history. I think about the Italians who have used these archways to sell fruit. I think about the balconies, and the black cast-iron fences draped with flowers and plant pots. I think about the colourful shutters and wonder who lives in these concrete flats – so airy, yet so warm. The columns are huge. I am loving this. I know it's not on my list of things to do in Bologna – but wow, I need this. Just escape.

I loved Bologna with all of my heart.

Goodbye, Bologna. Goodbye, Denise and Stephen!

Pamplona…

Okay… the following chapter will give you my very honest account of what Pamplona offers in terms of a globally recognised bucket list event. I knew I needed to attend cultural events that may be misunderstood. I needed to understand them for myself so I could appreciate the true meaning. And now I was about to experience something that – for 19 events out of 475 planned during this particular fiesta – was the reason animal rights groups protested against the city of Pamplona. Welcome to the Running of the Bulls – San Fermin Festival. Before we begin, let me confirm I do not agree with the idea of using animals for entertainment – but the story of San Fermin as a festival (without the bulls) is quite extraordinary.

Event 51: Running of the Bulls – San Fermin

8th July

Welcome to an event steeped in culture and tradition but also plagued by trouble. Sexism and animal abuse cloud an event that, for generations, has been symbolic in a small town in Spain. Culturally, San Fermin is a celebration of Saint Fermin, the patron saint of Pamplona. It's a celebration that blends culture and religion. It brings together millions to engage with trade stalls, fairs, drinking, food – oh, and the ever-debated bull runs, which then become bullfights at night. Over the years it has been told as a story of adventure and adrenaline. Unfortunately, I will not be able to describe, discuss or give you a blow-by-blow outline of the festival – because it was all too much.

My friends were Piers and Kelsey. We met in the hostel and I was able to go to the festival through their eyes. They had arrived separately and didn't know each other, but they each had a massive amount of knowledge about the festival.

Fortunately, I was able to get a media pass, which gave me an amazing insight and perspective. I needed to collect the pass ahead of the festival from the art exhibition hall. The streets were silent. You would never know that over 100,000 people were currently estimated to be in Pamplona, getting ready for the festival to begin the next day. I collected my bib and pass – which gave me two days' access to the bull run – and my other media items, including a handbook called *The Professional Guide to San Fermin*. It was a dossier of everything I needed to know; critical information including the dos and don'ts. The media pack was going to help me see a different side of the festival but still enjoy the event.

The festival of San Fermin dates back over 700 years and there is nothing comparable anywhere in the world. Across nine days, 475 events designed to encompass everything about Pamplona are held on the festival site and in citizen spaces. Many of the events are steeped in tradition, such as the *Chupinazo* (a rocket launched to start the festival), the *Riau Riau* (a dancing procession), *Comparsa De Gigantes Y Cabezudos* (a parade involving big-headed papier maché giants), *Estruendo* (a musical parade where people play whatever they can find, including pots and pans) and, of course, the *Encierro* – the running of the bulls. The city of Pamplona is surrounded by a fort but for nine days it was taken over by world adventurers who were seeking out more than just culture: they were looking for their bucket list moment. Backpackers had descended with the intention of getting drunk and taking the best Instagram photo, rather than asking questions about the cultural symbolism.

Let's get straight into it. Firstly, I had to look the part. Every second shop in Pamplona sold the 'uniform' of white trousers and white t-shirt.

The bus terminal had opened the floodgates and thousands of people were arriving every hour. It was mobbed with people with luggage, backpacks and accents from all over the world. Wearing the media bib meant I could get away with asking people where they were from. Austria, Switzerland, Brazil, America, Australia… it was like the United Nations of culture chasers.

Barriers had been erected early to stop people from going into certain areas, but the control mechanisms allowed a certain amount of normal life to carry on. I saw police being deployed around the city. I saw marquees and stages being rigged and positioned. Non-essential shops – sewing supplies, kitchen appliances and so on – were locked up with signs on the doors saying 'Closed for San Fermín'. The festival was closing local businesses but that was okay because no one arriving here now wanted a microwave or a washing machine anyway. On the other hand, restaurants and bars were full to capacity. It was all about feeding the party rather than feeding the community. Locals were also descending and celebrating – which added to the questions I already had about the authenticity of this festival.

The hostels were packed. Top tips being shared over the dinner table. Where to go and not to go. What to eat and, of course, what to drink. Most of the hostels were empty during the day but full between 2am and 4am. All you needed was two hours' sleep before you got up and started partying again. There were plenty of bags under eyes as people stumbled awake and got ready.

Let me introduce you to the opening event, the *Chupinazo*. I watched in wonder as a mass of red scarves were held to the sky and then wrapped around their owners' necks once a firework had exploded in the Pamplona sky. On the town hall balcony, from where the rocket was fired, the municipal representative, the manager of the city, the VVIPs, the VIPs and the rocket man stood. Quite a moment for them all. Music was played by bands on the ground who were being protected by police, who were surrounded by thousands of party-goers, mainly Spaniards, who controlled who was allowed to get close to the main attractions. All those who stood staring up at the balcony began to chant "San Fermin!" The neckerchiefs were once again held high. A song was sung. But it was all about getting as close as you could to the town hall. Thousands were crammed in.

They estimate that, during this event, 12,500 people are crammed into the square. There's a wave of heads – all bopping. The pure animation and enthusiasm of the crowd was all aimed towards the narrow balcony. The bands played loud. The festival had officially begun. I was in awe. *This was just outstanding,* I remember thinking. But still, I was confused knowing that tomorrow, bulls will be running through these streets.

The day of celebrations continued. I got four hours of sleep and was up at 4:30am. I am not kidding. The bars were still open. Literally, it's a 24-hour festival and thousands of people were still stumbling through the streets – but there were also hundreds of locals who were ready for the first day, which is the most important to them.

The running of the bulls begins at 8am and, in the four hours before it starts, the streets of Pamplona are prepared for something the whole world is watching. While I waited, I spoke to many police, medical and media people. I watched the barriers for the bulls being lifted into place by the team from the city council. The buzz became louder. Time passed quickly. By 6.30am, the police had begun patting down anyone in the running area. Cameras, phones and alcohol-scented breath were not allowed on the route. No one was allowed to be on the run that might jeopardise the safety of others – especially when several tonnes of bull was sprinting towards them. I appreciated the measures put in place but really, health and safety went out of the window. I suppose bulls with horns are not dangerous enough, never mind trying to take a photograph. It really was a mind twist.

I was about to witness bulls sprinting towards humans – but just a reminder: this was not the true essence of San Fermin; this was just one part.

A lot of those taking part were foreign tourists, engaging with activities they didn't understand culturally but had seen online or on television and decided they needed to try. I was astonished to hear the accents. The Spaniards and locals who were involved weren't dressed in the traditional white and red colours of Pamplona. Instead, they were wearing special tops in colours representing their home towns and villages. This was about pride and competition. They all knew each other and the police didn't search them; they were more focused on the tourists.

The night before, PETA (People for the Ethical Treatment of Animals) peacefully protested the event, as they do in Pamplona city hall square every year on the night before the first run. Because I had my red media bib on, I got to interview someone from PETA and understand why they had come – from the Netherlands, UK and France, to name but a few, as well as Spain – to spend three nights in Pamplona. Really, they were adding to the local economy – but when I mentioned this they said: "Well, it's important for us to be at the forefront of the argument and being here is critical. We must stop this through action and demand. We will not stop. We will do this for the bulls and for the future of culture. This is not culture."

They made it very clear to me what exactly it was that PETA does not like about the running of the bulls:

- Bulls being run through the streets after being steered into and held in small areas, which creates a blind rage in the animals, making them ready to run and be aggressive.
- Humans aggressively tormenting the bulls as they run.
- Running along cobbled streets.
- Being killed...

I felt sick, for sure, knowing the impact watching and, in a way, supporting an event like this would have. The run would end in Plaza De Toros and the people from PETA were disgusted, as was I, that baby bulls would then be sent into the arena for hundreds of runners and the 24,000 people cheering to goad and intimidate. The actual killing of the bulls was a sold-out spectacle for the Spanish middle and upper classes that I really did not wish to support or attend. PETA wanted the running of the bulls to be cancelled – forever. Unfortunately, the political pressure, cultural heritage argument and economic pressures will never lead to cancellation of the event.

So now you have an overview of the animal abuse issues at this event. Sexual harassment is another issue that has been covered by the media at the event for some years but has been happening throughout the event's history. In 2016, several sexual assaults were reported during the festival, which led to the implementation of new policies. I have never before heard of a global festival needing to implement policies and run a marketing campaign focused on promoting safe spaces, showing a commitment to eliminating sexual assaults and encouraging women to participate and feel safe.

The campaign's nine objectives were aimed at making San Fermin feel more equal. When I first arrived, I saw a giant red-handed statue and wondered why it was there and what it stood for. Later, I was given a small lapel badge to promote that the event was *Free From Sexual Harassment*. On a hoarding at the bottom of the statue was a telephone number set up specifically for sexual harassment complaints during the festival, and manned by the police and trained staff.

I can't even express how torn I am about being at this event, where animal abuse and sexual harassment are such huge issues. And yet the fact that Pamplona residents thrives off of the success and the history of the event is mind boggling. This indicates two different worlds that appreciate the event.

It's 7:48am and the first run is about to begin. All eyes are on the clock. The police have done the cordon and finished their pat-downs. The drunks have been ejected. The South Korean TV crew is beside me. The emergency services have their spinal boards ready on the other side. I perch on top of a fence post. Some men in their 50s arrive, wearing white trousers and green shirts with 'Pastora' on the back – they are herders. They stand bearing large sticks but most of the time they hit the people, not the bulls. Everyone knows them; they are royalty. Suddenly... BANG! And we're off. Cobbles tremble. I tremble. Mixed emotions are going through my mind as I cling to the side of the fence. 1,500 runners begin to sprint. For literally 10 seconds the bulls and screaming crowds are rushing past me. The emergency services pluck the unlucky ones over the wooden fence. The herders hit runners who are stopping and blocking other people's paths.

I could not understand what was going on. I could not describe it. But I could feel it. And I could smell it, as these literally raging bulls came closer and closer. I kept the finger on my camera and captured as much as I could – although I was struggling to understand what it was I was capturing. Animal abuse? Human bucket list achievements? Spanish culture? Historical misunderstanding of traditions? Pamplona was absolutely pulsing in a way I have never seen a city pulse before. On the slope of Santo Domingo, the bulls were running uphill but it was the flat turn that gave them the grip to push off and suddenly they were away towards Plaza De Toros. My heart rate went through the roof. The whole thing lasted about four minutes for the entire 800-metre route. Bars that had had to close because they were on the route opened their shutters and were soon full of runners wanting an early morning beer and to watch the replay on TV. I felt like I was on a television set where the director had shouted "Cut!" and normality had returned.

Apparently, everyone watched the TV replays to see who ran for the longest next to the bulls, the techniques they used, who ran the furthest and who got gored. I kept walking. Along the way I saw, on the first morning, ambulances picking up five people who had been injured. Two had been gored. The professional runners were sprinting back to try and figure out who had been injured. There was a very weird community spirit on the streets that I couldn't understand. The locals were peering over the paramedics' shoulders to see who was being treated and if they didn't recognise the shoes, the hair or anything else – they were off. At times I heard clapping as a runner was loaded up into an ambulance by the medics and taken to hospital. On the first day, one of the injured was a man from California who jumped across the fence line and tried to take a selfie with a bull. Yes... No one respected his decision and he was actually 'warned' by the police about his behaviour and not allowed back once he'd been released from hospital. The respect I saw on the course was another weird mix. The organisers, police, herders and bull handlers didn't want anyone to touch the bulls. There was a considerable amount of disrespect for anyone who whacked the back of a bull as it ran past. They were soon hit or arrested by the police – even though the runners all had newspapers rolled up like batons, ready to wage war against the bulls. So far, I am sure you feel as confused as I did.

The first run was over. "Well, what's next?" I hear you ask. It's time to go to mass, of course. After all, I am in Spain, where every cultural event has an association with religion. A procession of icons of Saint Fermin proceeded through the streets for an hour and a half. City councillors and the mayor left the town hall and met the procession at the Church of San Lorenzo. Everything was about the traditions. Here there was a completely different crowd. This was for the locals. The grandmothers, who were wearing the uniform but not interested in the tourist aspects of San Fermin. This was the spiritual side. This was the event that makes the festival interesting. This wasn't the tourist draw. The statue of Saint Fermin was made in 1584 – but no one who had come from Ireland or New Zealand cared. Only I did! It was no surprise then that just six police officers patrolled the whole thing. For many people, the festival was a revelation; a true spiritual event. No drunk people here. Instead, it was a sacred religious moment of celebration.

I needed to understand the festival a wee bit more, so I went to some of the family events. The one that was the most inappropriate and completely confusing was *Comparsa De Gigantes Y Cabezudo*: the parade of the Giants and Bigheads. The puppets danced in unison. One group of the Bigheads, the Kilikis, who were swinging large foam sponges around, were mean! Those foam sponges were used to literally smash spectators over the head. The mere fact that they were smashing kids over their head with sponges – maybe in 1860 that was okay, but now it was like – really? Yet the parents seemed fine with it and the children were laughing. This was another event intended for the locals. No backpackers came to this. The Giants stood at just under 4 metres and the Bigheads were 3.5 metres tall. The Bigheads were made in 1890. Just think about that. 1890. These things had been preserved for so long by whichever group in Pamplona had taken ownership. I loved the tradition. But whacking children? As it said in my Pamplona dossier: "The Kilikis were feared by the kids." Great. They literally were sprinting around whacking everyone who was in their way with the sponges.

Me included. It caught me by surprise and I quickly gave the guy a swift "What do you think you're doing?" The impact of the event was evident. Families had come together and the children were all dressed in white with red scarves. It could be viewed as a way of passing on tradition. It was brilliant and confusing and wrong.

Pamplona had so much going on. Sprawled across benches were revellers who'd had too much fruity wine. Residents had hoses and buckets on their balconies while below, hundreds of teenagers waited to be soaked. Backpackers walked around looking for the nearest bar. The authenticity of this festival has changed because of the globalised approach, yet the firework to begin the festival, the handkerchiefs worn as a symbol of identity – they were signs of a cultural celebration and recognition of history that the Spaniards focused on. But for the globetrotters, it was a rite of passage. However, overall, San Fermin is not about the bull runs. The charming elements of this festival give it another level to appreciate. I saw white marquees with large food stalls where people gathered.

I hope this chapter has helped you understand the construction of the event and the emotions it invokes. To lose the running of the bulls could mean the event would lose its other traditions, many of which date back to when Saint Fermin lived in the area.

If the bull running was cancelled, the overall economic impact (over €150 million in nine days) for Pamplona would most likely be diminished. I am not at all condoning economic gain over ending animal abuse – but that is the political stance. The dossier specifically highlights that the media who attend the event have a role to play. We are allowed – or advised – to post certain things. And here's the interesting part. The event organisers want to control what is reported about the festival. Why do they want control? Well, it's simple. They know about everything that goes on – but they want to hide it. Excessive drinking (mainly by tourists). Waste management issues. Animal abuse allegations…and so on. The whole thing is just complicated. I can't deny that I loved the festival ambience. There were hundreds of thousands of people in Pamplona during the three days I was there. In total, over the nine days, 1.3 million people would attend. There's no denying the event does do something to your emotions. For locals, it becomes a fountain of excitement. And for tourists it becomes a circle on their calendar that they look forward to attending.

You can try to argue with your conscience to say, "But what about the bulls...?" but at the same time the music, the art, the culture, the tradition and the religious elements, with the processions and masses – it was flabbergasting and astoundingly addictive. So, bull running – no. Everything else that comes with it – yes. You need to go to understand it. You need to watch for yourself and experience the happiness that comes from the main heart of the festival – the locals.

One thing to take away...

Did the global backpackers from Ireland and America appreciate the cultural importance of San Fermin? Probably not – but in reality, they didn't need to know about the cultural history. Instead, and somewhat grotesquely, a bull horn up their bum was more attractive and appealing...

Goodbye, Pamplona...

Pamplona airport was a shed. The check-in desks were packed and very few staff seemed to be working during San Fermin. We sat on the runway for an hour and ten minutes. My connection from Madrid to Milan was in another hour and five minutes. Yep. That's right...

THIS WAS NOT GOING TO BE GOOD.

After 55 minutes in the air, we arrived in Madrid. We were late but, instead of everyone supporting each other, a man pushed his elbow into my back. I told him where to go and then he pushed me to the side. As I picked myself up, the whole plane started screaming at the man in Spanish for being such a jerk.

Eventually we made it into the airport. The time was 3:53pm and my flight to Milan was due to take off at 3:54 from Gate J. I realised I was going to miss it so I ran as fast as I could, only to see the doors close. I waved towards the plane and was sure I could see the pilot sitting there, staring and thinking: "There's Matt...!"

This was the first flight I had missed – and it was not my fault. It was now time to recreate some scenes from the movie *The Terminal*. I got talking to someone else who had also missed the flight, and soon we became a big group, all laughing and chatting in four different languages. We shared stories, even though my new pals had absolutely no idea what I was saying. We were told there were eight seats on the Milan flight – but there were nine of us. So I decided it had to be me. I had no job to get to tomorrow. I had no family waiting for me.

After waiting for eight hours, the desk woman called me over. She said something to me in Spanish, which my new friend translated for me. "I have worked here for 20 years. Never have I had someone ensure that their passenger friends could go first. So here's your ticket. Enjoy Milan!" We all hugged and off we went – for dinner, using our free meal voucher. All part of the journey.

Hello, Milan!

Milan: the fashion capital of Italy. Famous, of course, for Leonardo da Vinci's The Last Supper. Milan had some really beautiful buildings. Very old, full of history. Cast-iron balconies. Scooters parked everywhere. My plan had been to see some of the Giro d'Italia Femminile, the Women's Tour of Italy, before heading off to Saint-Étienne for the Tour de France. Unfortunately, I had completely mixed up the dates so, in the end, my time in Milan was short and sweet, just a quick adventure. Having said that, I still took 500 photographs...

Saint-Étienne

I was in Saint-Étienne for the Tour de France – as were many other tourists who were arriving in their cars from all over Europe. I arrived on 11th July and the Tour De France was due to swoop in on the 12th and 13th July.

Saint-Étienne had an array of beautiful bandstands dotted around the city square, with an entertainment programme throughout the months of June and August. But during July it stopped, allowing the huge festivals taking place on the outskirts of the city to get a bit of attention. The French city is home to many amazing design organisations and companies, but there was nothing much to do. However, the cathedral was beautiful. An elegant water fountain splashed up as local children sprinted around while their families ate in nearby restaurants.

The forward team of the Tour de France had arrived in Saint-Étienne to put up directional signage. The event was about to take over this quiet town...

Event 52: Tour de France – Stage 8 Arrival and Stage 9 Departure

13th and 14th July

This was the Stage 8 arrival point; Saint-Étienne was one of the few towns on the Tour de France route that was also a departure point the next day. When I arrived, I saw a small gap in the crowd that I knew could be mine. The whole 'waiting for the arrival' was quite a thing. A few people had done this before, and some had tactics; others knew some of the people working on the event. I stood, protecting my barrier position and staring into the same gazebo at the finish line, for over six hours. I saw the teams arrive and watched them as they worked on the site. Occasionally, they would walk about with a cup of tea and a biscuit. I had a good wee spot, just four barriers along from the finish line, and it allowed me to capture the great moment when the winner of Stage 8 crossed the line.

Suddenly I knew what it was like to be a spectator, waiting for hours. Sometimes when you work in events and you see people standing, you don't understand what it's like for them. Being nudged in the ribs by your fellow spectators as they jostle for position. The psychological boredom. Gripping on and also trying not pee. That was the biggest challenge. Especially when Vittel, the water company, was giving away free water – but we will get to that. I was so bored. But every so often, my imagination would be captured or I would be roused from my stupor by some type of engagement, or a French person shouting to another, or pickpockets trying to get at people's bags and being taken down.

The Tour de France had signed an environmental charter that was introduced by the French Ministry of Sport, in association with the World Wildlife Fund (WWF). It introduced 15 principles with which event organisers must comply. While I was waiting at the barrier, I learned that, on top of the charter, the event had three themes: 'Cycling For Earth', 'Cycling Your Life' and 'In The Tour's Slipstream...'.

The event was thinking about the bigger picture. That being said, I stood for five hours and was given 56 items that were all going to be turned into waste. I received: 12 bottles of water, 2 t-shirts, 7 cardboard fans, 2 Continental foam hands, 24 packets of Haribos (lots – literally, you put your hat out and they filled it up), a Tour de France hat, Orange Mobile lanyards, 2 packs of cards from a coffee supplier, three keyrings and a glass cleaner. And this wasn't even part of the caravan, which carries a larger quantity of freebies to be given to spectators along the route. Post the event, everything that was handed out was either left lying in the gutter or chucked in the bins, which were overflowing. So disappointing. It was a real shame that products were now just left as waste – and TOTALLY against the principles committed to by the organisers. Or did they do it all just for show? You couldn't refuse the items they were giving away; it was like: "Oh, it's your problem to deal with now."

With 90 minutes to go, there was more activity at the finish line. The mascots were racing each other – unofficially. Team members were having dance-offs with the police officers – who all carried large machine guns and were designated to the Tour De France. It was one big happy family and every time another family member arrived at the finish line there were hugs and kisses. I didn't care about who was cycling; I was just enjoying the ambience created by the organisers – and not just by those in the white shirts, the race directors, but also by the activation staff, police commanders, VIP staff and so on. The scale and level of organisation really was quite remarkable.

An MC arrived in a black car and sped through the finish gantry to a chorus of cheers. *He must be a regular,* I thought. He jumped into the timing tower, where he was surrounded by staff members, with everyone laughing and joking. Watching him was like watching someone arrive on the Hollywood Walk of Fame and be deluged by fans. The MC came bouncing out of the tower with his mic and it began. Of course, it was all in French – even though most of the people at the finish line were not French. At times he would comment on what was happening out on the route. Every now and then he started a Mexican wave. I felt like part of the Tour de France family – finally. It only took five hours.

With 30 minutes to go, it was clear the peloton (the main group/pack of riders) was creeping closer – actually, flying closer. The helicopters – two in total – that accompany the race were zooming overhead. The police were redeployed to the finish line. The pickpockets were back in operation and getting caught 50 metres away from me; you would have thought they'd learned by now. The zone was full, and the excitement was building. And I really needed the toilet. But no way was I leaving. I needed to witness the end of the stage and feel the energy of the crowd. The people I was standing next to – Americans from Denver – were great about explaining what would be happening next. They understood the sport. I was enjoying being with them – but the sooner the cyclists arrived, the better. I was actually feeling quite bored now that the caravans, activations, dancers and mascots had disappeared. It's interesting, isn't it – the main reason we were all here was the cycling. But was it really?

Stage 8 really did include some great racing. The excitement was on – I could feel it – and the banging against the barrier was constant. And I was super excited to find out who had taken the lead even though I have absolutely no idea about cycling. While grappling with my freebies and holding onto my spot as a wee French woman pounded my ribs, causing me pain as she tried to move closer, I could see on the TVs that they were really close. I held my ground. It felt like I was battling for the front position. "Go away!" I felt like screaming in her ears – but I was nice about it and instead just stared along the finish line, waiting for the most amazing, weirdly emotional moment to happen. I don't know why I felt emotional. I had a tear in my eye – and I was not the one that had been racing! The winner – Thomas De Gedt – gripped into the saddle and suddenly the pace sped up as he punched his hand into the air. Both hands in the air. He flew through. The staff were waiting with his bike stand 100 metres away, so he had a chance to slow down and get control after cycling non-stop for 200 kilometres. Mind-blowing operation. The media were clicking away, trying to get that photo. The cars behind came flying through, still going at a crazy pace. The combination of people and cars together in the same space was scaring me.

Every day – with a few rest days in between – the athletes were doing quite extraordinary things with their bodies. Within three minutes, the rest of the peloton came flying past. Some knew they would probably never win a race – but they would never have the chance if they didn't apply themselves. Each cyclist looked absolutely knackered. I was knackered just watching them! Some arrived in rescue cars with their bikes on the roof rack. The whole operation at the finish line went smoothly. Watching it all, from its creation six hours ago to the finish, gave me a great insight. Well done to the Tour de France – and to Saint-Étienne. I did feel they could have done more considering thousands of people were in the city, but tomorrow was Bastille Day, which is a huge celebration in itself, and there was also the start of Stage 9 of the Tour de France.

Now I could finally run to the toilet...

One thing to take away...

The story of the Tour de France is a beautiful one. The event is more than just a bike race. Possibilities for opportunities are jumped upon. Everything is branded. Logos plastered on everything. But where will it be in five years? As long as the sponsors don't ruin it, it will still be selling France in a way no other marketing campaign ever could... but hopefully with less plastic and fewer giveaways.

Saint-Étienne to Lyon to Paris and then… farewell, Europe!

My European leg of the trip was almost over. Done. Finished. I couldn't believe it. Before I headed off, I spent one last night in Lyon before my train to Paris. Today was Bastille Day, a huge celebration in France. Because I had to be up at 4:30am the next morning for my train, I decided not to go to any celebrations, but I did catch some amazing fireworks and I treated myself to a nice fish and chip dinner, which was delicious.

From Lyon, I went to Paris. Charles de Gaulle Airport would be the last place I would see in Europe. The European leg of this adventure had encompassed 12 countries and numerous cities along the way. I had spoken to thousands of people – in broken English, broken every language possible – and drunk hot chocolate in the warmest of climates. I literally forgot at one point where I was and what I was doing. Reflecting back, it's funny; this whole idea spawned from simply thinking outside the box. Travelling around Europe was an honour. The cultural events were something else. We in the UK probably don't appreciate what Europe has to offer – and, most probably, our political correctness and health and safety wouldn't allow half of it to happen.

In some places I received beautiful help; in other places I was just a bit lost, and to be lost was even more beautiful. I got to explore areas I probably would never have found with a map. I didn't need or want to understand what was being said, yet I listened. I simply opened my ears and heard the world talking – and I got more from that than by attempting a Google translation. I made hundreds of new friends. These are called the 'five-minute WhatsApp best friend'… you speak for a few days on WhatsApp and then they disappear. Gone forever. Sad but true in many situations.

So… Europe. Thank you.

Now I was off to conquer North America. The flight took me over my house – literally – and at that point I had a tear in my eye. I cried because I knew that this was the final stage. This was it.

Calgary

Calgary had literally just hosted the Calgary Stampede, an event that brings a very American culture to thousands, with horses and cowboys and everything country and western, the day before. I couldn't go because of the cost. It was $500 for one night's accommodation… Yep. Instead, I booked two nights straight after in a five-star hotel for $114, because the price drops pretty quickly.

I arrived in Calgary at 6:30pm, checked into my hotel and stowed my jetlag in my backpack, expecting it to hit me hard in eight hours. By 7pm I was having dinner with my dear friends Chloe and Jon, who live up the road from Calgary. I literally lasted two hours – by 9pm, I was confusing my words! It was time to sleep. Chloe and Jon took me back to the hotel, where I couldn't even find the strength to put on my colourful pyjamas. Instead, I just starfished with my shoes still tied.

I rose at 4:30am with my shoes still on. Perfect! Just in time to see the sun rise. I went for a run in the city, which is very flat. Calgary is in the province of Alberta. The city is known locally as Cowtown – even though it has one million people and few cows.

This was the first time on my trip that I had visited a town *after* a major event. That in itself was a unique experience: the marquees coming down, the airport departures busier than arrivals. The place was slowing down. All the event branding was being dismantled in downtown Calgary and the regular normal quiet rhythm was being unpacked. The information points, which were bright with purple, orange, yellow and red stripes, were closed. The shopping centres were very quiet. Areas created specifically for the extra visitors had all gone. It was so strange – but this is exactly what happens. The stillness of the city gave me a unique perspective on what the true impact of an event is.

But today was a special day. I had arranged to meet a legend in the world of events academia: none other than Donald Getz. He began writing academically about events management in the late 80s and at the start of the 90s. For a long while his work went unnoticed but suddenly people began to pay attention and that was it, he became the most referenced events academic of the century. Literally, if you know anyone who has ever studied events management they will have referenced 'Getz (any year)' in every essay or assignment. And now I was going to have coffee with him – well, that's what I thought, anyway.

When I met him, I said: "I can't believe I am meeting THE Donald Getz!" We went first to the newly built Calgary Library, where we wandered around, appreciating the design and how it was being shaped by the community. We talked about the space and the use of the surrounding land. This public building and the consumption of it was dependent on the public. It was really interesting to walk around with an academic and hear his views on the impact places have on the community.

Next, we went to the National Music Centre. "So is this a PhD?" Donald asked.

"Nope," I answered. He was astonished – and so was I. "This was just a dream I came up with one day!" I told him. We shared some stories and I showed him photos of everything I had experienced so far: consumer behaviours, consumption of events, the impact of digital technology and the way events are changing people's lives.

It was awesome to be having this conversation with Donald Getz. It felt great to have this platform. "Let's get out of here and go to the Canadian Olympic Park," he suggested. Excellent – off to a government-funded park to see the legacy of the Olympics Games of the past.

We decided to explore Canada's Sports Hall of Fame, which cost $12 to enter. It was crammed with information and items from Canada's sporting history: Olympic torches, Olympic shirts, balls from famous matches and even a global corner. Unfortunately, there was just too much – and, worse, much of it didn't even make sense. When we went in, the staff were finishing their lunch at the reception desk. When it comes to customer engagement, setting a good first impression is crucial. We need to understand that the customer deserves the best experience, right from the get-go. I grabbed a map, which was quite poorly designed. I was confused about the fact that this was a national museum yet it felt like a school had been asked to complete a research project. Donald and I were both in agreement that the whole museum was missing successful engagement. The other thing was we were the only two visitors in the museum. This was Canada's Sports Hall of Fame; it should be an epic place with displays of some of the hottest sports equipment and sporting memories. But it was dark, boring and just not as amazing as it could be. There were some great activations – but most of them were broken. Not ideal. But… The actual bobsleigh that was used during the filming of *Cool Runnings* – the Disney portrayal of the Jamaican bobsleigh team from the 1988 Winter Olympics – was on display in the park! I took a quick selfie before Donald dropped me back in Calgary, where the weather was well and truly taking control.

Overall, my experience of meeting Donald was truly inspiring. He was brilliant to talk to and such a great sport by allowing me to have some of his precious time. Three and a half hours we spoke for! Goodbye, Calgary and thanks for two good nights.

The next day I was off to Seattle. Within the last ten days I had been on both sides of the world and had visited four countries, six cities or towns, used seven modes of transport, been in three time zones… and now I was in the west of America. I felt like a touring pop band – let's hit the road!

Seattle

Seattle – where do we begin? It's a destination for many tourists because of films and TV shows like *Sleepless in Seattle* and *Grey's*

Anatomy. But I saw a city in the grips of an epidemic of homelessness. I saw citizens walking around the streets suffering from mental health issues. I watched people smack their heads off walls and lie on the ground in front of traffic. Every shop had two security guards at the door because of shoplifting. A broken system was now too late to be fixed. This was a topic I discussed with many people I met in Seattle, but all they did was shrug their shoulders as they either weren't involved or didn't feel they could do anything. For me, there was plenty they could do: they could put pressure on government – local and federal.

I visited Pike Place Market, which is world-renowned. The Museum of Pop Culture, which was really cool. The Seattle Art Museum. The very unhygienic Gum Wall.

I contacted Seattle Tourism, who gave me an amazing goodie bag with a t-shirt, leaflets, a welcome note, a cool map – but the city itself was complex.

Event 53: Bite of Seattle

<u>19th July</u>

Welcome to the Bite of Seattle – or, to give it its full name, the *Albert Lee Appliances Bite of Seattle*. The event showcased 200-plus food and speciality cuisine vendors. Over 70 live bands performed throughout the weekend and there were cook-offs and sponsor activations. The event ran from 11am to 9pm, and I was a bit surprised that it closed so early, but I was advised it was because of licensing laws. Government control of cultural escapism – interesting, eh?

The event had a great marketing slogan, which I loved. #MeetMeAtTheBite. Date night sorted! This event was about bringing Seattle together. The weather was great and entry was free. It was a fabulously simple concept to attract people to come and stay at the event. Everything was about people spending dollars. Simple. Make sure they know what to expect.

Photo opportunities are something events have scattered around the site; places where people can take a photo to say: 'I am here'. *Bite of Seattle* was no exception and all the brand sponsors, including T-Mobile, Red Rock Deli and Nintendo, had platforms to engage visitors and create memorable experiences. I loved the sign at Red Rock Deli: 'I woke up like this… Hungry.' It was a great way of getting people to take a snap to keep on their phone or share online. It's that process of capturing an audience for free through someone wanting to show their location and their social status (as such!).

This food festival was about meeting people. Friends were meeting after work; families with newborns were strolling around for the first time through the park. As I looked up at the Seattle Needle and ate my overpriced burger, I felt there was something quite special about the city.

I did feel a bit lonely though. Food festivals are the perfect opportunity for people to come together, and everyone was here with friends. And then there was me. "Hello... Can I be your friend?" I sat alone, eating nachos and listening to *The Greatest Showman* soundtrack. But my job for eight months and two weeks was to be alone – kind of; to observe and just watch. I observed how laughter was the end result of food being eaten in circles of friends. I observed how people queued and understood how food units were missing a trick by not engaging with a waiting audience. There were so many ways of creating engagement: "Hey, let's have a singsong while we wait!" or even sending samples along the queue... but I suppose that is more work. So, to keep the labour costs as low as they can, nothing is innovative or different.

Bite of Seattle welcomed 400,000 people over three days. That is, 400,000 people who brought laughter and friendship to the park. I went for about four hours on the Friday night and enjoyed the festival (alone). I listened to music on Fountain Lawn Entertainment Stage, I watched Greek food being made, I saw the start of Movie Night and I charged my phone at the T-Mobile stand (where the reps had absolutely no conversation skills and were more interested in their clock-off time). It was so relaxed. After being in Seattle for two days, this showed a different side to the city and it was great to witness. I got the feeling that usually people were scared of coming into the city centre but for tonight, it belonged to them. The difference was unbelievable. But why that is... well, we'll get to that in a moment.

One thing to take away...

This was the first festival I visited in the USA. It was for sure the start of a rolling ball of wondrous experiences. Also – truck food can be expensive... and very small portions!

Back to the streets of Seattle…

Seattle really did have some great gems. Some lovely shops. Some amazing venues, which I took tours of. And the Space Needle, which gave great views to the horizon. But tomorrow it was time for a flying visit to the other side of the country… before coming back to Seattle (in 24 hours) – yep!

New York: Part One

Six hours to New York from Seattle. I got talking to the crew. They gave me double pretzels. I told them all about my trip so far. My story. Tonight, I was going to be catching up with a dear friend from Australia who was in New York after an epic adventure around the country. When I heard Rachel would be in New York for 24 hours before flying home to Melbourne, I said: "Same country – no problem. Let's do it!" After not seeing each other for months, we laughed at the situation – but there are always surprises attached. So, the agenda was planned. The only problem was when we got to Manhattan it was 43 degrees; it was the warmest weekend they'd had. We went up the Empire State Building at midnight with the lights of New York twinkling below; we went to the most amazing Italian restaurant; we cycled around Central Park in 43 degrees – bad idea! Then we visited an amazing book store for some light reading after the cycling. We packed in so much in less than 16 hours until, eventually, we had to say goodbye. I'd needed a boost on my trip and seeing my friend gave me it. The conversation we had at the top of the Empire State Building will always stay with me, because sometimes you miss deep and meaningful conversations when you're travelling by yourself. It was such a delight to just laugh and chat, rather than answering emails or worrying about the events I was missing in Seattle.

I arrived back in Seattle in the early hours and boarded a bus to my hotel. As I got on, the driver said: "Sit near me." I quickly understood why. This was the first bus on the route that morning and for many it would be their home for the day. As I looked down the bus I saw people sleeping under blankets and, at the back, drug users were shooting up with dirty needles. It really wasn't ideal. Again, I was seeing things many tourists wouldn't and the driver could sense the fear in my eyes.

As we drove along, I questioned why cities spend millions on events and tourism when their own people are sleeping on cold paving slabs with no cover. In the western world in the 21st century, poverty should be in a museum – locked up for people to look back on. But here it was right in front of me, on a bus. It was the problem of the city and a matter of ignorance... and yes, the city will most probably be reading this (or not) and disputing it.

When a bus is full of citizens carrying blankets and pillows and they're wrapping those blankets around them because they have nowhere else to sleep... Who needs to fix this? The city? I was only here to looks at events in the city. It is those people who choose to call Seattle home that need to challenge the situation. The city should not be financially supporting or hosting events when its streets are being used as beds for the night.

Okay. I am calm now.

Event 54: Seattle Mariners vs Texas Rangers (Baseball)

22nd July

This is a story about my visit to a baseball park on a warm Monday night where I saw absolutely epic strategies of customer engagement. The T-Mobile Park, in the middle of Seattle, has a retractable roof and its capacity is 47,929, although tonight it was slightly quieter. However, let me begin with how I got to this point. I love sending emails. Copy-and-paste emails to people I don't know, asking questions like "Can I get in?" If I don't ask, I'll never know. And the T-Mobile Stadium had said yes.

I was beginning to get used to walking into a stadium or venue and introducing myself at the reception desk. It was my new hobby. Usually I was greeted with a: "Oh my God, your Scottish accent is so good!" Well, thank you. I was also getting used to helping myself to the sweets that were always out on a table.

But this time I was met by two police officers. "Have you got an appointment or a VIP pass?" I told them I did, and they asked me to wait. Venue front offices always have something welcoming and here, at the home of the Seattle Mariners, the reception area was plastered with posters of the stadium's history and trophies from days gone by. Some magazines were scattered on the small coffee table and I waited patiently as I flicked through a few pages of *Woman's Weekly*. The reception was busy with guests coming through and they all looked at me. I loved that whole "Who's that guy sitting there? ... Oh, that's alright, he's from Scotland..." Literally three times the receptionist had to stop the security from throwing me out. Just as well I had worn my best shirt that day!

Eventually I met Sarah from the PR media team. She gave me a tour of the ground and some cracking perspectives. With over 15 years' experience at this ballpark, she took me through everything there was to know. Here, baseball is more than just a sport; it's a passion. In reality, baseball can be boring. But the stadium was a spectacle with many features of great interest that will keep you entertained for hours. Immediately, I had a lot of questions regarding the commercialisation impact of sport and the fans. With tickets costing over $50, a shirt on top of that, food and drink, half time raffle, a treat and so on... it can cost a lot. Usually, a night at the ball game for one person and two kids, with everything combined, can cost as much as $300.

A ball game is one thing; an appreciation of American fan engagement is another. T-Mobile had phone charging units on every pillar, where you could charge your phone and still see the game from where you stood. In the concourse was the Mariners' Hall of Fame where, instead of watching the game, you could learn about the history of Pacific Northwest Baseball in the *Celebration of a Rich Tradition* exhibition or take photos of the sculptures in the museum area. How about posing for a picture next to a statue of legendary pitcher Jamie Moyer while a live baseball match is in full play? I watched as parents encouraged their kids to get photos with the sculptures. I loved listening to them reminiscing: "I remember I sat up there when Jamie hit a home run..." Including a museum and a Hall of Fame feature in the ballpark allowed for an immersive experience. And that was all within the first 200 metres of my tour! Sport, history, nostalgia and many photo opportunities met me. Maybe because I was with Sarah, I saw so much. Up at the kids' area at the top end of the park was the Junior Mariners section, which was full of games for children with prizes to be won. It was a great way to give kids more than just a ball game experience – and all within the stadium itself. It was even staffed by some of the younger baseball players whose careers hadn't yet taken off!

But tonight was special for one woofing and barking reason... because it was *Bark in the Park* night. Tonight, dogs were allowed in the seated upper section of the stadium. Strict instructions had been given to the friendliest dog park in Seattle by the government and local lawmakers, including directions on how to enter the stadium and what was allowed and not allowed. A check-in station was set up outside the ballpark and guidelines were given to dog owners. It cost $50 for both dog and human and, on arrival, a release and waiver was accepted and signed. Obviously, it was the height of summer, so every precaution was put in place – including a vet on standby in the stadium, who was sitting literally in the medical room. Brilliant! Water fountains and paddling pools were everywhere for drinking water purposes (and fun), and machines dotted around the stadium were firing out dog treats. Perhaps the best feature was the 'real grass' that had been laid on concrete to ensure dogs would feel right at home and comfortable doing a pee. No stone had been left unturned, that was for sure.

Sarah explained the success of this event – and I totally understood it. This was not just about 'having dogs at the stadium'. It was about maximising as many ticket sales as possible. A ball game can last 3-4 hours and the owner of a dog might not want or be able to stay away from home for that long. A dog sitter might cost too much. So, if the club puts measures in place to encourage as many people as possible to bring their dogs to the game, they increase food sales, merchandise opportunities and the rest. The Seattle Mariners had become leaders within the sports entertainment market. *Bark in the Park* only happens at a few baseball stadiums around the USA, but Seattle spearheaded the idea.

As it was my first time at the ballpark, Sarah took me to receive a special souvenir certificate. The Guest Services agents were tremendous. We chatted and laughed for about 10 minutes and they made me feel very at home. Before I left, we got a photo together. I was very impressed with their engagement as well as the knowledge they bestowed on me about the stadium and the sport. Sometimes on my adventure it had been difficult to find positive customer experience but these three were beaming with pride, simply because they worked at a club they support. Having such a caring, passionate and exciting staff strengthens the experience for those who consume it.

I was at the end of the tour and Sarah showed me to my seat, which just happened to be directly behind the home plate. I was sitting with some top tech people who all knew each other and were all wearing relaxed summer wear. And then there was me, in my bright pink shirt and tight trousers. I looked totally out of place. These seats were comfortable and apparently extremely expensive. At the other end of the stadium I saw some dots walking about. Those seats were priced at $20 and the ones I was lounging in – well, shall we just say they cost so much more. Hawkers selling beer and chips walked up and down the aisles. They seemed to know all the tech leadership people because they knew exactly what they would order. Human interactions can be so important at events – and this was the perfect example.

At half time the cameras turned to the stands. It was time for the return of the 'Simba Cam', which has become a legendary part of *Bark at the Park*. All around the stadium, pet owners held their dogs high into the sky while the famous music from *The Lion King* was played over the PA. This was what the fans had been waiting for, and I watched in amazement as 150 dogs, from tiny terriers to huge Labradors, were launched towards the sky. Even a few newborn babies were lifted high in an imitation of the famous *Lion King* pose. Amazing work! I kept thinking, "Is this really happening?" I guess a happy dog means a happy owner!

Baseball is a sport that has innings, runs, strikes and so on. Construction of that is simple. The delivery of everything else is what fascinated me. I loved the fan engagement, the concept of *Bark in the Park*, the passion of the fans (even though the team were not so good) and the overall impact the ballpark has, especially as the team support communities and organisations in Seattle through charitable donations.

One thing to take away…

Stadiums deliver more than entertainment. However, this stadium was not just about adding things for the sake of it; it was about delivering a sense of community and fan experience that is incomparable to anything they would experience anywhere else on the west coast of America.

Back to Seattle…

I was very fortunate that the Space Needle was part of my CityPass. I booked my slot and off I went to stand in a queue for the lift. The horizon was just spectacular. I saw planes taking off from Elliot Bay and then, to the opposite side, the reflections on Lake Washington. I stood on the see-through glass and looked down on the city. I watched the crossing points. I watched the boats. I watched birds fly. I watched clouds float through the sky to another part of the world.

Seattle really was a city that, in small portions, was breaking my heart. The problem was the disjointed approach to everything the city was building. It didn't feel like it was quite together. It was all very abstract. The city has a lot to offer but please – first make sure the cold pavements and roads aren't being used as mattresses.

Bus to Vancouver… HELLO, CANADA!

I was taking the bus from Seattle to Vancouver, which meant crossing the international border. I get nervous for no reason at borders. I was also still jetlagged from France, so the three-hour bus journey was actually quite easy. When we arrived, I was asked: "What is your purpose in Canada? And can you show me you have enough income to support yourself?" It's very nerve-racking being asked that question. Your palms go sweaty as everyone around you seems to be looking at you… Luckily, the border control officer was lovely. She asked to see my bank account but then asked me about my adventure and shouted to her supervisor, "This guy's been around the world... literally!" I decided either this would end up in a sale of my book or I'd end up spending a night in jail! Luckily, it was neither and I was sent back to the bus with my bags. I was relieved that this was officially my last international border crossing!

Vancouver was going to be the longest stay on my adventure. It was also going to be the place I almost had a breakdown and decided to disappear into the wilderness for a while. But first, I had some events and meetings to attend.

At 6pm I had to be at a briefing for the first event I was volunteering at in North America, Honda's Celebration of Light. Here is a story about something that was interesting to be part of.

Event 55: Honda Celebration of Light

27th/ 31st July and 3rd August

At 6pm I sprinted into a community centre near David Lam Park. Unusually for a volunteer briefing, there was no registration point. Instead, the volunteer coordinators were walking around with pen and paper. No one was wearing a name badge or official t-shirt; it all seemed a bit disorganised. I was kind of like, "Okay, Matthew, just keep calm – you are here as a volunteer…"

I got the feeling this event would either be an absolute success or I would end up having to jump in to help… Guess which one it ended up being!

The Honda Celebration of Light is the largest offshore fireworks competition in the world. It takes place on three separate evenings across two weeks and this year Canada was going up against Croatia and India. The event attracts an estimated crowd of over 300,000 each evening, although weekday events are usually quieter, for obvious reasons. The event was now in its 29th year and was a staple event that showed Vancouver off (kind of). As well as the fireworks, it was all about sponsorship activations, stunt shows and hospitality – of course. This was a huge event for event suppliers. A lot of people depended on it. And the volunteering element of it was critical. But unfortunately, the people who came to volunteer probably did not understand what they were letting themselves in for – because I for sure didn't.

The presentation mentioned sustainability. Massive. Like a real push about not bringing plastic on site. I appreciated the drilled-in approach. I thought, "Brilliant! This is so good. Finally, we have an event that is thinking about its impact and footprint"

Volunteers were encouraged not to bring anything on site that would end up in the waste. However, in the hospitality area, free one-use plastic wristbands were being handed out. The argument, of course, was the impact on brand engagement and that it was only for 400 people in the bleachers. I sometimes think people are ignorant about some of the smaller things they should be open to.

I was offered a choice of volunteering roles – usher, hospitality, recycling or staffing the volunteer hub. I picked usher. I wanted to be at the forefront of the customer journey. But this would change on the night – quickly.

I arrived on the Saturday, ready to begin. The volunteer coordinators were trying their best despite the lack of information they had. My plan was to volunteer only for tonight, not for all three nights – but that soon changed. I tried to collect my t-shirt but they hadn't arrived in the volunteer hub yet. I was there so early that I helped clear out all the rubbish from the hub and ensure the area was safe for volunteers. First night organised madness. It was that chaotic I ended up being asked to help manage the volunteers and became an unofficial volunteer coordinator. And I would now be volunteering on all three nights. Sometimes volunteers are willing to do anything and everything – but when there's a Scotsman standing over you, saying, "Right, let's head over..." and there are thousands of people strolling in, it can be daunting. It didn't help that only half the volunteers who had signed up actually turned up. However, I was loving it and the organisers were loving having me chip in.

On the first night, India was setting off their production of fireworks. Having already ventured to India, I understood the passion that Indian citizens have for anything relating to national identity. Thousands of flags were flown that night and there was a real carnival atmosphere. It is estimated that 243,000 Indians live in Vancouver; tonight was going to be busy.

The site for the event was about 2km long, officially. In reality, it encompassed a much larger area. Most of the volunteers were engaged in the hospitality sections or were waving flags at the entrances. I was now managing the breaks, making sure all the volunteers were in position and organising everything that was needed, as well as understanding what my own role was. Floating. Superb. It meant I got to see everything. The official volunteer coordinators – a lovely mum and daughter duo – were lovely, but they were so grateful I was just willing to get stuck in.

Over the course of the event I observed the traffic management, signage plans, fireworks operations, police sweeps, and garbage trucks being used to mitigate traffic in case any vehicles needed to get through the crowds. Who would have thought garbage trucks would be used to welcome customers to events in 2019? Everything to do with the construction of a safe event was put in place. Seeing the police control the roads was interesting, especially the way they were stopping cyclists going through road closures and into the crowds by basically shouting "STOP!" I was especially excited to see the food trucks entice people in to buy food with free samples. I kept my eyes and ears open as I walked around (over 20km!) that night. I even spotted things you would never think about, like the firework tugboats out in the water surrounded by police to ensure no one had any crazy ideas. ("Let's go and see what dynamite looks like up close!")

Talking of fireworks, the show was spectacular on the Saturday – as it was every night. As the same people probably weren't there for all three evenings – and most certainly would not be sitting or standing in the same positions – I saw three different nights of engagement, spectator involvement and experience. The event was being covered in newspapers to increase commercial opportunities and consumer buy-in and it even made the 'Photos from Around the World' feature back home, which was cool to see.

The one thing I felt Vancouver was missing was the whole sense of 'THIS IS VANCOUVER'. Here was a chance to sell Vancouver to a bigger stage – I mean, this was one of the best-attended events in North America – and Vancouver, in my opinion, completely missed the opportunity to use such a massive event to say, 'Buy our city'. (And I told Tourism Vancouver this). When cities host events they have a goal in mind and in this instance

Vancouver should have used this as a stage to capture a new crowd and the one thing they can bring to the city – which is, in the nicest way, their money. Vancouver needed to push this message even more – especially as, while I was staying in the city, there were six events going on with a combined estimated crowd of 1.7 million.

The volunteers were excited for the second evening and knew what was expected of them. This was the first time during my trip that I had stepped in and used my skills to help with an event. I got us all into a huge circle and we put our hands in. Suddenly we were a team. I had built a team of volunteers. A team that was delivering a great event. We had our photo taken as a team and had lots of fun. Mind you, I still thought volunteers were being used in the place of too many paid staff at this event – and I did advise them of that.

But guess what? I finally got a t-shirt for my hard work! The fireworks brightened the skies and the volunteers, along with security and others at the forefront of customer service, made everything go with an amazing bang. Next time you're at an event, thank those who are greeting you – because their roles at times can be totally misunderstood.

One thing to take away...

Thousands upon thousands of people created the event for themselves. They brought blankets and friends. It was constantly busy right up until 7:30pm and then, for 30 minutes, the fireworks went off. And as soon as the display was over, and all at the same time, hundreds of thousands of people left.

Meetings in Vancouver

I made friends with Tourism Vancouver. The meeting began with them asking me, "What do you want from us?" I opened my laptop and showed them my presentation about my adventure – this was to the CFO of Tourism Vancouver and his colleagues, who didn't know me, and it was fabulous! It was a huge personal achievement to be presenting to such an innovative group. I then openly critiqued their programme of events, questioned why they weren't investing more into publicising things and asked them if they understood touchpoint engagement...Yep.

Vancouver was a ghost town in the winter and currently it was all about how to capture the local audience. My adventure was about creating relationships – and this was one to keep and cherish.

My next event was the Vancouver Vegan Food Festival, and it won't be a long chapter – simply because there was nothing happening for the three hours I was there – except queuing!

Event 56: Vancouver Vegan Food Festival

<u>27th July</u>

The Vancouver Vegan Food Festival was free to enter and explore. Veganism was fast becoming a trend and the festival was created as an opportunity to celebrate food within the vegan remit. Held in Vancouver Creekside Park, which was next to the Science Museum, the event was very open and a good opportunity to explore and learn about veganism. The event was literally pop-up tents, white-topped marquees and stalls. In the middle was a small amplifier, but there was nothing happening to amplify. I decided to try and delve a bit deeper to understand why the queues were so long.

Surveys in 2019 highlighted that British Columbia led the way when it came to the number of people who identify as being vegetarian or vegan. Nearly 40% of Vancouver residents under the age of 35 identified as vegan. So this was not a trend, really, more a lifestyle. Vegan foods did not occupy a token aisle in the supermarkets – there was proper produce, and it was pricey. But people flocked to this festival; they engaged and they learned about the products. It seems that those events that specialise in certain products or markets – for example, a festival of saxophones, or a festival of biological science, or a vegan food festival – experience a higher rate of direct engagement and conversation than more generic events, which have more passive engagement. These specialised events can impact and even change people's lives.

Those who chose to be at this event as stall holders – mainly start-up companies or sole traders – were keen to take a piece of the economic pie, which, in Canada, was estimated at around $14.2 billion in 2018 from the vegan industry alone. So those queues of consumers with their wallets and purses – well, they were helping to boost the share and impact of the vegan economy.

I walked around. I watched. I listened. I enjoyed it – but I didn't buy anything. I wanted to be doing something other than standing in line waiting for a vegan burger. But I did get some free vegan soap.

One thing to take away...

Why is the vegan movement so crucial for the future? Education around veganism is important. A vegan festival needs to have purpose and bring excitement – not just pop-up tents, but a microphone that can be used to get people sitting up and listening about a change for the future.

Now to get naked...

Event 57: Vancouver Naked Bike Ride

<u>27th July</u>

'Being free…' Literally. The Naked Bike Ride was a spectacle and a huge success. It was an open and honest way of being free. Riding along with the police motorbikes and enjoying the freedom were some naked Vancouver citizens. I had forgotten about being naked and stood there fully clothed.

A few hundred people cycling around Vancouver was not the main headline here. The event has a deeper meaning and has created a movement, not only in Vancouver but globally. It's a positive protest against car culture, pollution and oil. The purpose behind the event is to raise the awareness of those watching about the damage being done by pollution in our world. I totally appreciated what they were trying to say but I have to admit that all the viewing public saw was… well, you know – nothing much.

The question was: how do you create buy-in from those fully clothed people who were spectating from the side of Granville Street and the surrounding area? The event is about creating a reaction from those who are observing. Creating a connection. Creating a movement. Creating conversation. And the crack at this event was well and truly everywhere to be seen!

The event began at 12pm; it was the same day as one of the fireworks displays but I wasn't due there until 3pm. Around 100 people were part of the cycle and another 200 turned up for the social activities at the end of the ride. I walked out of my hostel to head down to the meeting point but the bikes came right past me as they had left their meeting point 45 minutes earlier than planned. Participants are encouraged to be creative with their attire – or lack of it. It is all about noise and 'baring as you dare'… Excellent entertainment on a Saturday afternoon! Only shoes and helmets were mandatory… so yes, you guessed it, everything else was flying free through the wind. Just make sure you're wearing a helmet... Some people had covered themselves in bright body paint and others did actually cover up – in quite hilarious ways. It was brilliant to see friendships being made between those who were just strolling around the park relaxing and others who were there to talk about the earth. The police, on pushbikes, were also being thanked for their presence. I loved that the officers – who were fully clothed – were really getting into the spirit of the event and had absolutely no problems with pushing people away if the naked bike ride was getting too much negative attention.

Globally, the World Naked Bike Ride is a 'thing'; a fun event with a deeper meaning. In Mexico City, thousands took part for the 13th year running, protesting against oil dependency in the world. Meanwhile in Cologne, Germany, 60 people participated to call for cleaner and safer streets in their city. With the correct positioning, this could really push governments into policies and laws that protect the future of our planet. However, in today's climate, environmental 'things' can be taken too seriously. It was reported on *5 News on Your Side: KSDK in St Louis* that the naked bike ride in that US city was slightly dampened by a man shooting paintballs at the cyclists as they rode through Tower Grove Park. You could say that would be a pain in the backside...

This was the first time the naked bike ride had been held in Vancouver and it will continue to grow. Go and bare it all – I'll pass!

One thing to take away...

Any event – whether naked or fully clothed – has a deeper purpose and understanding that purpose can help you appreciate the event more. Baring all is what everyone should do at events – because to be open means you will open your mind and heart to every conversation... (Deep eh?)

Now I am all clothed up, let's talk more about Vancouver...

I was fortunate enough to be able to visit some tourist attractions in Vancouver, the most amazing of which is called FlyOver Canada. I was strapped in and then 'flew' over the Canadian countryside across 18 screens, which combined over 100 hours of footage. Best thing ever!

Let's move on to the next event I experienced.

Event 58: Downtown Movie Night

29th July

Downtown Movie Night in Vancouver – when thousands came together to sit on cold concrete and watch a movie – was an escapist activity in an area of urban development. The space was intended to be for 'passing through' only, yet tonight the opposite was true; it was a destination, a place where people wanted to spend time. Why? Well, a large screen had been erected outside the Vancouver Art Gallery as part of a movie series that was, in my opinion, aimed squarely at the residents of the city. Tonight, the crowds were here to sing along to *Bohemian Rhapsody*. And I'd arrived at the event by accident.

The movie wasn't due to screen until 9:45pm but by 8pm, hundreds of people had arrived and set up their blankets and chairs. This was a constructed environment with food trucks, a warm-up DJ and a large screen. Deckchairs and blankets covered the entire space and people nibbled on snacks and chatted away as the sun set on a warm Monday evening. The secret of a 'downtown event' is to give the downtown area something vibrant to bounce along to; creating a different atmosphere to the concrete and glass of urban life.

Outdoor cinema is about disrupting the normal routine of the city streets, and this event was about more than watching a screen; it was about watching a city come together. The event was free, so it perhaps wasn't valued as highly as a ticketed event... Deep, eh. But thousands of people sitting on cement and watching the film really were buying into the fact that this was something different for them to consume. All around me, people were relaxing, all chitter-chatter until the movie began. Events can be stressful because of the pace, but this one, on a beautiful summer's evening, was pure bliss.

Next to the screen were large white letters that spelled out

V.A.N. This represented the message Vancouver wanted to get across – that this is *our* city and *our* space. However, the giant letters had been brought in by Downtown Vancouver, the company running this event, rather than the city council or Tourism Vancouver. I saw it this way. A movie on a screen is just a movie. You can go to a cinema to see one, where you sit in an enclosed environment. After it ends, that's it; there's no legacy. Or you can create an attachment – and these six-foot-high letters were just that.

As the film began, I watched the traffic go by, fast. I watched late-night shoppers heading home on the bus. I watched skaters whizzing past, curious and furious that their ramps and benches were unavailable tonight because Freddie Mercury was asking "Is this the real life?" on screen. And I admired the skyscrapers around me, which created a unique backdrop that was just mind-blowing and beautiful. Remember Bologna? The terracotta tiles and the buildings surrounding the square? Well, Vancouver may not have that history but the city still presented itself with class and splendour.

In Canada, the cinema industry is worth $1.9 billion in operating revenue. This includes motion pictures and video exhibition companies. Cities around Canada have increased the capacity of cinema output and opportunities. Outdoor cinema is included in that economic impact statement, but on this weekend alone there were five outdoor cinemas operating within a 20-mile radius of each other in the Vancouver area alone. The demand for this type of event was apparently high. The supply was there. But for me, what was missing was the idea of immersive movies. We were watching *Bohemian Rhapsody* but no one was singing. I mean... What?

As Freddie sang, "DOO-AO-AO-AO-AO-AO-AO-AO-AOOOOOOO," he got nothing in return. I understand that events are governed by rules and regulations, laws, signage, entrance times, and so on. But sometimes I wonder why events cannot be orchestrated more to focus on the customer journey? Why do organisers not understand fully what they could do, even on a low budget, to make the event even more of a spectacle?

So, let's talk about the *watching* of the movie. Literally, no one was singing, loud and proud. Well, maybe I did – or attempted to – but I felt socially awkward doing so. This could have been the biggest singsong ever heard on these streets. But the reason for the silence was obvious. Those who lived nearby probably wouldn't want to be disturbed by the noise. However, as I looked around, the occupants of nearly every apartment and hotel room were watching the film! This event had all the ingredients to be powerfully engaging. Imagine someone on a cherry picker, standing at the top of the screen and conducting the crowd in a singalong. Instead, it was just the crowd watching a movie. I really wanted *Radio Gaga* to be the moment where everyone erupted into song. Or the trembling and rumbling of *We Will Rock You*. Events are about these iconic moments and this movie night had the potential for several moments of pure joy. Regardless, I walked away singing to myself and my new hostel friend, Freddie (Yes, that was her name! Relevant, eh?).

So thank you very much, Downtown Movie Night. I experienced an amazing event that literally had thousands crammed in, relaxing together. Silence may be golden, but the setting was even more special.

One thing to take away…

Engagement. That is all that was needed to push this forward. Just a small tweak would have taken it from a standard movie night to a PROPER MOVIE EXPERIENCE! Widen the eyes of opportunities and broaden the minds of those engaging. But well done, Vancouver, for allowing residents and those passing by to engage with and enjoy the film.

So, Vancouver...

On 1st August I decided to book a getaway to Kelowna, a small town with a population just short of 100,000, a three-hour bus ride from Vancouver. Snap decisions, and all that.

Two days later, I was about to celebrate six months of the adventure. Crazy. I spent the evening sitting in the middle of a road in Vancouver. Every weekend the police close the main street to traffic at night so the clubbers can spill out. Every weekend it's party time. But I remember just sitting. Looking and listening. It must have been about 1am when I heard someone say: "She didn't love me the way I wish she did."

I was heartbroken for him – as he struggled to stay upright. Tomorrow, however, was not about my six months on the road, it was about Pride... and oh my days, it was an adventure.

Event 59: Vancouver Pride

4th August

I was meant to be at the meeting point for volunteers for Pride at 9am. I lifted my head from the pillow two hours later. I felt so bad. I was letting myself down. I was letting the Pride Society down. But sometimes I had to admit defeat – and I was admitting defeat today. I grabbed my hat and bag and decided to experience Pride not as a volunteer but as an attendee. Walked out of the hostel at 11:30am my body was telling me to slow down.

Vancouver Pride left me with some mixed emotions. It was so well attended, which was critical to the message being sent out, but on the other hand, it was overly commercialised, which made me feel very uncomfortable. But let's talk about the positivity I witnessed first.

"Hello, guys and darlings!" The greeting came from a very well-dressed drag queen who was entertaining the crowds from a radio station sponsored truck. The LGBT community celebrates Pride with pride. The trucks were all logoed up. Approximately 650,000 people were attending the Pride parade here in Vancouver. It was the place to be, where liberation is celebrated. "HAPPY PRIDE!" is all I hear. Everyone is using the event to express themselves. I adore the expression, but I am slightly confused about those telling me 'HAPPY PRIDE'. The event is a colourful celebration of doing good but the origins of Pride are rooted in protest...

Vancouver Pride was a huge contrast to what I saw in New Zealand. In Auckland, the police were not welcome, yet in Vancouver I saw the LGBT community engage with each other and dance with the police. But this just made me more confused about the message behind Pride. The Auckland event was a throwback to the origins of Pride. It was a protest; it was about standing up for

311

the rights of those who had been pushed aside – now and in the past, across many sectors of society – for being part of the LGBT movement.

Here in Vancouver, I had to wonder what impact the branded floats would have, or whether the people running them would even care about the civil rights issues around being in an LGBT relationship, or about discrimination towards a schoolboy who just wanted to be accepted for being gay. Did they? Did Pride make the community more mainstream simply for the fact that Starbucks was here selling every type of rainbow-coloured cake they could? Could an online company really turn up and become LGBT-friendly for the day?

I asked someone about this, and they said: "Please do include this in your book." As a member of the LGBT community, they were sick of it all: Pride stickers whacked onto the floors of stores, colourful décor that screamed, "It's okay to be gay in this store!" which translated in business terms to "It is okay to spend your pink dollar in this store – we would love your money..." Free flags were being handed out to the crowds of thousands, who waved them for the day, before the plastic went to waste. Did it actually achieve anything beneficial?"

I think in one respect it did. I saw a group of 18-year-olds who were celebrating their first Pride and were somewhat overwhelmed by the size, scale and some of the sights. But did any of the brands help these 18-year-olds feel accepted? Well, some may argue they did, because the teens felt they were brands they can consume. But only for that day... They had the flags, the lanyards, the badges and the stickers, oh, and the beautiful window displays. But the next day – LITERALLY the next day – everything was gone.

The 'pink dollar' is the name given to the economic impact of the LGBT community. In North America alone, it is worth $790 billion a year. And it has the most unusual impact too. For example, Skittles created white (colourless) skittles to 'celebrate' Pride, so of course everyone bought them because they were available for one weekend only. Flight Center was offering LGBT-friendly holidays during the weekend. The danger is that companies do things for Pride weekend to hit their Corporate Social Responsibility targets and then forget about the LGBT community for the other 364 days of the year – in my opinion.

And then there's the suggestion that straight people love Pride because they can "be gay for the weekend". I asked people at the hostel and at the event about this and that's what they said. They told me they had never seen so many straight people together, wearing Pride colours and parading like it was a party. But I also spoke to two gay men, one of whom said: "We have been in love for 37 years, me and this guy here. We're too old for all this shit. But do you think, 37 years ago, all the straights would have been out? Not a chance. You know why? 'Cos it wasn't attractive for them to be part of us. To be with us. To be with the gays. So why the fuck do I need a machine to tell me on this day I need to wear a t-shirt and sing Cher with the straight people?"

Mind blown and very true.

Some floats were from the local and national radio stations. You know, being visibly seen to support and be at the forefront of the LGBT movement; apparently it gives you a greater audience appeal. And then... Well, you had the 'Dogs and Dog Handlers Association'. Yep. These were some very rough-and-ready guys who were pretending to be dogs with their handlers. I was a bit stunned by it at first but hey, if it makes them happy... for sure they were sweating in their leather bondage and dog masks. I admired their passion. But this was exactly what Pride is about – a diverse approach to expressing that you are part of the LGBT community. The fact that some of these men were wearing Apple watches, Asics running gear and purple masks ... it was a subculture. And then there were the well-groomed men with six-packs, strutting around like it was an episode of *Project Runway*. It was very clear that people wanted to portray their identity in different ways.

I saw flags being waved by people who had jumped onto a

commercialised bandwagon, in my opinion. For me, Pride has become something of a FOMO event. It's not acceptable to miss it. You must go. It's on the calendar for people of all sexualities. The celebration of love as one. Yet there is still injustice when it comes to equality for those people PRIDE is for – it's just not fought within these boundaries or at this event these days.

A few people protesting against the commercial side of the event walked through the parade carrying banners stating "Pride is a Protest..." I understood what it was these people were shouting about – screaming so loud it was actually upsetting. And I wasn't even part of the group. It was obvious that these members of the LGBT community – who were dressed all in black with masks over their faces – were fed up. It was the complete opposite to the drag queen approach of the floats.

Thousands of basically half-naked people were crammed in to enjoy a 'spectacle of gayness', as it was described by the MC. Loud whistles, glitter, colour and passion were part of the 'festival' starter packs being sold from all legit corner shops in Vancouver. Joining a movement should mean researching its origins and discovering the central point to what is being argued. The noise at Vancouver Pride was deafening but the changes that needed to happen... well, everyone was silent about that. I didn't see anyone talking about partner financial rights. Instead, I saw glitter, colour and corporate logos – which, once the mass crowds had disappeared, were taken down. Binned. Stored away. The next day, this 'mirage' of colour that reflected and represented Pride had gone. No more colourful cakes. I was so confused, but also upset for the LGBT community, who were basically being used...

This was the Pride I saw in Vancouver – and it was very different from Auckland!

One thing to take away...

We sometimes miss the true meaning behind an event. We

sometimes lose the direction of an event. We sometimes cannot appreciate why an event is so important. Yet it is key to understanding their production and manufacture. One of the most important factors is actually understanding the impact an event can bring. So – there is it. Pride is a complicated event with a complicated impact…

A break from Vancouver…

The night I arrived in Vancouver I'd gone to the hostel laundry room to see about sorting all the dirty washing I was carrying around with me. Sitting on the first washing machine was a woman who was focused intently on her phone. Every so often the machine would go full speed and she would hold on for 20 seconds. When she saw me she jumped off, thinking it was my washing. Having checked out the machines, I went to leave, at which point she said something I didn't catch, so I ducked my head back around. Two hours later we finally left the laundry room laughing and chatting. By the way, it was not romantic; it was travelling chat, but this chat was quite special.

Keira was a tour guide for a local company and she was departing the next day. Keira was the same age as me (27) and had visited over 90 countries… Her passion for travelling was on another planet. We spoke for hours and I loved learning about her mission and objectives in life. Her friendly personality was warm and welcoming and just what I needed.

After 12 days in Vancouver with a non-stop diary, I decided to take a break and now, with Keira's help, I was in Kelowna. The city centre was just WOW. It had a beautiful lake called Okanagan Lake and I had a great time exploring this small town. The cultural district was well advertised and promoted, and it was a very vibrant part of the area – a lot was going on. But my agenda WAS EMPTY! I was planning on doing nothing more than walking around the lake and observing the tourists.

I sat on the harbour wall, swinging my feet over the edge. I sat at the pianos that were randomly located around the town, lost in the music while some drivers stopped to listen. The pianos and busking spots around town were organised by the people at Festivals Kelowna, who I became very good friends with after I left. But the best bit of the whole weekend was the moment I hired a kayak and, for two hours, got lost in a circular lake. Don't get me wrong – I was having a great time, but there was something that was crippling me. Especially when I was a dot in a kayak in the middle of the lake. I was fast coming to the conclusion that I was lonely. But loneliness leads to reflection, and reflection leads to great discoveries.

I learned a few things while I was travelling. I was discovering that travelling is an art. I'd seen a psychological change within my mind. I'd discovered a fresh love and appreciation for everything I encountered. I understood the differences in cultures that I'd met. And although I was only experiencing places for a short time, I was leaving behind a footprint that would stay in the world forever. As I sat in that kayak in the middle of the lake, I realised how fortunate I was to be able to walk a path that only I knew and understood how to navigate. Did I appreciate how fortunate I was in comparison to those who were in a different boat? And could I inspire others to think about their own journey?

In Seattle, I was struggling to see the end of the trip. In Tokyo, a hospital visit meant I couldn't do my runs anymore. In Saint-Étienne, I'd watched cyclists compete to be the best athletes in the world. In Pamplona, I'd discovered a culture beset with animal rights issues. In South Korea, I'd rushed to see a motor show and bought Turkish ice cream in the middle of Seoul. In Christchurch, I'd discovered a city that was rebuilding. In Riga, I met the most unwelcoming doctors. Life is about walking a pathway that creates the best for you. Everything I did and had still to do was creating a pathway I never knew I would walk. And I was reflecting on all this in the middle of the most majestic hills of the Okanagan Valley.

There was more to go; more steps along the pathway. But for now, I needed to paddle fast. My two hours were up soon, I was a long way out and there was a $100 dollar fine for being late.

I was returning to Vancouver for one last night before I headed back to the United States of America. I met up with University friends Lauren and Conor and it was fab! Vancouver was brilliant. The culture. The atmosphere. The people. The streets. The diverse programme of events. The tourism board who, I am sure, were probably not ready for the whirlwind of a Scottish hurricane that smashed through their office. It was as if I had planned to be in the city when basically everything was happening. In one respect my time in Vancouver was really long but, thanks to Tourism Vancouver and all the events I attended, time flew. Thanks, Vancouver – I will be back! But now it was time to fly to San Francisco…

San Francisco

From the airport, I went to the railway station and immediately got stuck in a long queue for the ticket machine. When I eventually got my ticket, I inserted it in the barrier, where a waiting police officer asked me, "All good?" As I hauled my luggage through the turnstile, I felt like I was being checked out. However, he redeemed himself by spending five minutes explaining to me why San Francisco was dangerous. Excellent. Absolutely perfect arrival. He told me all about the areas to avoid – including Tenderloin, the neighbourhood where I was staying. He warned me to keep everything close to me when I got to the station, and he also said, "Don't walk anywhere where there are groups of people. Or anywhere that is dark!" At that point I was all for turning around and heading back to Vancouver or ANYWHERE ELSE, FOR THAT MATTER!

A man was lying down in carriage three, his body sprawled over the four seats, shoelaces undone and liquid on the floor below him. As with Seattle, from the moment I arrived I realised that San Francisco is on the brink of a social epidemic. Downtown San Francisco is a complete contrast to the famous Silicon Valley area. Downtown doesn't cover just two or three blocks; it's seven blocks long, four wide, with homeless encampments everywhere. One time I took the wrong turning back to my hostel and ended up being accosted by the police. When I told them where I was staying, they said: "Okay, let's go for a walk..." and escorted me back. Although I was never threatened or robbed while I was in San Francisco, I never once felt safe in the area I was staying. Even in the areas known to be safe. Even in the hostel.

Could I do anything? No, but what I did do was send a very to-the-point email to the San Francisco Tourism Board, who were too busy to meet me – and may I add it was the only city so far out of the whole of North America that claimed to be too busy to meet me.

San Francisco is best known for Fisherman's Wharf, Alcatraz Island, the Golden Gate Bridge and Golden Gate Park. It's also the location of two of my favourite movies, *Sister Act* and *Mrs Doubtfire*. Tourists flock to see the sights of the city, the air blasting up through their hair on the cable cars that take them to the summit of the mountains, where the main streets are. I had chosen San Francisco simply mainly to visit the bucket list sites, including the Golden Gate Bridge. But how people consume attractions is interesting. Who decides which bridge is the most famous and needs to be photographed by millions and have its own visitor centre? What about the one that sits further downstream, uncared for, lonely, but doing just as good a job? History is written by humans for a purpose. But enough about that... Let me tell you about my first event in San Francisco.

Event 60: Pistahan Parade

Today was a really important cultural celebration. Those attending the Pistahan Parade came from a suburb just outside San Francisco, which was the largest community of Filipinos outside the Philippines. The parade would see us meander through the streets – but currently, a tour bus was stuck in the middle of the road closure.

I had emailed three days before the event, chancing my arm to see if I could meet an organiser. They were kind enough to offer me John (name changed) as my babysitter for the day. He was heavily involved as a senior volunteer and I asked him everything I could think of. I was especially keen to find out more about the social issues in the city, and I asked him, "Do you think the homelessness issue in San Francisco is acceptable, especially when it is literally at the bottom of this street and the mayor is standing over there?" It was early in the morning and he rubbed his eyes, but we managed to have a great conversation about the situation and how this event aimed to help.

The Filipino community in San Francisco dates back many years, with the majority living in Daly City in the San Francisco Bay area. In 2004, a Filipino Community Center was created as a place for Filipino families to have a base in the city. The community focuses on engagement, services and support for those who have chosen the USA as their home – well, as the place where they are allowed to follow their dreams.

In a nutshell, the Pistahan Parade brings the community together to celebrate the culture and cuisine of Filipino life. The parade itself was full of floats, music, colour and ethnic dances that would transform the streets of San Francisco. Around 80,000 people were welcomed to the festival site to enjoy stage performances, talks, art and culture, dance, health, sport and much more. I saw pride in each person attending or performing. I felt the energy. This passionate community was driving forward Filipino culture and history.

It was not yet 9am and families had already started to arrive, dragging their yawning kids along to experience a memorable celebration. San Francisco was still waking up as the operation began. Police arrived with traffic enforcement officers and I watched their confusion about which roads the parade would go down.

A parade can have two very different impacts. Firstly, it disrupts daily routines and causes chaos to car users, who beep non-stop because they are stuck. But parades also provide a platform for celebration and community spirit. For a short while, they bring to life the concrete and steel buildings that suffocate town centres.

Before the parade really got started, the MC introduced a number of 'political faces' ranging from city councillors and representatives of the state senate to others who basically wanted – in my opinion – to be seen to be supporting the world's largest Filipino community outside the Philippines. It was all about the face. All about getting out there and being seen to be supportive. The perfect photo opportunity for them. But what did they actually do? John said to me: "You really think they care?"

I was quite amazed by the political positioning of the parade; it felt like it had moved away from being about cultural celebration and instead was a showcase for politicians. A real shame. It felt like these politicians were saying: "I support you... so you support me." Welcome to American politics.

And then it began. After the speeches – which, for sure, were not the priority of the event and in fact were a complete waste of time – came the beat of a drum. Children danced to the beat as bands marched by, and the adults were also tapping their toes. The flag of the Philippines, flying on the side of a float, was more than a symbol; it was saying: "We are here... Welcome to our community... Let's dance." The mayor, London Breed, was the first African-American woman and only the second woman ever to serve as the mayor of San Francisco and she was leading the parade, albeit from the very back. I found it very 'American' to see the police department and fire department forming a guard of honour along the route for her.

As far as I could tell, the true meaning of this parade was slightly ambushed by politics. However, it was led by community members and, at a time when America is so divided, this worked. The parade may have disrupted people's normal daily routine but it was also an opportunity to educate them about a minority community. Sometimes people will buy in to such opportunities; other times, it is ignored. In many ways, parades such as this are a way for communities to be given a right of passage in the country they have chosen as home. On this occasion you couldn't help but feel an electric vibe from the noise, energy and colour. You couldn't help but tap your toe along to this completely free opportunity for engagement and learning. You couldn't help but feel the community are attempting to be more mainstream while keeping their traditions – which is critical, for sure.

One thing to take away...

It's important to celebrate the different cultures within society – but it's equally important to ensure you get the inclusion right. I felt I was part of the Pistahan Parade. I ate Filipino food, I met Filipino people and I even got a flag to wave. Along the way, I saw the political impact that this large community has. Parades are more than processions; they are cauldrons of opportunity.

Now, let's go fly a kite...

Event 61: Presidio Kite Festival

<u>10th August</u>

I was standing in the Presido National Park and today was all about kites. As a child in Glasgow, I remember there was an *red ash pitches* across from where we lived. My mum and dad and I would go over with my supermarket-purchased kite and we would watch it dive up and down for hours until it got tangled in a tree or landed literally on top of the secondary school. It was such a simple pleasure. And that is what this reminded me of – the simple joys, which are often the longest lasting ones. Add in some families and hey presto, it's time to fly kites.

This was my second event of the day and it turned out to be one of my top five events of the whole trip. I was boiling hot because I'd walked here and it was 34 degrees. However, it was a great day for kite flying because the wind at Presidio Park was blowy, and the long green lawns were the perfect location. Organised by the national park's events and engagement team, this was a way of engaging communities in San Francisco with somewhere that is very leafy and quite intimidating for those who don't live in picket-fence houses.

The engagement team's aim was to create events that brought in people who wouldn't normally come to the park, perhaps because they were put off by economic factors – it costs to go on day trips – but also because it can be daunting going somewhere unknown. The hope was they would come to an event to see what the park was all about and hopefully in the future they would come again for more events or even just to relax. So it was about attracting locals and diversifying the product to being more than simply a park in a very affluent residential neighbourhood. The most beautiful thing about the park's focus and direction was the approach they had to San Francisco's underprivileged areas. The picket fences and perfect driveways were a million miles away from the reality of San Francisco City. But the event organisers had booked a bus to bring in people who lived in under-privileged areas, as defined by social and economic factors, to come and build a kite and fly it – for free. No cost. It was as much their national park as it was those who drove to the event. No judgement here. This was a great thinking-outside-the-box operation by the event organisers that allowed them to break down barriers. No one should feel awkward when having a fun day out. Kites have a way of bringing a family unit together and this was the perfect way of doing that and creating joy.

A week before the event I emailed to ask whether I could meet the organisers. To my surprise, I got a reply: "Yes, Matthew – we can't believe you have chosen our event!" I met Margaret, who was part of the events team and the person who came up with the idea for the kite festival. I walked into a huge marquee with her and the noise was so energetically positive. Families were sitting on white fold-down seats at picnic-style tables. All the materials they needed were laid out in colourful baskets – like being at primary school on induction day. Small chairs for the adults and smaller chairs for the children. Everyone collected a recyclable paper kite and then they designed it. No time pressure. No need to give their address or any details.

Have you ever been somewhere and felt good just by listening to the buzz? Children were laughing and grabbing crayons. Parents were focused quite seriously on designing the perfect kite. Some families were working in silent competition. I think some of the parents were more engaged than the kids! Everything about the approach the organisers had taken – the impact the event had, its construction, the family environment, the fact that it was for ALL of San Francisco – was just overwhelmingly positive. I thought there must be a catch; there must be some other agenda. But no – it was just this. The connection with nature and the community. The use of the wind that blows this stretch of the park every day. Making use of a piece of land with lawns cut to perfection and just as perfect for launching kites. There were no tourists in sight – except me. And Margaret could not have been any nicer.

I loved the idea that instead of children sitting indoors playing console games, they had a chance to get out and smell the fresh air. But this free event had another purpose: to enable the family connection to become stronger. I didn't see any mobile phones in the marquee. This was a bonding event where communication was developed. I saw laughter and frustration, in equal proportion. That in itself is priceless. To see fathers and mothers engaging with their children in a place that allowed them to be free – just like the kite. Laughter was the only sound I could hear; well, laughter and the wind. Oh, and the occasional cry from a child as their kite nosedived straight down and broke. Or one parent untangling the kite string and trying not to say: "This was your fault," to the other.

As well as families, the event was open to kite enthusiasts who loved being able to showcase their creations. There was a whale in the air and a dragon coming up as well. This was about bringing together people who love flying kites and passing their enthusiasm on to those attending. It does not need 20,000 people coming through the gates and giving their email addresses. It needs to keep its central purpose – cater for a few thousand and be an amazing addition to the park and the area. This wasn't about San Francisco's tourism strategy. It was about keeping the park engaged with the local community. Allowing people to see what they had on their doorstep – and not just the Golden Gate Bridge. Inspiring emotion and making memories. Taking a photo of a family day out and loving each second. Posting on social media and showing the family together. That is what this event was about.

This was the second time the event had taken place and the skies above were so much brighter for having colourful kites swirling around. There are things the event can build on, especially sustainability, by discouraging single-use plastic and encouraging people to take public transport and recycle the kites they have made

– or keep them forever!

Let me finish with one word: nostalgia. Our world is very fast-paced. We are always in a rush to do things. We tweet in 240 characters. We Insta for a 10-second story. We like and share constantly without giving any thought to what it is we're liking. We read books as fast as we can, simply to start another one. We watch sports highlights because watching the whole match would be boring. But then something that was first introduced to us as a child – a kite – is brought into our lives again. Suddenly we forget about rushing through life. We forget about time limits. Instead, we spend time together as a family, giving each other attention and using our imagination.

Just as with games like hopscotch or Snakes and Ladders, kite flying is a way of passing on a torch of tradition. It's something so simple that does not just pass time but embraces it. It allows time to come on the journey and not just be the leader of the journey. We are living in a world that needs to pause and stop coming up with so many new ideas or fast-forwarding through moments that would be better meandered through. So, next time you are in a shop – why not buy a kite? Why not fly it and feel what I felt? Why not stop and watch the clouds and the blue skies above be brightened by your design?

Today, the kite was the product but the family connections were the outcome. Crayons scattered everywhere and ripped tablecloths in the marquee were not a problem because the event was a success on every level. Except for the crying child whose kite took off and never returned from the nearby trees...

One thing to take away...

Kites. Such a simple thing, but such a massive impact. They bring happiness. They make memories. Most of all, they offer an experience for all to engage with. Events don't always need technology to be advanced in their impact. A kite festival in a national park – genius.

Returning to San Francisco...

There were no major sporting events taking place while I was in San Francisco, but I did manage to secure a volunteer opportunity at a fitness competition... Well, it was advertised as a fitness competition. Ladies and gentlemen, welcome to the Pole Dancing Championships in San Mateo.

Event 62: PSO US National Pole Championships

<u>11th August</u>

My understanding was that the National Pole Championships were based on fitness – but then I was introduced to Emily, who told me about the sexy element of the event. For 10 minutes she talked me through everything to do with the sport, including the use of two poles and the whole 'on the floor' piece. The show was sponsored by companies who also had stalls there, selling many items for pleasure and enjoyment. But how did I end up volunteering at the Pole Dancing Championships in the first place…?

I've said before that I needed to attend events that were different; I also wanted to find events that were not just in the middle of cities. So say hello to a two-hour train journey, followed by a one-hour walk to San Mateo University, where the National Pole Championships were taking place.

I'd emailed the organisers to ask if I could volunteer and suddenly I had an email from Amy welcoming me to the team. No questions asked, except for the type of role I would like to have. There were five options: pole cleaner, backstage assistant, MC announcer, registration and door usher. Originally, I put down to be an MC. I thought it would be funny for the announcer to welcome the next performer to the stage in the broadest of Scottish accents. However, these positions had been taken by regulars. Instead, I was allocated a role as a door usher. Perfect. The event attracted an audience of friends and families of the dancers. I was not a regular here, or even part of the 'pole community' and it became clear everyone knew this. Everyone could tell I was not a pole dancer. Everyone involved was involved through fitness clubs – so there was an immediate community feel to the event.

Before I started my ushering, I got talking to some of the stall holders. They were intrigued about what a guy from Scotland was doing at this event. I explained I wanted to see the fitness pole dancing competition as part of my journey. They laughed. "Fitness?" I laughed back – and then looked at some of the products on offer, which were not, shall we say, PG. Hard balls, whips and other sex toys. *Shit,* I thought. One woman had driven for six hours from LA to sell her very kinky clothing. She laughed at my innocence and lack of knowledge about the competition and I laughed too at the fact that I had totally misunderstood what this event was about. Thankfully, I was just the door usher. But try dealing with some of the feisty pole dancers, who were totally not happy when I blocked them and wouldn't let them in during someone else's performance. I had to be that guy, or else I would get looks from the judges who were literally staring every time the door opened. For volunteering today, I was given a $5 voucher in a plastic wallet to spend on the stalls at the event. Yep, I could buy a solid plastic ball. Never mind my travel experiences; I could go home with some memorabilia from my time here. I gave it to Emily instead.

From my vantage point at the back of the auditorium, I could see the stage had two poles screwed in place. I had never thought I would ever be volunteering at a pole dancing championships, but here I was. Remember, we were in a university complex – but of course the campus was being hired out. The first couple of dancers were all about fitness and believe me, it was exhausting just to watch them. Then Emily advised me to read the sign outside:

SEXY ALERT

Upcoming performances celebrate the sexy side of pole! If you have small children attending, or friends and family sensitive to the sensual nature of pole, please be advised that some content of the exotic performances may not be suitable for them.

You are welcome to exit the venue and re-join us for the awards ceremony. Thanks for helping to respect all aspects of the pole community.

Okay, it was about to take off. Literally. No nudity; just new ways of moving around the pole. I laughed as I saw a family in the crowd cover the eyes of a young boy who completely should not have been there. But it was down to audience discretion and the organiser said: "Let them stay – he's one of the performer's sons." Okay... Most of the performers competed in a 'leisure' way. Many were university professors, office workers and so on.

I ushered at the doors for about two hours and I began to get know the crowd and the dancers pretty well. There were about a hundred people coming in and out of the door. This may have been a quiet event, but it was full of characters. At one point, two women came in and asked if I knew if their friend had been on. Checking the schedule, I couldn't see her name. Now remember, some of the dancers here were purely fitness and performed under their own names. But now we were past the curfew and it was SEXY time... Another usher came across and asked them if they knew what her stage name was. I laughed when the woman said, "No, I just work with her." The two women were obviously not part of the pole dancing community but, worse than that, I don't think they knew what they were about to experience. Just as they sat down, having figured out who their friend was, she walked on stage...

They clapped and then the hilarity began – for me. One of the women took out her phone to capture the proud moment of her friend performing. The phone stayed locked in her hand as her jaw dropped in a kind of 'Oooo' motion. I was speechless as I watched them. The performer was brilliant and needed extreme strength for the moves she was undertaking – but I think for her friend, it was all a whirlwind of emotions – and it never was captured on camera. The hilarious thing was after the performance the two ladies got up and walked back towards my door. Halfway across the foyer, they met the dancer. The friend gave her some flowers she had brought, and then introduced her to the other woman. So, the dancer knew this woman from work, and the woman had brought another friend... and I could tell it was the first time either of them had been to a pole dancing event. I wonder how Monday morning coffee was? May I add, they left straight after she had performed – either they had a knitting class to get to, or they were dashing away to buy a pole.

Some people may ask me why I went. From my perspective, it was a gathering of people who were there to perform their passion and engage with their fans – and it was brilliant to be part of it. I was given a (small) t-shirt and I visited another interesting event. I got to really delve in and experience first-hand the world of pole, which was mind-blowing. It's not my world – but that is why going to such diverse events is crucial. We must go to events that are different. The organisation hosting this event wanted outsiders to engage with their community and in return, they got something from it too.

One thing to take away...

Events come in all shapes and sizes – and poles. Pole dancing is an admirable leisure activity, and the championships gave those who want to engage a safe space to enjoy it, be part of a community, develop friendships and be the best on the pole.

24 Hours in Sacramento

I literally had not stopped for two days in San Francisco, what with the kite festival, the Filipino parade and the pole dancing (and never in my life did I think I would ever write that!). And now I was in Sacramento... Well, how can I even begin to describe the 24 hours I spent there? Compared with San Francisco, it was chalk and cheese. The charming capital of California has a lot of potential. Getting off the train, onto the tram and off to my first of eight meetings was rather delightful – and exhausting. The City of Sacramento had arranged lots of meetings for me, which was so lovely!

Mary Lynn is a legend in the City of Sacramento Volunteer Department. Considering I was only there for one day, she booked me into eight meetings, introduced me to two events and gave me another destination to add to my list. Sacramento was buzzing with activity, despite the streets being eerily quiet; the place is amazing in terms of content output. The amount I did in Sacramento could fill a whole chapter but here is a snapshot:

- Meeting with Sacramento Tourism – twice. We even had our photo taken next to a large fork… Yeah, I know – the things I do for social media.
- Lunch with the founder and organiser of Wide Open Walls (the Sacramento mural festival).
- City of Sacramento Volunteering Department.
- Volunteer Sacramento – independent organisers of volunteer roles at events.
- Sacramento History Museum.
- Sacramento Cultural Advisors for events and culture.
- Crocker Art Museum.

Mary Lynn had put together an unbelievable agenda for me. Sacramento really did offer a lot to the state of California. However, San Francisco and Los Angeles are still bigger magnets of appeal to tourists. Even in the hostel, the 10-dorm room I was staying in was empty. Literally, it was me and me alone. And this was at the height of summer. Yet these organisations are really forward-thinking about how they can create local and national engagement. How to diversify. Sacramento was beginning to have an impact in the sporting world with the Sacramento Kings, which meant that travelling fans of other basketball teams were travelling to the city. This gave them a good objective for moving forward – every time the team played away, they were promoting Sacramento. Genius. The city has some fascinating and interesting museums but strangely they don't attract the same number of visitors as more average museums in other cities.

The people in Sacramento could not have been any more

welcoming. I really was flabbergasted by their welcome; it was quite overwhelming. I walked along old railway lines at the historical Railway Museum. I was taken around buildings that had a majestic feel to them. Somehow I got the idea that Sacramento doesn't get visitors like me; they're not used to people appearing and wanting to know everything about the place – so if they could show me their most up-to-date paper shredder, they did! I wasn't just strolling about like a visitor; I was being shown around these museums by the directors. "Why do you think people don't come to Sacramento?" The tough question had to be asked. A lot of the time the answer was that LA and San Fran have established tourism strategies, and so on. But one person said something really interesting and I knew I needed to record it:

"Sacramento hasn't been found yet. We are waiting. When we arrive into people's lives – we will not disappoint..."

BINGO!

The capital of California had not yet been discovered by many people, nor, in my opinion, by itself. And these people knew it. I had a great time taking photos, meeting the voices of the city and listening to Irish music being played in O'Neill's Irish Bar (where I had a steak pie – delicious!). Bye, Sacramento – thanks for the memory!

Instead of going home that night, I decided to go and visit a friend of a friend in Davis, a town with a population of just under 100,000 and most famous for UCD – the local university. We had dinner, relaxed, chilled and the next day I jumped back to San Francisco for my last event there as well as my birthday.

Event 63: Hamilton:
An American Musical

14th August

"How does a bastard, orphan, son of a whore..."

And so the show begins. In 2009, Lin-Manuel Miranda was invited to perform poetry and music from his Broadway musical *In the Heights* for Barack Obama's White House administration. However, going off script, he performed something he was working on. At first it was laughed at, but this was the first glimpse the world had of *Hamilton: An American Musical.* Why would anyone do a musical about the history of US politics? By answering this question, Lin-Manual earned awards and global success. And so *Hamilton* was born...

In 2015, the show was performed off-Broadway. Four years later, the show had toured the US, been on New York's Broadway and found a home in London's West End. It swept the floor at the Tony Awards in 2017 – they may as well have been called the Hamiltons. Lin-Manuel Miranda has become a household name, which is rare for anyone from the musical world. After seeing the show, I now understand the euphoric excitement. I have been fortunate enough to have followed its development since 2009 so I understood the show but, nearly 10 years on from that original performance, I was at the point of GET ME THERE! So when I had the chance to see the show in San Francisco, I jumped on it like an Olympic hurdler. I also wanted this to be my birthday treat. For eight months I had carried a birthday card in my bag that my mum and dad gave me. They wrote in it: "Get yourself something nice." So, having already bought a ticket, I decided to treat myself to an ice cream and a show programme.

Due to the popularity of the show, tickets were outrageously priced. I somehow managed – officially, through Ticketmaster – to get a ticket for $90. My seat was at the very back of the theatre, but I was so excited to be even walking through the doors. In New York, tickets can go up to as much as $600. Now, let's break this down. You are a musical lover. You absolutely adore *Hamilton*. $600 is a pay cheque in itself. How can musical theatre sustain these prices? I'm not talking about devaluing the show, but opening them up to new markets of consumption. This would also help with another factor: the lack of diversity in the audience. On the stage it was all diverse, but it was very obvious that those who could afford a ticket were mainly middle-class white people. The theatre was located in the middle of the Tenderloin area where I was staying and the people who lived there had no chance of buying a ticket. The people attending the show could not have been any further away from those who lived outside the walls of the theatre. I walked into the theatre behind people wearing pearls on a Wednesday afternoon... I'd forgotten my pearls that day, but I did have my pink shirt on – again, not washed, but the shirt was bringing in all the glam.

My impression of the Orpheum Theatre was mixed. The theatre was part of Pantages Theatres and opened in 1926. Based in the middle of San Francisco, it was the home of the big shows: *Miss Saigon, Hamilton, Bat Out Of Hell* and so on. In 1998, it underwent a renovation that completely changed the interior and freshened the place up. It could be a lovely theatre. But the seats are so close to each other, it's like being in the economy section on a very cheap airline and it decreases the experience for the consumer. Theatres are quite outdated when it comes to the customer journey. Putting the customer experience at the heart of what a theatre does is exactly what I think they have missed.

As I entered, I was met by a man who I think would rather have been at home watching Dr Phil on the TV with his feet up and a cold beer in his hand. He scanned my ticket without a smile. Instead, his face should have been saying, "YOU ARE ABOUT TO SEE A GLOBAL SPECTACLE... ARE YOU READY?!" Okay, maybe not that excited, but most certainly different to what I was seeing. Once I stepped into the theatre the usual carpet design met my feet – gold swirls on a bright red background. I was discovering that those events that hadn't thought about the customer journey were bucket list events and those in high demand. On the other hand, smaller, more niche events really put their heart and soul into making consumer satisfaction the most important thing. Free events, in my opinion, had happier staff, happier outcomes, happier moments of satisfaction and an overall higher success rate. This, of course, was not a bad event I was at – but the theatre was letting it down. *Hamilton* is on another level but despite the renovation the customer journey seemed old and rusty. Some theatres have just fallen into the trap of not evolving. Even the merch stand, with its torn poster displaying all the merchandise, didn't represent the show. The price list was literally held up with Blu Tack and the MERCHANDISE sign was sellotaped on. I felt like I was in a seaside gift shop full of tourist tat. It wasn't like 'Buy me – you need to take me home!' There was no illusion of perfection and the staff had no urgency to fix any of it.

The story of Alexander Hamilton was amazing. The show was powerful. The cast were just incredible. The set design, the emotional connection between the actors and the audience, the feeling you were left with, the interest the event inspired in you about American politics – it was all truly special. It was all quite incredible. The logo for the show and the impact it has made in society was totally backed up by the lyrical and musical performance. I was awestruck.

A performance on stage can create an emotional connection. As the performers whiz around the hydraulic-controlled stage, they capture the audience. They hold the audience in their arms. No one is allowed to escape the emotional power of this show. The couple next to me, who were 81 and 83, sang every word. Each word means something to those who are watching. You try not to sing out loud but there is something that makes you want to. It's the same with other shows, like *Mamma Mia,* maybe. Different, completely different, but very similar. We act the performance with the performers – because we have watched the YouTube videos and listened to the soundtrack (and now, probably seen it on Disney+). The stage is not only the stage we watch; it is the stage we sit upon. The seats may be laid out in a semi-circle, but the atmosphere is created all around and it's not only the stage that is lit up, decorated and acted upon. The audiences are extras – and extras are as important as the lead artists.

The costumes the performers wear take us back to an era we will never fully appreciate, maybe through ignorance, maybe because we were not previously open to let it into our lives. The costumes of the audience also tell a story – the story of the haves and the have nots. Those wearing designer gear wear it to tell their own story. I had now worn the same shirt for the last three months at most of the important meetings I had attended. I observed those around me and took in the shine of the shoes, the sparkle of the belt buckles – but then suddenly I saw someone in light green shorts and a pink shirt. Shorts in a theatre – I was in shock! His Ray Bans kind of gave it away but again, the costumes the audience wear can tell a story of their own. His story was 'I am allowed – I have money...' But sometimes it's about what's underneath the costume. The confidence. The approach to pulling it off. I was acting with what I was wearing – so this in itself was a performance.

It was never the intention for *Hamilton* to become a show for the elite. Lin-Manuel Miranda's breakthrough musical was *In the Heights* and he was all about equality. But now I realised how many barriers theatre still needs to break down. Maybe because it was launched in the White House, with those with money and power watching, *Hamilton* had now fallen into a trap and become something it never aimed to be.

I looked at those attending and thought, "What have they actually gained from being here? What is the takeaway message?" What if this show toured a hundred schools (which I know it has done) and those schools put on their own version of *Hamilton:* part educational and part fulfilling a dream. Imagine those kids getting on a stage. In 2020 they launched a programme to roll out to 250,000 kids a *Hamilton*-inspired educational programme. There's much more to be done to break down the curtain of class in this constructed division. And I know it can happen – but sometimes fame means people run away from the challenge and become too busy…

One thing to take away…

I fully believe *Hamilton* has the opportunity to break down social class boundaries – because of its influence on society. But please – go and perform a pop-up in deprived areas rather than only playing in positive financial pockets.

San Francisco… my last three days

So, my time in San Francisco was up. My last night was spent listening to the sirens of fire, police and ambulances racing through the city to another stabbing. The area where I stayed really did cast a cloud over how I perceived the whole city. Everyone I spoke to back home had said, "Oh, you'll love San Fran…" but my first impression unfortunately affected my thoughts and seeing 20 used needles scattered on a main street at 9am on a weekday was daunting. So, if you ever go travelling, don't listen to someone who has had the red carpet laid out for them. Listen instead to someone who has watched, smelled and felt the heartbeat of the city. San Francisco has a future; just not a present…

Los Angeles

I arrived in LA in the most glamorous way possible – on a sweaty smelly bus to the railway station. Hollywood has a way of sucking you in and for eight days I was going to be another tourist addicted to the bright lights and the idea of becoming a star. Los Angeles City has a lot of really interesting characters and areas. Actors in every subway and branch of McDonalds. Did you know there are at least 110 cities in Los Angeles County? Just take a moment to think about that. The area has a population of 10.4 million (double the population of Scotland); it is the most populous county in the USA. Because of its complicated mapping and geographical breakdown, there is no city centre. Bizarre, but it means each area has its own identity. I liked the place but, because I'd based myself in the most touristy district, I could only come to the conclusion that Spiderman likes McDonalds, Batman is overweight and has back issues and street vendors maybe have limited knowledge of health and safety when it comes to food handling – welcome to the Hall of Fame – which was truly not a side of LA that was at all appealing or attractive.

My time in LA began on the train from Union Station. I got on the red line, dumped my bags on the seat and tucked my body against them to make some space on the seat next to me. On came a family with a newborn baby. In the space of 20 minutes, the family and I got to know each other and had a great discussion about the world, how they had met at university and were now married with children and so on... They were lovely, but for the life of me I cannot remember their names. I wish I did – they were just a perfect family. But they said something I didn't forget. "Don't take your eyes off your pockets and listen to your heart..." Interesting. I was starting to see a theme in the areas I was visiting.

I settled into my hostel and somehow fell asleep despite the backdrop of continuous beeping from the traffic along the Walk of Fame. The next thing I knew, I woke up at 9am... to silence!

Event 64: CicLAvia

18th August

I definitely remember hearing horns when I went to sleep but, as I looked out of the window of the hostel, there was no traffic. I was so confused. Some cyclists sped past but there were no cars. Overnight, the street had become an event site. Marquees were being set up and speakers tested. It seemed there was a live event taking place on the Walk of Fame. Perfect. I was a bit tired this morning, so it was ideal to find an event literally on my doorstep.

Today was CicLAvia, which is held six times each year. It is organised by a non-profit organisation whose focus is on increasing awareness and benefits of cycling as well as a mode of travel in a county where cars are God. On Instagram, they have over 29,000 followers – I suppose out of a population of 10 million, it's a strong 0.2%. That's positive. I loved the focus of the event, which was about enabling people to cycle on streets that are normally full of cars. An area 2km long by 200 metres wide had been closed to motor vehicles. The police on duty were brilliant at engaging with visitors and telling angry motorists to go away. The event was not only to raise awareness of cycling but to act as a catalyst for change.

A sea of cyclists met me and I realised I was walking in an allocated cycle lane. I soon jumped onto the pavement. The organisation wanted to empower the residents of LA to take over their streets. They wanted to show how the streets of LA can be filled with bikes rather than filled with hotdog carts and lookalike Elmos and Mickey Mouses (who charge $15 and above for a group photo – don't get me started). I absolutely adored this event because of its objectives to have an impact on health, the economy and air quality. Reports estimated that over the nine years CicLAvia has taken place, over 1.6 million people had cycled as part of it.

The event was well manufactured and a real asset to the local economy. Cafes were mobbed with locals, shops full of people who didn't usually venture to this area and so on. I kid you not – people who live in LA don't come to Hollywood Boulevard. Organisers in branded t-shirts were welcoming visitors to the event – positive engagement. People had cycled from all across the county to get to CicLAvia and were celebrating an area that was slowly being re-captured by the locals – for a set period of time, of course.

I spoke to a representative of the city mayor, who was nowhere to be seen – but his pop-up and his staff were. When I explained what I was doing, they asked if I had arranged to meet LA Tourism. Sadly, they were one tourism board who hadn't replied to my emails but within 12 hours I was being introduced to their Vice President.

Celebrating the local area was important during this event. The stage had key speakers who were local cycling advocates – local celebs who cared about the environment but weren't looking for fame. It was pleasing to see real no political party representation here.

Air pollution on the route had decreased over the years by 20-40% and CicLAvia were the ones making a difference, not the celebs who lived literally 2km away up in the hills. This was a huge achievement by all involved. The decrease in pollution was slowly improving the disastrous impact LA has on the environment. Of the 10 million people who call LA home, 7.8 million of them have a car. Just think about that. Imagine rush hour...

CicLAvia was a carnival for cyclists. They felt safe cycling with no cars around. Nothing to disrupt their ride. On the event website was a whole host of studies regarding the scientific impact CicLAvia has on air pollution, climate change and so on. It was a bit different from your usual type of event advertising, but a positive way of showing the true impact it had. The website was a fountain of change. On the streets, the happiness of those attending was clear. Bells were rung and the streets were able to breathe again. I watched people securing helmets to bikes as they headed into shops they may never have visited before. No mass crowds or waiting at traffic lights. With a stage, marquees, a live zone, police and so on, this was a proper set-up for an event with purpose. Through their engaging programming, it was a great way of promoting the idea of cycling in the city. "We are getting closer to our goal... We are changing the mindset of thousands... We are CicLAvia." A very powerful and defiant speech closed the event.

Since it was a Sunday morning the tourists hadn't arrived in droves yet. But as soon as the bikes cycled away the crowds would arrive – and all of this would be gone, until the next one. Closing so many roads is a huge operational and logistical nightmare. I decided to take a quick hop outside to the left and right of the event and witness the traffic jams – it was a disaster. Literally. Cars were at a complete and utter standstill. At some intersections it was physically impossible to completely close the road. Instead, road marshals were waving orange flags at the cyclists and using yellow straps to control the groups. Police on bikes were enforcing the rules, including telling cyclists when to dismount because of crowd congestion, or instructing people not to cycle on pavements.

Sometimes, everything seems so perfect inside an event but on the outside there's madness. It's a reflection of an event's impact and legacy. Will car owners ever be happy with CicLAvia? Not a chance – but they could become part of it.

One thing to take away...

I think cycling is so important to a city. LA is never going to be Amsterdam. But when those people running the city look at how they can be impactful, change mindsets, create new ways of living and travelling, powerful change can happen. This was not only a big fancy cycling event; it was a movement. Movements are vital – but in LA, I suppose if it is not Instagram-worthy, it's simply seen as questionable and annoying. A movement of change was pedalling forward!

Back to Los Angeles...

Los Angeles is a magnet for tourists who want to get photos next to the Hollywood sign, outside the Staples Center, by the Hollywood Bowl – it was all very flashy. But on a street to the right of the Hollywood Bowl was a homeless encampment. I was beginning to see a trend on the West Coast. Homelessness and drug addiction were plaguing the streets. This was what I saw on my journey. On the buses, I heard local voices tell their stories. I saw train carriages abandoned on the tracks and set up as homes. Heart-wrenching. The inequalities on the streets of LA are apparent to those who look. And there's an obvious racial divide in some areas. These issues, combined with rising unemployment, were a recipe for disaster. Cities can run the best tourist campaigns. They can host the best events to bring in international visitors and sponsors. But their own people are sometimes left behind. City halls are often blind to the real problems when money is flashed in front of them.

Now it was time to go and see what making a TV show in LA is like.

Event 65: The Price is Right

Remember when you were a child, you would watch a TV show and think, "I wish I could be in that audience"? Well, tonight I was contestant number 005 and I was about to find out what it was like to sit in on a TV show...

The Price is Right is one of the most iconic TV programmes, and it has been beamed globally for decades. It began in 1956 and the show in America has been presented by Drew Carey since 2007. Contestants can win all sorts of things including fridges, boats, cars and even planes, but the thing they all want is the money. The programme is 30 minutes long and they record it just as if it's a live broadcast. The show always seems to be highly energetic on TV, and I wanted to find out how it was produced and how people consumed the live product. I wanted to see what it was like to be an audience member and a fan, and find out what the taping of a TV show is like. On top of that, I want to introduce you to some of the people I met – the Americans who absolutely love the show and wanted to be a part of it for many reasons.

It was 11:45am and there were only a few of us here at the moment. I was sitting on the bleachers in the shade but it felt like the inside of a slowly cooling oven. I was presented with a document that was 10 pages long – a legal contract with a lot of important information about being on the show. I'd gone simply to be in the audience; I hadn't anticipated being a contestant. However, I soon realised I wouldn't be allowed to because I was not an American citizen, so I couldn't pay the federal tax due on anything if I won. Yes, that's right – you win the money but the government is waiting to strip a large amount away. If you win something you don't want, like a boat, you have to keep it anyway and you pay the tax on its value. Quite a surprise if you live in a flat on the 23rd floor – you're stuffed with your boat. I witnessed the excitement of winning soon disappear after the show when the winners and their families realised they were not only going home with a TV, but with a bill they didn't ask for. I was so relieved that I knew I couldn't be picked. After signing the contract, my phone was taken away and I was whisked away for a photo – which I could buy for $10; smart business.

Now, I sat for five hours in the middle of the bleachers, getting to know those around me. I quickly learned when it was good to chat and laugh and when it was appropriate to be silent. Without us knowing, the producers had walked around the audience sussing everyone out before they introduced themselves four hours later. But I was not bothered at all and neither were the people sitting next to me. Husband and wife Bob and Anne from Detroit were on one side, and grandmother and grandson Nita and Steve from Phoenix, Arizona on the other. We had a blast. For hours we laughed and joked – without anyone else trying to step in. It was 33 degrees that day and we were sitting under a corrugated iron roof. It wasn't ideal for anyone who struggled with the heat, and I made sure Nita, who was well over 30 (well, maybe over 80) had enough water.

We had arrived here at 11:30am and had to be in position in the studio by 4:30pm. *The Price is Right* t-shirts (homemade) were being worn by nearly every other person. There were groups of hen parties of older women who had chosen the show as their final farewell to single life. Some characters were trying to ensure they were the number one pick for the producers. Bob and I sat analysing the crowd and discussing who would be chosen – and in three instances we were spot on. Nita and I discussed life. It was so lovely to get to know this woman, who was so excited to be here. It was the first time she had taken a flight to LA – or flown anywhere, for that matter. Before today we had never dreamt this bond would occur – but thanks to the bleachers, the steel benches of the studio and the ridiculous procedures, we were now family. The problem was there was nothing comfortable about these bleacher seats or the environment we'd been herded into. On the ticket it did mention we would be held – but it didn't say for how long. We weren't given anything, not even water, although there was a café where we could buy hot dogs and pizzas for $10. I bought a few slices and shared them amongst my friends, along with a bag of M and M's – which were soon melting in my hands.

With an hour to go, the audience was beginning to lose energy. Suddenly, previous episodes were beamed onto screens that had probably been installed back in the 90s. Although I was not asleep I was slowly drifting off and the noise woke me up. I had a feeling this was what you call brainwashing but thankfully, my friends and I were not buying into it. We were just here for the ride. Then the producers came along and lined us up like zoo animals along the barrier and we were asked to introduce ourselves: name, where we were from and why we wanted to be on the show. I said my name and immediately the producer shouted, "Freedom!" Excellent – I'm in. Well, no, I wasn't in because my next line was: "I'm a traveller… Writing a book about this…" He laughed. I don't think he realised I was serious. He walked on and I wasn't chosen, but being in the crowd was good enough for me. After another hour we were split into groups and taken into the studio. With my ticket being number 005 I was expecting to be near the front but that wasn't the case. However, I was seated with Bob and Anne, with Nita and Steve in front of us; maybe we looked like the perfect family. "Nita? You alright? You just tell me if you need anything and I'll get it," I said, and everyone around us howled at this Scotsman screaming across a studio. Thankfully I wasn't thrown out, and Nita's grandson Steve started to explain to those around us who I was.

The brightness of the studio was completely unexpected after sitting in what was basically an outdoor shed for five hours; now it felt like we were in a fish bowl. I watched as some people were moved to specific seats and everyone was like, WOW. I simply thought, "Cool – when can I eat my dinner?" Now remember, we didn't have our phones, so there was no way to capture this experience on screen, but it was actually nice to consume it with open eyes and heart – and, for those taking part as contestants, with their social security number, because the taxman was waiting. It hadn't happened often during my trip that I could enjoy the moment and keep the memories in my mind instead of in my photo gallery.

So… It was time for the show to begin. A warm-up artist was responsible for squeezing as much energy as he could from the audience. Placards with the names of the chosen few were 'hidden' in plain sight to the side of the stage. The crew were setting up and the models who present each prize were getting prepared to go into position. With their hair concreted with spray. Some music was playing but it wasn't doing it for me. But for many in the audience, this American staple of entertainment was just the perfect dose of an injection that was allowing them to 'feel free'.

We were given our instruction. It was simple. Be as excited as you can possibly be. I mean, some people were up and howling like they had just won $1 million. I laughed, and just kept clapping as Drew Carey came on with his long thin stick microphone. We knew when the cameras were pointed at us. It was all very staged. Well produced, but I would say only half the crowd were fully awake because it had been such a long hot day. If only they'd given us water; it would have been a nice treat.

One by one, contestants were pulled down to the front where they competed to go onto the stage to contend for those prizes. "What is the cost of 250 grams of sugar?" was one of the questions. I got that wrong. At one point I noticed the producer switch contestants; at the last minute they changed the prompt cards of who was going on stage next and wrote down a different name. When the whole audience is watching, I would recommend making such actions slightly less obvious – especially when the CBS security guards and all the staff knew the young man who went up, and was high fiving and hugging them all after the show. It was slightly staged. Occasionally, the producer would come out of the control room to the side and shout: "This side – I need more energy…"

So, after eight hours and being part of the show and adding to the fake energy, it was time to leave. We were held in the studio and instructed but everyone was like, "No chance, we are out of here!" So out we went and collected our phones. I have never seen a place go from being so loud to so quiet, so quickly. It was an interesting change in the dynamics as we transformed from a collective to individuals. For me, it was time to say goodbye to Bob and Anne and Nita and Steve. This was the hardest part. I hated saying goodbye to people I had connected with. But Nita and Steve had a plane to catch – they were literally only here for the day. However, Bob and Anne had offered to show me around Detroit when I arrived there in due course.

I had mixed emotions about my day. I thought the whole process was poorly organised. People pay to come to LA – and, specifically in a lot of cases, to be in the audience of a TV show. The Price is Right has hardcore fans. Planes, trains and hotels are booked and services bought so fans can get to this stage and be part of the show. But when you get here, it feels like you are being enrolled at a new high school. Some of the staff didn't seem to care and waiting in a really warm area was quite a contrast to the air-conditioned studio with the brightest of lights. The staff maybe need to be grateful they have work and grateful they are part of this show – and not dream about what it could be like to be on the stage and not behind it. It was as if this event and the stage setting was dazzling people from the truth. Well, it was. Win $10,000 and you get taxed – a lot. Win a boat that you don't want, need or use – but you still get taxed on it. Actually, the best thing to do was to be boring and not get picked.

One thing to take away…

Actually, my one thing was four people: Bob, Anna, Nita and Steve.

They were the best things about today.

Back to the streets of LA...

The streets of LA are plastered with artwork. Art murals painted everywhere many of them have now become tourist attractions. I mean, that's a chapter in itself. *'Art is more than paint...'* I was sitting at a table outside a cafe waiting for my food when a man sat down next to me. I still had my 005 number on, and he laughed. "You been in a TV show audience today?" he asked me, and we got talking. I told him all about my adventure and he talked about his role here in LA; he was heavily involved in charity work within the LGBT community. He had been part of Elton John's charities back in the 90s and had also done a lot of work with major events within the LGBT movement more recently. I gave him my thoughts, as an outsider, on Pride and the commercialisation and whether people actually understood the problems that affect the community. He said: "You've got it spot on. We live in a world where commercialisation is changing our ability to sometimes see the truth. It's masked." He talked about inclusion in education, he spoke about AIDS medication and so on. We chatted for about an hour as the sun was setting; the café actually closed but we stayed in the seats that were left outside. I loved that every time I had a chance encounter it filled me with joy and knowledge. His movement and his organisation were positively impacting people's lives in a way that a celebration with glitter and coffee chain sponsorship never will. And yet he was struggling for funding, and the organisation was struggling to survive.

Tomorrow I was meant to be going to see the filming of *America's Got Talent* but instead I changed my plans very suddenly, and changed from shorts and t-shirt to my fancy pink shirt and shiny shoes. Fortunately, it was a change of plan that worked...

Event 66: Will and Grace Taping

21st August

When I told my mate Ajay about my change of plans, he pleaded with me: "NO! Go to *America's Got Talent* – it will be SO much better for your project." But personally, I knew I would be more excited watching *Will and Grace*. I stood outside Universal Studios for three hours before the queue opened. Nothing would stop me getting in. It helped that the security guard at the gates became my new best friend. She was like, "I'll make sure you get in..."

Before we go into the details of the most exciting event ever, let's talk about the show *Will and Grace*. Created in 1998, it came out at around the same time as *Frasier* and *Friends* – shows that were having an impact on American culture. Over 22 years later and after 11 seasons, the show was calling it quits. But the impact it had was so much bigger. In America, coming out as gay on a TV show was a no go and crossed a fine line. As was noted by LGBT community forums and websites at the time, the social awareness, the breakdown of stereotypes and the acceptance of being gay was the biggest success and the biggest weapon the show had. The positive impact it made led to a more inclusive attitude in the world of showbiz.

The diverse audience was dressed very smartly. For many people this was date night; for others, it was a night for celebrating an anniversary, or a birthday treat. We had ethnic communities represented, and people of different sexual orientations. It was mind-blowing how different it was to *The Price is Right*. In a way, if you could compare it to American politics, this audience was a representation of the future of America!

The filming of *Will and Grace* was not just another TV comedy; it was a show like no other. The whole thing, production and management of the audience, was just so slick. Before we boarded the bus that took us to the studio complex, everyone who drove in was told to return to their cars and leave their phones. I had obviously walked here. As I stood in the queue I talked to one of the people wearing a headset – so they must be official – and was honest about having my phone with me. "Just keep it out of sight," they said. "You'll be fine." We were bussed across to the studio and put into groups. This was all so civil – there was no competing to get on the show. No personality clashes. I spoke to a lovely couple who had met at a taping of *Will and Grace* and were now returning for their anniversary. They both admitted that the show had helped them understand more about socially accepting the gay community and that was why they felt they needed to return this season. Others had been to the recording before and knew how to get the good seats. I was now with Dinita and Jesus (he was on my side), who were huge fans. The seats were up at the very back, high above the studio floor. The set was broken down into three main areas: office, apartment and then an area that could be chopped and changed to fit the storyline.

Music began and we were introduced to our amazing MC, Roger. This character entered the room with a huge smile on his face and took us through what to expect. I had been briefed by Jesus that he would ask the audience for questions. I immediately tried to think of something but was struggling. I didn't think 'What's your favourite breakfast cereal?' would cut it. Then the cast came out and bowed and Roger introduced them to the audience. He was up in the seats with us – not even he could get down to the studio floor, and they couldn't hear what was being said from above the gods. He advised us all about when was a good time to go to the toilet and so on; he was very engaging. As for what happened next... well... I'll never be able to fully explain my reaction...

The questions began. A sea of hands rose. The Aussies, of course, were in the house, the French and so on... I'm shouting "SCOTTISH!" but Roger was at the other side of the long studio, so I missed the chance. The lights dimmed and again we began,

Roger's voice slowly calming the crowd down. "And roll..." was what we heard from the set. The producers and directors had large boards that they pushed along to follow the script. They were watching the audience's reaction to the jokes rather than the actual scene, and in many situations the jokes were changed. Sometimes the producers asked the audience what we preferred. It was very engaging and led by the audience reaction.

During the next break in recording, Roger asked if anyone had any questions. Dinita and Jesus were pointing at me as I stretched my hand as high as I could. "You, sir in the pink shirt... Yes sir, what is your name?"

"Matthew..." I said. And then this is where it got special. Word for word – this is what happened.

"Matthew... I am going to guess you are from Scotland." I nodded. "Come on down..." He had no idea who I was or that I was on a journey. And then the music played and everyone was clapping. Down I went to the front of the area of the gods – with 240 people staring on. The energy in the room was electric so I thought, *Go for it.* I danced down the stairs. I was high fiving the front row and spinning my way to Roger. The way the seating bank was arranged, we were 10 feet up from the studio floor. Roger was howling as we embraced. "Matthew, yeah?" I nodded as he went back on the mic. I just got lost in the moment. I used this opportunity to captivate the audience. I wanted to ensure I didn't waste a second. At this point Roger was looking at me in awe and laughing. Once we hugged, he said: "Oh, this is going to be good!" He asked me a series of questions and then asked me what I was doing in LA. I stood and looked at the audience and said:

"I am about to become the first person in the world who has ever been 'Around the World in 80 Events' to 26 countries and 80 events, to understand what the events industry is like, globally. This is my dream and I am on a journey to inspire others to live theirs..."

I watched as a woman wiped a tear from her eye – she had something in it. Roger whispered in my ear, "That is amazing." He kept asking me leading questions about what the journey was about.

So I said to him: "Well, it's simple. Everyone in this room has a dream. We all have dreams that we sometimes think are not possible. We build barriers before we understand what we need to do to fulfil the dream. But together we can achieve our dreams…"

Roger was just brilliant. He asked me all about the countries and events I had visited. I explained that this was one of the events and I was trying to understand the impact of the show and the audience engagement. Suddenly he looked behind and winked. Down on the studio floor was a well-dressed man who looked up and said, "Who's this?"

I turned around and said: "I am Matt Lamb – I am going 'Around the World in 80 Events'." And I gave him my business card.

Unbeknown to me, the man was Steve, one of the executive producers at the channel. He was **the man**. He checked my website on his phone and said, "Well, you're legit." Roger kept asking questions until Steve said: "Have you got your phone?" I said I did and apologised. "Turn it on and take photos. Tell the world about us," he said.

Roger said to me, off mic, "That is huge – you just got permission to take photos."

Steve then said to Roger, "At the end we will get him on the set for a photo on the couch." I was like – NO WAY! Going back up to my seat, people were giving me high fives, waves, 'This is brilliant!' and so on. I was on cloud 109, never mind cloud nine.

So the show began and it was recorded. But my experience was not over yet.

At the end of the show, Roger told me that I was able to go on set after being given permission by Steve. He asked me to wait. Suddenly a queue was forming of people pleading with Roger to get them on set. This included some of the people I had met in the original queue, who were asking for autographs. It was quite interesting when Roger said no. At one point Roger and I both had queues in front of us, which was funny. One was pleading with Roger to be allowed on set and the other to ask me about my journey!

We went down some steps and suddenly we were on the set. Instead of just sitting on the couch for a photo, I heard: "COME ON, MATTHEW..." It was Steve shouting and beside him was *Will and Grace* star Debra Messing. Yep, Grace herself! She'd stayed on the set with her family and I got to meet her. Again I took advantage of the opportunity and asked Debra to do a video for me to say #comeonthejourney... It was so special! I couldn't believe what was happening. Roger stood at the side, just laughing as I lapped it all up. This was my adventure in a nutshell – seek something and in return, don't waste the opportunity!

Thank you to Roger, Steve and Debra for letting me be on the set of a show I have watched and laughed away to for years.

I absolutely could not have road mapped this part of the journey. Meeting Grace from *Will and Grace* was certainly not at all part of the plan. I was meant to be at *America's Got Talent* – but instead I created a memory that will live with me forever. Things often happen for a reason, even if we don't understand it at the time. And this is because if we did, we may not engage with it in the same way. If our lives are all prepared and we can't engage, react and energetically love each moment, we may not fully appreciate it. It is not for us to have it all planned out; instead, it is for us to be ready.

One thing to take away...

You never know what will happen in life – but whatever does happen, always take it with both hands and enjoy it! You never know who you will meet or what life will give you. Whatever it is – sing, dance and twirl – use every opportunity you have to be the best you can.

LA...

So, after that wonderful experience, I was still on cloud nine – but there was no time to rest. The next day I wanted to shed some light on the world of university (college) sport in America. But before then I went to a diner and ordered pancakes.

Event 67: UCLA Women's Soccer

23rd August

The University of California Los Angeles has some great sporting achievements to its name. Sporting activities alone incur budget expenses of over $125 million, and sponsorship and membership ($14 million achieved through 8,000 memberships alone) bring in an income that professional teams could only dream of in some countries. It is a quite extraordinary financial model within sport. In terms of funding and individual and corporate sponsorship, the structure is truly eye-watering – but the university is not actually the best in the state or even the country; it's more of a League One kind of university.

As I arrived to the university campus, which was its own city with its own shops, hospital and police department, I saw the stereotypical American alpha buildings – like delta houses with picket fences and cheerleading squad poms poms on the balconies. Entering the campus, I could see that this university had a lot of money, that's for sure. After some research, I found out that UCLA has a budget of well billions a year. Yes. In comparison to the GDP of a country, it is on the same level as Malawi and higher than Andorra and Bhutan and Tongo – combined. I mean. My mind was blown.

I went to two of the university shops, which are all within a mile of each other, to buy a lanyard and postcard. Welcome to the store of all stores. I walked in to what was probably the size of a soccer pitch. It sold everything – and it was on two floors. Upstairs was the book department and downstairs was everything else an American college student needs, from hoodies and t-shirts to a calendar of Scotland. Like, I mean – of course. In the travel section I even found a book about Glasgow. The shop was basically your local supermarket with everything stamped UCLA. It also had a post office, a police department booth, a bus station helpdesk and food markets – and that was just what I was able to access.

Tonight, it was UCLA Women's first soccer match of the season against Iowa Thunders. Fans from Iowa were sitting on the right of the bleachers and they were quite vocal considering only 50 of them had made the trip over. A thousand other spectators were on the bleachers singing along to the songs being broadcast around this very impressive and professional stadium. I had bought my ticket on Ticketmaster for $12; if I was a student here I could have free access to all the sporting events. Everyone was UCLA-branded – staff, students and fans alike.

The screen was the main fan engagement piece. As the music played, the screen showed pre-recorded headshots of the players coming up and staring the camera down. Even I felt intimidated. The floodlights were dimmed and then it began. The mascot. The music. And the mothers and fathers who all knew each other. "Yeah, I managed to get work to send me down on business; I'm staying at the (insert fancy hotel) here for four nights – she doesn't know I am here but I won't be able to see her because I need to get back for a call with Tokyo. But I'll see her in four months for Christmas." I mean. Wow. It felt like I was living in some type of elite world of separation by wealth but loneliness by choice.

I was so intrigued about everything that was happening on the bleachers, never mind the fierce football. It was like a cheesy American sitcom starring Z-list celebrities. The community of UCLA was tight. People came wandering down to catch a bit of sport after studying in the library, instead of going back to their dorms. The students had their own section and I was in the public domain with the families. The families all had their own spots and had brought chairs they connected to the bleachers. Occasionally the parents would shout: "Coach, what are you doing?" Well, firstly the coach was on an average wage (I discovered, after some research) so, considering he was coaching a Division 1 team, I don't think he deserved the abuse that this UCLA blue t-shirt-wearing mother was throwing at him. Mummy and Daddy were ensuring their children were getting as much play time as they could – even if they were shockingly bad. But also, the more time they spent on the pitch, the more chance there was a scout may spot them.

I'd smuggled in a Twix bar and ate it as I watched the game. I was getting right into it. Everyone seemed very upbeat – smiling but focused – and that was just the crowd. The way people were engaged with the game was quite extraordinary. Whenever there was a wrong tackle or a wrong pass there was a huge "OOOOOO!" or "REFEREE, YOU KIDDING ME?" I am always amazed by how people get so engrossed in something they cannot influence – but feel they can. The badge at their heart means they are connected. Engaged. The players are not paid but were treated like professional athletes. Does this special treatment prepare them for an unrealistic pathway into the real world?

Women's soccer in the USA has a large and positive following. Literally two weeks before I arrived in the States, the USA had won the Women's World Cup for football – which meant the sport had just been propelled even higher. Soccer had first seen a spike in popularity in 2009, which resulted in college teams beginning to pay more attention to the sport. An increase in women's football camps and sponsorship opportunities led to more success for the women's teams.

The whole thing was spectacular. Seeing the growth of women's football for the second time on my journey showed me how the availability of and access to the sport has improved. Yes, I was in a very over-protective but fake bubble here at UCLA, but this bubble had many opportunities to make an impact on the world of women's football. And it was absolutely brilliant to witness it.

One thing to take away...

This was football that was powerful, strong and engaging. Sport, generally, is like this... but the players at UCLA showed how delivering success at college level will drive it forward to create more professional opportunities for the future.

LA... time to fly

In many ways LA is a powerhouse, but the city is a bit of a hotspot for racism and poverty. The homeless encampments are not condoned by the local government; they are hidden away. We are now living in a world where anything perfect is great to share but whatever needs improvement is painted over. LA had something about it that felt a bit lost but unfortunately, the glitz and glam of the city still ensured millions walked through the gates of LAX airport. Footprints left their mark on the stars of the Hall of Fame. Mickey Mouse was probably still going to be fat and Batman would be forever trying to fight Robin.

Denver

I was on a United Airlines flight with an epic flight crew. We got talking about my adventure and before you knew it, I was at the back, eating Pringles and having a laugh with the crew. One of the crew, Derek, had flown to 126 countries. He was 50 and had been cabin crew for 25 years. He met his wife at United Airlines and forever flying high in work and love. I was standing in the middle of the gantry telling a crowd of seven people about the Tour De France, jazz festivals, Minsk and so on. This was one of the perks of travelling alone – you just talked to everyone.

When I got off the plane I struggled to catch my breath. Welcome to Denver, the Mile High City, 5,280 feet above sea level. In LA, at maximum I was 285 feet above sea level. Most places I had visited were nowhere near this elevation so, as I walked into the airport, I could feel my breath being snatched away. I grabbed my inhaler and took a quick puff. I had been warned it would take me a few days to adjust, but I had literally no time to waste. My 13 days in Denver would be a sprint of activities, so get ready...

Event 68: One Republic at Red Rocks Amphitheatre

Red Rocks was part of Denver City Council. It was 17 miles outside the city and had been open to the public since 1941. I had arranged to meet Brian on the Thursday, which was ideal, but he wanted me to appreciate the venue live. "What show would you like to see?" WOW! I opted to see OneRepublic, who are local to Denver. He gave me a seat 14 rows from the front, in the middle of a crowd who were treating this like a homecoming, and I got to experience the most amazing performance I had seen – literally 55 minutes after I got off the flight.

Red Rocks is a one road in, one road out venue, carved into vertical rock in the 1900s. The view from the steep seating bank was of the vast landscape behind the stage as it disappeared into the distance. I cannot emphasise this enough – Red Rocks was in the middle of absolutely nowhere. The natural formation of the rocks had created a near-perfect venue that is constantly sold out. Curiously, The Beatles played here as part of their 1964 tour of America but it was the only show that did not sell out – because (fun fact) there was no highway and it was a struggle to access. Mary, Peter and Paul were regulars here. The Blues Brothers in 1980. Any artist you can think of has most likely played at Red Rocks.

Venues sometimes lack character, but this place was so different from the usual emotionless retractable roof, bricks and mortar. The best part of a venue tour is always to experience the route the artists take from the stage door. The walls here were covered with photos of artists who had played Red Rocks. Some bands had even brought their own stencils and paints. Everyone who has performed here was on that wall and it was a real testament to the venue for its success in drawing these names in. Internally, the backstage café was home to the artists, crew and staff of the venue, which meant it could get really cosy. And they liked that approach – everyone involved with making the show a success would eat from the same buffet table.

One thing I was intrigued about was the way the flight cases for each performance were transported – they are all winched up the amphitheatre rows, hauled up by a rope for every single show. Because of the structure of the venue, no change can be made.

There were water stations all around the venue and heart monitors at the top of the stairs. This is because Red Rocks is 1,000 feet higher than Denver city centre and the air up here is even thinner. And I felt it. Those who have never performed at Red Rocks before always struggle, apparently, and usually, located at the back and as part of the artist rider, there is an oxygen tank. Artists are advised against putting any alcohol on their rider and recommended to take a break halfway through the show for an oxygen boost.

On the evening of the show, my ticket had been loaded onto a new app, Flash Tickets. It's very similar to other ticket company apps but quite clunky. On top of the app, I'd also been given a printed ticket with my name on it – so really, I have no idea why the app was used. I went in as the sun was setting and realised why Red Rocks is probably one of the most amazing venues in the world. I then took off down the stairs. Thousands of people now surrounded me. The stage was the focal point, but because of the design and natural rock, everything was 100% more intense. Any show would rock this venue in a way that would never be able to be replicated in a metal-structured arena.

OneRepublic are world-renowned and Grammy Award-nominated and tonight they were playing to a home crowd, because, just one hour down the I-25 S from where we were, was Colorado Springs, the home town to these global stars. As well as

OneRepublic, for the first time two collectives from other genres of music were collaborating for this show. So I was going to see OneRepublic, the Colorado Symphony Orchestra and a gospel choir, whose name I unfortunately can't remember. Not only was tonight about music but it was about collaboration and showing how three different genres can fit together – and believe me, they fitted more than can be explained.

The most powerful moment was when Ryan, the lead singer, talked about the work he put into the music. The band had a successful run after a number one song with Timbaland (*Apologize*) and for them the struggle was to maintain that success. I don't think the public realise when you have such a big hit how hard it is to keep the momentum going. In the crowd was the producer who had worked with them after that hit. Ryan talked about how the producer's encouragement led to him writing songs for other artists as well as the band. What I found quite amazing about this live performance – and, sometimes, live performances altogether – was the honesty from the performers. It's like they're in their living room – a bit like George Ezra in Brussels – and you're there with your cup of tea. Ryan's passion and commitment to music couldn't be any clearer. I felt like he was talking to me. I felt like there were not thousands surrounding me – it was truly incredible. He had this way of attracting you into a zone and engaging with more than just words. This show was triggering moments of escapism. It wasn't about being on phones taking photos; it was about capturing moments to reflect on and remember.

The lyrics to some of the songs were so touching, especially *I Lived* and *Somebody to Love*. The band really did have a collection of underestimated songs. Sometimes you see a band and wonder why they are not bigger; OneRepublic is, in my opinion, this band. At one point Ryan spoke to his friends and family, who I think were probably all of five rows in front of me. He ran down and hugged them and suddenly he was up on top of one of the rocks. I don't think it was planned – but my god, it looked good. Sometimes impulsive moments at events allow certain memories to stick – and that stuck. Especially when his bodyguard was clambering up to try and make sure Ryan didn't fall. But instead, Ryan was balancing literally on the energy of the world.

The lights illuminating the rocks and the sound of the Colorado Spring Orchestra was simple yet so powerful. I was in the middle of the wilderness. Snakes and bears live just over the rocks, I kid you not. When events take over unusual spaces, they create something special that, in return, changes people's lives. Tonight wasn't about seeing OneRepublic (although they were amazing); it was about taking in something that could be described as a once in a lifetime opportunity, and I soaked up all the emotion around me. I had arrived in Denver three hours earlier and now I was sitting here reflecting on having seen a band in concert at Red Rocks. That's not something you can say you do every day, and I will probably never experience anything like this again.

At the end of the night I knew there was only one way out. Literally. Because of the single-track road I knew I had to leave early to avoid the other 9,000 people departing. I reached the designated pick-up point, which was managed by Lyft, the online internet taxi app. They were the official providers of taxis and no one else was allowed in the area to pick up. Anyone using Uber would have to wait. Interesting. Eventually I found my ride, and the driver was so excited I was Scottish. I told her all about the show, and then I heard the best line ever: "Your English is so good for being Scottish…"

I kind of gulped and laughed and then realised she was 100% serious. How do you respond? Well, I said, "Yes, we learn it from an early age…" I mean, get me out of here. I just want to sing OneRepublic songs.

Red Rocks. The grandeur. The space. The emotional connection. The history of such a wonderful place lies within the future of possibilities. But of course only a few people will ever experience it, because it literally is in the middle of nowhere.

One thing to take away…

OneRepublic blew me away. The venue blew me away. The whole packaged experience was just a WOW. This wasn't about sweat pouring from a bland venue; it was a mixture of talent and uniqueness working well together.

Denver, the next day

I was heading to Ruby Hill to meet the Pineapple Agency. They were an experiential marketing company that organised big bold experiences for their clients – mainly festivals. They transformed ideas into reality. My email had been replied to by Alison, who explained that they were more than happy to meet – which was fantastic. I sat with Alison and Justin and we talked about the importance of emotional connection at events. Justin was the founder who was so welcoming, and I was engrossed in everything he had to say. We spoke about how emotional management is critical for success in the industry.

The company really had an amazing client base for their 'anything but ordinary' approach. I loved the design of their logo, a sliced pineapple shaped like a lightbulb. Clever. It was all about contacts and connections: who knows who in Denver, especially since it was such a small industry in Colorado. It was so small that basically everyone I had emailed knew each other – which was great. The next week I gave them a 40-slide presentation about customer emotional connections at events around the world. I explained, over a Mexican meal, some of the amazing things I had seen: the different approaches to planning, the various marquees, cultural celebrations and so on. Meeting the people from Pineapple Agency was brilliant, a great insight into understanding the thought process that organisers go through to create an event. They fly all over the place to work on projects and I wish them well and look forward to continuing our friendship in the future.

I wanted to meet someone from Denver Botanic Gardens and to

my surprise I was successful and met the director of events and the events manager. The venue holds some amazing and special events. Weddings take over the beautiful grounds. A summer concert series was held in the York Street grounds. Sponsored by a major bank (who got naming rights), the partnership involved local community music projects. *Fete Des Fleurs* was a gala that raised funds for the gardens. In October, for Halloween, they invited people along to events like the Pumpkin Festival and Glow at the Gardens, which was a wonderful luminous show. The gardens may have been an agricultural space but they were also an unusual space for events. It was all so open. They were diversifying the product. Being different. Gaining new audiences. Our discussion was full of laughter but I took away the vision that they had.

Next, by chance – or by the way of planning – I was going to see my first ever NFL match…

Event 69: NFL Pre-Season Denver Broncos

29th August

I was very fortunate to be able to catch a warm-up American football match in Denver at the Mile High Stadium. Denver Broncos were playing Arizona Cardinals and I experienced a half-empty stadium – but it was an intriguing insight into NFL. This game was an opportunity for rookies from both teams to be able to make the cut onto the main roster for the NFL season, which started very soon. Technically, an NFL match should last 60 minutes plus breaks – so let's say 90 minutes. On average, NFL matches last for three and a half hours...

Tailgate parties are a tradition before a match, with many clubs hosting tailgate concerts where everyone brings their truck or car, lifts the boot and has a party out of the back of the vehicle. The Broncos had an official tailgate concert sponsored by Ford Country, with large pick-up trucks on display. There were even some fans doing wheelspins in their cars because they felt so honoured to be close to the stadium.

In the public domain area there were giveaways, a chance to win prizes and so on. I was given a whirly material thing. Sponsorship opportunities attached to the NFL are massive deals and everywhere I went, everything was sponsored. I was surprised that the toilet pans weren't sponsored – but the toilet doors had sponsorship from a local pizza place... Interesting. The food court was called 'Mile High Mountain Village' but sponsored by Bud Light. Everything was named. On the screen alone, there were 14 different brand logos surrounding the televised coverage. People know the NFL to be an engaging sport, entertaining and a food-consuming machine. In Mile High, a cheeseburger and pretzel bites cost me $13.50. To go to an NFL match would cost, on average, $240 per game – plus the ticket. Food and drink, merchandise, half time draw tickets, fan engagement games at the tailgate party, a few dollars here and there into charity buckets and so on.

The longer people were sitting in a seat, the hungrier they would become, the more time they had to eat and spend more money – and the more air time there was for companies to buy to advertise their products to an audience who had nowhere else to go. Whether this is televised or in the stadium, it's a clever tactic and people do spend.

Stadiums in America had started to focus on inclusion, which I had been told was a recent trend. It was all still a bit disjointed but fans who feel vulnerable in large crowds were given support through different mechanisms, including sensory bags, shuttle carts and rest rooms as well as permits for service animals – and not just guide dogs. The plans, signed off with Denver City Council and accessibility organisations, showed Mile High Stadium's focus on delivering equal access and also – as stated on their website – complying with local laws and regulations. The sensory bags were becoming especially popular as they included fidget spinners, colouring pens and pencils, notepads and more.

Off to my seat. You know when you go into a stadium and the first thing you do is look around? Well, I was in section 420, Upper. And remember I said Denver is mile high? I was literally sitting at the top of the 75,000-plus seater stadium. Although Bolivia has the highest stadium in the world, at over 14,000 feet, Mile High Stadium was certainly an experience and as the night progressed the air became thinner and clouds were nowhere to be seen as it turned from a beautiful day to a cold night. My seat gave me an amazing bird's eye view of the pitch but it was also great for watching other people.

Here are some facts about the Denver Broncos. Once upon a time their nickname was Orange Crush. They have two mascots: Thunder II (a horse, literally forced to sprint for the entertainment of the applauding fans; I didn't like this) and Miles (a costumed character). The first ever male cheerleader at the Denver Broncos was the late great acting supremo and comedic genius Robin Williams, who turned up during a game in 1979 in full cheerleading outfit, complete with pom poms (all part of a stunt, but it did make history!). The team has a membership programme for kids called 'BUNCH - Broncos Kids Club'; a $25 enrolment pack includes a t-shirt, height chart and other things to get kids involved in the sport. There's also the Broncos Brigade, which is for those who served in the military, active or prior.

One of the most important parts of the whole game was at the beginning when the national anthem was played. America is very patriotic. I had been in the country a month and I think I had sung the national anthem eight times at different events and places I visited. I mean, it's interesting, for sure, and there's a lot to be discussed about the importance of national pride. Here in the stadium, everyone got on their feet and the players of both NFL teams stood proudly. Hats off and we all faced the flag. Chewing gum out of mouths and held during the singing. The words had so much importance to these people. And all this was during a time when discussions were rife about some NFL players taking a knee during the national anthem, which had divided opinion and the country.

Following an American football game can be tricky. First downs and all the numbers on the screen, flags, violations and so on. Even the numbers painted on the pitch were confusing me. The snap happens. The quarterback decides where to throw the ball. The coach is at the side, giving signals. The running back (I think) catches the ball and off he runs. He is slammed to the ground by the defending team. And the crowd claps. For 30 seconds, nothing happens on the pitch – or on the screens. Then the replays show the strength of the hit. An MC gets everyone to swing towels in the air; I think this is a 'thing'. The play begins again. Coaches screaming from the sidelines. The quarterback throws the ball and it's caught by the Cardinals – they have the ball – this is an interception. UNBELIEVABLE THAT I KNOW WHAT THIS MEANS...! And suddenly we had a sprint on for the opposing touchdown. The fans went from clapping to booing. And then the teams switched. Large brutes of humans came off and more machines came on. And on we went, on repeat. Throw. Catch. React. Repeat. Throw. Catch. Call a time out. React. Throw. React. And so on.

No wonder people bought as much drink as they could. Watching American football was now the chance not only to watch a game but also to see commercialisation in action. The fireworks erupting, letting the fans know it was time to celebrate and cheer. The stadium was still only about 70% full – because it was a pre-season match – so the noise wasn't quite at a level to pulsate my ear drums.

This was alright. It was what it was. What I think the NFL needs to learn is that a consumer experience is only manufactured and delivered well when everyone buys in. There was no excitement from the security guards. On the other hand, the guest relations team – an older group of staff, many of whom were retired and doing this on the side for pocket money – had amazing energy. It was great to experience. Yes, security is there for safety, but their body language can affect the consumer experience.

Eventually, the game ended. Some people chose to jump onto bikes with coloured lights wrapped around them and baskets for the passengers, which were flying at 20mph. As I left, I felt part of the fan community. Literally – I was in the middle of hundreds of people pushing me towards each other. Proper immersion.

One thing to take away...

Stadium events are what they are. Concrete-constructed emotionless places of power. Power used sometimes more for business than for human interactional success. The customer journey should always be one to remember – but after you've spent over $240 on a three-and-a-half-hour American Football match, it would need to be truly spectacular.

More from Denver...

Next day I was heading to Roller City, a skating rink in Lakeland, just outside Denver. This was an indoor roller-skating rink that had recently been restored to its former glory. After 22 years of being a thrift factory store, it had been taken over by Bry, who wanted to show me the rink and tell me about the direction of roller-skating and why it was important to have escapes in life – as well as the importance of roller-skating in the community.

Bry grew up roller-skating and he told me all about his connection with the rink and its decline. My focus was on understanding how roller-skating was embraced by the community. I wanted to see how the community had brought back roller-skating after years of absence and find out what the appeal was. The rink had everything you would expect. Arcade machines. A diner. Funky carpets. And, of course, the rink itself. It was well looked after by Bry and the rest of the team, who were more like family. Many of the members of Bry's team were fortunate to have him in their lives but for Bry, there was not just financial pressure on this venture but also the pressure of historical success and reputation. Sometimes you need to take a step away from normal engagement and socialising to find something special, and that was what I was doing. This wasn't about saying: "Look at roller-skating." Instead, I was brought in for five hours and welcomed by a community.

I was allowed to go on the skating rink and fell flat on my face. As people laughed, I felt accepted. Bry was really trying everything he could and throwing everything he had into his dream, which he knew would become a successful business. For me, it was about going for an hour on the number 60 bus to Lakewood and enjoying a place I probably would never have explored as a tourist. I left knowing I would return one day to this place that was at the beating heart of the community and a place of leisure. I wish Bry all the best, because I know his hard work and his team's commitment will deliver another 50 years of roller-skating memories.

Denver had a strategy for 2020 – IMAGINE 2020: Denver's Cultural Plan. This creative plan's direction was to look at how arts and neighbourhoods could meet to make Denver an international cultural destination. After being in the city for only three days I could see how the city was shaping up. I saw the vision. I felt it. A cohesive cultural roadmap for social empowerment. I could see places of 'outreach' move forwards.

Event 70: The Wedding Party

1st September

Have you ever heard about nine weddings happening at the same time, with festival vibes, sponsorship from Pepsi and Stella Artois, some of the finest Denver restaurants giving out free food, Jack Daniels galore, ice sculptures, 700 people buying a ticket to be a wedding crasher and more... Nope, neither had I – until I was introduced to *The Wedding Party.* A wedding like no other... and, as I strolled along the long flat roads of Westminster, I knew love was in the air. This was the beginning of the most bizarre event in the most luxurious surroundings – which were being built on a golf course.

Wearing my extremely well-pressed shirt, I was already sweating as I arrived at the golf club early. The setting was lovely. The marquee was beautiful. The surrounding landscape was glorious. And I was about to be confused by what I would witness.

This was the idea of a Denver events company that specialises in food and drink events. However, I'd been introduced to the event by Allison at Pineapple Agency, who was attending as a guest. The ball was rolling. I checked in and was given an extremely tight volunteer t-shirt and immediately given things to do. Before I could put my water bottle and jacket down, I was lifting tables and chairs, collecting food from delivery trucks – it was pleasantly chaotic, but I was in my element. I was teamed up with one of the paid crew, Zac. He was a great guy and laughed when I told him about my adventure. "You writing about this?" he said. We were the best team – as we put up umbrellas and tables and loaded things like we were professionals, you would have thought we'd both done this before! We were roving about in our buggy and being sent all over the place to get things done. Zac was well known by all the traders and he introduced me as: "This is the Scottish guy writing a book…" Zac was absolutely brilliant. We were laughing and joking like we were best buds from years gone past. This is what events are all about: making new friends in new environments, especially in the middle of something that is completely new to you on so many levels.

On arrival, everyone was given a Stella Artois glass. I mean – WOW! Already the guests were excited and they hadn't even seen the whole site. There were photo opportunities on flower swings decorated with sponsor logos, and ice sculptures, which we had to carry carefully. My heart was on a different level. "You drop this – you're fired…" I thought. Technically, they couldn't fire me – but I think I would probably have been marched out of Denver. The ice was melting from the heat coming off my hands as the clumsiest Scotsman carried the amazing sculptures across the site. The large marquee in the middle of the site was the heart of the event and it was fabulous to see everything come to life as time progressed and the voices got louder.

The brides arrived on one bus and the grooms in another. The number of people going into the event was incredible. The ice sculptures were sponsored by Korbel Californian Champagne; the pink lights beaming on them would probably melt them pretty quickly. Oh, and the llamas. Yes, of course this exuberant event needed llamas. I mean – llamas. Truly unique. I didn't agree with the llamas being there – I don't think they enjoyed being prodded by guests wanting a photo for their 'Gram. Japanese sushi. Chocolate doughnuts. Photo booths. A Smirnoff tasting booth. The whole event was a plethora of brands and it felt like a who's who of Denver's social elite had taken an Uber out to the sticks and were here just to post on Instagram. I was told that this was the hottest ticket for some of the wannabe celebs… Excellent.

Usually only friends and family would be part of a couple's big day – but oh no! Not here. On top of around 30 family and friends of each couple, a paying audience was able to be part of this. Because of course. WHY NOT! Nine couples walked into the event –

their wedding – to videos that had been shot prior to the day. Under a white marquee, with hundreds seated inside and zones created for the brides' and grooms' family and friends, it felt like a proper festival; there were even wristbands for certain VIP areas. With the brides on one side of the 30-metre wide marquee and the grooms on the other, the music played and down the aisle they came. I was completely in awe and I tried to understand why I was crying when I didn't even know the happy couples!

I sneaked a few of the bacon sandwiches from the BBQ and stood at the back chatting to the chef. I asked him if he'd ever been to anything like this before and he said, "Nope – I'm here because we need to be…"

Nine couples stood on a three-foot-high stage. It took 45 minutes for the next steps of love to occur. The 'minister' – or conveyor of love – was one of the hunky contestants from a famous USA TV show called *The Bachelor* – which meant he was perfect for the event to get some credit and social media coverage. As he walked past me I was literally knocked out by his aftershave. He asked me where the toilet was. "Aye, the loos – across there."

To be fair, there was a great show of respect for all the couples. They all had their moment. Brief maybe, but it was their moment. "We do" was screamed out by the audience in excitement as each couple embraced hands. I mean, just take a moment to think. Orchestrated demonstrations of love. As the banners at the side of the stage said, 'LOVE IS DOPE.' This was a niche product. A festival of love. The unique selling point is there – you want to be a celeb – so this is the event to attend.

We'd packed away the final tables and chairs and now it was time to find my bride… Just kidding! Zac was like, "Right, Lamb – time to enjoy the party." And I did. Because I had helped out many of the vendors, it was easy getting the last samples. I can't describe the relationship between people who work at events like this – but there is a very special bond. Yet at the end, the rapid relationship comes to an end. And with that, I finished, and left on the bus back to Denver.

One thing to take away...

Love is not easy to understand but it's easy to share and apparently even easier to make money on. If you ever walk into a wedding environment and see large umbrellas sponsored by a drinks company – it all started in Denver!

Denver... more adventure

The logistics to arrange everything perfectly for my 13 days in Denver was full-on. The city was special, but the day after the wedding I decided to take a day trip to Boulder.

Event 71: The Pearl Street Stampede – University of Colorado, Boulder

6th September

I travelled to Boulder, which was only a 45-minute bus ride straight from Denver, to attend The Pearl Street Stampede, the warm-up 'party' for the University of Colorado's American football game. This is when the students and the community kick off a weekend of sport with a wonderful display designed to put fear into the opposition and create fan unity.

I was standing in the middle of Boulder wearing my new Colorado Boulder hoodie and carrying a paper bag with my two other branded University of Colorado tops. I thought if I was going to be standing watching the stampede, I should be dressed in the colours of the college team. The shopkeeper laughed at me – but she was a student at the university, so she got it that I needed to blend in to understand the event. The tradition was to wear your colours and have a greasy fish supper – so I did. The stampede was to wish the University of Colorado football team good luck for their match the next day. The college band, the cheerleaders, the mascot and the community – including police and politicians – were all out. The football team arrived on their bus and were escorted like celebrity sports stars. Armed police created tunnels through from the bus – while the players had headphones on and were staring like they were about to enter the Superbowl.

The musicians performing on the grass in the middle of Pearl Street were absolutely amazing. A total of about 150 musicians from the university band were creating rhythm in the town centre. The music was loud. *Can't Wait to Be King* from *The Lion King* was one of the top crowd pleasers as about 800 people gathered to watch and get ready for the most passionate display of being a sports fan I had witnessed on my trip. Everyone was pumped with the usual YESSSS! approach. The whole parade was led by a 1948 fire truck owned by a member of the Boulder community. The event had been advertised as an opportunity for the team and staff to high five fans of all ages along the route. But this year – well, it was a bit different...

This event really did do well in helping the local economy and apparently the mental focus of the players was psyched. Draped in their white and gold colours, the stampede began. Tomorrow, 55,000 people would arrive at the stadium to watch the football match. It's similar numbers to an English Premier League or Australian football crowd – huge. And remember, this is college football.

Outside the county courthouse the crowd had grown from 800 to over 2,000 people surrounding the gardens as 7pm approached. But unfortunately, so did rumbles of thunder from above. The fire truck started its sirens and some of the football players stood on the back, holding tight as they began the parade. Suddenly, the heavens opened, more footballers jumped onto the fire truck, the cheerleaders got absolutely soaked and the streets were soon deserted. All that was left was the fire truck in the middle of the road with about 40 players on the back, squeezed together and pelting out small rubber footballs to fans, who had taken cover in nearby bars. It was a frantic scene, with speakers being thrown into vehicles and the fire truck going as fast as it could. I decided to run along with it. Even the police officers couldn't keep up as the fire truck flew through the streets. Believe me, this was chaos. Lightning strikes and thunder every minute. The players weren't wearing jackets and a team manager was shouting: "COME ON!" The musicians were scrambling to cover their instruments, which were getting soaked. The fire truck met up with the team bus and all the footballers jumped onto it as fast as they could; the 40 on the fire truck jumped off the sides and made a beeline for the bus. Random people started throwing towels for the cheerleaders. The parade is called a stampede because it's about the roar that the town makes to celebrate the sport and wish the team all the best. Unfortunately, this roar had come from above.

To be honest, I don't think there was a plan in terms of safety. On the other hand, I have never seen rain that bounced so hard. The police officers looked at each other and high fived as they swept the water off their waterproofs. When I say I was wet – my feet were swimming and, even better, my new jumper needed to be put in the dryer when I got back to Denver.

I was impressed overall. The pride on display was cool. It was very American. I can't imagine the same passion and over-the-top approach towards sport in Europe. I love the tradition that is the Pearl Street Stampede. Obviously, the event didn't fully flourish as it usually does – but it does show the importance of having a weather plan and a brolley on standby!

If you live in the middle of Colorado, you support that team. You turn out. And the next day, when Nebraska showed up (which they did, in large caravans) you show them that this is *our* town. This is *our* sports team. This is *our* Superbowl. It's not just an add on.

One thing to take away...

The brand of the university has taken control of the town of Boulder, and the local community are able to associate themselves with everything the brand offers. College sporting events are truly a power source of their own.

A bus to sleep and a bus to go...

So now I was going home to Denver from Boulder – but in eight hours I would soon be rising to go back on a bus past Boulder to Estes Park...

Event 72: Scottish Irish Highland Festival

You know I have been saying throughout this book that my trip was all about adventuring and seeking out things that would throw me out of my comfort zone? Well, unbeknown to me, that was about to happen! It was 6:30am and I thought I was going to Estes Park – but actually I arrived in a well-produced mini Scotland. Today was a celebration of Scotland and Ireland in the hills and valleys of Colorado. I could not be any further removed from Scotland if I tried, yet so close to everything that is packaged as Scottish. Estes Park was shadowed by the Rocky Mountain range and has a population of approximately 6,310 people. I couldn't believe my eyes at how beautiful it was. And I couldn't believe I was here. I was 7,500 feet above sea level, and I was about to witness pipe and drum competitions, Highland Games, a culture exchange, clan heritage, kilts on sale – and I could win a trip to Scotland. Ideal!

So how did this festival come about? Some 43 years ago, a man called Dr James Durward created the event to celebrate his links with Scotland and Ireland. The retired dentist aimed to bring tourists to Estes Park for Labour Day – but it turned into so much more. Dr James organised the festival to try and boost business engagement and that first year, four families attended. From these roots (not a dentist joke…), it grew arms and legs – but not overnight, and not without challenges. The weekend of celebrations had now become a festival that was not just part of the Scottish and Irish celebrations in America, but the event of all events. It was THE event to attend if you had one drop of Celtic blood in you.

Immersing visitors in this historic culture was exactly what the event aimed to do – especially when everyone looked like an extra out of *Outlander* or *Braveheart*. It had successfully grown such a reputation that it has created a proud unofficial partnership between Scotland and Colorado. This year, 75,000 people visited over three days. A town of 6,000 was being submerged with Celts. Not that I was homesick – but this insight was TRULY FANTASTIC! As for seeing the Scottish flag fly in the shadows of the Rocky Mountains... Emotional...

On the bus, I got talking to a few groups of people. "Oh my days, you're actually Scottish..." Well, funnily enough – yes I am. I am Scottish, I live in Scotland, I was born Scottish. The woman – a Campbell – could not believe someone from Scotland was actually at the event, rather than Americans seeking their Scottish roots – this truly was a wonderful experience for her to meet someone from Scotland! My accent seemed to be working wonders when one of the women said "You will so get an American girlfriend with that accent..." Every police officer was in a kilt and I soon realised I was the only person not to be wearing some type of tartan. Everyone around me was showing their heritage – but the only Scottish person with an actual Scottish accent was the one who looked the least Scottish – ME!

The $15-dollar entry ticket bought me tradition and what the Americans thought was an authentic Scottish experience. The Campbells wanted me to hang with them but instead I went to the information desk to find out if I could get a five-minute word with James Durward or someone from the family. And this is where the story becomes crazy.

As I looked around, everyone behind the information tent was wearing a kilt. They were all James' family – his daughter, her children and their children. Everyone was literally more Scottish-looking than Scottish people are in Scotland (I mean, with kilts and heather in their hair...). The announcement for the Highland Games had just gone out and the Tug of War was on in 50 minutes. The tannoy system made it feel like I was in an American high school movie where the carnival was just about to begin. And then James' daughter Peggy gave me the unique chance to be with James for a while, but not before saying, "Remember, Dad, you're on stage in 15 minutes."

I sat on a buggy while James showed me around like I was a celeb. "This is Matthew from Scotland. He is writing a piece about us." James' vision was inspirational. I held his walking stick and he talked to everyone that stopped us. He told me some brilliant stories about getting to this point. "We wanted people to feel connected with what they think is home – but also to find home here." He spoke about the 80 clans that come to the event, the Scottish weapon displays, the British Isles dogs… but one of the main things I got from him was his commitment to the festival. This was a project that had encompassed his whole family. Running it had become a family tradition and one day his daughter would be handed the reins. Suddenly, he said: "Right, we have to go to the march past. Okay, let's go." Through a gap in the rope fence we went, entering the parade grounds where what I would estimate to be 20,000 people were waiting. I took a step back as James launched himself up the metal stairs. Slightly confused, I followed him. It was time for the Clan March Past and I was invited to be on the stage. WHAT? Wait. WHAT? So up I went. James introduced me to some of the dignitaries. "This is Matthew…"

"Hello, I am from the Consulate Office of Canada" … "I am from NORAD and part of the Canadian Armed Forces." Oh, excellent. And then there was me. "Hello, I am writing a book about events in the world and I am actually Scottish." Even the MC looked confused. As I stood there in my light blue jeans and worn-out trainers, I was not ready to be introduced as 'the author from Glasgow writing about this event' to the thousands of people waiting for their clans to march past. Yet I was about to be part of the group of eight people who would be saluted. I was confused, that was for sure! And so it began, with *Scotland the Brave* played by about 80 pipers and drummers walking straight towards the stage and me feeling a little more homesick.

While I was on the stage I decided to be sneaky and Facetime home. Literally in the middle of the march past, I decided to call Mother and Father Lamb. They had front-row seats as the hundreds of participants walked past with the flags of their clans. Each clan held the clan emblem up high and shouted the name of the clan as the MC introduced them to the crowd, who were cheering everyone on as if we were in the middle of a coliseum. "CAMPBELL... MCTAGGART... MCDUFF..." they screamed, at the tops of their voices. The roar was so passionate. I was so confused yet so honoured.

And suddenly James said, "Watch this." My heart just about stopped as I wondered what could be even more perplexing than this right now. In the middle of the parade, in the middle of a clan, one of the members of a group got down on one knee. I was screaming in my head DON'T DO IT! DON'T DO IT! I'll be honest – there was a moment where it didn't look like she was going to say yes. I was sitting next to the Consulate General, who said: "Well that's going to be awkward." But with about 20,000 people staring at her, she had no choice. They were begging her for an answer really. Congratulations to them. And then the clan – who, may I add, wore a beautiful tartan, as did everyone dressed and draped in Scottish 'traditional wear' – marched off, all hugging each other. After the final clan had gone past I was allowed to depart the stage – because I really was not dressed for the event.

The park was filled with marquees, Highland Games, pipe bands, a flyover and more. The marquees had brilliant musicians and trade events and I worked my way around the site – until, that is, I was introduced to Michael, the Irish leprechaun. Michael took his role extremely seriously. He had been involved in the event as an assistant site manager for many years and was good friends with James' family. Michael was what I would call dedicated. But literally, he was a *leprechaun*. In his allocated green leprechaun buggy and wearing his bright green suit, he drove around the site. At first, I thought he had an Irish accent, but I soon realised he didn't. However, I liked hearing him talk just as he was. He was one of the star attractions and popular with all the spectators. We had lunch. We saw Seamus Kennedy perform. We saw some famous 'Scottish artists' and I laughed when Michael said, "Yeah, they're huge in the US, but I don't think they have ever played in Scotland." The poster that was draped across the tent said 'Scotland's hottest talent...' Bizarre was one way to describe it, that was for sure.

I went across and met with the guys in the Highland Games. Suddenly I was towered over by a man who was the organiser of the folks taking part in the competition. They had everything they needed – hammer throwing, caber tossing and every other Highland Games sport. The athletes were huge. Absolutely built like tanks, and even the main organiser was six foot four and built bigger than some of the planes I had been on. He was such a lovely, softly spoken man though, and told me about the competitions, the athletes and the importance of the Highland Games traditions. We got a photo together, but I totally forgot his name. I am sorry.

After the Highland Games, Michael took me over to the weapons section. I went to the stalls that were showcasing 'ancient Scottish weaponry'. I really was quite intrigued because I don't think we are taught about ancient Scottish weaponry in Scottish schools. Strangely, it's taken an event in the middle of Estes Park in Colorado to teach me about the history of Scotland!

Personally, I didn't understand the pride people took in being linked to Scotland. I think that we who live in Scotland don't realise how much our culture and traditions are celebrated and applauded around the world. And now I was standing in the middle of a park near the Rocky Mountains, surrounded by thousands of people who had never been to Scotland but loved it as much as I do. We don't understand what it means to them to say "I am Scottish – fourth generation." Being here today and meeting people like the Hayes and the Camerons and being accepted by them – it felt like I was home. I literally felt like one of them. I was being hugged and thanked for coming. Hearing everyone's stories was actually reaffirming my love for Scotland and for what we try to sell to the world. Someone asked me: "Does this not offend you, that people are celebrating Scotland?" No – the opposite was true. I mean, except for the fact that it looked like *Outlander* and *Braveheart* had had a baby and it had created a festival. It was actually encouraging to see people wanting to engage with Scottish culture.

Whether it was about local businesses selling tablets (as were a family from Paisley who moved to America three years ago) or allowing kilts to be part of the police uniform, everyone here was proud to be linked to Scotland and happy to spend money to demonstrate and celebrate their heritage. There were no questions asked when it came to money. Without it, this festival would never have been possible. Celebrations and traditional events face huge issues regarding funding because of policies and council regulations. But the opportunities they bring, if not neglected or built for commercial purposes, demonstrate community cohesion, cultural affirmation and diversity through sharing local history. The meaning of an event is key. The authenticity is key. The identity it holds is key.

Would this event have been so successful and grown so fast if it took place in a city centre? Probably not. Firing empty cannon balls from the site and having a flyover right over the event could only happen on the outskirts of a city. This festival has been so successful and popular over the last 40 years and I'm sure it has many more to come.

One thing to take away…

People who live in Scotland could learn a thing or two from this type of event. Our culture is adored, and we must realise the impact it has on millions around the globe. Scottish people don't know what they have. If people in a park in Estes Park can engage so passionately with Scotland, why can't Scottish people celebrate everything we have as well? Maybe not ancient weaponry though!

Denver

Well, Denver – it's over. I do not think I will ever be able to say thank you enough. I timed everything perfectly. The majority of my time in Denver was like being in a fancy sports car with the accelerator stuck at 170mph. Denver has so much in common with Scotland. I saw, first-hand, Denver's cultural output. It's a massive part of the job economy. People spend time together in constructed social moments – festivals and so on. In Denver, the majority of situations where people are together is at events or in hospitality settings. Denver has a great strategy and a great vision. It has great organisations. It has great people. As the capital of Colorado, for me, Denver is a future leader in so many different industries. It has epic character. It may have a grid-lined street pattern but it also has winding roads that can take people on a journey of awesomeness – and I cannot wait to return. Goodbye from Denver Airport...

Well... hi, Chicago!

I was in Chicago for three days and was adamant I didn't want to see another building or museum. Instead, I wanted to lie on my bed and wake up three hours later than scheduled. What a delightful idea. But of course, I didn't do that...

I was coming to an interesting conclusion about railway stations. Those that are located in the middle of the community are not just places where people wait for trains; they are community centres where people hang out, partly waiting for family to arrive back but often just to take up office. The Latino lifestyle and culture is very important to many people in Chicago, but locations and spaces – and what they did with the spaces – was even more important.

In the area of Pilsen, culture is especially important – it is life. Flags flew high and everyone spoke Spanish or Portuguese. When I arrived, people were cooking in gazebos on the street during what turned out to be a parade to celebrate South American culture. Children ran out of their houses carrying vegetables freshly chopped by the grandmother, who was now tired and leaning against the door, while the father sparked up the BBQ and the mother stirred the pot.

One of these streets was home to a beautiful venue called Thalia Hall. The hall was originally built by Croatian immigrants 120 years ago as a place for the immigrant community to get together and enjoy leisure activities. It grew in popularity over the years but was then left to rot. A few illegal raves happened, with people bunking down In the roof. But now, Thalia Hall had been completely restored. Once again, the venue was providing the community with an opportunity to gather.

Sarah from the venue was so kind and gave me the most amazing tour. I took a few videos from the stage – the theatre made it seem like I was in Hollywood and I felt like I was presenting at an awards ceremony. Then she said: "Right, let's go and see something special. Do you like heights?" I said I didn't have a problem and suddenly we were in the attic. She opened a hatch and we looked down on the venue below. I was really impressed by how the venue looked from above. Then Sarah pulled down a ladder from the ceiling and we went up one more level. And then... we were outside on top of the building. Holding onto the wobbly handrail, we went to a door and I saw the dome of the theatre from above. I saw history. I'd become so excited about exploring everything venues are about – including the engineering – and it was really special to be given an opportunity like this to get in and see the spiderwebs, and to think back to when this was built. Who sat up here 120 years ago and enjoyed this view? Whose footsteps had I followed? I was standing on beams placed hundreds of years ago by workers who didn't know the impact this building would have.

Next, Sarah took me to a compact Green Room where we sat for over two hours talking. I felt really honoured that Sarah had spent so much time with me – especially when she had a wedding coming in shortly. The dome, the boxes, the staff and the balcony made it not only a theatre but a beacon of cultural engagement. A hub for illuminating opportunities. Every bare wall was bare for a reason. Every hole that hadn't been plastered had a story to tell.

We walked out to the piano bar and met Bobby. He said something really interesting to me: "I do this role to curate events for the community." He could work at any major venue in the city – they all could – but this venue was something different. Its aim was not simply to make money (although it has to survive); it was in the middle of the community, and hosting performances, meetings and other events that give something back was critical.

I began to play the piano in the bar and Sarah disappeared, only to return with a snow globe, which she gave to me as a gift. I was honoured. "You now have Thalia Hall with you, wherever you go," she said. I now had a glass snow globe to try not to smash for the remaining 35 days. This was going to be a challenge!

Both Sarah and Thalia Hall were truly special – thank you!

Now let me introduce you to my only event in Chicago…

Event 73: Riot Fest

13th September

PUNCH, WHAM, BAM... and onto the floor he went. When someone tries to start a mosh pit next to a guy who is protecting his girlfriend who is trying to enjoy Blink-182, that's what happens. Welcome to Riot Fest. I hadn't been to a rock festival before, and this was going to be very different to the Penis Festival in Tokyo or *Will and Grace* in LA. Today I was about to observe a festival that was happening in the middle of a dangerous part of Chicago. The majority of this area was run by gangs (as I had been advised by the police) and the festival was attended by mainly middle-class white people who loved rock music. On Reddit, people were saying Douglass Park was seen to be safe if you didn't go there...

I picked up my ticket and walked through security. In Christchurch they searched inside wallets; in Chicago, they didn't even acknowledge you had a wallet. But guns and knives weren't allowed. Sometimes I think certain festivals (not this one in particular) have a policy of 'Drugs will enter – what can we do?' Cannabis is legal in Chicago. I could even buy marijuana products on the site. I was patted down, but I could have had anything between my legs. It seemed like most of the protection was outside the venue, where the police were stopping members of the local community from getting anywhere near the music fans coming to the festival.

Riot Fest was in its 15th year and the audience had bought into the event. The organisers needed people to post positive social media comments – they had to make sure those attending were protected and had a positive experience. The festival moved to Douglass Park in 2015 despite police statistics showing it was a breeding ground for heroin dealers and gun crime. Visitors were recommended not to walk in or through the park at any time.

Events are usually used to boost areas, but in discussion with a few people I met, I heard that this festival did nothing for the local area. Interesting. In reality, Riot Fest is like a circus – it rolls in and rolls out and that's it; it gets out of there – fast.

Music events are for socialising in an environment that meets the needs of the audience. With my index and pinkie finger raised in the classic rock and roll symbol, I watched people do exactly this – I felt as one. Phones were in pockets and people were launching themselves at each other, with crowd surfing more prominent than posing for the perfect Instagram photo. In comparison to other festivals, it was clear the audience here was more down with listening to the music, feeling the music, immersing themselves in the music – being the music – than getting more social media followers.

The festival had five stages which were all different. The five stages – Riot Stage (Main Stage), Roots Stage, Rise Stage, Radical Stage and Rebel Stage – were really spaced out across the park and each had its own 'diehard' supporters, who sat at the barriers waiting for their favourite musicians. I picked up a Riot Fest timetable and map. I didn't know half these bands. I watched Pennywise from a distance, then Taking Back Sunday, The Flaming Lips, Dashboard Confessional and Hot Snakes, who I liked. Of course, I knew absolutely none of the songs by any of these bands (except Blink 182); it was going to be an educational experience. I also wished I had a film crew with me, because you would have seen the fear in my eyes when I walked into some of the crowds during performances. Like a twig snapped in half. So I stood to the side and watched the crowds meander past each other to get to their next performance. Deliberately not getting in the way and deliberately enjoying the observational role.

Illegal vendors were selling bottles of water for $3 each in the middle of the site. Interesting. You couldn't bring knives in but this guy had smuggled 72 bottles of water. Then you had the beer on sale from Goose Island Beer Co. that had an unusual fan engagement piece. When you peeled a sticker off the can it revealed the stage timings for all three days of the festival. Clever.

There were plenty of merchandise stalls around the site and fans could purchase items and then leave them in lockers. Vince was the man who owned the lockers. They had to be booked in advance and Vince told me they sell out at the same rate as the tickets and it's usually the same people, year after year. You're probably curious why this such is an important piece of the furniture and why I wanted to tell you about it. Well, rock festivals are known to be the best type of festival for merchandise income. Eventbrite wrote in 2017 that on average, a rock festival consumer in the USA will spend $60-$100 – and at this event it was at the higher end, simply because they could put their new souvenirs in a locker and not worry about them until the end of the night. Instead they could head back into the mosh pits with their posters stored safely away. I watched as people bought t-shirts, prints and band merchandise – including a Blink-182 clock. Put the provision in place and the merchandise will sell – very clever, and I think a lot more events should think more about what they could gain from fans with some investment. Alongside the lockers were rehydration stations and the queues were ridiculous for these. Putting on my customer journey hat, I could see so many issues. Queue jumping, security guards who were more focused on their DMs or having a smoke, non-existent signage or instruction on how to queue... But hey – this was a rock festival.

One part of the site was set up like an American gala day with an old rickety Ferris wheel, bright lights, lollies and overpriced candy on sale (MASSIVE QUEUES). I laughed as I strolled through the crowds waiting to buy over-priced chicken and a pre-heated crepe. Most of those attending had disposable income, so it was easy for people to throw money at chicken stalls and vending machines without any problems.

It seemed like people thought I needed a friend and I met loads of people, including one guy wearing a kilt, just because he loves kilts. He said to me: "Don't walk out of here yourself... You'll get robbed!" Even the customers of the festival knew it was a dangerous area. He was a banker from Chicago who wore his kilt to all the rock gigs he attended.

A stall in the charity section that seemed very out of place, I thought, was an HIV testing unit and awareness programme. It was run by a charity that had brought together trained nurses to do on-site testing. I was so surprised to see this here, at a rock concert, but, as they explained to me, in many circumstances rock fans are not openly confident or comfortable enough to allow themselves to be tested. So they brought it to them. They wanted to be accessible and the process was 100% confidential. The charity is very prominent within the gay community and they told me about their history and charities focus. They explained that if two men walked in today, that was two more than yesterday – and two more than would be tested if the charity was not present at the festival.

Riot Fest was a complete riot. There was no real plan on how to enjoy the festival and no scenario planning from the customer's point of view. It's very much led by the inspiration of the music and the behaviour of the fans who attend. For me, the best thing was watching the fans. But actually, I'll throw out this argument. Who is the audience at a concert? I fully believe the audience is also the artist. They observe each other. The reaction they give leads and influences the next move of the performer. As I watched the fans releasing pent-up energy, a thought occurred to me. At both the Jakarta Jazz Festival back in March and here now, I saw fans react to music, hands in the air and singing loud. This wasn't anything like the jazz festival – but at the same time, it was. It was an escape from normality.

Blink-182 were certainly one of the best things to witness. I was excited to see them and as they were introduced, people surrounded me, ready to flatten the idiots wanting to mosh in a non-mosh pit area (okay, not really a thing). Sadly, due to faults with the speakers, the booing began. And it was loud. A lot of outrage was being hurled at the stage, along with pint glasses, shoes and anything else to hand. The speakers were not working on the right-hand side, which meant the fans from that side started to try and squeeze over. Suddenly it felt dangerous. With about 40,000 people and no barriers separating us – it was time to go. Of course, the fans weren't disappointed with the band – it was the opposite. The band were being let down by the organisers and the contractors and I was literally face to face with the people complaining. As I tried to leave, you could sense the fans up the back had just given up and were talking to each other instead of enjoying a band who had returned after having to cancel unexpectedly the year before.

As I left, about 30 police were standing next to their vehicles, hands on their guns and blue lights flashing. I wasn't sure why really, because the stream of fans wandering back towards the railway station were walking past houses with smashed windows, cars with flat tyres, and families selling water, sausages and cocaine. Although I was starting to fall in love with areas that host events, as I walked along I could see the people lurking in the shadows, scoping out those tourists who were obviously on their own – so, without really meaning to, I locked onto a couple so I looked like I had friends.

Next day on the Reddit forums, the sound issues were discussed. '*Sound is not Riot Fest's forte...*' And for me, this summed up the Riot Fest customer journey. Believe me – it was bad. At something like this, the fans are just there for the music. But when the music doesn't play and the fans can't hear the main product of the experience, then the festival needs to start looking at changes – immediately.

One thing to take away...

Rock is rock. But I feel the spectators here probably deserved a better experience. There were plenty of good things, like the lockers. But when I read back through my notes, I tallied up 64 changes they could make – 64 things to improve on – and that was just from one day.

Chicago...

As I was eating my dinner I flicked through Instagram and saw that Lewis Capaldi had reposted that a very famous British DJ, Greg James, was in Chicago for one night only. Greg is one of the most popular BBC Radio 1 presenters. He ain't showbiz and he ain't celeb driven; instead, he is well-liked, down to earth and he loves his fans. He is a great presenter – occasionally on TV as well as radio – with a real sense of purpose for what he does. He is now building a children's book portfolio with his co-author Chris Smith, a very successful author. And tonight, he and Chris were here in Chicago as part of a North American tour for their children's book. So, of course I would now do anything and everything I could to meet him! Let me just bullet point what happened to speed up the excitement:

- I quickly finished my dinner (a microwaved hostel meal).
- I found out that Greg and Chris were doing a book signing at Anderson's Bookshop (16 miles outside the city centre).
- The book signing was due to finish at 9pm.
- I worked out it was going to take me an hour and a half and two trains to get there.
- My pal Rachel phoned from Australia as I was rushing through Chicago. She laughed as I screamed: "I need to be on this train!"
- I got on a train – going in the wrong direction. So I got off and had to wait for another train back.
- I was losing time but bought a ticket for a third train, which was the suburban slow train to La Grange, where the bookstore was.
- Once I was on the train I Instagram-messaged Greg (who didn't know me) to say I was en route.

- He messaged back to say they had already left. It was 8:30pm and I was only halfway to La Grange.

I was gutted – and in the middle of nowhere. Like literally, in the middle of a suburb that didn't even have street lights. To my surprise, Greg messaged me back and asked a few questions, like how long I was here for and so on. Probably seeing if I was a real person. Suddenly he invited me to come and see him during his meal back in Chicago town centre. WAIT! WHATTTTT! REALLY???? Okay... Don't panic! We can do this! As I leapt from my seat I smashed my head on the luggage rack. I absolutely gave my head the biggest smack; it was that hard I dropped everything and fell to my knees. I still have the bump to this day. My head was spinning. But I had to get to Greg James! I could feel my brain pulsing as I gathered all my things and got off the train. I needed a plan. I stood up and look above me. "Wow... those lights are so shiny!"

I was now 15 miles from the restaurant where Greg was, no trains were due, and I was literally in the middle of nowhere. OH GREAT! I was having a great day! So I jumped onto an internet taxi app and grabbed a vehicle. My driver was Abdul and he was from Saudi Arabia. He was fantastic. We got a selfie together and he said, "You'll be famous one day with your book." It was lovely encouragement, but I don't think my head had stopped spinning the whole trip.

Feeling sick, I entered the restaurant for my big moment. Greg James was sitting with Chris Smith and a few others from the publishing company. My head stopped spinning. Greg saw me and said: "Matt!" and it began. We spoke for 45 minutes – or maybe even longer – and it was honestly one of the most amazing conversations I've had. Greg was just so welcoming and curious about what I was doing as he scrolled through my Instagram. I told him about the Penis Festival and being on the set with Grace from *Will and Grace* and living my dream. At one point he said: "I am sure our paths will cross one day." Well, hopefully they will if he reads this book – or feel free to tweet him and tell him that you read about him in the most amazing book! He was humble. He was lovely. And we got a photo and a video together and when I posted it online – well, people just couldn't believe it! I left him to eat his dinner in peace... At least, I tried, but it's hard when you know you're never going to have this opportunity again. Thanks, Greg and Chris!

I didn't have much more planned for Chicago, but I did stand outside the Chicago Cubs baseball ground (sadly there were no tours on the day I visited) and went to the world-famous United Center, which was literally just bricks and concrete.

Thanks, Chicago – you ended up really interesting and left me with a cracking big lump on my head.

Now for the bus to Detroit...

Detroit

I arrived in a city that I wanted to get to know better. I left the city with my heart wanting more. As I walked towards my hostel in the middle of Detroit, I was unsure why I had picked this place. My first impression of Detroit wasn't good. Houses flattened. Fences overgrown. Branches growing out of the windows of abandoned houses. Trees covering the roofs and slates lying on the street. No pavements. I was so confused about what had happened to this city. The area I was walking through was truly on its knees. No buildings over one storey high. Rooftops had become oases of flowers and foliage. Unfinished roads. Holes in the tarmac. Some houses with boarded-up doors. Others with large painted Xs to show families still lived there. Homes with their hearts left broken.

Detroit went bankrupt in 2013, because of mismanagement by city officials. Five years earlier, in 2009, the biggest recession ever hit the town when the collapse of the motor industry left Detroit almost on the brink of extinction. The horizon was busy with skyscrapers but most of them were empty. Literally, you could see empty desks through the curtain-less windows. This was a city in decline.

I was here to look at the events industry. I had meetings arranged with music promoters, entertainment providers, Foot Locker Detroit's marketing manager and many more. The purpose of my visit was to witness hope.

My first meeting was with Olympia Entertainment, a sports and entertainment company that owns and manages various teams and venues in Detroit. Basically, Olympia Entertainment is the saviour of the city when it comes to creating jobs and opportunities to bring life back to the streets of gloom. I was fortunate because by the end of the trip I would have visited three of their seven Detroit venues. Little Caesars Arena opened in 2017 with a construction cost of $862.9 million.

I got a tour of the arena, which was very modern, very glitz and glam. The Coca Cola Fan Experience activation was fun. Large lightboxes with photos of athletes that lit up the concourse via virtual touchpoints as it took you on a journey of education to learn about the players and coaches of the Detroit Red Wings, the ice hockey team that called this place home. It felt like I was in an arena with a museum in the middle. The venue was also very focused on the community impact. It had a great outlook and a genuine focus on development for the benefit of the community. Across the road were local families who could now afford to rent a flat because they worked at the arena.

The next day I would return for the ice hockey...

Event 74: Detroit Red Wings vs Chicago Blackhawks

17th September

Ice hockey – another staple American sport that's part of life. But a very different audience. It's weird, actually; the crowd was evidently different from American football fans. Ice hockey is a global sport but there is nothing like 20,000 American fans in an ice hockey arena. After my two-hour n the day before, I had been asked to be a secret shopper and check out the customer experience during the game. I was invited to ask difficult questions and, after 73 events, I was more than happy to be the most awkward customer ever! But unfortunately I stumbled across an obstacle. Amanda, who was just fabulous and worked in the customer relations department, met me inside and asked me to go back out with my ticket and come in a different door with another ticket. But the police officers standing outside were a bit suspicious that I was leaving so early. So I got really nervous and told them I was a secret shopper. *Well done, Matthew.*

This was a pre-season match and everything was being warmed up for the season ahead. Had the venue come back as strong as it could? Well, I was about to rip everything apart. The first security check was poor, and I quickly identified that they weren't properly set up to do a thorough check. There was no signage set out. The staff didn't fully understand how to use the wand. And it didn't help when all my stuff fell out of my bag (not deliberate at all…). The second it was exemplary. I mean, I was so surprised I wasn't clocked on the CCTV cameras. The friendliness of the guard was just brilliant. He identified I was from Scotland and that was it. He loved the accent and I asked him about his travel plans to come to Scotland – to try and distract him, in a way –

but everything was done correctly and smoothly.

The next thing to check was the recycling. Great to see the recycling bins in place – but suddenly the waste management team came along and put both bins into the same bag in the same bucket… So close to success.

Bud Light had a throne made of their boxes in the middle of the concourse for people to take a photo of. Comerica Bank had bank machines lit up for the world to see, that charged $2 per transaction. All the food and drink outlets were interestingly bright. Attractive to the eye. Well maintained, with serviettes stocked up and cleared away at every opportunity to make sure it looked appealing. Because of the low numbers expected for the pre-season game, some of the outlets weren't open tonight. This was the first time some of the newly designed units (by Delaware North) had been used so of course there were some teething issues – but they had good offerings. Very American. The small merchandise store inside the venue wasn't easily accessible for two spectators in wheelchairs. The area was tight and there was no way of getting to some of the items that were displayed at least 10 feet up. Unfortunately, the staff in the merch stall had struggled to understand customer service – but that was soon sorted out.

BANG… The player smashes into the glass. A fist is thrown. The gloves are off. The helmets scatter all over the place and then two players are sin-binned. *Love this… Boxing and ice hockey – perfect,* I typed into my notes on my phone. Apparently, fighting is all part of ice hockey. The guy next to me – well, five rows away – had a pair of binoculars so he could see every single punch. I just saw the pile-up and the smashing against the shaking glass screens. Ice hockey is similar to NFL, with a lot of starts and stops. This means creative direction is needed and it resulted in dance cams and a lot of singalongs. For many fans, being on the TV screen means they are famous for ten seconds, the sole focus of attention at their favourite sports team's arena. And there was dancing – I mean proper dancing – on the stairs, but this was all because of viral videos from other stadiums over the years. People think they can recreate this and, in return, have their 15 minutes of fame on YouTube. It's more about the psychological journey than the ice. The added extras bring the game to life.

I was sitting in the gods so I got to take it all in and see the fans high five each other when the puck went into the goal. That community celebration, I ask myself – what does that do for the team? Why do fans high five each other? Well, you could say it's the norm. I love trying to understand how people get so involved and connected to players and a team that, you could argue, they don't actually know. They're connected by merchandise and a ticket, but in no way did any of these fans have a natural connection to the team.

At the end of the game I received my first ever ice hockey match certificate as well as a 2018 calendar from Amanda, the guest experience manager, who then introduced me to some of the guest experience team that I had been grilling earlier. "Oh, so you're the one who is bringing your cousins from Chicago to the ice hockey and is interested in the sensory bags," they said. They were stunned to hear I had been asked to check out the customer service – and they passed. It was a great experience overall but the hockey for me was just – well… on thin ice. Everything else – the sponsorship, the activations, the food and so on – was more exciting. Stadiums are often so big that they can at times miss the smaller details but thankfully Little Caesars Arena captured my attention and I walked away happy.

One thing to take away...

I loved seeing the fans turning up in their colours; I think that is one of the key things about sport. What are the opportunities that other 'events' create to ensure people buy in and show their colours? Detroit Red Wings have given people the chance to be part of the club and ensure community is back within this broken city.

Detroit... Time to explore

Remember back in LA when I met Bob and Anne at *The Price is Right?* Well, they are from Detroit, and Bob was more than delighted to give me a guided tour of the city. I was going to see Detroit in a way tourists rarely do.

We met at a deli near my hostel. The staff welcomed me and 'my dad', and we laughed as we explained our story. The waitress was super interested but I think more in awe at my accent. "OMG, you're actually Scottish – I love Outlander!" Great. Personally, I've never seen the show. Bob was trying hard to get me a dinner date but the waitress was busy; maybe I should have been offended when she laughed and said – and I quote – "Having dinner with a Scottish person would be hilarious."

Bob drove us to places I couldn't get to on foot. The area around the former grand city station was quiet and eerie. The building, in Corktown, had been abandoned since 1988, but in 2019 a $350 million renovation project began. Funded by Ford Motor Company, it was to become the home of their innovation and research departments and would open in 2022. Bob showed me an old rowing club and a membership golf resort and then he decided he wanted to take me out of the city limits. Of course, it's rare to have the opportunity to visit the suburbs with a local. In the space of seven blocks, we travelled through two different 'cities', each with its own mayor, police force and rules. I was so confused. Maybe this was why Detroit and the surrounding area had so many problems. However, one thing I did notice was that out in the suburbs were mainly white people. The crime rate was not that high, and the American flag was flown proudly from the gardens. Then, as you got closer to the city, the flags were torn and sometimes lying on the ground. Maybe this was a representation of how certain communities had been let down.

I couldn't grasp the difference I saw in some of the residential areas 10 miles from the city. I couldn't help but wonder what the solution was. Along one side of the road the houses were beautiful, big, gated – and then two blocks down there was grass growing from the guttering, and empty patio chairs with ripped pillows; the houses were old and broken, much like Detroit's future. But there were people who would bring about change – slowly. Bob drove me around for about five hours, at which point I was so comfortable sitting in the passenger seat I fell asleep. I felt so bad because Bob was talking, but after 10 minutes of me snoozing I said "usually I put people to sleep!"

A friend back in Glasgow had arranged a meeting for me with Donald, Foot Locker Detroit's marketing manager. We met in the most urban and out of place hipster café. Donald was a gently spoken, modest man who was just finishing off some Excel documents when I arrived. We settled in and began our discussion. His job was based around Detroit's Foot Locker community store, which was a successful hub for culture, art, music and fashion. They organised competitions, music events and collaborations that brought people into the local neighbourhood and created opportunities and – once again – hope. Donald had spearheaded the initiative for the benefit of the residents of Detroit – and he loves sneakers. That culture was something that transformed his life and gave him purpose. You're probably wondering why Donald was important within my journey. He, like many others I met, had a vision that could shape, change and influence the future of the city. Donald is not only a Foot Locker worker but also a serious trendsetter in terms of successful community projects. He is the kind of person who can inspire an American kid who thinks they have no future to believe their dream is possible. Well done to Donald and his vision – I know for a fact he will inspire many more kids in the future.

I had also arranged a meeting with Brian and Alannah, who brought music events to Detroit. For three generations Brian's family had had a great relationship with the city, and he knew first-hand how much Detroit had changed – and was still changing.

Brian and Alannah were both open to the challenges ahead in the music industry. Brian's business was booking artists and creating music events at venues he managed. We met in the Fisher Building, which was about three miles from the city centre and just the most amazing building.

I want to explain from the get-go – this next event was attended by many people who were caught up in the troubles associated with this city, but for one night only it was all about the music and culture. Welcome to a party…

Event 75: Detroit Eastern Markets: After Dark

19th September

"I see what's going on…" the MC said as he got shed one bouncing. "Bounce bounce bounce bounce… Detroit – let us drop!" And immediately, the music dropped. I was in a trading market shed at a rave (all legal).

This was an area of Detroit that had fallen off the cliff and into a deep ravine. But a few companies there had a dream. Cultural arts and the council wanted to put Detroit back on the map by using the Eastern Market area, which was very run down. Brick walls smashed to the ground and factories abandoned. The story of manufacturing in Detroit was history; there was no future. Those walls that were still standing and the old steel beams left leaning against them had been turned into art. This was all part of a strategic plan to bring new audiences into this complex area. But persuading the middle classes of Detroit to come and visit this area was a challenge. Equally difficult was encouraging the working-class community here to show people what this area was all about. So they designed it to be explored and appreciated. Colourful lions, pandas peering out of gaps in walls, sunflowers, portraits along a makeshift skateboarding alleyway; bricks on the ground turned into Brussels sprouts, all green and lying there just waiting to be served. A mural festival was held to display the amazing talent Detroit has. Art is more than paint on walls – it is a way of defining an area. This was bright, powerful imagery with a clear message to the locals of Detroit, inviting them to visit and see for themselves the beauty the area holds.

Eastern Markets is open every day to sell fresh fruit and veg, flowers and fish to traders, local shops and restaurants. The markets have been here for 150 years but sadly the locals of Detroit don't come. The area became very run down, the nearby flats were demolished and many businesses that surrounded the market had to lock up and leave. On one retail unit was yellow paper sellotaped to the window stating: 'The City hiked our rent up – and now we can't afford to serve you...' The note went on for a total of seven A4 pages condemning the local council.

In 2012, someone had the idea of producing an event in conjunction with Detroit Month of Design – and Eastern Markets After Dark began. It's a free event and gives a platform to designers, businesses, creatives and those intrigued by Detroit to come together into a melting point and experience the markets as they have never been experienced before – after dark. Detroit is noted to be a hub for creative textiles, but it is also a UNESCO City of Design. I didn't realise the success or the scale of the design industry here until I walked into After Dark and meandered through the different displays.

This was a locals event; no tourists here. Actually, I think there were five tourists and they were all from the hostel where I was staying. The police had closed the road off because it was so busy and, as the music took over everyone's movements in one of the five sheds being used, it reminded me of the reason for my whole trip: escaping normality. When I saw After Dark listed on the Detroit Events page it was under the category of 'experience'. I found this fascinating and wanted to find out more. Experience. What does that mean? Do we not do this in every corner of the events industry? As I draw upon what I witnessed, you'll understand how Eastern Markets: After Dark was just something else – on a different level.

After an hour of strolling around the murals, Karen – my new friend from the hostel – and I wandered around listening to the live artists playing in the alleyways. A Mexican band, a rock band and a solo artist were all singing away, adding to the atmosphere of the market. We walked into one of the sheds where a lot of the stalls were still setting up. All five sheds would soon be 'lit up'.

Detroit City's engagement team were here with postcards on a washing line. A very simple but effective method of engagement. Visually pleasing, with five rows of colourful cards attached to the beams. The idea was to get visitors to write their vision for Detroit on a postcard and place it on the line with a peg. The prompts on the postcards were things like: 'My favourite thing to do in Detroit is…' and 'Some of the non-profits I am involved with in Detroit are…' Remember what I said about experience. Keep thinking about that as we progress through the sheds.

The five sheds all had different themes and items for purchase and engagement techniques. Shed one and two were for sure the best sheds – the most colourful and predominantly the busiest. Three was where the Detroit Design Awards was kicking off. Shed four had some epic projects to do with local crafts and shed five had some more market stalls and a wee soft shuffle going on at the back with a DJ.

We also saw 'live art' where the artist was there with a baby in a carrier on their chest, and they were literally flinging paint at an empty canvas. "IT'S ART, BABY!" Yes, I actually did hear this from one of the exuberant, energetic and cheerful painters, who was throwing his brush while the baby slept. This part of the shed, with its collective congregation of chilled, relaxed and very loosened-up artists, had real bounce.

Every item for sale had some type of logo of Detroit on it. This was the first city I had visited that did not put the city on clothing to make money from tourists (mostly because tourists weren't coming to Detroit anyway). Instead, this was a city keen to reaffirm connection with its residents and there was a sense of pride to be gained when you wore your Detroit-branded t-shirt. It was about saying Detroit is in your heart. Detroit is in your kitchen, in your living room, in your car, on your chest and on a bumper sticker. The city needs more events like this that share goals and visions, and accessibility is vital – this means easy parking, convenient timings, easy access, good toilets, clever marketing and clear instructions on what to expect. Eastern Markets needs After Dark – but the people of Detroit need After Dark even more.

There was a dance floor in shed one and, at 8:20pm, the live music began. It suddenly became the place to be. And now I was about to witness a shed and a city come alive like never before. Here is a story that will warm your heart. On the dance floor were six Black American women who were absolutely killing it on the floor. About 10 people were watching – not really a crowd, and they were aged around 65 (although they looked much younger). The women performed *The Shuffle* and then they had the time of their lives dancing along to Michael Jackson: "I want to rock with you... All night..." Some other people around the edges started to watch but at 8:28pm there were still only 20 people watching and eight people dancing.

And then a young Black American man joined in with absolutely no hesitation. He knew the dance and was laughing away with his new friends. He was wearing the most amazing pristine white tracksuit which had the badges of every NBA basketball team printed on it. His shoes were gleaming and his sunglasses – worn despite the darkness of the shed – were grooving in the light. Suddenly, another seven people joined into this most liberating of moments. The elders were now dwarfed by the other 20 people who had joined in. Now there were around 50 people in the middle of the dance floor – all Black Americans. By 8:36pm, 70 people were dancing, and people were flocking to shed one because of the noise. It had become a party magnet.

By 8:52pm we had seen a complete shift and the lines of dancers had become a large group. But suddenly a circle opened up. One young soul of man dared to be the first in and drop some moves. An older Black man ran over with his jacket and cooled him off because the moves were so hot. Everyone started clapping; the energy pulsing from this zone was addictive. I was thinking, "THIS IS GOLD! "Some of the organisers, still wearing headsets, came over and broke out some moves. I was in shed one for about an hour standing and it was the most magical and random moment of my entire trip. I saw the concrete floor and wooden beams become the location for a congregation of all genders, races, lifestyles, classes and dance move abilities as people lost themselves in the beat. No matter what anyone says about Detroit – this was the Detroit I was falling in love with. It took Eastern Markets to define it – it really did. That moment is stored in my 'best moments of the adventure' and if we ever meet, ask me to show you the videos and you will understand the true beauty of what I witnessed. Or, if you are ever in Detroit – go to Eastern Markets: After Dark.

I'd seen destruction all around the city, in many different ways – but tonight I saw a thriving community. Togetherness. Affection. I don't know how to conclude this event except to mention the division of Black Americans. After Dark aims to address integration and it did that!

One thing to take away…

Art, music, markets and more… I wish every city had an event like Eastern Markets: After Dark. It brings a new lease to life to an area usually used only by wholesalers. It gives spaces the chance to come alive. It gives the area hope. It gives businesses a chance to find new audiences to engage with. It's a great place to eat, drink and enjoy the atmosphere. After Dark – you were truly amazing.

Detroit… The story continues

Remember Olympia Entertainment? Well, I managed to secure a tour of two of their other venues on my last day. The first was Fox Theatre, where I was welcomed by Tony, one of the best operations managers I have ever met. Tony was truly spectacular. He talked me through the décor, much of which was designed by the original owner's wife Mrs Fox over a hundred years ago. The building is 10 storeys high and has the largest single-piece wool rug ever manufactured, and it has held up well considering the number of people who have trundled over it. Everywhere there was a big Indian and Chinese influence; even the columns on the stairs were inspired by Indian art and the lions at the base of the stairs have welcomed hundreds of thousands of people since 1928, when the theatre first opened. I was awestruck as we walked in. It reminded me a lot of the opera house in Mumbai, India. It was grand and charming, and I was overwhelmed to be standing in the empty 5,000 seat theatre.

Tony was so enthusiastic about his place of work, and so positive about everything to do with the theatre. "Let's go backstage," he said, and suddenly I encountered a sight similar to one I'd seen at Red Rocks. The walls in the backstage area had all been painted with the names and logos of various shows over the years, and signed by cast members. *Lord of the Rings* was there, and *Cats,* and *Cinderella.* My favourite was *Sesame Street,* which had a 24-show run in 2013 – the same year the city went into bankruptcy. When you think about it, the world can be falling apart but people still want entertainment. It's a bit like standing in an underground bunker, protected from the chaos outside once the large gilt-painted doors close behind you. The city was crumbling away, jobs were being lost and houses repossessed –but Big Bird and the gang still entertained Detroit.

My next stop was Comerica Park, where I was visiting as a secret shopper. I was going on a public tour and my job was to blend in and report back. I had all my bags with me, and Tony found someone to walk over with me. "You must be important to get escorted over by someone," I was told.

"No, I am just a lost Scotsman – you ever spoke to a Scottish guy before?" I said. This resulted in laughter and led to a great conversation that threw them off the scent of me being a secret shopper.

Comerica Park, again operated and owned by Olympia Entertainment, is the home of the Detroit Tigers. It is located in downtown Detroit, literally just along the road from Little Caesars Arena and across from Fox Theatre. The stadium opened in 2000 and replaced Tiger Stadium, which was down near the river. Comerica Bank had naming rights worth over $60 million, but the bank was founded in Detroit so it also had a local connection. The stadium has some quirky features, like a fairground in the middle of the concourse and an astronaut spacesuit on display to celebrate the anniversary of Apollo 11.

I was on the verge of being sussed out as a mystery shopper. "So you just got your bags carried over here? You a reporter?" the tour guide asked. I made some excuse about my friend's cousin working at the theatre and bringing me here, only for him to say, "Who's your friend's cousin then?" I was already sweating, but now in double time. So I said it was Fred, who works in the lighting department. Thankfully neither of the retired part-time tour guides knew Fred, who doesn't work in the lighting department. I think my fellow tour group members now believed me and I was welcomed into the pack.

Sadly, the tour wasn't up to Tony's standards. Shall we just say the tour needed work and after my feedback, hopefully the tour would be changed!

Detroit made it into my top five cities on my trip. I will definitely go back – and, if this book is ever made into a Hollywood blockbuster, I will ensure Detroit has a leading role. Because Detroit does have a leading role in the world and the empty plots, the broken homes and the roofs growing forests will turn into areas of opportunity, that is for sure. Detroit has something untapped. It has a special atmosphere. Yes, the bus station gave me a rough welcome – but every city has its rough edges.

If, every day, one brick can be taken down from the divide and used to build hope then this city will survive. A city like Detroit has been through more than most places and the people will love it with their hearts and minds and ensure the city flourishes through whatever problems are thrown at it in future.

Boston... YESSSSSSS!

Boston would be my fourth-to-last city. FOURTH! And I was going to see my very good friend Vicky, who would be joining me for three days. Boston is a city I didn't know much about, but Vicky had been preparing the agenda – so I would just go with it and add a few of my own surprises along the way.

At the very last minute, Boston Celtics invited me to meet with the vice president of media services, Jeff. I was so honoured to have a chance to meet Jeff and discuss the importance of media, the changes in sports consumption, fan engagement, community involvement – EVERYTHING to do with the success of a club. Okay, the Celtics haven't won much recently but sometimes the brand is bigger than trophies. They were also the only team to win 17 championships during the 20th century. I was checked in by the security guard at the front door and asked to sit in the reception area. In front of me was a 20-foot Boston Celtics logo. The receptionist said: "You're the guy going around the world?" and I laughed. They had an email go around with the visitors that week and I was on the list.

Jeff popped his head through the office door and said, "You're Matt!" I grabbed one last sweet from the reception desk and followed him down the corridor. Jeff's office was packed top to bottom with everything he had accumulated during his 39 years at the club – snippets of articles, books, tops, t-shirts and more. Jeff was a fount of knowledge when it came to Boston Celtics and I learned a lot in the hour and a half we were together. Jeff taught me about loyalty in sport, and about the vision a club can have and the importance of understanding the vision from the perspective of the players, staff and owners. We spoke about the increase in sports wages and how the 'fame game' can change the ways players behave and are received by fans and staff, and he commented gingerly about the 90s compared to now. Relationships in sport are critical, as is networking – not just within your club but throughout the league. You need to be liked. Jeff has stood courtside while the club went through disruption and changes, wins and losses. I asked him why he'd been here so long. Sitting back in his large black chair with his hands clasped, he took a moment. Eventually, he replied: "For the love of this club." And you could see it. Our discussion gave me an insight that was truly invaluable, not just in sport but in becoming a leader. I was sitting in front of someone who had worked his way up to becoming the vice president of a major team, and that was a story in itself.

We wrapped up the discussion and Jeff walked me back to reception. We meandered along corridors full of pictures celebrating the club's success. As I was leaving, he turned to me and said, "Okay, one last photo..." Then he said to the receptionist: "That's them." He walked over to two large black flight cases. At first, I thought they were speakers. Suddenly he revealed the trophies. One was the 2008 NBA Championship and he said, "Right, here you go," and passed it to me! I didn't have gloves on, which I knew was breaking protocol, and it was heavy. "Don't drop it!" he said. No pressure. We'd laughed, we'd talked about the future but, most importantly, I had made a friend. Thanks, Jeff – both for the chat and the confidence to push forward in life.

Event 76: What The Fluff?

In a supermarket near you, in the baking aisle, there are usually four tubs of a thing called 'Fluff': the sticky marshmallow stuff that can be truly addictive and damaging to your teeth. It is not a product you would go to the shops solely to buy. It's not a staple ingredient in any recipe. But Fluff is very popular and Somerville, a city outside Boston, is the home of Fluff and has created an event dedicated to Fluff. This year was the 102nd anniversary of the invention of Fluff but the 14th anniversary of the What The Fluff? festival, and I was right in the middle of it.

The What The Fluff? festival is a combination of selling the city, drawing opportunities to local businesses and bringing unity to the area and it really has a unique way of bringing Union Square to life. There was a great partnership between the city, the local businesses and Fluff. When I arrived, I noticed yellow dumper trucks sitting at the festival entrance, being used as an engagement tool. Some roadworks were going on and the building company had agreed to let people sit on the diggers! Streets had been closed to traffic and there were stalls run by schools, charities and random kids selling Fluff and jam sandwiches in plastic bags to raise money for their local Boys' Brigade. I was like: what is going on? Thousands of people flocked to the festival with their dogs, children, bikes, scooters and the rest. The festival was a community event and an estimated 20,000 people visit throughout the day. It was constantly busy. Families all knew each other; stall holders were locals who had side hustles like painting and baking. This may have been a street festival about marshmallow fluff but really it was a chance for the community to escape their homes and come downtown for something to do. And, of course, it was a celebration of Fluff and the positive impact it has had on the town.

I was really curious about why it was called 'What the Fluff?' and I managed to speak to Jess, the executive director for Union Square Main Streets; I also got five minutes with the Mayor of Somerville, Joseph Curtatone. He was very popular at the festival and lots of people were surrounding him. But me being me, I was straight in there. "Can I have five minutes with the mayor?" Not a problem. I asked him why this was an important event and he talked about the unity and economic benefits (very political answer) but as I listened to him I realised it was actually a way of promoting certain aspects of Somerville, including the business technology area which was one of the key sponsors. This wasn't about selling lots of Fluff. It was using Fluff to get people together to impact business agendas and build community spirit. It wasn't so much a hidden agenda, but certainly there were sponsors and partnerships for a reason. The event was organised by Union Square Main Streets and The Somerville Art Council and sponsored by Allstate Insurance. Interesting. Especially interesting to see an insurance company supporting this quite upmarket event when insurance is such big business in America.

I found the theme of this year's festival interesting. All the maps and information were designed like a pirate island. The staff all wore t-shirts that said 'Captain'. An interesting way of trying to show authority. An event needs to take the people with it and this theme was well received. Everyone had something pirate-y going on around their stalls and people really seemed to enjoy that sense of discovery. Some families had even turned up with their children in pirate costumes.

The festival tagline was 'All Roads Lead to Fluff' and I liked the idea that Fluff is from Somerville so all roads, whether for locals, businesses, or tourists, should lead to Somerville. Because for now, sadly, Somerville is not a tourist destination. It's miles from anything that would be worth visiting – but this is why entertainment magnets and the large crowds they attract are invaluable to businesses here. The area is represented by 50+

languages, with neighbourhoods and communities from all over the world. The corner shop was run by a Chinese family, but only the daughter spoke English. The Indian takeaway was owned by a family from Mumbai, who had a stall at the festival. And a Croatian family were wearing pirate hats and flying their national flag on their stall. A very multicultural street with multicultural objectives.

On the merch stall, everything had Fluff stamped on it. Hats, magnets, stickers... everything. I paid $15 for a Fluff hat for Mother Lamb – she absolutely loves this marshmallow stuff. So the hat was more than a photo, it was a tangible memory. Never mind the fact that I took her up the Eiffel Tower or to see Elton John. Me giving her a Fluff hat – life made. And I think this is an important point when it comes to merchandise. Something so simple can mean so much for so many people. A hoodie with a logo on it will probably never be taken off by a die-hard fan because for them it shows loyalty and a connection they can never explain. And, in a way, this is the same with the idea of a captain.

One thing to take away...

Buy-in to this event by the mayor and local businesses allows for genuine engagement. It makes a novel idea work. Oh, and the reason the festival got its name? Apparently someone at a council meeting who wanted to reject the plans for the festival said, "What the fluff are we doing?" Immediately the name was carried. Promoting a sugary product is never going to be on the agenda of people trying to stamp out obesity, but for one day a year Somerville used it to be the captain of the area.

Back to Boston...

Vicky had planned some great activities for me, but I was all good to just chill. Exciting times! It was the first time I had really allowed myself time to relax. We went on a boat tour, we went down to the harbour and ate chips, we ate cake and we also went to an improv show. The construction of improv shows means you take a risk on whether or not you will find it funny. Apparently two people in the front row decided they didn't and left. I grabbed a chat with one of the comedians, James, who was a big brute of a man and very funny. I also liked the show's tagline: 'Can we get a word, any word, and get us started.' Genius.

Looking online, we found out that we would be able to visit Harvard University and go to an event at the same time. Perfect! Just excellent!

Event 77: Concert for One

<u>22nd September</u>

One musician and one spectator in the middle of a refurbished shipping container. I mean – wow! Today, at the Harvard Science Center Plaza, I witnessed a combination of music and escapism in action. The event was run by a company called Celebrity Series. It's an annual event and the main purpose is to immerse the public in music they have probably never heard before via a unique platform. A key point to make was that this was the first time I had seen anything like this on my journey – an event that combined music and an unexpected surprise. Events should be about surprise and emotional engagement – but usually you know everything that will happen.

As a non-profit organisation, its mission is to introduce the performing arts to people's lives and inspire dreams through innovation and excellence. The organisation has venues all across Boston that create individual and partnered performances, including diverse line-ups. Today I was experiencing – Concert for One – within this shipping container.

The tagline for Concert for One was 'One musician. One listener. One minute of music.' The shipping container was laid out like a well-decorated cabin. A flowery carpet and a table lamp made the place look very homely. In the cabin sat a musician with his instrument. Only one attendee walked in at a time. The event is so simple. You walk over, queue and then enter. Staff wait outside and ask your name, which they then use to introduce you to the musician – genius. Remember – the biggest flashiest events with all the money sometimes don't offer the best experiences. The free ones are often the ones that are created with love. I loved the personal approach here – it was beautiful. This wasn't you competing with 50,000 others to experience an event – you were speaking to the event directly.

Inside the container I was introduced to Mario, who was playing a lute, a plucked string instrument dating back to the 16th century. As I sat in a cabin that felt like home and listened to the sound of the lute, it was so peaceful and a complete contrast to the world outside. I was inside this cabin for only one minute. For 15 seconds Mario introduced me to the instrument and for 45 seconds he played it. And then my time was up. The door opened, I thanked the musician and I left. No tip jars – the whole thing was at no cost and no email address was taken. There was just Mario's business card, which you could pick up if you chose to.

I was absolutely stunned and amazed by how perfect this event was. It was really interesting to sit face to face with a musician. When have you ever taken the time to listen, engage with and appreciate a musician like that? The face to face idea is so clever and has so many benefits for the future of music. I can see it as a new form of busking. Of course, it will be difficult to get a cabin for every busker, but give it a shot – it's something different.

We went to a half-cabin where there was an information board covered with cards, and shelving that held a lot of different things to read and engage with. I spotted a large 'thank you' banner with all the sponsors' logos, a mirror engraved with #concertforone to take selfies, posters asking 'What is your neighbourhood?' and encouraging you to 'Share the experience', with a list of social media handles. There were also cards that said 'Tell us what you thought about your one minute experience…', with pins to stick them up, similar to the washing lines of cards in Detroit. It was an excellent way of getting people's immediate feedback and first impression of their Concert for One experience.

The fact that the capsules were so bright and the whole thing was positioned in a high footfall area gave people the opportunity to engage; it disrupted their usual routine. It wasn't about taking me off my path but about adding to my path. However, I do feel the physical positioning of the event was negative. It was in the middle of a wealthy area – we were literally on the Harvard University campus – which wasn't a problem for us; in fact, it was a positive association in many ways, and I'm sure the thousands of students on campus would visit. But I don't know if people from the surrounding neighbourhoods would venture in. I would love to take the cabin to the roughest of areas and see whether something that is welcomed in a place like Harvard would be equally appreciated in the rougher streets. I think it would. I think every city needs a cabin with a musician. And I think it could open creative opportunities not only to musicians but to ballet dancers, poets, even a triangle performer…

One thing to take away…

Events can instrumentally deliver an experience that takes people to another level without being complex. I think the concept of Concert for One could be a global project that one day could for one moment allow everyone to share one minute of music…

Boston… Tourist time

My last night in Boston was great. Vicky and I relaxed at the harbour, devoured chips and watched some buskers. We sat and reflected – a lot. It was so nice to have someone to talk to, moan at and celebrate with. Boston was more than just a flying visit.

Now the bus to New York…

The bus from Boston to New York was the opposite of pleasurable but certainly entertaining. I am not going to miss travelling on buses and not knowing whether the person next to me will pee in the provided toilet or on the seat. But I wasn't here to hear the buzz of the city but to explore the events industry and relax at my cousin's home in New Jersey.

My first stop in New Jersey was Newark City. As I asked the

way to the symphony hall, each police officer I spoke to said: "Be careful." I don't why they felt they had to say this to the hardest man from Glasgow – I was wearing a pink shirt, shiny black shoes and my grey trousers and carrying a black briefcase. I arrived at the front of a locked-up building with iron bars across the windows. Smashed glass had been replaced with wooden panels. Dirt on the walkways – and not only trash. This was the home of Newark Symphony Hall. Of course, absolutely no one knows about this place. It's not a tourist attraction. From the outside, it's a historic but run-down building that no tourist groups come here wanting to see. Inside, the theatre has seats that are dusty but filled with years of memories. It's a place that just needed to be loved by the community – and investors.

I entered the ticket office, which was open despite there being no shows booked for the next six months. After my name was taken I was told to go through and I was met by two of the most dedicated staff members, who were from the local community – Jos and Ebony. I could have stayed with them all day. We sat and discussed life like long lost friends. We were from different sides of the world and opposite ends of the spectrum, but we had the same energy. It seemed they were nervous but there was no need; I was the nervous one. They talked about the lack of shows and their desire to do so much more than they could. One had just graduated college and come back to support the growth of their community symphony hall. The other was the janitor turned general manager. Both had a stake in this place. Jos had a vision that was amazing and was backed by the CEO, who was well known but not from the community. They both cared more than anyone would if they were just employed with a payroll number. Each day they walked to work along streets paved with trouble. The hall is in a predominantly poor black area where employment opportunities are rare. Instead, gang shootings and drugs are common activities.

First, we headed up in the lift to the performing arts academy area. This is a summer programme run by the most amazing

418

woman, Ms Cisely. The CPAASP (Children's Performing Arts Academy Summer Program) aims to help the children of the neighbourhood reach their potential and find hope. It wasn't just about getting children into a summer program for six weeks but inviting 8 to 15-year-olds into a space where they learned the skills to one day potentially perform on a stage on Broadway. I honestly believe this programme needs more attention from Broadway and the musical theatre companies. They need to see the dedication Ms Cisely gives it and, believe me, these kids who come in with a dream can reach it. After a sing-song and a wee dance in the mirrored room, it was time to see the theatre.

The crystal chandelier lit up the most beautiful ceiling. This wonderful theatre has been loved by all over the last 94 years and the marble archways have welcomed thousands to enjoy performances on a stage framed by gold-edged red drapes. I cannot explain how I felt as I stood here. I just kept saying: "WOW. WOW, WOW!" This theatre would be sold out if it was in the middle of Manhattan, but because it is in Newark it misses so many opportunities. I was told about the shows that do come here and there was a sense of 'Everyone laughs at us...'

Newark Symphony Hall didn't have the same appeal as other places, and no one but me was attracted to this place. I was attracted because of the huge love and heart that each row of seats possessed and the stories the stage could tell – even in the dim light. Unfortunately, other than some political rallies held in the ballroom, no shows had taken place here for a few months. I stood on the stage and made a video on my phone, where I said: "With the wallpaper peeling off the walls you would be right to think this is disused – but it's not. Instead, it is a place with more love than theatres only 16 miles away. It's not about commercialism, it's about community. Upstairs is a place where children find their love for singing and dancing. They don't pay ridiculous prices for a summer camp so mum and dad can swan away for a break – instead, this camp is run by those who passionately care about the arts and the children of this community. A theatre with seats that have dust on them is not a theatre in disarray – it's a theatre just warming up to the possibilities it will one day encounter..."

Newark Symphony Hall – the place where, one day, dreams will come true. If you are reading this and live in New York or the New Jersey area, I hope you will go and see the hall. Believe me, you will fall in love with it as much if not more than I did. I came to see an old, rundown but up-and-kicking venue and I left with a new appreciation for what community means.

After a 90-minute train ride, I was delighted to be welcomed with open arms by my family – Michael, who is my second cousin, and his amazing family! I felt so at home. There was even a pantry with snacks. Michael's aunt and uncle were also in town, so we had an amazing time together.

You may recognise the band I am about to meet...!

Event 78: Lucky Chops Album Release in Manhattan Subway Station

27th September

It was 27th September and on this Friday morning I was going to an album launch. My family laughed when I said I was going to the subway to watch a performance. I was so excited to see this band again after meeting them in Jakarta. Their music had stayed with me and had become the unofficial soundtrack to my adventure. Lucky Chops, who are an American band, had gathered a huge social media following after going viral and now had over 1.2 million likes and a global audience. A European tour was happening in October 2019 but for now, the subway was their stage.

Memorable performances are exactly what Lucky Chops deliver. I emailed them about catching up in Manhattan and immediately got a reply saying they were dropping their new album where it all began – in the middle of 42nd Street Station. How much more random could it get? I was now going to an event that would literally disrupt people's day and hopefully help them discover a new band in the most amazing venue and part with some money when they were simply going about their daily business. See, you can have events in subway stations – you just need the permit, which Lucky Chops did.

So, let's figure out what it is like to play at a subway station in New York. Firstly, the smells are palpable (it was that intense). The NYC website highlights that to perform in a public area you must have a permit. However, to perform on the subway platform you must conform to all Metropolitan Transportation Authority (MTA) rules of conduct. The subway stations have a Music Under New York busking programme and performers have to go through an audition process to be part of it. It's a very exciting project. But today was completely different. The band had permission to hold their album launch and also include amplification – which is usually banned. The subway manager, with his hundred keys hanging to the right of his waist, came along and the band showed him the permit. They were asked to move back a bit and a flag was tied to a water pipe above them to mark the boundary.

As I watched the band set up I had to remember where we were standing – in the middle of 42nd Street subway station in Manhattan, with thousands of people passing through every five minutes. Tourists were here. Locals were here. Disgruntled humans were here. Every three minutes the doors of a subway train opened on platform C and a new audience arrived for Lucky Chops to immerse in their music.

The band actually became famous because of their viral videos shot in subway stations showcasing their high octane performance about 12 years ago. So let's talk about how viral videos are mass events. Viral events can catapult people to another level in terms of their talent. As people scroll through social media, they engage with the video and if it is positioned correctly it can lead to success very quickly. How the performers in the video then use it – well, that is another story. In this case, it worked well and has resulted in world tours for Lucky Chops, thanks to their music being accepted and enjoyed by millions around the globe. Now these very talented musicians and composers have created works of art that have allowed them to enjoy a life that many musicians can only dream of. But this dream did not come easy. It came through hard work and a lot of tough decisions.

As I stood behind the band, I watched the crowd gather. Most of those passing by had no intention of seeing an instrumental band play today. But that is the art of busking. People stop for five seconds to listen to the music and decide whether they like it. If they enjoy it, they stand for another minute before realising their train is leaving. At one point I counted a hundred people crowded around, tapping their toes. Some put money in the bucket and some were just standing there soaking it up. Keeping a crowd is a feat of engineering. You have to know how to manage, lead and influence them – and Lucky Chops did. I had witnessed it in Jakarta, but the levels of attention from those here, who were simply going about their daily business, were different from those seeking out entertainment at a music festival.

This was why this type of event was so unique – it had no confirmed audience. The band were streaming the show live, and it received an amazing 275,000 views online – amazing! Combining virtual platforms and real-life experience was an unusual hybrid approach. The crowd at the station was getting a first-hand experience that the online audience would never be able to appreciate. Although the filmed one-angle approach looked good, it was still nothing like being in the middle of the smelly tunnels of the New York subway. It was warm down there, that was for sure. I mean, a BOILING September day. I could hear the trains arriving below and the announcements: "This train is for the Bronx." The new audience shuffled in, letting people pass, some wearing earphones and ignoring what was going on. Ignorance, but not arrogance. This subway tunnel offered something adorable and well suited to the times we are living in.

Album releases are critical for bands. They have to be creative and you could not be any more creative than going down on 42nd Street Station in Manhattan. I still couldn't believe I was standing watching this band again after seeing them in Jakarta in March. Things happen for great reasons. During their interval, I ran across and saw Josh. We chatted. He was even more sweaty here than he was in the 38 degree, 100% humidity of Indonesia. I was laughing as the rest of the band came over. "Matt!!!! You've lost weight!!!" *Thanks, guys! I work out – I know.* But we talked about what it was like to perform in the station. They laughed as one of them said, "It's funny watching people who want to stay but can't. It's intriguing to think – what are they willing to miss to watch us perform?" That last part is interesting. Were people willing to change the course of their day in order to enjoy this spectacle?

This was the band's bread and butter. All their income comes from music, through things like this. Their success all over the world was great – but nothing was quite like going back to the place that made them what they are now. Lucky Chops performing in a subway... I never thought I would have that on my list, that is for sure. But that was the funny thing. Who was to tell me what type of events were possible? The venue in itself is a great story and insight and has the potential to hold whatever it wants. I watched, leaning against a pillar, and thought about all the people going past. Okay, maybe the subway was not somewhere to hold a cocktail dress auction or a movie night – but it was the perfect place for a spontaneous music concert to bring joy to people's lives.

One thing to take away...

Events can happen anywhere. They can shape someone's day. They can change someone's life. I have a feeling a few people missed their train simply because they were immersed in the most energetic performance ever. Events can create a positive distraction and give people a moment of unique engagement. And the subway station and Lucky Chops delivered just that. Down the escalator I went, shouting "Bye!" to a band who had basically completed the trip with me!

New York with the family...

Staying in New Jersey, it was great to relax with the family. We laughed. We joked. We cooked together (well, I didn't; I cleaned up). We had a night at the pub. We spent an evening with Michael's friend. I was becoming better at reflecting as I was becoming closer to the end line.

'No matter what is typed, it was all a memory. No matter where it was typed, it was all written from a place that I would probably never return. Soak up each sight, smell and taste and

understand what you get from each place. The next day and the next place may not be as pretty, but it will all convert from a moment to a memory.'

To everyone in New Jersey – thank you. Including the Trader Joe staff, who just laughed when I told them all about what I was doing at the till. They didn't understand a word I said.

Nashville...

I'd now arrived in the State of Tennessee. It's loud. It's bright. It's colourful. Welcome to Nashville – a complete contrast to what I expected. After my relaxing time in New Jersey and the luxury of having a room to myself for seven days, I got straight back into hostel life – I was sharing a room with nine people.

I would be spending the next few days with Chloe and Jon – remember the amazing couple from Calgary? We were going to see the sights together and I was very fortunate because they had planned my agenda; I just needed to float along.

Between First and Fifth Avenue is what is known as Honky Tonk Row. Every bar had the windows open and a band playing to the crowd inside – but also to attract people from outside in. Exhausting to experience on the fourth night, but exciting on the first. Bright neon lights everywhere. On the stages were a mixture of bands: those who have played here for years and are waiting for their big break; resident musicians who are happy to jump from bar to bar and play for free; people who work in Nashville and come to sing in the bars after 5pm for some side cash; and people who came to Nashville to make their dreams come true. Nashville is known as the capital of country music and it is a destination for every music lover. And there's no off switch. It's a constant round of noise and frantic tourist-like behaviour – which we will get to...

So let's hit the first note...

Event 79: Grand Ole Opry 94th Birthday

5th October

Firstly, thanks to Jon and Chloe for this moment!

The sun was scorching. The small stages outside the Grand Ole Opry were warming up the crowd, who were arriving for a big day in the history of the venue as it was the Grand Ole Opry's 94th birthday – epic, eh! I managed to include this special occasion on my trip thanks to no careful planning and sheer luck. Today I was attending two different shows in the Opry. The first show was half empty; it was an older audience and it was quite flat with engagement. Most people were having a nap, to be fair. I wasn't prepared for a show in the Opry to be quite so boring – but it was. The crowd weren't bothered about where they were. Either it was not the priority of their trip, or they were knackered from the night before. I don't think the prestige of the surroundings was really exciting them too much. Yet I was over the moon to be here. I couldn't believe it, to be fair! Every time the music started, I was like a five-year-old in a candy store.

The Grand Ole Opry is, in my eyes, a musical wonder of the world. Originally it began as a radio show; it is currently the longest-running broadcast radio show in US history. It was founded in 1925 by George D Hay, and its aim is to attract and celebrate the diverse range of musicians within the different genres of country, from bluegrass and Americana to folk and gospel. Visitors from all over the world come to buy a fridge magnet (which, of course, is the main purpose of being a tourist).

In 2010, the Grand Ole Opry House was flooded, along with much of Nashville, and it was closed for five months as restoration took place. Interestingly, the Opry is the place that defines

Nashville, but The Grand Ole Opry House is actually nowhere near the heart of Nashville. As I walked into the Grand Ole Opry I could understand the impact this venue has on so many people. The venue may not be near the centre of Nashville, but it's held close within the hearts of those who visit.

The celebration today was being broadcast live on WSM Online. There were USA flags everywhere. I felt naked without one, to be fair. The website said everyone was invited – but the reality was you could only come if you had enough money for a ticket. This was a 12-hour birthday bash; a long day. Chloe, Jon and I sat for hours critiquing the whole thing. It was fab!

During that first show, an interesting thought came to me. It felt more like we were in a bingo hall than a music event. So did the age and financial stability and riches of the people attending mean they thought they had control over how they engaged and behaved, rather than conforming to the regular activity of audiences at the Opry? It seemed as though they were taking the whole experience for granted. It kind of felt like a bus tour had turned up and were disappointed after being told they were going to the best place in the world – and their reaction was as if you had stolen their teabag out of the tea before it was brewed.

As I glanced around, a few people had nodded off. At one point one usher did actually go up and smile at one gentleman (I was guessing he was a regular) who was perched back ready for his snooze. But I remembered something I had been told earlier in the day. The one thing that the world of country music should be worried about is the demographic of the audience. And I could see why. The future audience of country music was not in this room, that's for sure. They go to the Country Music Awards or the more out of the way country shows like Stagecoach Festival or Country Jam in Colorado. How do you change the Grand Ole Opry's demographic? In a way, the venue was very much focused on engaging with the older generation. The staff for this show were even older. Everything was at a slower pace. Outside, before the show began, there were 100 spaces on the pre-show musical bingo cards that was played on the buses that brought some of the guests in. I kid you not! This was proper bingo; I mean, will that draw in the country music fans of the future? But I don't think they have thought about assessing the crowd dynamics in terms of success for the future.

But it all changed when we got to the 7:30pm show. The demographic approaching the door was immediately noticeably different. The place was full – upstairs and downstairs. There was no tour bus bingo to be seen and there was a whole different approach towards customer engagement. A team of young ushers had arrived with big smiles and name badges. It was party time. There was a fair amount of hustle and bustle in the air. Everyone was wearing cowboy boots and hats – and then there was me, in my pinkest of cotton shirts and even pinker face.

This time we had seats on the other side in the stalls, which was brilliant. There was a host. There was a warm-up act. And, importantly, there was life in the auditorium. The pulse had just been restarted. It felt like I was now in one of the Grand Ole Opry's marketing videos. Before the show, the warm-up was all about getting everyone up and out of their seats. Those who know me will know you don't need to ask twice for me to dance. "We want energy and we want people to be contestants on the Plinko game tonight during the performance," the host said. All I had to do was dance and impress the host – who was about 50 metres away. I danced that hard I was picked out of an auditorium of 4,000 as the only one to play. Yes – to the absolute horror of those who of course had been trying for years to get on this stage, there was me straight up there. Perfect. Instead of just watching the show, now I was part of it. We will get to what happened soon…

Because tonight was the 94th birthday party there were huge names on the bill. Some absolute legends of the Nashville music community. Trace Atkins – who, apparently, was a country heartthrob – was on stage strutting his stuff and the female members of the audience were loving every minute. He knew how to control a crowd and had been successful at doing just that over the years. Everyone knew the words to his songs. The place was alive. I was oozing with excitement because I was in the Grand Ole Opry – that in itself was HUGE! A duo was on next – and then I was approached by the stagehand. Now it was my time to be 'on stage'.

On the stage was a famous country music duo (so famous I forgot their names). And suddenly it was the interval on the radio show – which means it's time to play Plinko. "So it's simple. Answer the question, I'll give you the token and you play the game." Before we walked on from behind the curtain I was told: "The question is very straightforward – you will know the answer." I tried to explain I knew nothing about country music. I pleaded with them. "No, it's easy, don't worry... You'll know it." By now I was begging the stagehands to give me a clue. "You'll know the answers."

"No, I won't – I am from Scotland and I hate quizzes!" I told them. Even as we were walking out towards the big game board I was begging them: "Please!"

And then we were out. Hello, Nashville! The presenter, who was not that nice to me, was doing this for the first time ever. She had never done this type of interval entertainment before. Oh, and she couldn't understand me either. "Okay Matthew from Scotland, you will now answer this question..." I froze. I had no idea. The artists on the stage were screaming. The 4,000 people were screaming. I was looking at the stagehands, who were mouthing something. I had no idea who sang a number one hit in a certain year– I had warned her before – but now I had every jealous event attendee screaming at me!

Jon and Chloe tried to help but they were in zone Z, which may as well have been in a different state to me. But, to my surprise, I managed to guess – with the help of the screams – that it was the band standing on the stage. Winning the game was one thing; winning the prize, which was women's jewellery worth $270, was interesting. It was a set of earrings – they just didn't suit me. We wheeled off and the presenter was obviously not happy. "You didn't know that?" she barked at me, before walking back to her dressing room with a very 'I am more important than you will ever be…' attitude.

The stagehand said: "Right, Matthew, let's get you back to enjoy the show." As I collected my earrings I told them I had warned her. "You did," the guy said. "She should have just told you. We couldn't tell you because – well, she would have got us sacked if we helped you." It kind of said it all. The stagehands weren't fans of the host either. As I returned to my seat I remember Jon and Chloe just laughing and hugging me. Everyone was giving me one of those awkward rounds of applause as the show continued. The engagement was… ugh. It needs work. It wasn't the best. It wasn't the worst.

By 9:15pm, the show was over. At 9:30pm, the next show was to begin. Yes – that is right. Only 15 minutes to empty, clean and refill. The show had to be reset and go on the radio again. As 4,000 people were exiting straight into a small concourse area, another 4,000 were waiting to come in. It was EXTREMELY busy.

The show that night was fantastic. The atmosphere in the Opry is unique. I managed to feel my way around the world of country music while rubbing shoulders with fans who had travelled from all over the States for this night. Using my compasses – Jon and Chloe – I could appreciate the buzz and the noise and navigate my way quite quickly through how the music world appreciates the Opry as a shrine. Draped in history, it's a place of pure country for gun-wielding, cowboy-boot-wearing, constitution-abiding citizens.

Finally, let me share with you the story of the earrings I won.

A burst of applause occurred outside the venue. "He just proposed!" someone shouted at their friend.

I looked at Chloe and Jon. "Chloe, hold my jacket…"

So this couple had just got engaged about 50 metres from us and all of a sudden, William Wallace was chasing after them.

Without me knowing, Chloe was recording me; Jon was simply confused that I had sprinted away from the only two people I knew. Slightly out of breath, I got to the couple just as they were coming to the realisation that they had just joined hearts and decided to marry each other. "Hi," I said. "Congratulations on getting engaged. So I just won these earrings and I don't need them – so happy engagement…" Then I ran away without stopping for breath, or a conversation. Happy engagement!

One thing to take away…

There was cake, fan engagement and country singers galore. To be there was special and to understand the demographic was cool – but change is needed to keep this amazing place going in the future. The audience sleeping at the 3pm show does absolutely nothing for the future or even the current image of country music. Luckily, the 7:30pm show redeemed itself.

Returning to Nashville…

This city may be best known as the heart of country music but it is also home to Nissan, The Saturn Corporation, many leading universities and the world's largest publisher of the bible. Skyscrapers fill the city centre and bars are located around these developments. In comparison, East Nashville has taken a different approach to urban regeneration and is strikingly flat. In Downtown Nashville, 'bar bikes' roam the streets, with 12 to 20 people on these capsules of alcohol-fuelled excitement whizzing around. The driver, who rents his 'tourist capsule', was sober, while the passengers were balancing on the edge of the vehicle as they cycled along while singing and being served shots. The noise alone had resulted in petitions being launched against the owners of these bikes. Suddenly, tractors were ploughing through the streets trailing large wagons with dancing party-goers; it was quite extraordinarily dangerous to witness. In Nashville, boundaries for tourism experiences had all but gone. As they thundered through the streets, they brought a special variety of tackiness to the city.

I wanted to experience as many aspects of Nashville as I could so I went to the Nashville Country Music Hall of Fame, a fantastic museum that was really interactive and busy. It was a contrast to the chaos outside and allowed those who love country music to appreciate its history in many different ways. Costumes, song-writing sections (sponsored by Taylor Swift), lyrics painted on walls, singalong song booths, drum kits, photo opportunities – the place was full of opportunities of engagement, with so many things to enjoy. I was in activation mode. Some museums seem to have lost their way; there's no real depth to the experience and the visitor leaves without understanding what the point was. What I loved about this place was that everything was so easy to access. You knew what was there and where to go next. And I got my photo with the plaque of one of the country's greatest artists, Charley Pride. The circular room where the plaques are displayed is truly a great way of reminding visitors of the country royalty who have passed through the city. Well done, Country Music Hall of Fame; you have my seal of approval.

Jon, Chloe and I also ventured to the Parthenon. Yep – here in Nashville is the most random thing to be recreated from Ancient Greece. It was built for the 1897 Centennial Exposition and forms part of Nashville's art museum. It felt so out of place yet was so wonderful. The art collection is permanent and includes 63 paintings by American artists. There is also space for temporary shows. The tragedy was there were no visitors – anywhere. It was literally the three of us, despite it being just two corners away from the busiest 500 metres of road I had ever seen at 2pm on a Tuesday – anywhere. The only thing that brought tourists close to the history and culture of Nashville were the tractors decked out in American flags and blasting out music while flying past. This time the song was so appropriate: *Born in the USA...*

I had organised through a friend to meet a man called George

Gruhn. George is the owner of a very famous guitar store and people literally fly here from all over the world to show him their guitars and try to sell them to him! What I didn't realise was that George was also an accomplished author and he has another interesting hobby too, as I would soon discover. I was taken upstairs to a special entrance through two doors with code access. And then I met a softly spoken, quiet man wearing very modest clothing. His green cord trousers and plain shirt were really not what I expected.

Now, you're probably curious about why I had come to meet George and why I am about to tell you all about him. Well, have you ever thought about the difference one guitar or another can make to a performance? Or wondered who advises musicians on which guitars to buy? Well, George is the man.

On the first day we met for an hour and George invited me to return to do a recorded interview. I was kind of like, "Oh... okay." So we did. Chloe and Jon were my production team. We talked about George's personal guitar collection and also the popularity of the guitar industry. George told me about amplification in theatres and venues but also his access to the music industry in Nashville. He told me the best music he has experienced in Nashville is at the jamming sessions: "Backstage at the Opry, the best session players bring their friends and the spontaneous backstage show can be so much better than a scripted show..."

Then I asked George about the impact of music on society, but the conversation took an interesting turn because he started to tell me about his childhood. He grew up in New York City and when he was eight, he started a zoo in his home. By the age of 12, he was now living in Chicago and his animal collection had grown and was making headline news. Here in his office – five metres from where we were sitting – he had a collection of snakes. These were his passions: music and animals. And then this bizarre conversation turned to banjos, when George talked about the golden period of their manufacture...

By this point, I was totally blown away by the amount of knowledge George had. No wonder he had become such a respected individual – but I noted one simple thing. Everyone knew him as the man who knows guitars. But for three hours I got to know the real George. I let him tell me all about his animals and he described the nature study walks he would go on. It was nothing to do with what I wanted to hear – I wanted music to be the focus – but I was so happy just to learn all about George, who, on film, was so much more engaging. I honestly could not have picked a more interesting man to speak to. After the interview, a thought came to me. When someone lives in a world that they have totally become known for – like guitars – it's always good to remind people this is a person with many interests – and that was what George was doing here.

I spent my last evening in a restaurant three streets away from the madness. However, on the 7th floor was a restaurant that was open 24 hours a day. It sold beer for 22 of those 24 hours. I got talking to a couple from Phoenix who loved country music. We agreed that the character of Nashville was being ruined by what was happening three streets away. The history had been lost. The music scene was on the verge of being laughed at. And absolutely nothing was being done to quieten the streets. Instead, because of how busy the streets got at night and for safety reasons, the police literally had to close about a mile of the main street for four hours every night. This meant people could walk safely on the road and not be crushed on the pavements. The waitress was very frank with us. She said being from Nashville was great, but this was not the real Nashville.

Nashville was fab and it destroyed me all in one go. The tourism strategy needs to be ripped up and written again! Chloe and Jon: once again – thank you for an amazing experience!

Nashville airport...

This was it. I was almost done. Pfft. I cried writing this part. I walked into Nashville airport past a lovely mural and thought: "Oh well, last flight before home..." I was about to become the first person to ever go to 80 events in 8 months and 2 weeks. I had just about completed *Around the World in 80 Events* and now I was to visit my last city.

We boarded the plane and a voice came over the tannoy. "Ladies and gentlemen, this is your captain speaking. We will be delayed for the next hour..."

Toronto...

The day I arrived in Toronto I had a meeting with someone from the Rogers Cup. The tennis tournament is played at the Aviva Centre at York University, which is a 45-minute train ride out of Toronto. The tournament, known as the Canada Masters or Canadian Open, is sponsored by Rogers Bank and was founded way back in 1881. I met Jack, who is from England and had recently taken on a role with the Rogers Cup communication team. He was brilliant as he spoke about how the area really changes when the tournament is on; everything comes alive. Right now, it was silent. Only the noise of the machines cleaning the courts could be heard. Tennis was one sport I never got to see on my adventure, as no matches were scheduled. However, meeting Jack helped me to understand what it is that makes the Rogers Cup so amazing. The surface is hard, the Centre Court audience is 8,000 and the fact that this event actually alternates between Toronto and Montreal, with the women's and men's tournaments flipping over each year – if you get what I mean – was a really interesting concept.

My next meeting was about Toronto Buskerfest, a world-renowned event organised by a charity, Epilepsy Toronto. I met someone from Epilepsy Toronto in a café and they took me through the concept, the organisation and the fundraising method. It was all very simple. The festival space is a gated area within Woodbine Park in Toronto. There's a suggested donation of $5 to enter. That money goes to Epilepsy Toronto. Each busker who performs then has a hat and can collect money at the end of their performance. Clever way to operate. A superb idea and a great opportunity for the charity to be seen to deliver something unique.

So, ladies and gentlemen... I said this would be a wild journey. I said this was going to take you to places the likes of which you've never been before. Here it is – event 80. Yes, that is right... we're going to the very last event of my adventure...

Event 80: Pumpkin Festival

12th October

Did I ever imagine I would get here? Nope! Seven years ago, I had dreamed of this moment – of arriving at my 80th of 80 events. But I didn't know what the dream would look like. I didn't know I would be dragging myself to Downsview Park to go to a pumpkin festival. Yet here I was, standing at the railway station on a very cold Saturday morning. I was unbelievably exhausted, but this was it.

Organised by Superior Events, the Toronto Pumpkin Festival was 700 metres from the station. In between here and there was a large silver warehouse. I caught sight of a giant orange pumpkin about 200 metres away and walked slowly towards the entrance of this free event. A quarter of the field was full of greasy spoon food vans, and in the middle of the field was a pumpkin patch. This wasn't a festival with high-end cuisine. For sure, it wasn't a tourist attraction. A picnic fence around the pumpkins was the classiest thing about the 'festival'. The pumpkins were being thrown around by the 'event staff'. Signs told me it was $4 for a pumpkin (small) or $6 for a large one. I laughed. Inflation comes in all shapes and sizes and this was the perfect example of how some events really do take the biscuit with their captive audience. The supermarket across from the silver warehouse was charging $2 for a large pumpkin, but the excitement of taking your children to pick their own was what the organisers betted on.

"Mum, look!" A child was running excitedly through the small field, grabbing pumpkins and laughing. The parents encouraged them to drop the three pumpkins they had picked up. Around the pumpkin patch were inflatable slides, mechanical rides and a few other attractions. I stood in the middle of the patch, laughing. It seemed so bizarre that all these people were part of the last event of my journey, but the priority right now for them was to find the biggest pumpkin.

Parents threw money at mechanical ride tokens; $25 for 5 rides. Immersion was the key factor for this event – but in a completely different way to most of the other events I had visited. I mean, this didn't have a million-pound budget. It was about getting people into a field and giving them something to do. The event was free to enter and walk around but I think the organisers missed a trick here in not creating a story. I knew from my travels that events – mainly the free ones – can be packaged in some amazing ways that take simple ideas and turn them into journeys.

This event seemed to be about people spending money rather than buying into the concept. Families could easily spend $100 – and that's just the basic maths I could work out. This might seem like a lot of money but if the Toronto Pumpkin Festival billed itself as THE BEST PUMPKIN FESTIVAL IN THE WHOLE OF PUMPKINVILLE and if they built a pumpkin village and made it a proper experience rather than just picking a pumpkin, $100 would have been no problem.

As this was my last event, of course, I looked at it differently and critiqued it harder than usual. The highlight for me was taking my photo next to the large inflatable pumpkin. I laughed as I cried... This was it. The last photo at my last entrance to an event.

One thing to take away...

Pumpkins. Something that is associated with Halloween, autumn and Thanksgiving. Using the symbol of a pumpkin can create a certain feeling and excitement – and they did just that.

Toronto...

I was really ill. During that last event, I could hardly stand up. I was knackered and so tired that I checked out of my hostel and into a fancy Hilton for three nights. (Worst decision ever!)

But, ladies and gentlemen – I had done it. In the space of eight months and two weeks, I had visited 26 countries and immersed myself in 80 events. It felt slightly underwhelming celebrating by myself. When I got back to the hotel (having been there for three days before the pumpkin festival), the receptionist said: "You look better but still tired... but did you do it?" They high fived me and gave me some cookies from underneath the desk. This was my celebration.

And So...

You're nearly at the end of the book. Tired? So was I! Completing my mission was tiring. I hope while you were reading this you have begun to think about your own dreams – or even started to realise them.

So, what did I learn about the events industry? Well, lots – but here are just a few things...

Waste

Events can create a lot of waste. Whether you are bringing 400 or 40,000 people into an area will create waste that is not normally there. And much of that waste, especially the marketing materials and freebies, goes straight in the bin. San Fermin, Jakarta Jazz Festival, Tokyo Baseball and Auckland Pride, among others, all sent a positive message about sustainability and waste management. I enjoyed checking out bins and watching how waste became recyclable materials.

Customer Engagement

How does an event engage with its customers? Well, I'll be honest, the customer journey was variable. Some events, including the Jakarta Jazz Festival, Tour De France (with the freebies) and Seattle Mariners did understand what engagement is and created a connection, a real sense of purpose to what they delivered. But many organisers need to realise that the event itself is not the most important factor; it is the emotional attachment that is left with the consumer. It's all about putting plans in place to ensure the special moments are created to leave a positive impression even after the event has ended.

Meetings

Some of the people I met were so open; others said things like, "Please don't include that in your book..." and I didn't. But the reason I wanted to tell you about the meetings was because I wanted to show that the events industry is so open to conversation. Event organisers thrive upon delivering the most amazing social experiences. They give up their own social lives to allow others to enjoy theirs. When I met Jeff, Nadja and Steffi, Donald and the others, I could tell that the projects they work on are their life passion.

What would I have changed on my adventure?

I would have taken fewer flights. Unfortunately, I only considered flights rather than seeking alternative travel options at the beginning of the planning. That was a huge mistake.

I also really should have had a five-question survey about what events mean to people. I could have had over 3,000 views about how people enjoy events and what events mean to them – but sadly I missed the opportunity. I could have got people to fill it out on planes, trains, buses... and the global audience and reach would have been unbelievable – maybe next time...

I would have filmed more and posted more videos and done a few Q&As on Facebook Live. I would have created a much more marketing strategy.

The one thing I would never have changed is the amount of fun I had. The amount I laughed, whether it was alone or in dorms or at events.

And then COVID-19 came

A big wrecking ball smashed into the events industry in 2020 and killed it. Literally, for months globally, nothing was happening. Mass gatherings were finally recognised as something that has an impact on people's lives – not only from the social element but through the sharing of germs. COVID-19 has completely flipped the way we will see events in the future. And it has reminded me that the trip I took highlighted some of the best of what the events industry has to offer – and more than that. Whatever happens next, the industry is in good hands. Social interaction may change but I saw for myself the psychological benefits of events. I saw children laughing at puppets, elders enjoying drumming, and speakers pushing forward agendas in a way that hybrid and virtual events can never recreate. Whatever happens, I feel sure events will innovate and have the same impact they had before the pandemic.

No online event can ever replicate an experience like a physical in-person event does. In-person events are not just about being there; they shape who we are. Together, the humans on this planet have created social interaction that makes us happy. Allows us to meet people. Frees us to sing songs back to our favourite bands in a way online videos never will. Events do all this and more...

'At the planning of events, the gates of a festival, the side of a stage or in the middle of a race, remember the feeling that events bring. A laugh. A smile. A photo. A singalong. A new friend. A new t-shirt. A journey to escapism. Those memories will return... and when they do, they will be bigger than before...'

But the COVID-19 pandemic also shows us that we should never wait for our dreams to fall into our laps. Instead, we should chase them when we think that time is right. We should leap at possibilities and enjoy each moment when we can. And I hope after reading this book you are doing just that.

Well... It's over. Thank you. I don't have enough pages left to thank every single person that supported me, liked my statuses, shared my posts, sent me emails, sponsored my 10km runs (which I completed in 2020, with all money going to charity), messaged when I was away to check in, understood I was sometimes not able to wish people happy birthday, kept me awake with their snoring in the dorms. Thanks to my mum and dad, and to you –you know who you are. Thank you. It's done – for now...

Around the UK / Around the World in 80 Events, Post the Pandemic?

Let's just see.

The End ☺

PS It was all about the journey...
#thatwasthejourney